ΑΡΙΣΤΟΞΕΝΟΥ ΑΡΜΟΝΙΚΑ

ΣΤΟΙΧΕΙΑ

THE HARMONICS OF
ARISTOXENUS

EDITED WITH TRANSLATION NOTES
INTRODUCTION AND INDEX OF WORDS

BY

HENRY S. MACRAN, M.A.,

FELLOW OF TRINITY COLLEGE, DUBLIN
AND PROFESSOR OF MORAL PHILOSOPHY IN THE UNIVERSITY OF DUBLIN

OXFORD
AT THE CLARENDON PRESS
1902

PREFACE

THE main object of this book is to introduce, to such English readers as may be curious in the matter of music, the writings of the foremost musical theorist of Ancient Greece; and with this object in view I have endeavoured to supply a sound text and a clear translation of his great work, and to illustrate its more obscure passages by citations from other exponents of the same science. But further, since the mind of the modern reader is apt to be beset by prejudices in respect of this subject—some of which arise from his natural but false assumption that all music must follow the same laws that govern the only music that he knows, while others are due to the erroneous theories of specialists which have been accepted as certain truths by a public not in possession of the evidence—I have thought it necessary to deal at some length with those prejudices; and this is the chief aim of the Introduction.

The critical apparatus differs from that of Marquard in including the readings of H as given by Westphal, and correcting from my own collation of the Selden MS. many incorrect reports of its readings.

I wish to express my thanks to the Provost of Oriel College, Oxford, Mr. Mahaffy, and Mr. L. C. Purser, for reading the proofs, and for many useful suggestions; to Mr. Bury for advice on many difficult passages of the text; and above all to another Fellow of Trinity College, Dublin, Mr. Goligher, for most generous and valuable aid in the preparation of the English Translation.

HENRY S. MACRAN.

TRINITY COLLEGE, DUBLIN.
Sept. 1902.

CONTENTS

INTRODUCTION—

PAGE

A.—ON THE DEVELOPMENT OF GREEK MUSIC . , 1

B.—ON ARISTOXENUS AND HIS EXTANT WORKS . 86

TEXT—

BOOK I 95

„ II 122

„ III 149

TRANSLATION—

BOOK I 165

„ II 187

„ III 209

NOTES 223

INDEX 295

INTRODUCTION

A.—On the Development of Greek Music.

1. Music is in no sense a universal language. Like its sister, speech, it is determined in every case to a special form by the physical and mental character of the people among whom it has arisen, and the circumstances of their environment. The particular nature of music is no more disproved by the fact that a melody of Wagner speaks to German, French, and English ears alike, than is the particular nature of speech by the fact that the Latin tongue was at one time the recognized vehicle of cultivated thought throughout the civilized world.

Further, this limitation which is common to music and speech leads to a more complete isolation in the case of the former. The primary function of language is to give us representations, whether of the facts of the world and the soul, or of the ideals of thought, or of the fancies of the imagination: and to appeal to our emotions through the representation of such facts, ideals, or fancies. This service, so far as we are capable of perception and feeling, any strange language may be made to render us at the cost of some study. But we are aware that our own language has another power for us; that of waking immediately in us emotions in which are fused beyond all analysis the effects of its very sounds and the feelings that are linked to those sounds by indissoluble association. It is here that begins the real isolation of language, the incommunicable charm of poetry that defies translation. But the whole meaning of music depends upon this immediate appeal to our emotions through the association of feeling with sensation;

and so the strangeness of the foreign music of to-day, and of the dead music of the past is insuperable, for they are the expressions of emotions which their possessors could not analyse, and we can never experience.

2. The same contrast appears when we consider music in relation to painting and the other arts of imagery. These latter appeal to the emotions no less than music, but they do so in the first instance mediately, through the representation of certain objects. It is quite true that here, as in the case of the emotions indirectly raised by language, the cultivation of a certain mental habit is a necessary condition of our receiving the proper impression from any work of art. But in painting and sculpture the mental habit consists primarily in our attitude not to the manner of the representation but to the object represented, whereas in music it consists in our attitude towards the expression itself.

The incommunicable character of music finds a striking illustration in the effect which the remnants of ancient Greek melody produce on the modern hearer. Some years ago, for example, Sir Robert Stewart delivered a lecture in Trinity College, Dublin, on the Music of Distant Times and Places; and illustrated it by specimens from various nationalities and periods, an ancient Greek hymn being included in the number. It was the unanimous verdict of all the musicians present that, while the music of the less civilized nations was often crude, barbarous, and monotonous in the highest degree, the Greek hymn stood quite alone in its absolute lack of meaning and its unredeemed ugliness; and much surprise was expressed that a nation which had delighted all succeeding generations by its achievements in the other arts should have failed so completely in the art which it prized and practised most. Yet all this criticism is an absurdity based on the fallacy that music is a universal language. It presupposes

2

absurdly that a melody is meaningless if it means nothing to us, and it forgets with equal absurdity that the beauty of anything for us is conditioned by our power to appreciate it, and our power to appreciate it by our familiarity with it.

3. But though it is impossible for us now to recover the meaning of this dead music of ancient Greece, and well-nigh impossible to accustom our ears to appreciate its form, we can at least study as a matter of speculative interest the laws of its accidence and syntax as they have been handed down to us by its grammarians. To this end our first step must be to make our conceptions clear as to the formal nature of music in general. We have already seen that the function of music is to evoke certain moods in us by the association of feelings with sensations. But the material of these sensations it does not find in nature, but provides for itself, by creating out of the chaos of infinite sounds a world of sound-relations, a system in which each member has its relation to every other determined through the common relation of all to a fixed centre. The idea of such a system implies two facts. In the first place, no sound is a musical sound except as perceived in its relation to another sound; in the second place, there is a direction in this relation in that one of the two related sounds must be perceived to be the inner, or nearer to the centre [1]. Thus in the chord

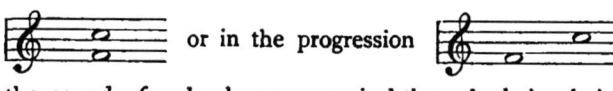 or in the progression

the sounds f and c become musical through their relation to one another, and through the perception in any particular case that one of them is more central than the other; in the key of C for example that the c, in the key of $\flat B$ that the f is nearer the musical centre or tonic.

[1] Nearer, that is, in respect of similarity, not of contiguity. In this sense, the nearest note to any given note is its octave.

But just as the arithmetical intuition cannot apprehend all relations with equal ease, but finds for example the relation $\frac{1}{2}$ more intelligible than $\frac{68}{147}$; and as the sight apprehends the relation of a line to its perpendicular more readily than the relation between two lines at an angle of 87 degrees, so there stand out from among the infinite possible sound-relations a limited class, commonly called concords, which the ear grasps and recognizes without effort and immediately, and these form the elements of every musical system. Not indeed that all musical systems are founded on the same elementary relations. Universally recognized as belonging to this class are the relations between any sound and its octave above or below, either being regarded as tonic; the relation between a sound and its Fourth above, the latter being regarded as tonic; the relation between a note and its Fifth above, the former being regarded as tonic. But the relation of the Major Third which plays such a prominent part in modern music has no place as an elementary relation in the system of Ancient Greece.

4. But evidently these few relations would go but a little way in the constitution of a system, and music to extend its sphere has recourse to the mediate perception of relations. Thus there are sound-relations, which the ear, unable to grasp them immediately, can apprehend by resolving them into the elementary concords. In our diatonic scale of c for example, the relation of d to c is resolved into the relation of d to g, and of g to c. Thus there enter into a musical system, besides the elementary concords, all those sound-relations which result from their composition; and to the complexity of such compound relations there seems to be no limit either in theory or in practice. There is no chord, no progression however complex, however unpleasant at first hearing, of which we can assert that it is musically impossible. The one thing needful to make it musical is

4

that the relation of its parts to one another and to the preceding and succeeding sounds be comprehensible.

It is also possible, though perhaps a sign of imperfect development, that a note may enter into a musical system through being related *indeterminately* to a member of that system. Thus we might admit a passing note as leading to or from a fixed note, without the position of the former being exactly determined.

Sound-relations can be perceived between simultaneous and successive sounds alike. In the former case we have harmony in the modern sense of the word, in the latter melody; the difference between these phases of music being accidental, not essential.

The development of a system such as we have been considering will proceed upon two lines. On the one hand the craving for diversity will lead to new combinations of relations, and so to the widening of the system and the multiplication of its members; while on the other hand the growing sense of unity will press for a closer determination of the relations, and result in the banishment of those notes whose relations cannot be exactly determined.

5. In the music of Ancient Greece we are able to trace, though unfortunately with some gaps, the first steps of such a development. The earliest students of the science, in endeavouring to establish a scale or system of related notes, started as was natural from the smallest interval, the bounding notes of which afforded an elementary relation. This they found in the interval of the Fourth, in which the higher note is tonic; and this melodic interval, essentially identical with our concord of the Fifth, may be regarded as the fundamental sound-relation of Greek music. When they had thus secured a definite interval on the indefinite line of pitch, their next concern was to ascertain at what points the voice might legitimately break its journey between the boundaries of this

5

interval. But how were these points to be ascertained? Plainly, not by the exact determination of their relation to the bounding notes; for the Fourth was the smallest interval the relation of whose bounding notes the Greek ear could immediately apprehend; and for mediate perception the musical idea was as yet immature. Consequently, the intermediate notes, whatever they might be, could only be apprehended as passing notes, indeterminately related to the boundaries of the scale. Evidently then the number of such notes must be limited. The sense of unity which suffers by any inadequate determination of relations would be completely lost if the indeterminate relations were unduly multiplied. From these considerations resulted one of the first laws of Greek melody. The scale that begins with any note, and ends with its Fourth above is at most a tetrachord or scale of four notes—two bounding or containing notes, two intermediate or contained.

6. Again; although for the theorist a minimum of musical interval is as absurd as a minimum of space or time, yet, for the purposes of art, it was impossible that any two of these four points of the scale should lie so close together that the voice could not produce, or the ear distinguish the interval between them. Was it then possible to determine for practical purposes the smallest musical interval? To this question the Greek theorists gave the unanimous reply, supporting it by a direct appeal to facts, that the voice can sing, and the ear perceive a quarter-tone[1]; but that any smaller interval lies beyond the power of ear and voice alike.

Disregarding then the order of the intervals, and considering only their magnitudes, we can see that one possible division of the tetrachord was into two quarter-tones and

[1] The tone is musically (not mathematically) determined as the difference between the concord of the Fourth and the concord of the Fifth. These latter again are musically determined by the direct evidence of the ear.

6

a ditone, or space of two tones ; the employment of these intervals characterized a scale as of the Enharmonic genus.

Or again, employing larger intervals one might divide the tetrachord into, say, two-thirds of a tone, and the space of a tone and five-sixths : or into two semitones, and the space of a tone and a half. The employment of these divisions or any lying between them marked a scale as Chromatic. Or finally, by the employment of two tones one might proceed to the familiar Diatonic genus, which divided the tetrachord into two tones and a semitone.

Much wonder and admiration has been wasted on the Enharmonic scale by persons who have missed the true reason for the disappearance of the quarter-tone from our modern musical system. Its disappearance is due not to the dullness or coarseness of modern ear or voice, but to the fact that the more highly developed unity of our system demands the accurate determination of all sound-relations by direct or indirect resolution into concords ; and such a determination of quarter-tones is manifestly impossible [1].

7. But the constitution of our tetrachord scale is not yet completed. We have ascertained the maximum number and the various possible magnitudes of the intervals; but their order has yet to be determined. In the Enharmonic genus, for example, when we are passing to the tonic from the Fourth below, shall we sing quarter-tone, quarter-tone, ditone; or ditone, quarter-tone, quarter-tone; or quarter-tone, ditone, quarter-tone ; or are all these progressions equally legitimate? To these questions the Greek theorists give the unqualified and unanimous answer, not defending it by any argument, that in all divisions of a tetrachord in which the highest note is tonic, and the lowest a Fourth below, the lowest interval must be less than or equal to the middle, and less than the highest.

[1] See below, note on p. 115, l. 3.

Thus the schemes of the tetrachord scales in the three genera are finally determined as they appear in the following table:—

TABLE 1.

SCHEME OF THE ENHARMONIC TETRACHORD SCALE
OF THE TONIC *A*.

SCHEME OF THE CHROMATIC TETRACHORD SCALE
OF THE TONIC *A*.

SCHEME OF THE DIATONIC TETRACHORD SCALE
OF THE TONIC *A*.

In this table the following points are to be noted :—

(1) The sign x is used to signify that the note before which it is placed is sharpened a quarter-tone.

(2) The distinction between the definitely determined bounding notes, and the indeterminate passing notes is brought out by exhibiting the former as minims, the latter as crotchets.

(3) Several divisions are possible in the Chromatic and Diatonic genera (see below, p. 116): those taken in this table are merely typical.

8. The importance of this tetrachord scale can hardly be overrated, for it is the original unit from the multiplication of which in various positions arose all the later Greek scales : and it is to be observed that the tonality of this scale is most distinctly conceived and enunciated by the theorists. Aristoxenus is never weary of reminding us that the mere perception of intervals cannot enable us to under-

8

stand a succession of notes; that we must also apprehend the δύναμις or function of each individual in the series. Thus the highest note of the tetrachord, which at a later period when the scale was enlarged, obtained from its position the name of Mese, or middle note, holds in relation to the lowest note the function of an ἀρχή or foundation, in other words of a tonic. For just as cause and effect, though they exist only in their relation to one another, do not discharge like functions in that relation inasmuch as the effect leans upon the cause, but not the cause upon the effect; so though the highest and lowest notes of the tetrachord are musical notes only through their relation to one another, yet that relation is conceived as implying the dependence of the lower upon the higher, but not of the higher upon the lower. The intermediate notes again are regarded as mere stopping places of approximately determined position in the passage between the boundaries. According to the Greek terminology they are κινούμενοι or movable notes as distinguished from the ἱστῶτες or fixed notes, between which they stand. For since the essence of a note is not its place in a group, but its function in a system, an Enharmonic, a Chromatic, and a Diatonic passing note are not to be regarded as three notes, but as one variable note in three positions.

Even if we disregard the Enharmonic and Chromatic genera, and confine our attention to the Diatonic, we shall seek in vain for a parallel to this tetrachord scale in the classical system of modern music. We can descend from the tonic a to the e below it by the progression

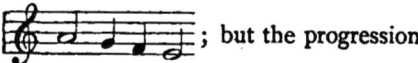 ; but the progression

to the tonic a, though of frequent occurrence in local music, has passed completely out of classical use.

9. When this meagre group of four notes was felt to be inadequate to the expression of human emotion, a ready method for the production of a more ample scale was sought in the addition to the original tetrachord of a second exactly similar to it. But immediately the question arose, How was the position of the second tetrachord to be determined in relation to the first? Or, to put it more generally, Supposing a scale of indefinite length to be constituted by a series of similar tetrachords, how was the position of these tetrachords to be relatively defined?

To this question it seems that there were three possible answers for the theorist, each of which no doubt found support in the art product of some tribe or other of the Hellenic world. The method of determination proposed in each answer constituted (as I shall here assume, postponing my arguments for the present) a distinct ἁρμονία or Harmony[1]; which term I believe to have meant primarily an 'adjustment' not of notes (for these are not the units of music) but of tetrachords.

10. According to the first of these answers, the tetrachords might be so arranged that the highest note of any one would coincide with the lowest note of the next above it. This method of *conjunction*, or the coincidence of extremities I believe to have been called the Ionic Harmony; and it resulted in a scale of this character :—

TABLE 2.

SCALES OF THE IONIC HARMONY IN THE THREE GENERA INDEFINITELY EXTENDED.

ENHARMONIC

---

[1] When I use the word Harmony as an equivalent of the Greek ἁρμονία, I shall employ a capital H.

If in the Ionic scale of any genus we take any consecutive pair of tetrachords, we obtain the Heptachord scale
of the seven-stringed lyre.

TABLE 3.

HEPTACHORD SCALES IN THE THREE GENERA WITH
THE NAMES OF THE INDIVIDUAL NOTES

11. These names were derived not from the pitch of the

respective notes, but from the place on the instrument of the strings which sounded them. Thus *a* as the note of the middle string was called Mese or 'middle'; *e* was called Hypate or highest because sounded by the top string; *d* which was sounded by the bottom string was in like manner called Nete or lowest. The note below the Mese was called Lichanus or 'forefinger,' because the string that sounded it was played by that finger. The names Parhypate, 'next the highest,' Paranete, 'next the lowest,' and Trite, 'third,' require no explanation.

It is important to observe exactly what these names do, and do not denote. They do not denote the members of a scale as points of pitch determined absolutely or in relation to any other scale. Let us take the scale

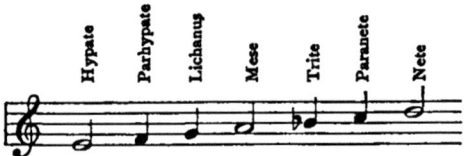

and transpose it, say, a tone higher

the individual notes of the resulting scale will bear the same names as the corresponding members of the original scale.

Again, these names do denote the points of a scale the order of whose intervals is determined. Thus, if we take the enharmonic scale

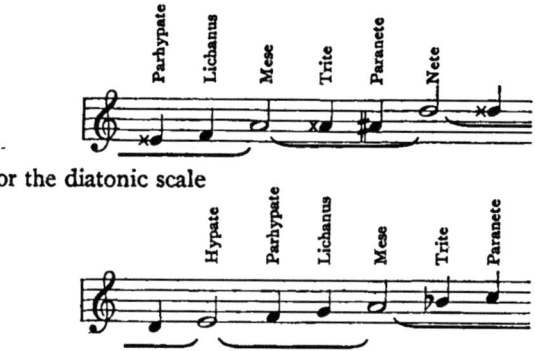

or the diatonic scale

consisting not of two complete tetrachords, but of one tetrachord and a fragment at each end, the notes of these scales will take their names from their place not in their own scales, but in the typical systems given in Table 3.

Once again, it is not implied by these names that the intervals between the designated notes are exactly determined in magnitude; for they are applied to the members of Enharmonic, Chromatic, and Diatonic scales alike.

12. The second method of forming a scale of tetrachords left the interval of a tone, called the *disjunctive* tone, between each pair of them. This Harmony by *disjunction*, or the separation of extremities, I shall assume to have been called Doric. It substituted for the Heptachord the Octachord, or scale of the eight-stringed lyre.

TABLE 4.

OCTACHORD SCALES IN THE THREE GENERA WITH THE NAMES OF THE INDIVIDUAL NOTES.

The scale of this Harmony, when indefinitely prolonged, resulted in the following succession :—

TABLE 5.

SCALES OF THE DORIC HARMONY IN THE THREE
GENERA INDEFINITELY EXTENDED.

The appearance of the octachord scale necessitated an alteration in the nomenclature. The old names were employed to represent the four lowest and the three highest

14

members of the new system, and the title Paramese, or 'next the middle,' was given to the note above the Mese.

13. The third method of adjustment employing *conjunction* and *disjunction* alternately interposed a tone between every second pair of tetrachords, while every other pair were *conjunct*. This Harmony I shall assume to have been called Aeolian; it resulted in the following scales :—

TABLE 6.

SCALES OF THE AEOLIAN HARMONY IN THE THREE
GENERA INDEFINITELY EXTENDED.

The alternation of conjunction and disjunction which is the characteristic of this Harmony is exemplified in the following eight-note scales:—

TABLE 7.

OCTAVE SCALES IN THE THREE GENERA WHICH
EXEMPLIFY THE AEOLIAN HARMONY.

ENHARMONIC

CHROMATIC

DIATONIC

14. If we employ modern nomenclature we may distinguish the first two Harmonies from the last by saying that the former give rise to modulating scales, the one passing over into the flat, the other into the sharp keys, while the latter maintains the same key throughout. But we must examine more closely into the nature of this difference. In the scale of the first Harmony we have a series of lesser tonics *B, E, A, d, g* [1]; that is, each of these notes serves as tonic to the notes that immediately precede it. What then is the relation of these tonics to one another? Each serves as a tonic of higher rank to the lesser tonic immediately below it and mediately through this to all below, so that we are necessarily driven upwards in our search for the supreme tonic, and are unable at any point to reverse the process; for no note can serve as immediate tonic to the Fourth above it. Consequently our progress towards the supreme or absolute tonic becomes a process *ad infinitum*.

When we pass to the second Harmony we find an opposite condition of things. Here the series of lesser tonics is *D, A, e, b.* Any one of these serves as tonic of higher rank immediately to the lesser tonic next above it, and through this mediately to all above, but cannot discharge a like function to those that are below it. Here then the necessary order is the descending one, but the progression

---

[1] When any scale contains the same note in two different octaves, we shall represent the higher by small, the lower by capital letters.

is equally *ad infinitum*; and our search for an absolute tonic is again fruitless. But when we arrive at the third Harmony we find for the first time the object of our search. In the series *E*, *A*, *e*, *a*, *A* is tonic to the *e* above through the mediation of *a*[1], and directly to the *E* below, and through them to all the lesser tonics of the scale.

15. The distinction, then, that holds between these three Harmonies corresponds in no wise to the distinction between our Major and Minor modes. All three of them alike recognize no fundamental relations outside that of a note to its Fourth above or Fifth below, and that of a note to its octave; and all three alike place their passing notes in the same position. But our distinction of Major and Minor has arisen through the recognition of two fresh elementary sound-relations unknown to the Greeks, those of the Greater and Lesser Third; and according as a scale embodies one or other of them, it is denominated Major or Minor. Thus the essential characteristic of the major scale of *A* is the immediate relation of ♯*C* to *A*, and of ♯*G* to *E*; and of the minor scale of *A*, in so far as we have a minor scale at all, the immediate relation of *C* to *A*, and of *G* to *E*; and these relations are not present in the scales of any of the three Harmonies. One might illustrate the contrast by representing the modern minor scale of *A* as follows :—

[1] The relation of a note to its octave above or below approximates to identity.

and the diatonic scale of the third Harmony as follows :—

in each case supplying the most fundamental relations of
the scale in the form of a bass.

16. From the comparison above instituted between the
three early Harmonies of Greek music, it was clear that
the third possessed a consistency and unity which were
wanting in its rivals. Accordingly we are not surprised to
find that they fell into disuse, while the Aeolian won its
way to predominance, and finally to exclusive possession
of the field of melody. But the process was a gradual
one, and there were many attempts at combination and
compromise before it was accomplished. Of such attempts
we have an example in the so-called Phrygian scale, the
earliest form of which is given us by Aristides Quintilianus
(Meibom, 21. 19).

TABLE 8.

(a) ENHARMONIC PHRYGIAN SCALE OF ARISTIDES
QUINTILIANUS.

(b) OLD DIATONIC PHRYGIAN SCALE ON THE ANALOGY OF (a).

Here we have a scale which, though containing two dis-
junctions (between D and E, and between A and B), yet
produces an octave by combining conjunction with disjunction at A, and in so doing embodies the distinctive

feature of the first Harmony, the relation of the tonic *A* to *d*, its Fourth above.

17. The perverse artificiality which is conspicuous in this scale is a common feature in the musical science of the period. It does not by any means follow that the music of the time suffered from the same vice. For the sake of brevity, we have regarded the theorists as gradually evolving the system of Greek music; but of course their province as a matter of fact extended only to the analysis and explanation of what the artist created. As the theorist of metrical science arranges in feet the rhythm to which the instinct of the poet has given birth, so the theorist of scales offers an analysis of the series of notes in which the passion of the singer has found expression. Now, the art which in the beginning had created the tetrachord and then passed on to the various combinations of tetrachords came to require for some song or chorus the following diatonic series of notes :—

This scale the theorist applied himself to read, and the scheme of Table 8 is the fruit of his first attempt. When the distracting claims of the First and Second Harmonies had become silent, and the Third had come to be recognized as the normal method of combining tetrachords, the true reading of the scale became apparent

18. Aristides Quintilianus has preserved for us several other examples of these perverse scale-readings. Composers found room for variety within the Aeolian Harmony by employing now one, now another segment of the indefinite

Aeolian scale, not of course with any change of tonality or
modality, but simply as the melody required this or that
number of notes above or below the tonic. Thus there
arose a series of scales which offered material for the analysis
of the theorist—an analysis that was not by any means so
easy and obvious as we might at first suppose. We seem
immediately to recognize that they are not essentially in‑
dependent of one another, but differ merely as various
portions of one scale; and we are disposed to wonder that
the Greeks should have deemed each of them worthy of
a separate analysis and a name to itself. But there are two
important considerations which are apt to escape us. In
the first place, at the period of musical science which we
are now considering, the contending claims of the three
Harmonies, and the possibility of combining them produced
an uncertainty in the analysis of scales, of which music,
through the simplifying tendency ever present in its development, has since cleared itself. In the second place, we are
accustomed to instruments of great actual or potential
compass, in which the relation of such scales to one another
as segments of a common whole is immediately and palpably
evident. But for any performer on a limited instrument,
say, one of eight notes, it would be impossible to pass from
one of these scales to another except by a fresh tuning, or
in some cases by a change of instrument; and from these
practical necessities the scales would derive a character of
independence which does not belong to them in the nature
of things. We should never think of differentiating and
distinguishing by name the octave scales in which are
respectively contained the opening phrases of Handel's
'I know that my Redeemer liveth,' and his 'But thou did'st
not leave his soul in hell.' But it would be natural enough
for a player on the pipe to do so when he found that the
two themes could not be rendered by the same instrument.

19. Again, these scales that had to be analysed were in common vogue, and so belonged to the Diatonic Genus. For here it is to be observed that the Enharmonic and Chromatic scales seem to have been esoteric or academical in use, and the pre-eminently natural character of the Diatonic was recognized even by those theorists who defended the other genera (see below, p. 111, l. 9). We append a table of the scales to be analysed.

TABLE 9.

VARIOUS SEGMENTS OF THE DIATONIC SCALE OF THE
AEOLIAN HARMONY.

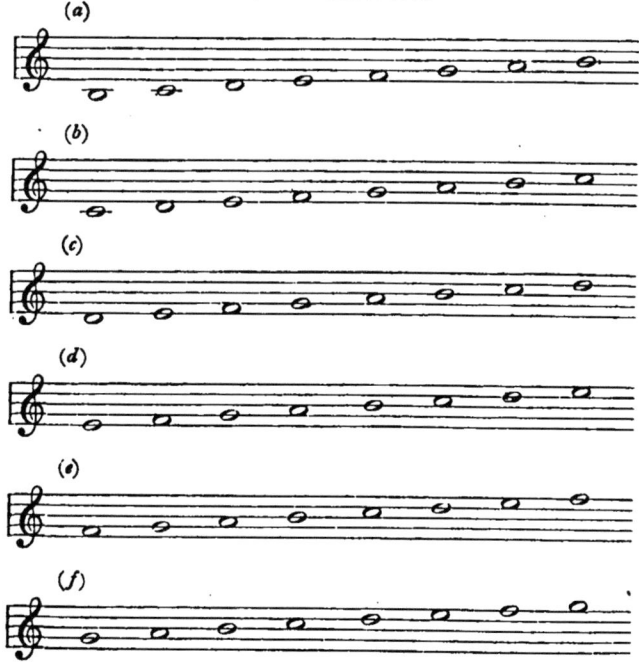

(*g*)

It is most carefully to be noted that, in order to conceive of these scales as did the Greeks, we must entirely abstract from the pitch relation which is necessarily introduced into them by representing them according to modern notation. Any one of the above scales may lie higher, or lower than, or in the same compass as any other of them.

20. To guide them in their analysis the theorists were not without certain clues. No note, they knew, could be the tonic or Mese of the scale unless the fourth note below it stood to it in the fundamental relation of a note to its Fourth above. And the increasing influence of the Third Harmony made it necessary to find the tonic in a note next above which lay the disjunctive tone. But even with these clues the scales often baffled their analysis. Authorities differed, and in one case at least a historian[1] records the discovery in later times of the true reading of a scale which had formerly been misinterpreted. Nothing, perhaps, contributed more to these doubts and failures than the endeavour to find a distinctive plan of formation in each scale. In accordance with this principle (*d*) in the above table was construed as two complete tetrachords of the Dorian Harmony, and was augmented by a tone so as to represent adequately the nature of that adjustment by dis-

---

[1] See Plutarch, *de Musica*, 1136 D Λύσις δὲ Λαμπροκλέα τὸν Ἀθηναῖον συνιδόντα ὅτι οὐκ ἐνταῦθα ἔχει (ἡ Μιξολυδιστί) τὴν διάζευξιν, ὅπου σχεδὸν ἅπαντες ᾤοντο, ἀλλ' ἐπὶ τὸ ὀξύ, τοιοῦτον αὐτῆς ἀπεργάσασθαι τὸ σχῆμα οἷον τὸ ἀπὸ παραμέσης ἐπὶ ὑπάτην ὑπατῶν. 'But according to Lysis Lamprocles the Athenian saw that the Mixolydian scale had its point of disjunction, not where it was commonly supposed to be, but at the top ; and accordingly established its figure to be such a series of notes as from the Paramese to the Hypate-Hypatôn.'

junction only. According as this tone was added at the
bottom or at the top, the scale would seem to have been
called Dorian or Hypodorian (that is, Lower Dorian). The
appropriateness of this latter name will appear in the
sequel.

TABLE 10.

OLD DORIAN SCALE.

OLD HYPODORIAN SCALE.

The reading of (*c*) resulted in the Phrygian scale, the
scheme which we gave in Table 8 ; (*b*) and (*e*) were identified as illustrating alternate conjunction and disjunction,
and, as typical of the Aeolian Harmony, were called Lydian[1].

TABLE 11.

OLD LYDIAN SCALES.

Again, (*f*) was read as in the following table, and, as
essentially similar to the Phrygian scale, was called Hypophrygian.

[1] For the relation between the terms Aeolian and Lydian see
§ 41.

TABLE 12.

OLD HYPOPHRYGIAN SCALE.

(*g*) does not appear in the oldest lists of scales. Perhaps the extreme position of the tonic made such a segment of rare occurrence. The same fact may have helped to obscure the analysis of (*a*). Certain it is at any rate that not only the true plan, but even the position of the tonic of this scale remained for a long time undiscovered (see note on p. 22). Aristides Quintilianus (Meibom, 21. 26) has preserved for us the old reading which is curiously interesting.

TABLE 13.

ENHARMONIC MIXOLYDIAN SCALE OF ARISTIDES QUINTILIANUS.

OLD DIATONIC MIXOLYDIAN SCALE ON THE ANALOGY OF THE PRECEDING.

In fact it was conceived as a scale constituted by the election of certain parts of two overlapping scales of the Aeolian Harmony; namely,

and

THE DEVELOPMENT OF GREEK MUSIC

We have already seen that the term Lydian was applied to the scale that was typical of the Aeolian Harmony; and consistently with this, (*a*), as a mixture of two such scales, was called Mixolydian or Mixed Lydian. It was an example of what Aristoxenus calls a double scale; that is, it had two Mesae or tonics, *d* and *e*.

21. Each of these scales might, at any rate theoretically, appear in Enharmonic and Chromatic as well as in Diatonic form. The following is a complete table of them in every genus.

TABLE 14.

SIX ANCIENT SCALES IN THE THREE GENERA.

(*a*) MIXOLYDIAN.

ENHARMONIC

CHROMATIC

DIATONIC

(*b*) LYDIAN.

ENHARMONIC

CHROMATIC

DIATONIC

INTRODUCTION

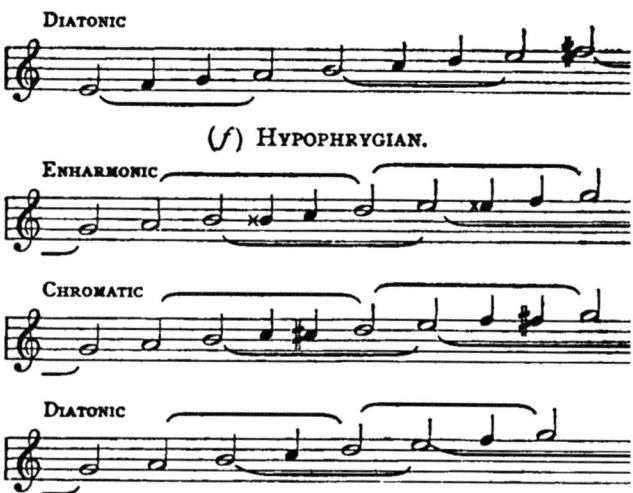

(*f*) HYPOPHRYGIAN.

It is to be noted that in the Enharmonic and Chromatic scales it often appears that more notes occur than in the corresponding Diatonic. The reason is this. If a diatonic scale exhibits, say, the combination of the conjunction *e–a* along with the disjunction *e–♯f–b*, the fixed note *a* of the conjunction will coincide *in pitch*[1] with the second passing note *a* of the disjunct tetrachord ♯*f, g, a, b*; and so will not be a different note from it according to our notation. But in the corresponding Enharmonic and Chromatic scales there will not be such a coincidence, and consequently our notation is able to distinguish such notes in these genera.

22. As soon as the formal essence of these scales had been established we find the Greek theorists exercised with the question of their proper keys, in other words of their pitch. At first sight the question seems an absurd one. In the nature of things no scale, regarded as a mere order

[1] Not in function.

of intervals can be determined to any particular pitch; and though practical necessities reduce the possible pitch of all scales within certain limits, they do not define the relative position of different scales within those limits. Let us take for example the Lydian and Phrygian scales; and, that our conceptions of them may be wholly free from any admixture of pitch relation suggested by our modern notation, let us assume as scheme of the Lydian :—

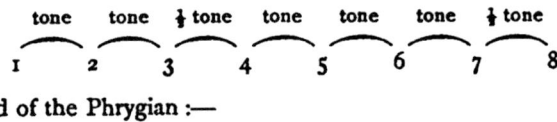

and of the Phrygian :—

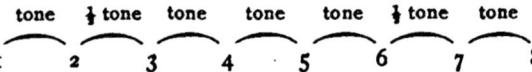

If then we suppose the limit of practically possible sounds to be two octaves, from

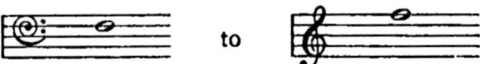

one might take as Lydian scale

and as Phrygian

in which case the Lydian is higher than the Phrygian : or again, one might take as Lydian

and as Phrygian

in which case the Phrygian is higher than the Lydian: or again, one might take as Lydian

and as Phrygian

in which case the scales coincide in pitch.

23. An explanation of the question that would naturally suggest itself to any modern reader is that the Greek theorists desired to reduce these scales to segments of one universal scale, and establish thereby a theoretical relation of pitch between them; just as we, finding types of most of the scales of Table 14 inside the series of the white notes of a piano, theoretically regard (*c*) for example as a tone above (*b*). But this explanation is immediately confronted by two objections, each of which is fatal to it. In the first place, the Greek theorists attributed to each scale in virtue of its formal essence an absolute ethical character, and they conceived that character as dependent on its pitch. Its pitch, then, must have been something more than a mere theoretical relation. And in the second place the answer actually given to the question is precisely the reverse of what it must have been if the above explanation of the question were true. For the Greek theorists state that the Phrygian scale whose scheme is (*c*) in Table 14 is one tone not above but below the Lydian, whose scheme is (*b*).

We must conceive, then, this question of the pitch of the scales as implying the possibility of determining each of them to a particular pitch, not arbitrary, but arising necessarily from the order of its intervals; not theoretical, or relative, but serving as the ground of an absolute ethical character; not leading to such an order of the scales as would arise from the reduction of them to segments of one series, but to precisely the reverse order.

24. To understand the possibility of such a determination we must take into account an important distinction between ancient Greek melody, and the melody of modern music. We have seen that the essential feature of music is the relation of all the notes of a scale or system to its central point or tonic. To maintain the sense of this relation, it is necessary in every musical composition, that the tonic should be expressed with due frequency; and all the more necessary when the musical consciousness is immature. Modern music indeed can fulfil this requirement by means of harmony; and so it is not unusual to have a melody of any length in which the tonic seldom or never occurs. But the music of Ancient Greece, lacking the assistance of harmony, could not thus dispense with its tonic; and accordingly we find Aristotle[1] enunciating the law that melody should constantly recur to the Mese, as to the connecting note from which the scale derives its unity. Now, let us suppose a singer, boy or man, or a performer on lyre or flute to have at his disposal only eight serviceable notes; and let us imagine him to sing or play a melody in the Lydian scale. Here the Mese is third note from the top, and sixth note from the bottom. Consequently it lies in the higher part of his register, or among the higher notes of his instrument; and the melody necessarily gathering itself around this note, and constantly repeating it, will assume a high-pitched tone. But now let us imagine him to pass to a melody in the Hypophrygian scale. Here the Mese is second note from

[1] *Problems*, xix. 20.

the bottom, and seventh from the top.   Therefore it lies in
the under part of his register or among the lower notes of
his instrument ; and the melody gravitating towards this
note necessarily assumes a low-pitched character.   Thus
the pitch of a Greek scale is determined not by the absolute
position of its tonic, nor by the pitch relation between its
tonic and the tonic of any other scale, but by the position
of its tonic in relation to its other notes.   When for example,
it is asserted that the Lydian scale is a tone higher than the
Phrygian, the meaning is that, while the Phrygian tonic lies
two and a half tones from the top, and three and a half
tones from the bottom of the Phrygian scale, the Lydian
tonic lies one and a half tones from the top, and four and
a half tones from the bottom of the Lydian scale.   Thus it
is seen that the relative determination of the pitch of these
scales is only made possible by the fact that each has an
intrinsic pitch character of its own, consisting in a pitch
relation between its own members.

25. The relative pitch of the six scales of Table 14 may
be presented to the eye by placing them as in the following
table between the same limiting notes, except that the Dorian
and Hypodorian will extend a tone lower inasmuch as they
exceed the others by a tone.

TABLE 15.

SIX ANCIENT SCALES IN PITCH RELATION.

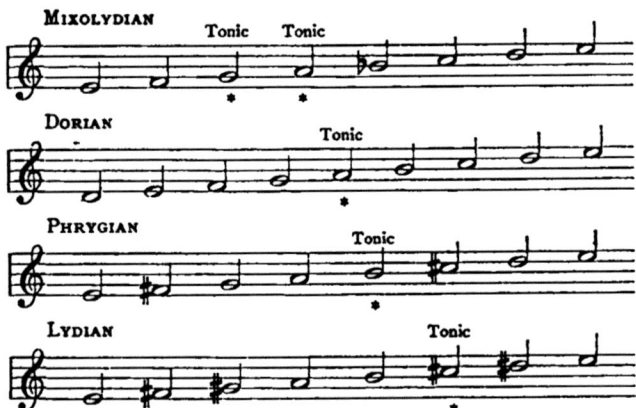

I have omitted the Enharmonic and Chromatic scales in this table, as the Diatonic are sufficient to illustrate the principle before us.

If we assume the pitch of the Mixolydian tonic to be ♯*G* which lies intermediate between the two Mesae *G* and *A*; the tonics of these scales taken in the above order are ♯*F*, *G*, ♯*G*, *A*, *B*, ♯*C*. We naturally conclude that the lowest scale is the Hypophrygian, and the Hypodorian, Mixolydian, Dorian, Phrygian and Lydian follow it at intervals respectively of a semitone, a semitone, a semitone, a tone, a tone, a tone. When at a later time the true construction of the Mixolydian was discovered, and its Mese was seen to be *D*, its position in the pitch series was changed, and it became the highest of the scales. (See below, p. 128.)

26. Besides these scales, all of which are complete or continuous in the sense that they employ all the notes melodically possible between their extremities, Greek art made use at this time of certain deficient scales which were called transilient, because they skipped some of the possible stopping places in their progression. The following

transilient scales in the Enharmonic genus are recorded
by Aristides Quintilianus (Meibom, p. 21).

(a) IONIAN

(b) HIGH LYDIAN

Another example is the well-known scale of Terpander
[see Aristotle *Probl.* xix. 32 and Nicomachus (Meibom,
p. 7)].

In the passage in which Aristides quotes these defective
scales he promises to supply on a later occasion the reasons
for the omission of the wanting notes. Unfortunately the
promised explanation is not to be found in his extant
writings, and it is impossible for us to supply the loss. But
we may conjecture that one cause of transilient scales was
the adaptation of an instrument to a scale larger than that
for which it was originally intended. Thus the scale of
Terpander would naturally find a partial explanation at any
rate in the attempt to get as much as possible of the
octachord scale

out of a seven-stringed lyre originally constructed to meet
the heptachord

INTRODUCTION

The Ionian scale of Aristides Quintilianus would seem to
have been obtained from the scale of two conjunct tetrachords by the omission of the two passing notes of the
upper tetrachord, and the introduction of one of the passing
notes of the disjunct tetrachord

It is thus an example at the same time of deficiency and of
the mixture of *conjunction* and *disjunction*; and the comparison of it with the Phrygian scale supports us in our view that
the characteristic feature of Phrygian and Ionian music alike
was the retention of the Fourth above the tonic.

27. From this point the development of the Greek musical
system proceeded upon lines which are easy to trace. The
most prominent moments in that development were the
growing importance of the Diatonic genus in comparison
with the Enharmonic and Chromatic, and the disappearance
of the Dorian and Ionian Harmonies. Thus the development was a process of simplification in which the artificial
scale-readings which we have been considering were gradually
eliminated. It was seen that the section of the diatonic
scale of the Aeolian Harmony from D to d (see Table 9)
contains all the same characteristic features as the so-called
Phrygian scale in the same genus. Similarly the Hypophrygian scale was seen to be the segment from G to g. Similarly,
as we have already said, the Mixolydian scale was seen to
be that portion in which the Mese stands second note from
the top. The Dorian and Hypodorian scales were deprived
of the second disjunctive tone which was their distinctive
feature, and were merged by coincidence in the one scale
called Dorian which was the segment between E and e.
Thus finally all distinctions of Harmonies perished; henceforth all scales were but the τρόποι or modes of one note-

34

series. To complete the number, the modes from *F* to *f* and from *A* to *a* were called respectively Hypolydian and Hypodorian on the analogy of the Hypophrygian. The results of this process of simplification are given in the following table :—

TABLE 16.

THE SEVEN MODES IN THE THREE GENERA.

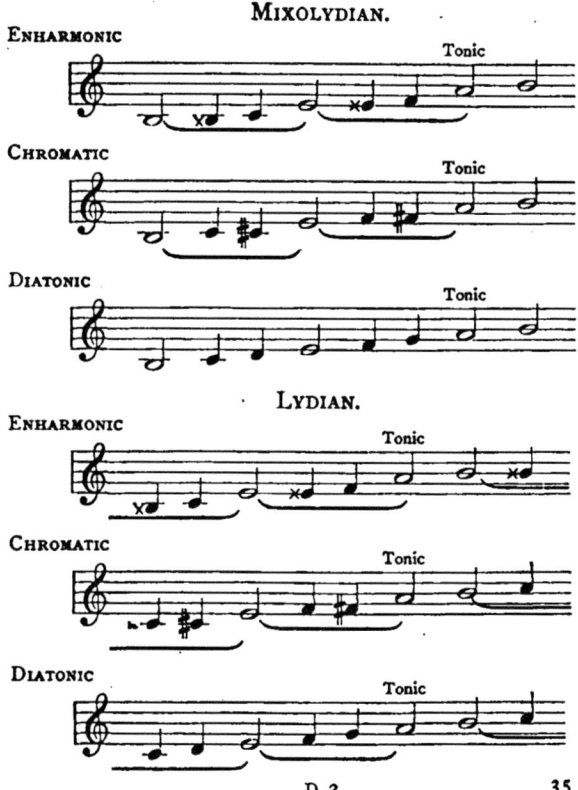

MIXOLYDIAN.

ENHARMONIC

CHROMATIC

DIATONIC

LYDIAN.

ENHARMONIC

CHROMATIC

DIATONIC

INTRODUCTION

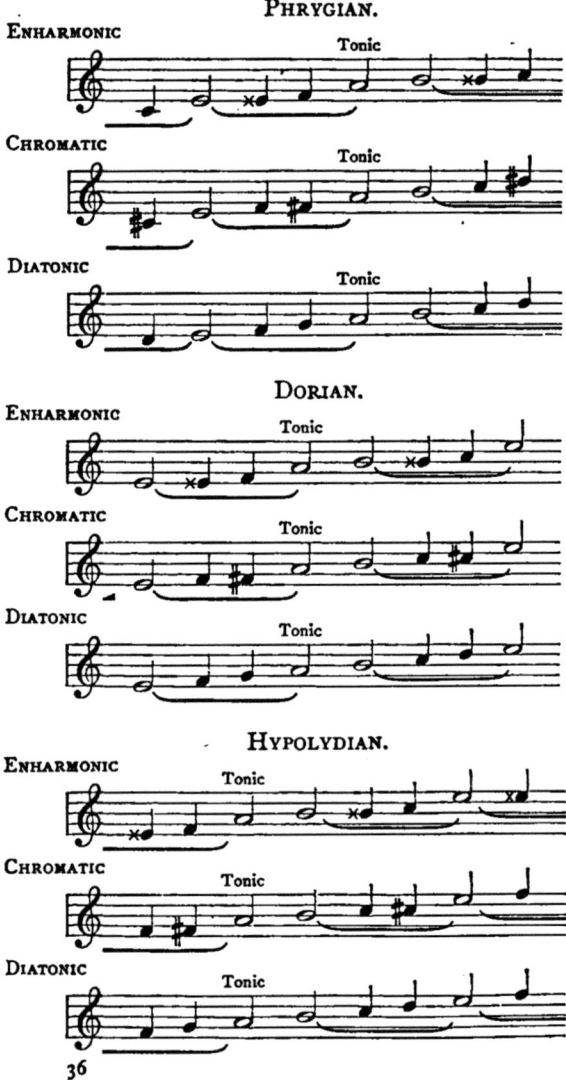

36

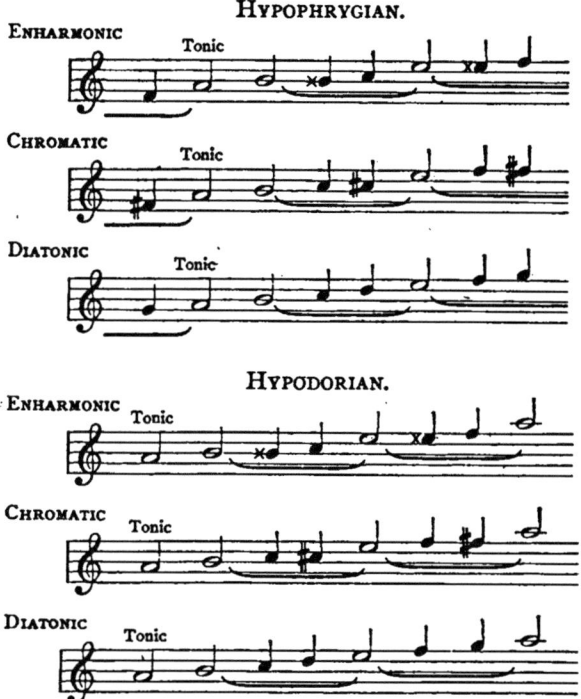

The pitch relations of the seven modes are exhibited in the next Table.

TABLE 17.

THE SEVEN MODES (IN THE DIATONIC GENUS) REPRESENTED IN THEIR RELATIONS OF PITCH.

LYDIAN   Tonic

PHRYGIAN   Tonic

DORIAN   Tonic

HYPOLYDIAN   Tonic

HYPOPHRYGIAN   Tonic

HYPODORIAN   Tonic

From this table it appears that the Hypodorian with its tonic *F* is the lowest of the modes, and the Hypophrygian, Hypolydian, Dorian, Phrygian, Lydian, and Mixolydian follow at intervals respectively of a tone, a tone, a semitone, a tone, a tone, a semitone.

28. At the risk of falling into vain repetition, let us again consider the essence of the distinction between these modes. It is not a distinction of modality such as exists between our major and minor scales. The development of Greek Music preserved, amidst all its changes, the original tetrachord as the permanent unit of composition. And even the differences that came into being through the various Harmonies had not survived, so that the principle of construction remained identical in the change of mode. .

Again, it is a distinction in the order of intervals, but only in so far as the several modes are different sections of one common whole.

Again, it is a distinction of pitch, but not such as exists between our keys, for it arises immediately from the order of intervals. The Mixolydian is a high mode because any melody composed in it, whatever be the absolute pitch of its total compass, must necessarily lie for the most part in the upper region of that compass.

Finally, because it is such a distinction of pitch, it is also a distinction of ethos or mood. To understand this, let us assume that high tension of the voice is the natural expression of poignant grief, an easy relaxation of it the natural expression of sentimentalism ; let us suppose, too, that to represent these emotions respectively a musician desires to write two songs, neither of which is to exceed the compass of an octave. How, then, shall he bestow the required character on each of these melodies? Evidently not by choosing a low key for one and a high key for the other, in the modern sense of the terms 'high' and 'low' key ; for this would imply that all first treble songs must be tragic, and all bass songs sentimental. He must, instead, leave the general pitch of the songs undetermined, so that either of them may suit any voice ; but he must so compose them that the one will lie chiefly in the upper, the other in the lower region of the undetermined eight-note compass. And this a Greek musician could only effect by choosing, for his pathetic song, a scale in which the tonic lay near its upper extremity, and for his sentimental, one in which its position was the reverse [1].

---

[1] Cp. Ptolemaeus, lib. ii, cap. 7 οὐδὲ γὰρ ἕνεκεν τῶν βαρυτέρων ἢ ὀξυτέρων φωνῶν εὕροιμεν ἂν τὴν σύστασιν τῆς κατὰ τὸν τόνον μεταβολῆς γεγενημένην, ὁπότε πρὸς τὴν τοιαύτην διαφορὰν ἢ τῶν ὀργάνων ὅλων ἐπίτασις ἢ πάλιν ἄνεσις ἀπαρκεῖ, μηδεμιᾶς γε παραλλαγῆς περὶ τὸ μέλος

INTRODUCTION

29. At this stage the compass of the Greek scale, whose growth from tetrachord to heptachord, and from heptachord to octachord we have already witnessed, underwent a further extension. To the typical scale

were added at its upper extremity a conjunct tetrachord

and at its lower extremity a conjunct tetrachord and an additional note below (called the προσλαμβανόμενος) at the interval of a tone

The resulting scale was called the Greater Complete System,

ἀποτελουμένης, ὅταν ὅλον ὁμοίως ὑπὸ τῶν βαρυφωνοτέρων ἢ τῶν ὀξυφωνο-
τέρων ἀγωνιστῶν διαπεραίνηται· ἀλλ' ἕνεκα τοῦ κατὰ τὴν μίαν φωνὴν τὸ
αὐτὸ μέλος ποτὲ μὲν ἀπὸ τῶν ὀξυτέρων τόπων ἀρχόμενον, ποτὲ δὲ ἀπὸ
τῶν βαρυτέρων, τροπήν τινα τοῦ ἤθους ἀποτελεῖν. 'Nor should we find that modulation of key was introduced for the sake of higher or lower voices ; for this difference can be met by the raising or lowering of the whole instrument, as the melody remains unaffected whether it is performed consistently throughout by artists with high or by artists with low voices. The object of modulation is rather that the one unbroken melody sung by the one voice may produce a change of feeling by having its tonic (lit. ' having its beginning') now in the higher, now in the lower, regions of that one voice.'

40

TABLE 18.

THE GREATER COMPLETE SYSTEM WITH THE NAMES OF ITS NOTES.

As will be seen from this table, all the notes of the Greater Complete System with the exception of the Proslambanomenos were distinguished by the same names which had been employed for the eight-note scale with the addition of a term to mark the particular tetrachord to which each belongs. The tetrachords were named in order Hypatôn i.e. 'of the lowest[1],' Mesôn i.e. 'of the middle,' Diezeugmenôn[2] i.e. ' of the disjunct,' Hyperbolaeôn i.e. ' of the highest ' notes.

Side by side with the Greater Complete System there stood another scale called the Lesser Complete System, in which was preserved the tradition of the Ionian Harmony and the heptachord scale. The following table exhibits its scheme and nomenclature :—

TABLE 19.

THE LESSER COMPLETE SYSTEM WITH THE NAMES OF ITS NOTES.

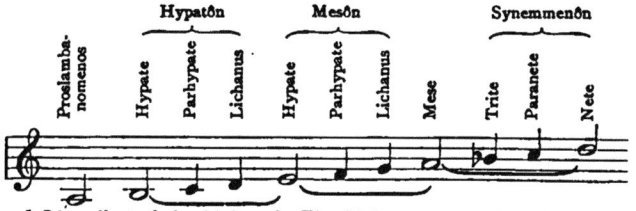

[1] Literally ' of the highest.' The *highest* or top *string* of the lyre gave the *lowest note*. [2] Also called Netôn.

INTRODUCTION

30. The following table exhibits the seven modes with the names of their notes according to the nomenclature of Table 18 :—

TABLE 20.

THE SEVEN MODES WITH THE NAMES OF THEIR NOTES.

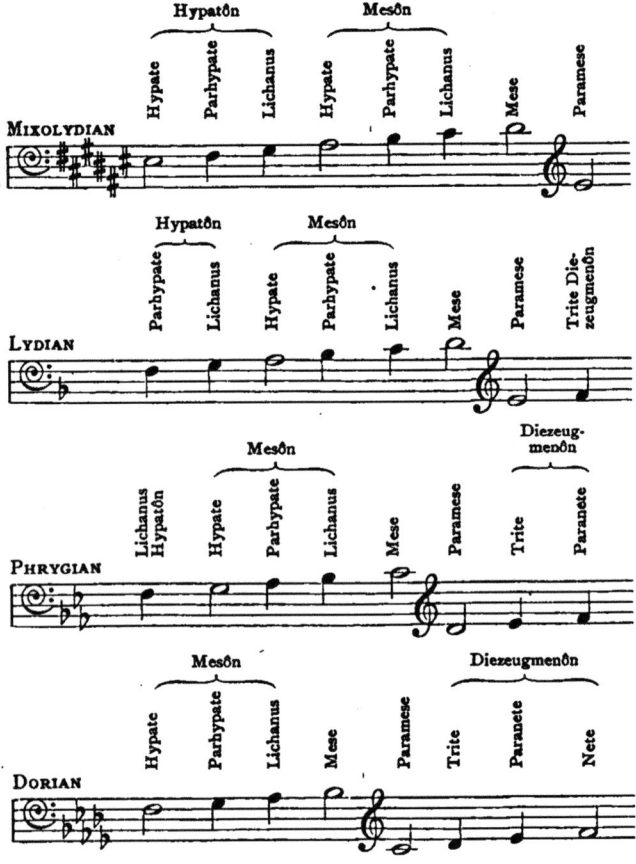

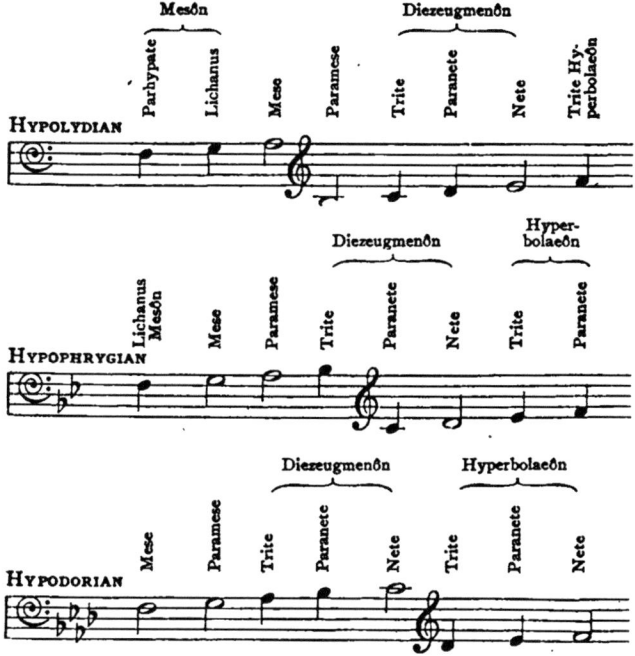

The nature of each mode as merely a segment of the typical scale of Table 18 is here apparent ; and the theorists showed their full recognition of this fact by extending, as is done in the following table, each of the modes to the typical compass of two octaves. The result is a series of seven scales identical in figure or order of intervals, but determinately distinguished from one another by the relation of their pitch. In other words, the modes or τρόποι have become τόνοι or keys.

INTRODUCTION

TABLE 21.

THE SEVEN KEYS.

The modes are marked off by bars.

This is a very striking change of conception. It means that the sense of the independent and distinct character of the modes was almost extinct. But this was an inevitable consequence of musical development; for that sense presupposed the limitation of the scale to an octave, and this limitation necessarily vanished before the widening demands of a growing art, and the larger possibilities of more elaborate instruments.

31. The number of the keys was afterwards, apparently by Aristoxenus, raised to thirteen by the addition of (1) a key at a semitone below the Phrygian, called the Second Phrygian or Ionian; (2) a key at a semitone below the Lydian, called the Second Lydian or Aeolian; (3) a key at a semitone below the Hypophrygian, called the Second Hypophrygian or Hypoionian; (4) a key at a semitone below the Hypolydian, called the Second Hypolydian or Hypoaeolian; (5) a key at a semitone above the Mixolydian, called the Hyperionian; (6) a key at a semitone above the Hyperionian, called the Hyperphrygian. In this scheme the Mixolydian key took the name of Hyperdorian on the analogy of Hyperionian and Hyperphrygian. At a still later date two higher keys were added at intervals of a semitone and tone above the Hyperphrygian, and were called respectively the Hyperaeolian and Hyperlydian. Thus we obtain the full number of fifteen keys which we find with their notation in the fragment of Alypius.

In the following table for the sake of completeness and convenience of reference, we present these fifteen keys with their notation [1], and in the three Genera, including the tetrachord Synemmenôn of the Lesser Complete System.

---

[1] On the question of the Greek notation, the reader is referred to Westphal, *Harmonik und Melopöie der Griechen* (c. viii); Gevaert, *Musique de l'Antiquité* (t. I. pp. 244 ff); Monro, *Modes of Ancient Greek Music* (§ 27). Each sound was denoted by two characters, one for the voice, and one for instruments. The vocal characters are plainly derived from the ordinary alphabet; but both the forms and the order of the instrumental characters raise great difficulties.

TABLE 22.

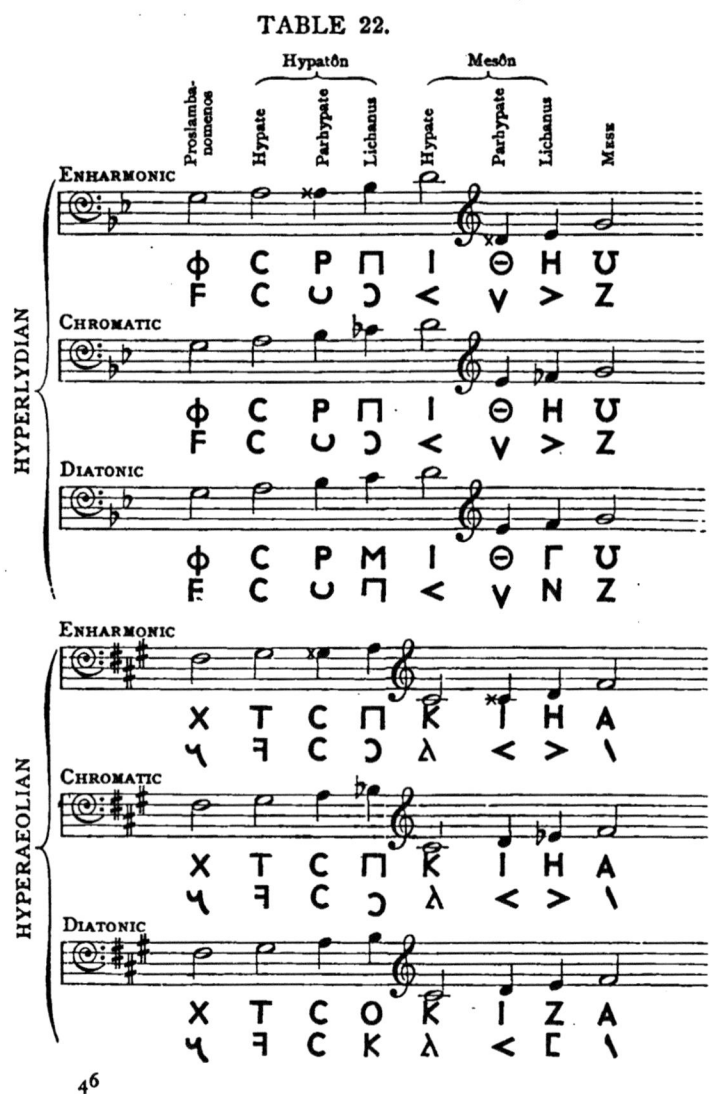

TABLE 22.

50

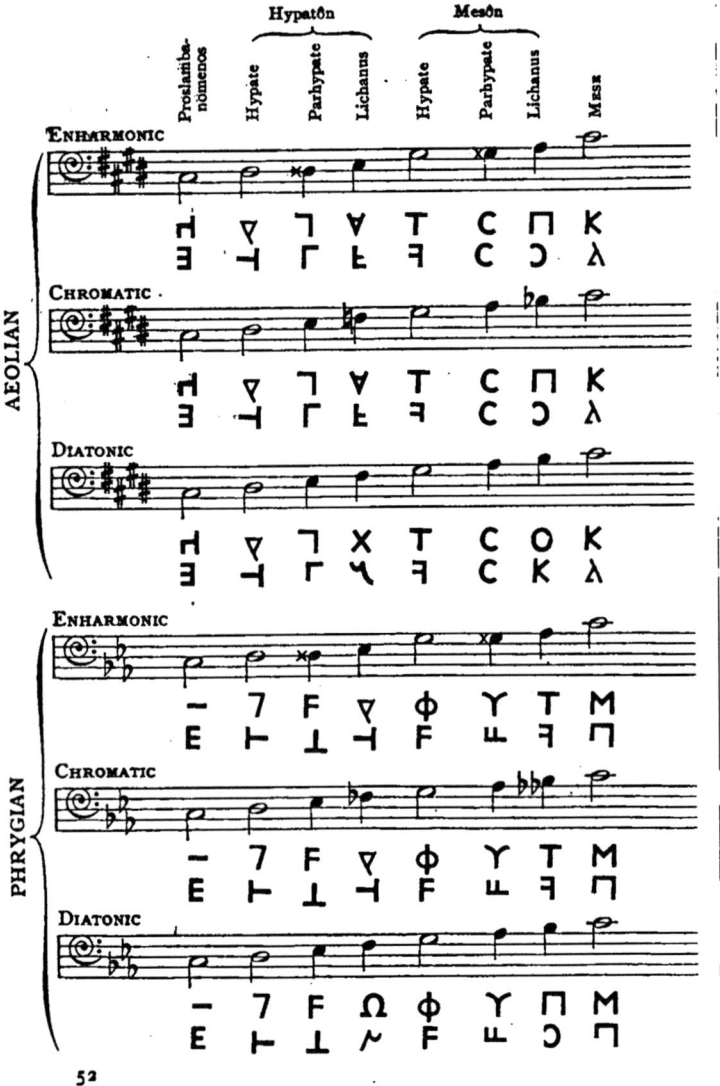

INTRODUCTION

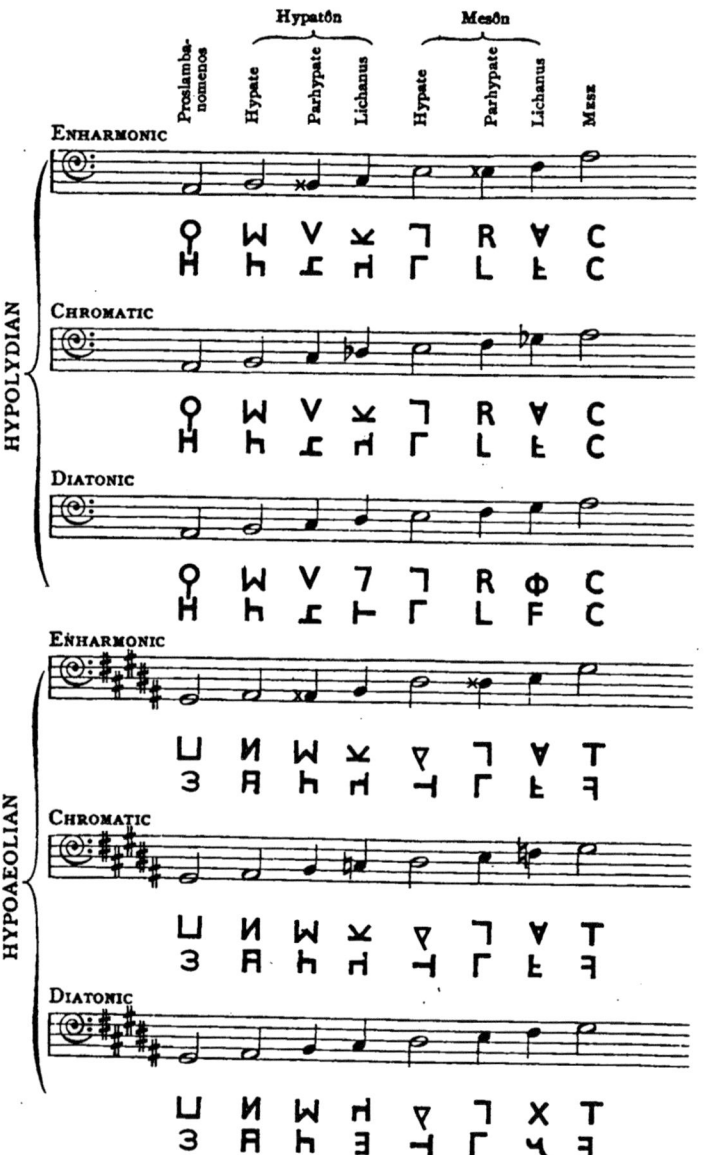

56

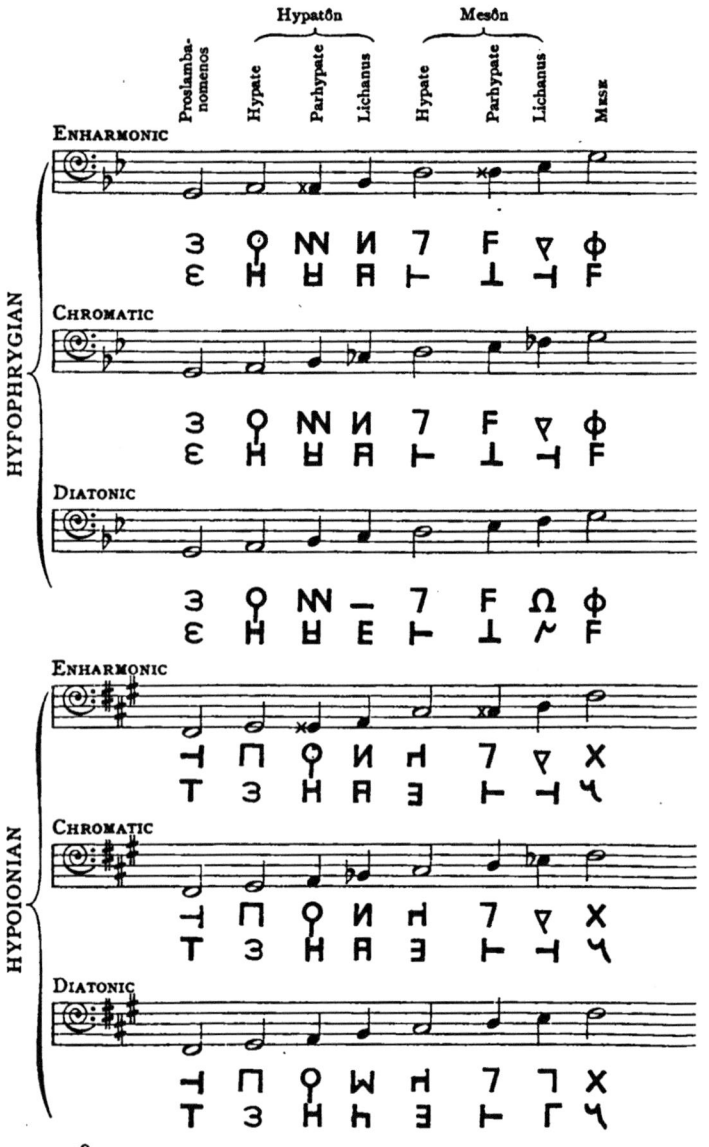

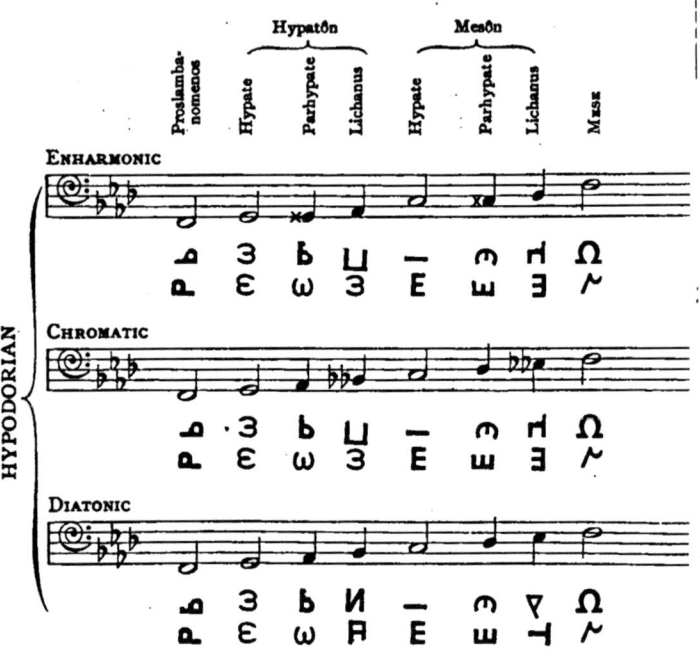

32. At this stage then the musical science of Greece found the material of all musical composition in a certain number of two-octave scales, uniform in construction, in the order of intervals, in the relation of the other notes to the tonic, but constituting in pitch a regular series spaced by equal intervals, admitting also theoretically the three genera of Enharmonic, Chromatic, and Diatonic, though the two former would seem to have fallen into practical disuse. And these scales may be resolved into the following elementary relations :—

(a) The relation between a note and its octave above or below ;

(b) the relation of a note to its Fourth above ;

(c) the relation of a note to its Fifth below ;

(d) the relation of two passing notes to the extremities of a tetrachord determined in so far that of the resulting intervals the lowest must be less than or equal to the middle, and less than the highest.

The scheme of these scales, as has been already said, must not be identified with either our major or our minor mode. In the Greek scale of the Diatonic genus the notes follow one another, it is true, at the same distance as in our descending minor scale, but the δύναμις or function of the notes is different, and the essence of a note is its function. The essential feature of our minor scale is the concord of the Minor Third which makes part of its common chord ; and this was to the Greek ear a discord, that is, a sound-relation not to be immediately recognized or permanently acquiesced in, but demanding resolution and change.

33. We have seen that in this conception of the keys the distinction of modes is virtually ignored. But it was destined to be revived by the revolution in musical science which was effected by Ptolemy, the celebrated mathematician of Alexandria. This theorist observing that, by the extension of the modes illustrated in Table 21, their distinc-

tive feature of supplying certain segments of the common
scale for the use of composers and performers had been
sacrificed, reduced them again to their original compass;
and, to emphasize the fact that their very nature forbade
their extension, he introduced (or made popular) a new
nomenclature by which the several notes of any mode were
designated in relation to that mode only, and not in relation
to the common scale of which they were all segments.
Thus the terms Hypate, Parhypate, Lichanus, Mese, Paramese, Trite, Paranete, and Nete were employed to signify
the First, Second, Third, Fourth, Fifth, Sixth, Seventh, and
Eighth notes of all the modes alike. These names were distinguished from those of the old system by the addition to
the former of the term κατὰ θέσιν 'in respect of position,' and
to the latter of the term κατὰ δύναμιν 'in respect of function.'

TABLE 23.

SEVEN MODES WITH THEIR OLD NOMENCLATURE AND
THE NOMENCLATURE OF PTOLEMY.

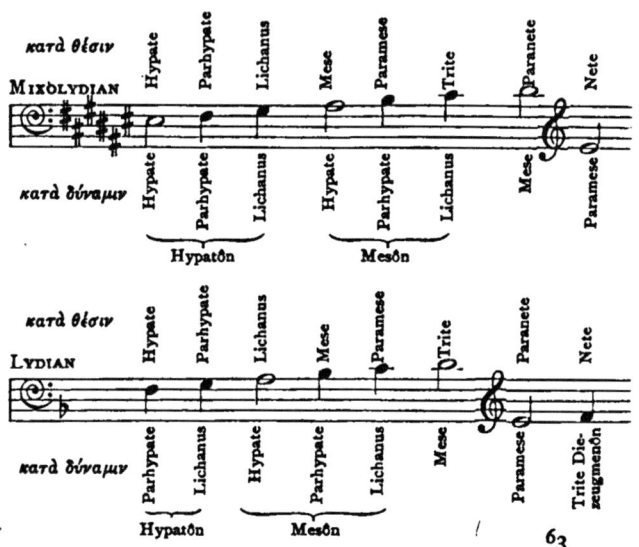

INTRODUCTION

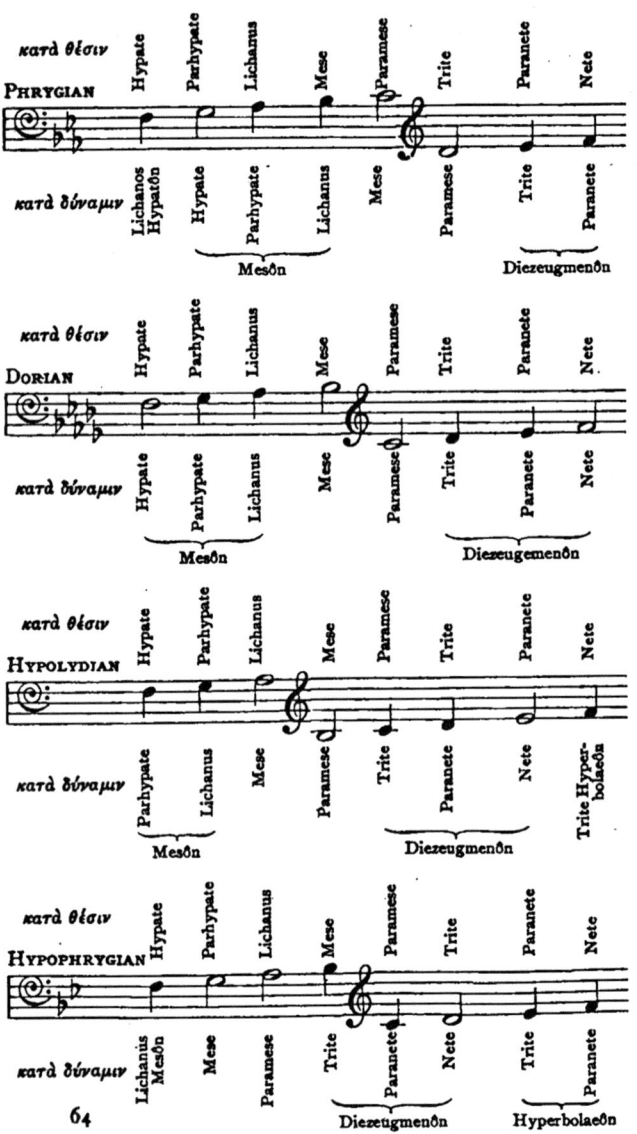

But even in this innovation we are not justified in tracing any new sense of the possibility of different modalities. For Ptolemy himself asserts that the object of passing from one mode to another is merely to bring the melody within a new compass of notes.

At this point we may close our investigation, as the further development of musical science belongs to the history of Modern Europe.

34. For the sake of conciseness I have adopted in the preceding paragraphs the somewhat misleading method of presenting, in the form of an historical statement, what is in reality a mere hypothesis. For the same reason I have omitted details, and restricted myself to the most general features of the development. The latter of these deficiencies will to some extent be made good in the notes on the text of Aristoxenus; the former demands our immediate attention. Strict demonstration of the truth of our hypothesis is in the nature of the case impossible; but we must at least examine the rival hypotheses and satisfy ourselves that the facts which tell fatally against them leave it unassailed. At the same time we must not be disappointed if many facts remain unexplained. In the development of any branch of human activity there is much that is accidental; accidental, in the sense that the explanation of it is not to be found inside the sphere of that activity. We shall be satisfied

then if we find that our hypothesis accounts for many of the recorded facts, and is not irrefragably refuted by any of them; while the other intrinsically possible hypotheses—there are but two—are put out of court by the weight of unanswerable argument and evidence.

35. Of one of these hypotheses the essential thesis is that the seven modes of Table 16 differ from one another as do our major and minor scales, that is in modality, or in the relations which the other notes of the scale bear to the tonic. The tonic of each scale it finds in the fourth note from its lower extremity, the μέση κατὰ θέσιν of Ptolemy.

According to this view the seven modes and their tonics may be represented in the following Table. In (a) the scales are given in the Greek form, with the tonic in the Fourth place from the bottom; in (b) they are given in modern form, and start from the tonic.

TABLE 24.

THE SEVEN MODES ACCORDING TO THE MODALITY
THEORY.

66

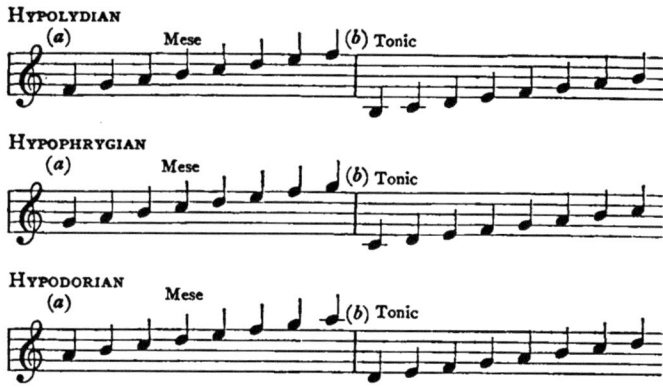

36. We cannot deny that at first sight this theory has
much to recommend it. It affords an adequate explanation
of the striking names bestowed upon the seven modes; for
if these differed in modality, they certainly deserved distinctive titles. It enables us too, on the analogy of our major
and minor scales, to conceive how the Greeks might have
found in each mode a distinctive Ethos or emotional character. Doubtless the objection at once presents itself that
the ancient nomenclature of the notes recognizes no such
variety of modality, that the note before the disjunctive tone
is the Mese in every scale, no matter what its place therein
may be. But this objection the theory finds little difficulty
in answering. For it is quite permissible to suppose that
one mode, because it was most common or most ancient,
or for some other reason, was regarded by the theorists as
typical, and that the nomenclature of the notes, originally
applicable to that scale only, came to be applied at a later
date to scales of different modality. Besides we have
seen that, in the time of Ptolemy, if not earlier, there was
a second system of nomenclature by which notes derived
their names from their positions in their respective scales,

and according to this system the fourth note of every scale was its Mese.

37. Nevertheless this plausible hypothesis is absolutely untenable, as the following considerations will show.

In the first place we must note that the modes are not the invention of theorists, but scales in practical use. Now, it is hardly conceivable, and in the absence of evidence or parallel wholly incredible, that an early and undeveloped artistic impulse should have produced such a variety of modalities, so many distinct languages, as one might say, of musical expression, not distributed through different regions and races, but all intelligible and enjoyable alike to a Hellene of Hellas proper.

In the second place, the distinction which is here supposed between the modes is essential not accidental, and as such, it is wholly impossible that it should have been overlooked by the Greek theorists, who have proved themselves in other respects the most subtle of analysts. Yet in all the extant authorities there is not one hint of such a distinction. Nay, we might go further and say that we cannot admit this hypothesis without convicting these theorists of a radically false analysis. If the tonic of the scale

is *C*, the scale must divide itself into the tetrachords

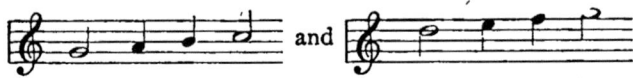

in which *G*, *c*, *d*, and *g* are the fixed, and *a*, *b*, *e*, and *f* the passing notes. But the theorists recognize no tetrachord of either of these forms; but insist that in all tetrachords of which the extreme points are the fixed notes, and

68

the inner the passing notes, the lowest interval must be less than the highest, and equal to or less than the middle. To take one from the countless instances we read in the *Isagoge* (Meibom, 3. 4):

Γένη δέ ἐστι τρία, διάτονον, χρῶμα, ἁρμονία, καὶ μελῳδεῖται τὸ μὲν διάτονον ἐπὶ μὲν τὸ βαρὺ κατὰ τόνον καὶ τόνον καὶ ἡμιτόνιον, ἐπὶ δὲ τὸ ὀξὺ ἐναντίως κατὰ ἡμιτόνιον καὶ τόνον καὶ τόνον. τὸ δὲ χρῶμα ἐπὶ μὲν τὸ βαρὺ κατὰ τριημιτόνιον καὶ ἡμιτόνιον καὶ ἡμιτόνιον, ἐπὶ δὲ τὸ ὀξὺ ἐναντίως κατὰ ἡμιτόνιον καὶ ἡμιτόνιον καὶ τριημιτόνιον. ἡ δὲ ἁρμονία ἐπὶ μὲν τὸ βαρὺ κατὰ δίτονον καὶ δίεσιν καὶ δίεσιν, ἐπὶ δὲ τὸ ὀξὺ ἐναντίως κατὰ δίεσιν καὶ δίεσιν καὶ δίτονον.

Here we find a certain order of the intervals of the tetrachord affirmed without qualification. This affirmation implies that all diatonic scales can be reduced to compositions of tetrachords of the form

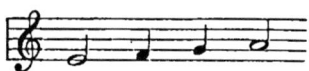

But the scale

if *C* be its tonic could not be so reduced except by an analysis extending to the superficial qualities only, and leaving the essential nature untouched.

Take again the following passage from the *Isagoge* (Meibom, 19. 1) ἀπὸ δὲ τῆς μέσης καὶ τῶν λοιπῶν φθόγγων αἱ δυνάμεις γνωρίζονται, τὸ γὰρ πῶς ἔχει ἕκαστος αὐτῶν πρὸς τὴν μέσην φανερῶς γίγνεται. 'It is from the Mese that we start to discern the functions of the other notes; for plainly it is in relation to the Mese that each of them is thus or thus;'

Or this still more striking passage from Aristotle (*Problems*, xix. 20):

INTRODUCTION

Διὰ τί, ἐὰν μέν τις τὴν μέσην κινήσῃ ἡμῶν, ἁρμόσας τὰς
ἄλλας χορδάς, καὶ χρῆται τῷ ὀργάνῳ, οὐ μόνον ὅταν κατὰ τὸν τῆς
μέσης γένηται φθόγγον, λυπεῖ καὶ φαίνεται ἀνάρμοστον, ἀλλὰ
καὶ κατὰ τὴν ἄλλην μελῳδίαν· ἐὰν δὲ τὴν λιχανὸν ἤ τινα ἄλλον
φθόγγον, τότε φαίνεται διαφέρειν μόνον, ὅταν κἀκείνῃ τις χρῆται;
—Ἡ εὐλόγως τοῦτο συμβαίνει; πάντα γὰρ τὰ χρηστὰ μέλη
πολλάκις τῇ μέσῃ χρῆται, καὶ πάντες οἱ ἀγαθοὶ ποιηταὶ πυκνὰ
πρὸς τὴν μέσην ἀπαντῶσι, κἂν ἀπέλθωσι, ταχὺ ἐπανέρχονται,
πρὸς δὲ ἄλλην οὕτως οὐδεμίαν. καθάπερ ἐκ τῶν λόγων ἐνίων
ἐξαιρεθέντων συνδέσμων οὐκ ἔστιν ὁ λόγος Ἑλληνικός, οἷον τὸ
τέ καὶ τὸ καί. ἔνιοι δὲ οὐθὲν λυποῦσι, διὰ τὸ τοῖς μὲν ἀναγκαῖον
εἶναι χρῆσθαι πολλάκις, εἰ ἔσται λόγος, τοῖς δὲ μή. οὕτω καὶ τῶν
φθόγγων ἡ μέση ὥσπερ σύνδεσμός ἐστι, καὶ μάλιστα τῶν καλῶν,
διὰ τὸ πλειστάκις ἐνυπάρχειν τὸν φθόγγον αὐτῆς.

[Translated by Mr. Monro, *Modes of Ancient Greek Music*,
p. 43: 'Why is it that if the Mese is altered, after the
other chords have been tuned, the instrument is felt to be
out of tune not only when the Mese is sounded, but through
the whole of the music—whereas if the Lichanus or any
other note is out of tune, it seems to be perceived only
when that note is struck? Is it to be explained on the
ground that all good melodies often use the Mese, and all
good composers resort to it frequently, and if they leave it
soon return again, but do not make the same use of any
other note? Just as language cannot be Greek if certain
conjunctions are omitted, such as τε and καί, while others
may be dispensed with, because the one class is necessary
for language, but not the other; so with musical sounds the
Mese is a kind of "conjunction," especially of beautiful
sounds, since it is most often heard among these.']

It is hard to imagine how the nature of a tonic could be
more clearly and truly indicated than it has been by the
author of this passage in his description of the Mese. And
as he expressly states that the Mese is the centre of unity

in all good music, he must have recognized only one modality. An attempt has, indeed, been made to evade this conclusion by supposing Aristotle to refer not to the μέση κατὰ δύναμιν, but to the μέση κατὰ θέσιν. But this supposition is quite untenable, not only because the nomenclature κατὰ θέσιν in all probability was the invention of Ptolemy, but also for this much more convincing reason that the terms κατὰ δύναμιν and κατὰ θέσιν seem framed with the direct intention of precluding such a supposition. The μέση κατὰ θέσιν is merely the note which is located in the centre of a group; the μέση κατὰ δύναμιν is the note which discharges the function of a centre of unity to a system. The first is a mathematical, the second a dynamical centre. When, therefore, the whole train of Aristotle's reasoning is based on his conception of the Mese as the connecting bond of musical sounds, can there be any manner of doubt to which Mese he refers?

38. Again, we have seen that one attractive feature of this hypothesis is that it offers a plausible explanation of the fact that the Greeks attributed a distinct Ethos or emotional character to each of the modes. It now remains to show that this plausible explanation is refuted by the express statement of the authorities as to the conditions of this Ethos.

Consider the following passages :—

(a) Plato, *Republic*, iii. 398 E:

Τίνες οὖν θρηνώδεις ἁρμονίαι; . . . Μιξολυδιστί, ἔφη, καὶ Συντονολυδιστὶ καὶ τοιαῦταί τινες.—Τίνες οὖν μαλακαί τε καὶ συμποτικαὶ τῶν ἁρμονιῶν; Ἰαστί, ἦ δ᾽ ὅς, καὶ Λυδιστί, αἵτινες χαλαραὶ καλοῦνται.

'What then are the scales of mourning?' 'Mixolydian,' said he, 'and High Lydian, and some others of the same character.' 'Which of the scales then are soft and convivial?' 'The Ionian,' he replied, 'and Lydian, such as are called slack' (i.e. low-pitched).

INTRODUCTION

(*b*) Aristotle, *Politics*, vi (iv). 3. 1290 a 20 :

Ὁμοίως δ' ἔχει καὶ περὶ τὰς ἁρμονίας, ὥς φασί τινες· καὶ γὰρ
ἐκεῖ τίθενται εἴδη δύο, τὴν Δωριστὶ καὶ τὴν Φρυγιστί, τὰ δὲ ἄλλα
συντάγματα τὰ μὲν Δώρια τὰ δὲ Φρύγια καλοῦσιν. μάλιστα μὲν
οὖν εἰώθασιν οὕτως ὑπολαμβάνειν περὶ τῶν πολιτειῶν· ἀληθέστερον
δὲ καὶ βέλτιον ὡς ἡμεῖς διείλομεν δυοῖν ἢ μιᾶς οὔσης τῆς καλῶς
συνεστηκυίας τὰς ἄλλας εἶναι παρεκβάσεις, τὰς μὲν τῆς εὖ κε-
κραμένης ἁρμονίας, τὰς δὲ τῆς ἀρίστης πολιτείας, ὀλιγαρχικὰς μὲν
τὰς συντονωτέρας καὶ δεσποτικωτέρας, τὰς δ' ἀνειμένας καὶ
μαλακὰς δημοτικάς.

'Some would have it that it is the same in the case of
scales ; there too they posit two species, Dorian and
Phrygian, and all other systems they class as either one or
the other of these. Such is the common view of forms of
government. But our analysis was truer and more satis-
factory, according to which of perfect systems there are but
one, or two, while the rest are deviations, in the one case
from the scale of proper composition, in the other from the
best possible government ; those that incline to high pitch
and masterfulness, being of the nature of oligarchy, those
that are low in pitch and slack being of the nature of
democracy.'

(*c*) Aristotle, *Politics*, v (viii). 5. 1340 a 38 :

Εὐθὺς γὰρ ἡ τῶν ἁρμονιῶν διέστηκε φύσις ὥστε ἀκούοντας
ἄλλως διατίθεσθαι καὶ μὴ τὸν αὐτὸν ἔχειν τρόπον πρὸς ἑκάστην
αὐτῶν, ἀλλὰ πρὸς μὲν ἐνίας ὀδυρτικωτέρως καὶ συνεστηκότως
μᾶλλον, οἷον πρὸς τὴν Μιξολυδιστὶ καλουμένην, πρὸς δὲ τὰς
μαλακωτέρως τὴν διάνοιαν, οἷον πρὸς τὰς ἀνειμένας.

'To begin with there is such a distinction in the nature
of scales that each of them produces a different disposition
in the listener. By some of them, as for example the
Mixolydian, we are disposed to grief and depression ;. by
others, as for example the low-pitched ones, we are disposed to tenderness of sentiment.'

THE DEVELOPMENT OF GREEK MUSIC

(*d*) Aristotle, *Politics*, v (viii). 7. 1342 b 20 :

Οἷον τοῖς ἀπειρηκόσι διὰ χρόνον οὐ ῥᾴδιον ᾄδειν τὰς συντόνους ἁρμονίας, ἀλλὰ τὰς ἀνειμένας ἡ φύσις ὑποβάλλει τοῖς τηλικούτοις.

' Thus for those whose powers have failed through years it is not easy to sing the high scales, and their time of life naturally suggests the use of the low.'

From these passages it is clear in the first place that the Ethos of the modes was dependent on their pitch, and in the second place that the pitch on which the Ethos depended made them severally suitable for voices of a certain class or condition. But, if the distinction between the modes is one of modality in our sense of the word there is no reason in the nature of things why they should differ in pitch at all. And though we might assume for them a conventional distinction in pitch by regarding them theoretically as fragments of one typical scale shifted from one point of pitch to another, the assumption would not help us to meet the facts. A conventional distinction of pitch cannot be the basis of an absolute distinction of Ethos, nor can it account for the practical suitability of certain scales to certain voices.

39. The weight of these arguments is so irresistible that we are not surprised to find Mr. Monro substituting a new hypothesis in his *Modes of Ancient Greek Music*. Unfortunately this substitute, though it embodies one most important truth, is open itself to objections no less grave. The fundamental principle from which Mr. Monro's theory starts is that the Greeks knew but one modality, that is one set of relations between the notes of a scale and its tonic ; and the establishment of this principle by argument and evidence is the great·contribution of Mr. Monro to the study of Greek Music. Proceeding from this principle, he maintains that the terms Dorian, Lydian, Phrygian originally designated merely so many *keys*, that is so many scales identical in their intervals and in the order of them, but

73

differing in pitch. The connexion of these names with certain modes or scales of different figures arose in his opinion at a later period from the fact that practical limitations restricted composers and performers to a certain compass, and the name of the key was transferred to the particular order of notes which it afforded within that compass. Thus the term Mixolydian and Dorian originally denoted the two keys

MIXOLYDIAN

and

DORIAN

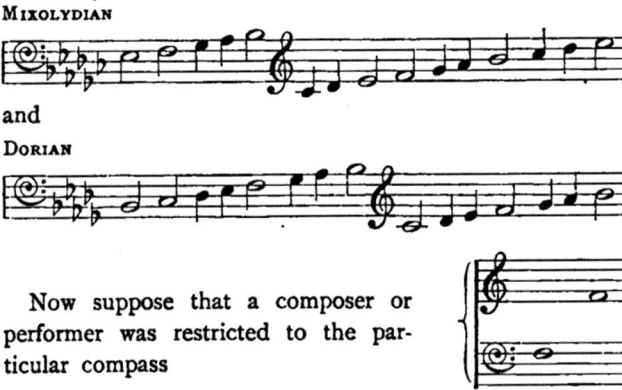

Now suppose that a composer or performer was restricted to the particular compass

Within that compass the Mixolydian key would give the series

which is of the form

and the Dorian the series

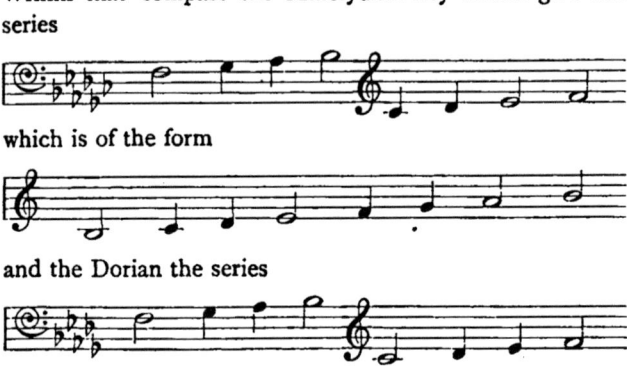

74

which is of the form

and in this way the terms might come to be applied to certain orders of intervals.

40. The objections to this theory are many and fatal. At the very outset, we are repelled by the supposition that such a striking nomenclature should have been adopted to denote such a superficial difference. Again, how are we to explain the distinct ethical character of the scales ? If the pitch of the Dorian, Phrygian, and other keys be only determined by their relation to one another, their emotional character must also be only relatively determined ; if, for example, high pitch is the natural expression of pathos, we can say of the higher of two keys that it is more pathetic than the lower, not that it is absolutely pathetic ; yet the Greeks always attribute an absolute character to each of the scales. It would follow that the pitch of the keys must have been absolutely determined. But of such absolute determination there is not a word in our authorities. Even if we assume it, in spite of their silence, surely it cannot have been exact. Absolute and exact determination would presuppose the universal recognition of a conventional standard embodied in some authorized instrument, or expressed in a mathematical formula ; the first alternative is precluded by its absurdity, and there is no evidence for the second. But if the determination, though absolute, was not exact, while we might admit an absolute difference of Ethos between a scale of extreme height and one of extreme depth, there could have been no such absolute difference between scales separated only by a tone or semitone ; for let there be but a slight variation between the tuning of one day and another, and the Phrygian of to-day will be the Lydian of to-

morrow. And even if we make Mr. Monro a present of all these objections, and grant the existence in ancient Greece of an absolute and exact determination of pitch, will any one venture to affirm that the difference of a tone or semitone in the pitch of two keys could result in such an antagonism in their moral effects, that Plato should have retained one of them as a valuable aid to ethical training, while he banished the other relentlessly from his ideal republic?

Again, it is not uncommon[1] to find the names of musicians recorded as inventors of certain scales. Would Mr. Monro have us believe that the only claim of these musicians to the regard of posterity is that they stretched the strings of their lyre a little more loosely or a little tighter than did their predecessors?

41. Returning now to the hypothesis which we have above proposed we shall consider a few passages which seem to offer striking confirmation of its truth.

(a) Heraclides Ponticus apud *Athenaeum*, xiv. 624 c :

Ἡρακλείδης δ' ὁ Ποντικὸς ἐν τρίτῳ περὶ Μουσικῆς οὐδ' ἁρμονίαν φησὶ δεῖν καλεῖσθαι τὴν Φρύγιον, καθάπερ οὐδὲ τὴν Λύδιον, ἁρμονίας γὰρ εἶναι τρεῖς· τρία γὰρ καὶ γενέσθαι Ἑλλήνων γένη, Δωριεῖς, Αἰολεῖς, Ἴωνας . . . (625 d) καταφρονητέον οὖν τῶν τὰς μὲν κατ' εἶδος διαφορὰς οὐ δυναμένων θεωρεῖν, ἐπακολουθούντων

---

[1] For example see Plutarch, *de Musica*, 1136 C-D Ἀριστόξενος δέ φησι Σαπφὼ πρώτην εὑρασθαι τὴν Μιξολυδιστί . . . ἐν δὲ τοῖς Ἱστορικοῖς τῆς Ἁρμονικῆς Πυθοκλείδην φησὶ τὸν αὐλητὴν εὑρετὴν αὐτῆς γεγονέναι . . . ἀλλὰ μὴν καὶ τὴν Ἐπανειμένην Λυδιστί, ἥπερ ἐναντία τῇ Μιξολυδιστί, παραπλησίαν οὖσαν τῇ Ἰάδι ὑπὸ Δαμῶνος εὑρῆσθαί φασι τοῦ Ἀθηναίου.

ἡ Ἐπανειμένη Λυδιστί, or low-pitched Lydian, is probably the same as the later Hypolydian. By the Ionian is probably meant the Hypophrygian. The Hypolydian in its schema, that is in the position of its tonic in relation to the other notes, is very similar to the Hypophrygian and most unlike the Mixolydian.

δὲ τῇ τῶν φθόγγων ὀξύτητι καὶ βαρύτητι καὶ τιθεμένων Ὑπερ-
μιξολύδιον ἁρμονίαν καὶ πάλιν ὑπὲρ ταύτης ἄλλην . . . δεῖ δὲ
τὴν ἁρμονίαν εἶδος ἔχειν ἤθους ἢ πάθους.

'Heraclides Ponticus in the third book of the *de Musica*
asserts that the term ἁρμονία should not be applied to the
Phrygian or Lydian scales ; that there are three Harmonies,
as there are three tribes of Hellenes—Dorians, Aeolians,
Ionians . . . We must conceive a very low opinion of the
theorists who fail to detect difference of species, while they
keep pace with every variation of pitch and establish a
Hypermixolydian Harmony and again another above that.
. . . But every Harmony should possess an ethical or
emotional character peculiar to itself.'

Mr. Monro, by a curious misapprehension, as I think, of
this passage, has accused Heraclides of carrying Hellenic
exclusiveness to the extreme of refusing the title of ἁρμονίαι
to the oriental scales of Lydia and Phrygia. But the
meaning of Heraclides' statement is that the seven scales
of Table 16, inasmuch as they are only so many segments
of the one scale, are all instances of the one ἁρμονία or
method of formation, and so cannot properly be termed so
many ἁρμονίαι. It was a different matter, he says, with the
three ancient Harmonies, the Dorian, Ionian, and Aeolian.
These were really distinct adjustments ; they were scales,
the principles of whose construction were essentially dissimilar. Difference of pitch, he proceeds to say, does not
constitute a new ἁρμονία.

(*b*) Aristides Quintilianus (Meibom, 21. 11) :

Τὸ μὲν οὖν Λύδιον διάστημα συνετίθεσαν ἐκ διέσεως, καὶ
διτόνου, καὶ τόνου, καὶ διέσεως, καὶ διέσεως, καὶ διτόνου, καὶ διέ-
σεως· καὶ τοῦτο μὲν ἦν τέλειον σύστημα, τὸ δὲ Δώριον ἐκ τόνου,
καὶ διέσεως, καὶ διέσεως, καὶ διτόνου, καὶ τόνου, καὶ διέσεως, καὶ
διέσεως, καὶ διτόνου· ἦν δὲ καὶ τοῦτο τόνῳ τὸ διὰ πασῶν ὑπερέχον.
τὸ δὲ Φρύγιον ἐκ τόνου, καὶ διέσεως, καὶ διέσεως, καὶ διτόνου, καὶ

τόνου, καὶ διέσεως, καὶ διέσεως, καὶ τόνου· ἦν δὲ καὶ τοῦτο τέλειον διὰ πασῶν.

'The Lydian scale they'[i.e. ancient musicians] 'composed of diesis, ditone, tone, diesis, diesis, ditone, diesis; this was a complete scale. The Dorian was composed of tone, diesis, diesis, ditone, tone, diesis, diesis, ditone; this scale again exceeded the octave by a tone. The Phrygian was composed of tone, diesis, diesis, ditone, tone, diesis, diesis, tone; this too was a complete octave.'

(c) The *Isagoge*, (Meibom, 20. 1):

Λύδιοι δὲ δύο, ὀξύτερος καὶ βαρύτερος, ὃς καὶ Αἰόλιος καλεῖται· Φρύγιοι δύο, ὁ μὲν βαρύς, ὃς καὶ Ἰάστιος· ὁ δ' ὀξύς. Δώριος εἷς. Ὑπολύδιοι δύο· ὀξύτερος καὶ βαρύτερος ὃς καὶ Ὑποαιόλιος καλεῖται. Ὑποφρύγιοι δύο, ὧν ὁ βαρύτερος καὶ Ὑποϊάστιος καλεῖται.

'Two Lydian keys, a higher, and a lower, also called Aeolian; two Phrygian, one low also called Ionian, and one high; one Dorian; two Hypolydian, a higher and a lower, also called Hypoaeolian; two Hypophrygian, of which the lower is also called Hypoionian.'

It appears from passage (a) that there was a period in the development of the Greek musical system when there existed three distinct Harmonies, i. e. three scales distinguished by the different methods in which their units were put together; and that these three Harmonies were termed Dorian, Aeolian, and Ionian. Now the units of Greek music are the tetrachords; and we cannot conceive how tetrachords could have been put together except by the method of conjunction, the method of disjunction, the method of alternate conjunction and disjunction, or a combination of two or more of these methods. It is probable then that the three Harmonies were the products of these three methods. But the characteristic feature of the Dorian scale of Aristides Quintilianus (see passage (b)) is

78

that it contains two disjunctive tones in succession ; from which we may reasonably conclude that the Dorian Harmony was the method of disjunction.

Again in passage (*c*) we find that when the number of the keys was raised from seven to thirteen, the terms Ionian and Aeolian were employed to denote respectively the duplicate Phrygian and Lydian keys. This implies a connexion for purposes of music between the terms Ionian and Phrygian, and between the terms Aeolian and Lydian. But the Lydian scale of Aristides is plainly a scale of alternate conjunction and disjunction ; and the characteristic feature of the Phrygian [1] is that it introduces the Fourth above as well as the Fourth below the tonic ; in other words, that it retains the essence of conjunction. It seems a fair inference then that the Ionian and Aeolian Harmonies are identical respectively with the method of conjunction, and the method of alternate conjunction and disjunction.

(*d*) Plutarch, *de Musica*, 1137 D : δῆλον δὲ καὶ τὸ περὶ τῶν ὑπατῶν ὅτι οὐ δι' ἄγνοιαν ἀπείχοντο ἐν τοῖς Δωρίοις τοῦ τετρα-

---

[1] The mistake has commonly been made of explaining the upper

tetrachord of the Phrygian scale as a mixture of enharmonic and diatonic notes, *d* being the second

passing note of the diatonic tetrachord But this interpretation ignores the distinction between fixed and variable notes, a distinction which Aristoxenus and other theorists are never weary of repeating. If *d* in the Phrygian scale were merely a passing note of the diatonic tetrachord, its position would not be exactly determined ; and as the lowest interval of the scale is exactly determined as a tone, the compass of the whole could not be definitely estimated as an octave. Besides, we should then have three passing notes in succession, and two λιχανοί ; the impossibility of which will be obvious to any one who has grasped the Greek conception of a note as a δύναμις, not a point of pitch (see § 8).

χόρδου τούτου· αὐτίκα ἐπὶ τῶν λοιπῶν τόνων ἐχρῶντο, δηλονότι εἰδότες· διὰ δὲ τὴν τοῦ ἤθους φυλακὴν ἀφῄρουν ἐπὶ τοῦ Δωρίου τόνου, τιμῶντες τὸ καλὸν αὐτοῦ. 'With regard, too, to the tetrachord Hypatôn, it is plain that it was not through ignorance that they' (οἱ παλαιοί, the ancients) 'abstained from this tetrachord in the Dorian Scale. The fact that they employed it in the other keys is proof that they were acquainted with it. But they dispensed with it in the Dorian because they respected the beauty of that key, and were determined to preserve its character.'

We saw above (§ 29) that to the early scale of the form

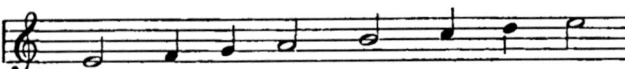

was added at a later period a conjunct tetrachord at its

lower extremity  and that this

addition was called the tetrachord Hypatôn. In the passage before us Plutarch informs us that for some time an exception was made in the case of the Dorian scale because it was felt that such an alteration would imperil its Ethos. Mr. Monro endeavours to reconcile this statement with his hypothesis of the keys by pleading that the character of moderation inherent in a key of middle pitch would be sacrificed by the addition to it of a series of lower notes. To which we may reply 'Would not the pathetic character of a high pitched scale suffer equally from such an extension?' But on our hypothesis Plutarch's statement is quite intelligible. Obviously the distinctive character of a disjunct scale would perish on the addition to it of a conjunct tetrachord.

(ε) See again the passage from the *Politics of Aristotle*, v (viii). 7. 1342 b, quoted in § 38.

Aristotle here recommends the use of certain scales to voices that are impaired by age. What then must have been the special property of these scales, that justified this recommendation? Evidently not a particular modality, for one order of intervals does not involve a greater strain on the voice than another. Nor can it have been a mere difference of key or general pitch. How should the same keys suit the failing tenor, and the failing bass? The property of these 'old men's scales' must have been such that the melody composed in them, whatever the pitch limits of its compass might be, made but a slight demand on the physical powers. And this is the essential property which our hypothesis attributes to the Hypolydian mode for example. For whether that mode occur as the scale

for a treble voice; or as the scale

for a tenor voice; or as the scale

for a bass voice; it necessarily results from the position of its tonic that any melody composed in it must gravitate towards its lower notes.

42. Many persons are under the delusion that to solve the problem of ancient Greek music means to bring to light some hitherto overlooked factor, the recognition of which

will have the effect of making the old Greek hymns as clear
and convincing to our ears as the songs of Handel and
Mozart. Very curious is this delusion, though not astonishing
to any one who has reflected on the extraordinary ignorance
of mankind about the most spontaneous and universally
beloved of the arts, and their no less extraordinary in-
difference to its potent effects on the mental and moral
character. Who would take up a book on Egyptian or
Chinese painting in the expectation of learning from it some
new knack of placing or viewing an Egyptian or Chinese
picture, by which it will come to please the eye as much as
a Titian or a Turner? Who would demand from metrical
science that it should supply us with some long-lost spell by
the magic of which we shall discern in

μὴ φῦναι τὸν ἅπαντα νικᾷ λόγον· τὸ δ᾽, ἐπεὶ φανῇ,
βῆναι κεῖσ᾽ ὁπόθεν περ ἥκει πολὺ δεύτερον ὡς τάχιστα

the movement of

> 'We are such stuff
> As dreams are made on, and our little life
> Is rounded with a sleep.'

Yet no less absurd is the supposition that any, even the
most perfect, knowledge of facts could lead us to the love
of these unfamiliar old-world melodies.

To some cold appreciation of their form we may perhaps
attain if we are willing—sacrilege and destruction as it may
seem—to strip them of those external accidents which are
peculiar to the music of their age, and invest them instead
with the habits of modern fashion. Otherwise the novelty
of the unfamiliar features will engross our ear to the
exclusion of the essential form. To render an ancient
melody note for note is to render it unfaithfully to ears
unaccustomed to its dialect; just as to translate an ancient
poet word for word is to misrepresent him, inasmuch as the
attention is thereby misdirected away from the sense to

the strange idiom. Nay, further, as a literal translation may often give a directly false impression of the meaning, so strict adhesion to the notes of a foreign melody will often lead us astray as to its essential form. As Aristoxenus would say, in attempting to preserve the pitch, we are sacrificing the all important δύναμις. If, for instance, we express the Greek enharmonic progression to the tonic through Hypate, Lichanus, Mese, by

not only are our ears revolted by the unwonted progression, but we are even distorting the real form of the melody. For, to take one point only, the Lichanus being the highest of the passing notes to the tonic from the Fourth below is for the Greek ear the next note to the tonic ; while we feel that in passing from F to A we are skipping several notes which the melody might have employed.

Let us apply, then, this method of paraphrase to the familiar Hymn to the Muse, one of the compositions of Mesomedes, a Cretan musician who lived in the reign of the Emperor Hadrian. The words and ancient notation (as far as it is extant) of the hymn are as follows :—

C Z Z   Φ Φ   Φ   C C
'A - ει - δε   Moῦ-σά   μοι   φί - λη

     I   Φ M M
μολπῆς   δ' ἐμῆς   κα - τάρ-χου,

Z Z   Z   E   Z   H H I
αὔ - ρη   δὲ   σῶν   ἀπ'   ἀλ - σέ -ων

M Z H   I   Φ C   P M Φ C
ἐ - μὰς   φρέ - νας   δο - νε - ί - τω

C P M P C   Φ C
Καλ·λι - ό - πει - α   σο - φά,

We shall (*a*) substitute for the Greek modality our major scale ; (*b*) substitute Diatonic notes for those of other genera ; (*c*) add simple harmonies [1] ; (*d*) make slight alterations in the melody so as to preserve as easy a progression in our major scale, as is the original progression in the Greek scale.

HYMN TO THE MUSE.

---

[1] Professor Prout has supplied the harmonies ; but he is not otherwise responsible for this well-intended mutilation.

INTRODUCTION

B.—ON ARISTOXENUS AND HIS EXTANT WORKS.

1. Our knowledge of the musical theory of Ancient Greece we owe almost entirely to Aristoxenus, or the Musician (such is his regular title in ancient writers). This philosopher was born[1] in Tarentum, and received his earliest instruction from his father Spintharus (also called Mnesias), a well-known musician of that town, who had travelled much, and come into contact with many of the great men of the day, and, among others, with Socrates, Epaminondas, and Archytas. Some part of the youth's life was spent in Mantinea, the inhabitants of which city were remarkably conservative in their musical tastes; and it was probably from this sojourn, as well as from the teaching of Lamprus of Erythrae, that he derived his intense love for the severity and dignity of ancient art. On his return to Italy he became the pupil and friend of the Pythagorean, Xenophilus of Chalcis. Something of the austerity of this school seems to have clung to him to the last; he bore, for example, the reputation of having a violent antipathy to laughter! We next find him in Corinth, where he was intimate with the exiled Dionysius. From the lips of the tyrant he took down the story of Damon and Phintias, which he incorporated in his treatise on the Pythagoreans. Lastly we hear of him as Peripatetic and pupil of Aristotle. His position in this school must have been one of importance; for he entertained hopes of succeeding the master, and his disappointment and disgust at the selection of Theophrastus betrayed him into disrespectful language towards the mighty dead. Indeed, if report speaks truly, want of reverence must have been his besetting sin;-he

[1] For everything that is known about the life of Aristoxenus, and for the references to the ancient authorities, see the excellent article in Westphal's *Aristoxenus*, vol. ii, pp. i–xii.

would seem to have consistently undervalued Plato, and to have maliciously propagated scandalous stories, which he had gleaned from his father, about the domestic life of Socrates. Besides his works on musical theory he wrote philosophy and biography.

2. The signal merits of this philosopher do not flash upon us at the first reading of him. The faults of his style are so glaring—his endless repetitions, his pompous reiterations of ' Alone I did it,' his petty parade of logical thoroughness, his triumphant vindication of the obvious by chains of syllogisms—that we are apt to overlook the services which such an irritating writer rendered to the cause of musical science. And yet these services were of great importance ; for they consisted in no mere improvement of exposition, in no mere discovery of isolated facts, or deeper analysis of particular phenomena, but, firstly, in the accurate deter-mination of the scope of Musical Science, lest on the one hand it should degenerate into empiricism, or on the other hand lose itself in Mathematical Physics ; and secondly, in the application to all the questions and problems of Music of a deeper and truer conception of the ultimate nature of Music itself. And by these two discoveries it is not too much to say that he accomplished a revolution in the philosophy of the art.

Until Aristoxenus appeared upon the scene the limits of Musical Science had been wholly misconceived. There existed, indeed, a flourishing school of Musical Art ; there was conscious preference of this style of composition to that ; of this method of performance to that ; of this con-struction of instruments to that ; and the habits formed by these preferences were transmitted by instruction. To facilitate this instruction, and as an aid to memory, recourse was had to diagrams and superficial generalizations ; but with principles for their own sake the artist, empiricist as he was, did not concern himself, and it is with principles for their own sake that science begins.

Over against these empiricists there stood a school of mathematicians and physicists, professing to be students of music, and claiming Pythagoras as their master, who were busied in reducing sounds to air vibrations, and ascertaining the numerical relations which replace for the mathematical intellect the sense-distinctions of high and low pitch. Here we have a genuine school of science, the soundness of whose hypotheses and the accuracy of whose computations have been established by the light of modern discovery. Nevertheless, musical science was still to seek. For if the artists were musicians without science, the physicists and mathematicians were men of science without music. Under the microscope of their analysis all musical preferences are levelled, all musical worth is sacrificed ; noble and beautiful sounds and melodies dissolve, equally with the ugly and base, into arithmetical relations and relations of relations, any one of which is precisely as valuable and as valueless as any other.) True musical science, on the contrary, accepts as elements requiring no further explanation such conceptions as voice, interval, high, low, concord, discord ; and seeks to reduce the more complex phenomena of music to these simple forms, and to ascertain the general laws of their connexion. Yet, while it will not be enticed to transgress the limits of the sensible, within those limits it will aim at thoroughness of analysis, and completeness of deduction. Such is the science which Aristoxenus claimed to have founded.

And with this clearer perception of the scope of musical science there came also a deeper conception of music itself. So busy were the Pythagoreans in establishing the mere physical and mathematical antecedents of sounds in general, that they never saw that the essence of musical sounds lies in their dynamical relation to one another. Thus they missed the true formal notion of music, which is ever present to Aristoxenus, that of a system or organic whole of sounds, each member of which *is* essentially what it *does*, and in which a sound cannot become a member because merely there is room for it, but only if there is a function which it can discharge.

The conception, then, of a science of music which will accept its materials from the ear, and carry its analysis no further than the ear can follow; and the conception of a system of sound-functions, such and so many as the musical understanding may determine them to be, are the two great contributions of Aristoxenus to the philosophy of Music.

3. Suidas credits Aristoxenus with the authorship of 453 volumes. Of these nothing considerable has survived save an incomplete treatise on Rhythm, and the so-called 'Three Books of the Harmonic Elements.' That the last title is an erroneous one has been established by Marquard and Westphal, who appeal to the following facts among others.

(*a*) Porphyry cites the first of these books as πρῶτος περὶ ἀρχῶν, and the second as πρῶτος τῶν ἁρμονικῶν στοιχείων.

(*b*) Though the usual titles of these three books are supported by most of the MSS., there are some important exceptions. The Codex Venetus (M) has for initial title of the first book 'Αριστοξένου πρὸ τῶν ἁρμονικῶν στοιχείων (though a later hand has crossed out πρὸ τῶν and added πρῶτον), and similarly the Codex Barberinus reads πρὸ τῶν ἁρμονικῶν πρῶτον. The concluding inscription of this book in M is 'Αριστοξένου τὸ πρῶτον στοιχεῖον, but the third hand has written πρὸ τῶν over πρῶτον, and ω over the latter ο of στοιχεῖον. In the same MS. the title of the second book is 'Αριστοξένου ἁρμονικῶν στοιχείων (the ω in the latter words is a correction of the second hand for ο) β, but an α has been written through the β by a later hand ; the concluding inscription of the same book is 'Αριστοξένου στοιχείων ἁρμονικῶν a, but the a is crossed out, and β written beside it; the heading of the third book is Ἀριστοξένου στοιχείων ἁρμονικῶν β, with the β crossed out and γ written beside it.

((c) The text of the 'Three Books' contains matter of three distinct classes; firstly, introductory matter or exposition of the scope and divisions of the subject; secondly, general principles or expositions of primary laws and facts; thirdly, propositions of details, following one another in logical order like the στοιχεῖα or Elements of Euclid.)

(d) We find in several cases more than one treatment of the same subject.

(e) We find certain inconsistencies. Thus μελοποιία, or musical composition, is sometimes included in, and sometimes omitted from, the list of objects with which Harmonic science is concerned.

Westphal, not content with negative criticism, has endeavoured to reconstitute from the extant fragments the scheme of three works of Aristoxenus on the Theory of Music; each containing a προοίμιον or introduction, a statement of ἀρχαί or principles, and a system of στοιχεῖα or elementary propositions. His idea may well be correct; but the result is so unsatisfactory from the utterly fragmentary nature of the *data*, that we need not enter into the details of his attempt.

4. The most important MSS. of the 'Harmonic Elements' are the following:

The Codex Venetus (in the Library of St. Mark), written by one Zosimus in Constantinople in the twelfth century. It has been corrected by many hands; but two of especial importance have been identified, one older than the fourteenth century (denoted in the Critical Apparatus by Mb) and one of that century or later (Mc). Ma denotes the first hand; Mx a hand not identified; (a later manuscript in the same library is denoted by m):

ON ARISTOXENUS AND HIS EXTANT WORKS

The Codex Vaticanus of the thirteenth and fourteenth centuries, which appears to have been directly copied from M. In the Critical Apparatus the first hand of this MS. is denoted by Va, a corrector by Vb:

The Codex Seldenianus (in the Bodleian Library), dating from the beginning of the sixteenth century. It is denoted by S in the Critical Apparatus. Mr. H. S. Jones has demonstrated (*Classical Review*, VII. 10), that this MS. depends closely on V throughout, though its exact relationship is hard to determine, since in some places it adheres to the original reading (Va), and in others adopts the corrections and additions of Vb. I have collated this MS. afresh:

The Codex Riccardianus (in Florence) of the sixteenth century (collated by van Herwerden), which shows relationship with Mc:

The Codex Barberinus (in the Bibliotheca Barberina in Rome) of the first half of the sixteenth century. From page 95 to 121 of the text this MS. shows agreement with Mc and R; but from page 121 on, it appears to have been copied from V *after* the corrections of Vb. This MS. has numerous corrections in the margin, which, however, are in the same hand as the original:

. A Codex of great value which belonged to the Library of the Protestant Seminary at Strassburg, and perished when that building was burned down by the German troops on the night of August 24, 1870. It was collated by M. Ruelle, who published the results with his translation of Aristoxenus. It seems to have been independent of all the other MSS. that we possess, none of which can be regarded either as its ancestor or its descendant. M. Ruelle attributes it to the fifteenth century. It is denoted by H in the Critical Apparatus.

The 'Harmonic Elements' were first published at Venice

INTRODUCTION

in 1542, in a Latin translation by Antonius Gogavinus, a worthless work crowded with errors. The first edition of the Greek was printed in Leyden in 1616 by Elzevir, with the corrections and commentary of Johannes Meursius, who displays gross ignorance of the general theory of Greek music, and of the doctrine of Aristoxenus in particular. Meibom's well-known edition with the Greek text, Latin translation, and commentary, was published in 1652 at Amsterdam by Elzevir. The text of this work is poor and the translation often obscure, but the commentary is valuable, and shows a thorough acquaintance with the system of Aristoxenus. Paul Marquard's edition with a German translation (so literal and servile as to be wholly useless) was issued at Berlin in 1868. The chief value of this work lies in the new light thrown on the text by the author's collation of the Codex Venetus. Westphal's exhaustive but diffuse and garrulous book on Aristoxenus was published at Leipzig in two volumes, the first in 1883, and the second in 1893, after the author's death. It is most valuable as a storehouse of facts. M. Ruelle's French translation of Aristoxenus, to which I have referred above, was published in Paris in 1870.

The following authors and works are referred to in the present volume:

The Εἰσαγωγὴ ἁρμονική (referred to in this volume as *Isagoge*) formerly attributed erroneously to Euclid (and so inscribed in Meibom), but probably the work of one Cleonides, of whom nothing else is known. It exhibits a strong resemblance to the doctrine and arrangement of the ' Harmonic Elements ' of Aristoxenus :

Nicomachus of Gerasa, who flourished in the second century, A. D. ; a Pythagorean mathematician, and musician ; author of a manual of Harmonic :

Bacchius Senex, a musician of the time of the Emperor

ON ARISTOXENUS AND HIS EXTANT WORKS

Constantine. The so-called 'Introduction of Bacchius' is a mass of excerpts of unequal value, some showing agreement with the doctrine of Aristoxenus, and some directly contradicting it:

Gaudentius the Philosopher, a musician of uncertain date, though he certainly was not earlier than the second century, A. D. His 'Introduction to Harmonic' is an eclectic work combining views of the Aristoxenean, Peripatetic, and Pythagorean schools:

Alypius, of uncertain date, whose 'Introduction' exhibits the complete scales of the three genera in all the modes, with their notation:

Aristides Quintilianus, a musician of the first century, A.D., author of a treatise in three books on Music, in which the theory of the Aristoxenean school is presented in detail:

Anonymi *Scriptio de Musica* (referred to in this volume as Anonymus) a cento of the works of Aristoxenus, Aristides Quintilianus, Alypius, Ptolemy, &c., probably of very late date.

The works of Nicomachus, Bacchius, Gaudentius, Alypius, and Aristides Quintilianus, and the *Isagoge* are comprised in the *Antiquae musicae auctores septem* of Meibom. The same works, with the exception of Aristides Quintilianus, have been edited by Karl v. Jan in the Teubner edition of the classics under the title *Musici Scriptores Graeci.* The Anonymi *Scriptio* was edited by Bellermann, and published at Berlin in 1841.

ΑΡΙΣΤΟΞΕΝΟΥ ΑΡΜΟΝΙΚΩΝ
ΣΤΟΙΧΕΙΩΝ ΠΡΩΤΟΝ

Τῆς περὶ μέλους ἐπιστήμης πολυμεροῦς οὔσης καὶ διῃρη- **Ι,** 11
μένης εἰς πλείους ἰδέας μίαν τινὰ αὐτῶν | ὑπολαβεῖν δεῖ τὴν 15
5 ἁρμονικὴν καλουμένην εἶναι πραγματείαν, τῇ τε τάξει
πρώτην οὖσαν ἔχουσάν τε δύναμιν στοιχειώδη. τυγχάνει
γὰρ οὖσα τῶν πρώτων θεωρητική· ταῦ|τα δ᾽ ἐστὶν ὅσα 20·
συντείνει πρὸς τὴν τῶν συστημάτων τε καὶ τόνων θεωρίαν.
προσήκει γὰρ μηθὲν πορρωτέρω τούτων ἀξιοῦν παρὰ τοῦ τὴν
10 εἰρημένην ἔχοντος ἐπιστήμην. τέλος γὰρ τοῦτό ἐστι τῆς |
πραγματείας ταύτης. τὰ δ᾽ ἀνώτε||ρον ὅσα θεωρεῖται χρωμένης 2
ἤδη τῆς ποιητικῆς τοῖς τε συστήμασι καὶ τοῖς τόνοις οὐκέτι
ταύτης ἐστίν, ἀλλὰ τῆς ταύτην τε καὶ τὰς ἄλλας περι-
εχούσης | ἐπιστήμης δι᾽ ὧν πάντα θεωρεῖται τὰ κατὰ μουσι- 5
15 κήν. αὕτη δ᾽ ἐστὶν ἡ τοῦ μουσικοῦ ἕξις.

· · · · · · · ·

Τοὺς μὲν οὖν ἔμπροσθεν (ἠμμένους τῆς ἁρμονικῆς πραγματείας συμβέβηκεν ὡς ἀληθῶς) ἁρμονικοὺς εἶναι βούλεσθαι
μόνον, αὐτῆς γὰρ τῆς ἁρμονίας ἥπτοντο μόνον, τῶν | δ᾽ ἄλλων 10
20 γενῶν οὐδεμίαν πώποτ᾽ ἔννοιαν εἶχον. σημεῖον δέ· τὰ γὰρ
διαγράμματα αὐτοῖς τῶν ἐναρμονίων ἔκκειται μόνον συστη-

De variis Titulorum lectionibus vid. Intr. B § 3   7 τῶν πρώτων
θεωρητικῇ Westphal : πρώτη τῶν θεωρητικῶν codd.   8 τόνων] τῶν
Mx   9 παρὰ τοῦ R : παρ᾽ αὐτοῦ τοῦ VBS : παρ᾽ αὐτοῦ Ma, sed add.
τοῦ Mx   14 τὰ add. Mx : τὴν (a suprascr.) B   17 ἠμμένους
. . . ἀληθῶς restituit Westphal ex Procli *Comm. in Plat. Timaeum* (ed.
Basil. 1534) p. 192, ll. 1, 2   20 ἔχων Ma : corr. Mb   21 αὐτοῖς]
αὐτῆς S   ἐναρμονίων Marquard : ἁρμονικῶν H : ἁρμονιῶν rell.

95

μάτων, διατόνων δ' ἢ χρωματικῶν οὐδεὶς πώποθ' ἑώρακεν. |

15 Καί τοι τὰ διαγράμματά γ' αὐτῶν ἐδήλου τὴν πᾶσαν τῆς
μελῳδίας τάξιν, ἐν οἷς περὶ συστημάτων ὀκταχόρδων ἐναρμονίων μόνον ἔλεγον· περὶ δὲ τῶν ἄλλων μεγεθῶν τε καὶ
20 σχημάτων ⟨τῶν⟩ ἐν αὐτῷ | τε τῷ γένει τούτῳ καὶ τοῖς λοιποῖς 5
οὐδ' ἐπεχείρει οὐδεὶς καταμανθάνειν, ἀλλ' ἀποτεμνόμενοι τῆς
ὅλης μελῳδίας τοῦ τρίτου μέρους ἔν τι [γένος] μέγεθος [δέ],
25 τὸ διὰ πασῶν, περὶ τούτου πᾶσαν πεποί|ηνται πραγματείαν.
ὅτι δ' οὐδένα πεπραγμάτευνται τρόπον οὐδὲ περὶ αὐτῶν
τούτων ὧν ἡμμένοι τυγχάνουσι σχεδὸν μὲν ἡμῖν γεγένηται 10
30 φανερὸν ἐν τοῖς ἔμπροσθεν ὅτε ἐπεσκοπούμεν τὰς | τῶν
ἁρμονικῶν δόξας, οὐ μὴν ἀλλ' ἔτι μᾶλλον νῦν ἔσται εὐσύν-
οπτον διεξιόντων ἡμῶν τὰ μέρη τῆς πραγματείας ὅσα ἐστὶ
καὶ ἥτινα ἕκαστον αὐτῶν δύναμιν ἔχει· τῶν μὲν γὰρ ὅλως
3 οὐδ' ἡμ||μένους εὑρήσομεν αὐτοὺς τῶν δ' οὐχ ἱκανῶς. ὥσθ' 15
ἅμα τοῦτό τε φανερὸν ἔσται καὶ τὸν τύπον κατοψόμεθα τῆς
πραγματείας ἥτις ποτ' ἐστίν.

5   Πρῶτον μὲν οὖν ἁπάντων τὴν τῆς φωνῆς κίνησιν
διοριστέον τῷ μέλλοντι πραγματεύεσθαι περὶ μέλους αὐτὴν
τὴν κατὰ τόπον. οὐ γὰρ εἷς τρόπος αὐτῆς ὧν τυγχάνει· 20
10 κινεῖται μὲν γὰρ καὶ | διαλεγομένων ἡμῶν καὶ μελῳδούντων
τὴν εἰρημένην κίνησιν, ὀξὺ γὰρ καὶ βαρὺ δῆλον ὡς ἐν
ἀμφοτέροις τούτοις ἔνεστιν—αὕτη δ' ἐστὶν ἡ κατὰ τόπον

---

1 διάτονον δὲ ἢ χρωματικὸν corr. ex -ων δὲ ἢ -κῶν S   2 ἐδήλω S
3 ἐναρμονίων Marquard : ἁρμονικῶν H : ἁρμονιῶν rell.   4 ἔλεγεν R
μεγεθῶν conieci : γενῶν codd.   5 τῶν post σχημάτων addidi
τε om. R   6 οὐδεὶς ante οὐδ' ponunt B R   ἐπεχείρει B V (ex
ἐπιχ.) : ἐπεχείρει A : ἐπιχειρεῖ rell.   7 γένος et δέ seclusi
8 πεποίηκε R   πραγματίαν B   9 ὅτε (ι suprascr.) B   δ' om.
M Vb S   οὐδὲ ἕνα S   πεπραγμάτευνται B V (ν fortasse postea
additum) : πεπραγμάτευνται rell.   οὐδὲ] ὃ δὲ H   11 ὅτι (ε
suprascr.) B   ἐπεσκοπούμεν H : ἐπισκοπούμεν R   12 οὔ μὴν ἀλλ' R
14 ἕκαστον] στ Mb corr.   ἔσται R   16 ἡμῖν post φανερὸν add. B, rubra
linea subscr. R   ἔσται R   17 ἐστίν] deinde lac. 3 litt. M
19 μέλλον τι M   αὐτὴν om. H   20 τὴν supra lineam S
23 ἔνεστιν B R : ἐστίν rell.   ἢ B

καθ᾽ ἣν ὀξύ τε καὶ βαρὺ γίγνεται—ἀλλ᾽ οὐ | ταὐτὸν εἶδος 15
τῆς κινήσεως ἑκατέρας ἐστίν. ἐπιμελὲς δ᾽ οὐδενὶ πώποτε
γεγένηται περὶ τούτου διορίσαι τίς ἑκατέρας αὐτῶν ἡ διαφορά·
καί τοι τούτου μὴ διορισθέντος οὐ πάνυ ῥᾴδιον εἰπεῖν | περὶ 20
5 φθόγγου τί ποτ᾽ ἐστίν. ἀναγκαῖον δὲ τὸν βουλόμενον μὴ
πάσχειν ὅπερ Λάσος τε καὶ τῶν Ἐπιγονείων τινὲς ἔπαθον,
πλάτος αὐτὸν οἰηθέντες ἔχειν, εἰπεῖν περὶ αὐτοῦ μικρὸν
ἀκριβέστερον. τούτου | γὰρ διορισθέντος περὶ πολλὰ τῶν 25
ἔπειτα μᾶλλον ἔσται σαφῶς ⟨λέγειν⟩. Ἀναγκαῖον δ᾽ εἰς τὴν
10 τούτων ξύνεσιν πρὸς τοῖς εἰρημένοις περί τ᾽ ἀνέσεως καὶ
ἐπιτάσεως καὶ βαρύτητος καὶ ὀξύτητος καὶ τά|σεως 30
εἰπεῖν τί ποτ᾽ ἀλλήλων διαφέρουσιν. οὐδεὶς γὰρ οὐδὲν περὶ
τούτων εἴρηκεν, ἀλλὰ τὰ μὲν αὐτῶν ὅλως οὐδὲ νενόηται τὰ
δὲ συγκεχυμένως. Μετὰ ταῦτα δὲ περὶ τῆς τοῦ βαρέος
15 τε καὶ ὀξέος διαστά||σεως λεκτέον πότερον εἰς ἄπειρον 4
αὔξησίν τε καὶ ἐλάττωσιν ἔχει ἢ οὐ ἢ πῆ μὲν πῆ δ᾽ οὔ.
Τούτων δὲ διωρισμένων περὶ διαστήματος καθόλου λε-
κτέον ἔπει|τα διαιρετέον ὁσαχῶς δύναται διαιρεῖσθαι, εἶτα 5
περὶ συστήματος· καθόλου δὲ διελθόντα λεκτέον εἰς ὅσας
20 πέφυκε τέμνεσθαι διαιρέσεις. Εἶτα περὶ μέλους ὑποδη-
λωτέον καὶ τυπωτέον οἵαν ἔχει | φύσιν τὸ κατὰ μουσικήν, 10
ἐπειδὴ πλείους εἰσὶ φύσεις μέλους, μία δ᾽ ἐστί τις ἐκ πασῶν
αὐτοῦ ἡ τοῦ ἡρμοσμένου καὶ μελῳδουμένου. διὰ τὴν ἐπα-

---

1 οὔτ᾽ αὐτὸ H : ταυτὸ M, sed postea una litt. eras.   2 τῆς] τῆς
τῆς S   ἐπιμελὲς conieci : ἐπιμελῶς codd.   3 γεγένηται ex δὲ.
γένηται B   τίς] τῆς B   ἢ om. S   4 μηδὲ ὁρισθέντος R
post ὁρισθέντος lac. 7 litt. M ; lac. 8–9 syllabb. R   de B ita scripsit
Marquard 'alinea B quod alibi nusquam fit'; quod non intellego
6 Λάσος (sic) M, sed acut. ab alia manu : Λαῦσος R : ὁ Λάσος H : Λάσος
rell.   Ἐπιγονίων BVS : Ἐπιγονείων sed εἰ e corr. M   ἔπασχον
R   9 σαφὲς Meibom   λέγειν addidi   13 οὐδὲ νοεῖται MS :
οὐδ᾽ ἐννοεῖται BR   14 συγκεχυμένως Marquard : συγκεχυμένα
codd.   15 διατάσεως BSR   17 δὲ om. VS   λεκτέον
conieci : δίκαιον codd. : post δίκαιον add. εἰπεῖν H   19 ante
συστήματος add. τοῦ VbB   διελθόντα Marquard : διελόντα codd.
20 μέλους ex μέρους corr. M

15 γωγὴν δὲ τὴν ἐπὶ τοῦτο γιγνομένην κατὰ τὸν χω|ρισμὸν τὸν
ἀπὸ τῶν ἄλλων ἀναγκαῖόν πως καὶ τῶν ἄλλων ἐπαφᾶσθαι
φύσεων. Ἀφορισθέντος δὲ τοῦ μουσικοῦ μέλους οὕτως ὡς
ἐνδέχεται μηδέπω τῶν καθ' ἕκαστα τεθεωρημένων ἀλλ' ὡς ἐν
20 τύ|πῳ καὶ περιγραφῇ, διαιρετέον τὸ καθόλου καὶ μεριστέον 5
εἰς ὅσα φαίνεται γένη διαιρεῖσθαι. Μετὰ τοῦτο δὲ λεκτέον
περί τε συνεχείας καὶ τοῦ ἑξῆς τί ποτ' ἐστὶν ἐν τοῖς
25 συστήμασι καὶ πῶς ἐγγι|γνόμενον.

Εἶτ' ἀποδοτέον τὰς τῶν γενῶν διαφορὰς [αὐτῆς] τὰς
ἐν τοῖς κινουμένοις τῶν φθόγγων, ἀποδοτέον δὲ καὶ τοὺς 10
τόπους ἐν οἷς κινοῦνται· τούτων δ' οὐδεὶς περὶ οὐδενὸς
30 πώποτ' ἔσχηκεν ἔν|νοιαν οὐδ' ἡντινοῦν, ἀλλὰ περὶ πάντων τῶν
εἰρημένων αὐτοῖς ἡμῖν ἀναγκαῖον ἐξ ἀρχῆς πραγματεύεσθαι,
παρειλήφαμεν γὰρ οὐδὲν περὶ αὐτῶν ἀξιόλογον. Μετὰ δὲ
5 τοῦτο περὶ διαστημάτων ἀσυν||θέτων πρῶτον λεκτέον, 15
εἶτα περὶ συνθέτων· ἀναγκαῖον δὲ ἀπτομένοις ἡμῖν συνθέτων διαστημάτων οἷς ἅμα καὶ συστήμασιν εἶναί πως συμ-
5 βαίνει περὶ | συνθέσεως ἔχειν τι λέγειν τῆς τῶν ἀσυνθέτων
διαστημάτων. περὶ ἧς οἱ πλεῖστοι τῶν ἁρμονικῶν οὐδ' ὅτι
πραγματευτέον ᾔσθοντο· δῆλον δ' ἡμῖν ἐν τοῖς ἔμπροσθεν 20
10 γέγονεν. οἱ δὲ περὶ Ἐρατο|κλέα τοσοῦτον εἰρήκασι μόνον
ὅτι ἀπὸ τοῦ διὰ τεττάρων ἐφ' ἑκάτερα δίχα σχίζεται τὸ
μέλος, οὐδὲν οὔτ' εἰ ἀπὸ παντὸς τοῦτο γίγνεται διορίσαντες
15 οὔτε διὰ τίνα αἰτίαν εἰπόντες οὔθ' ὑπὲρ τῶν ἄλ|λων διαστη-
μάτων ἐπισκεψάμενοι τίνα πρὸς ἄλληλα συντίθενται τρόπον, 25
καὶ πότερον παντὸς διαστήματος πρὸς πᾶν ὡρισμένος τίς
20 ἐστι λόγος τῆς συνθέσεως καὶ πῶς μὲν ἐξ αὐτῶν πῶς | δ'

---

1 δὲ om. Va : add. Vb   τοῦτο γενομένην B R : τούτῳ γιγνομένην
rell.   κατὰ τὸν S : καὶ τὸν rell.   6 γένη Meibom : μέρη codd.
9 αὐτῆς seclusi : αὐτὰς Westphal : αὐτῆς ante διαφορὰς ponit H
10 δὲ om. S   11 δ' om. B   12 ἡντινοῦν Ma Vb B R, S linea
subducta : accent. acut. supra ην et a supra τιν add. Mc   18 τι]
τε R   21 ἐργατοκλέα V   22 δίχα σχίζεται] διαιρεῖται H
23 οὐδὲ εἰ H   25 εἴ τινα S

οὐ γίγνεται συστήματα ἢ ⟨εἰ⟩ τοῦτο ἀόριστόν ἐστιν· περὶ
γὰρ τούτων οὔτ᾽ ἀποδεικτικὸς οὔτ᾽ ἀναπόδεικτος ὑπ᾽ οὐδενὸς
πώποτ᾽ εἴρηται λόγος. οὔσης δὲ θαυμαστῆς τῆς τάξεως
περὶ τὴν τοῦ μέλους σύστασιν | ἀταξία πλείστη μουσικῆς 25
5 ὑπ᾽ ἐνίων κατέγνωσται διὰ τοὺς μετακεχειρισμένους τὴν
εἰρημένην πραγματείαν. οὐδὲν δὲ τῶν αἰσθητῶν τοσαύτην
ἔχει τάξιν οὐδὲ τοιαύτην. ἔσται δ᾽ ἡμῖν δῆλον τοῦθ᾽ | οὕτως 30
ἔχον, ὅταν ἐν αὐτῇ γενώμεθα τῇ πραγματείᾳ. νῦν δὲ τὰ
λοιπὰ τῶν μερῶν λεκτέον. Ἀποδειχθέντων γὰρ τῶν ἀσυν-
10 θέτων διαστημάτων ὃν τρόπον || πρὸς ἄλληλα συντίθεται 6
περὶ τῶν συστάντων ἐξ αὐτῶν συστημάτων λεκτέον περί
τε τῶν ἄλλων, καὶ τοῦ τελείου, ἐξ ἐκείνων ἀποδεικνύντας
πόσα ἐστὶ καὶ ποῖ᾽ | ἄττα, τάς τε κατὰ μέγεθος αὐτῶν ἀπο- 5
διδόντας διαφορὰς καὶ τῶν μεγεθῶν ἑκάστου τάς τε κατὰ
15 σύνθεσιν καὶ τὰς κατὰ [τὸ] σχῆμα διαφορὰς ὅπως μηδὲν τῶν
μελῳδουμένων μήτε μέγεθος μήτε σχῆμα μήτε | σύνθεσις 10
[μήτε θέσις] ἀναπόδεικτος ᾖ. τούτου δὲ τοῦ μέρους τῆς πραγματείας ἄλλος μὲν οὐδεὶς πώποθ᾽ ἥψατο· Ἐρατοκλῆς δ᾽
ἐπεχείρησεν ἀναποδείκτως ἐξαριθμεῖν ἐπί τι μέρος· ὅτι
20 δ᾽ οὐδὲν εἴρηκεν | ἀλλὰ πάντα ψευδῆ καὶ τῶν φαινομένων 15
τῇ αἰσθήσει διημάρτηκε, τεθεώρηται μὲν ἔμπροσθεν ὅτ᾽ αὐτὴν
καθ᾽ αὑτὴν ἐξητάζομεν τὴν πραγματείαν ταύτην. τῶν δ᾽
ἄλλων καθόλου μὲν | καθάπερ ἔμπροσθεν εἴπομεν οὐδεὶς 20
ἧπται, ἑνὸς δὲ συστήματος Ἐρατοκλῆς ἐπεχείρησε καθ᾽ ἓν
25 γένος ἐξαριθμῆσαι τὰ σχήματα τοῦ διὰ πασῶν ἀναποδείκτως

---

1 εἰ addidi   5 ὑπ᾽ Meibom H : ἐπ᾽ rell.   μετακεχρισμένους Ma
V, B in marg. : μεταχειρισμένους R : μετακεχειρισμένους rell.   8 τῇ
om. H   9 ἀποδεχθέντων M : ἀποδειχθέντων Mc et rell.   10 ὃν
sed post o et ν ras. M   13 πόσα ἐστὶ plerique : πόσατ᾽ ἐστὶ B R :
ποῖά ἐστι H   ποῖ᾽ ἄττα Meursius : πόσ᾽ ἄττα V S : πόσά ἄττα H :
πόσ᾽ ἄττα rell.   15 post σύνθεσιν lac. 30 fere litt. M   καὶ τὰς
κατὰ τὸ σχῆμα διαφορὰς H : om. rell.   καὶ κατὰ θέσιν add. Marquard
post σύνθεσιν   17 μήτε θέσις om. H   ἀναπόδεικτον H   ᾖ H :
om. rell.   18 ἐργατοκλῆς V   25 ἀναποδείκτως Monro :
ἀποδεικτικῶς codd.

25 τῇ περιφορᾷ τῶν διαστημάτων | δεικνύς, οὐ καταμαθὼν ὅτι
μὴ προαποδειχθέντων τῶν τε τοῦ διὰ πέντε σχημάτων καὶ
τῶν τοῦ διὰ τεσσάρων πρὸς δὲ τούτοις καὶ τῆς συνθέσεως
αὐτῶν τίς ποτ' ἐστὶ καθ' ἣν ἐμμελῶς συντίθενται πολλα|-
30 πλάσια τῶν ἑπτὰ συμβαίνειν γίγνεσθαι δείκνυται· ἐτιθέμεθα 5
δ' ἐν τοῖς ἔμπροσθεν ὅτι οὕτως ἔχει, διόπερ ταῦτα μὲν
7 ἀφείσθω, τὰ δὲ λοιπὰ λεγέσθω τῶν τῆς πραγματείας με||ρῶν.
Ἐξηριθμημένων γὰρ τῶν συστημάτων ⟨τῶν⟩ καθ' ἕκαστον
τῶν γενῶν κατὰ πᾶσαν διαφορὰν τὴν εἰρημένην μιγνυμένων
πάλιν τῶν γενῶν ταὐτὸ τοῦτο ποιητέον· ⟨περὶ οὗ οἱ πλεῖστοι 10
5 τῶν ἁρμονικῶν οὐκ ᾔσθοντο ὅτι⟩ πραγματευτέον· οὐδὲ γὰρ
αὐτὴν τὴν μίξιν τί ποτ' ἐστὶ καταμεμαθήκεσαν. Τούτων δ'
ἐχόμενόν ἐστι περὶ φθόγγων εἰπεῖν, ἐπειδήπερ οὐκ αὐτάρκη
10 τὰ διαστήματα πρὸς τὴν τῶν φθόγγων διά|γνωσιν. Ἐπεὶ
δὲ τῶν συστημάτων ἕκαστον ἐν τόπῳ τινὶ τῆς φωνῆς τεθὲν 15
μελῳδεῖται καὶ, καθ' αὐτὸ διαφορὰν οὐδεμίαν λαμβάνοντος
αὐτοῦ, τὸ γιγνόμενον ἐν αὐτῷ μέλος οὐ τὴν τυχοῦσαν |
15 λαμβάνει διαφορὰν ἀλλὰ σχεδὸν τὴν μεγίστην, ἀναγκαῖον
ἂν εἴη τῷ τὴν εἰρημένην μεταχειριζομένῳ πραγματείαν περὶ
τοῦ τῆς φωνῆς τόπου καθόλου καὶ κατὰ μέρος εἰπεῖν ἐφ' 20
20 ὅσον ἐστὶ | δίκαιον· ἔστι δ' ἐπὶ τοσοῦτον ἐφ' ὅσον ἡ τῶν
συστημάτων αὐτῶν σημαίνει φύσις. περὶ δὲ συστημάτων
καὶ τόπων οἰκειότητος καὶ τῶν τόνων λεκτέον οὐ πρὸς τὴν

2 προαποδειχθέντων Monro: πρὸς ἀποδειχθέντων Β: προσαποδειχθέν-
των rell.   τῶν τε τοῦ] τούτων Μ: τούτων cum τε suprascr. Mc: τοῦ
τε m: τῶν τε Β Η: τε τῶν τοῦ Vb e corr., S   3 τοῦ om. Η
καὶ Β R: om. rell.   5 ἐτιθέμεθα Meibom: τιθέμεθα codd.
6 τοιαῦτα R   8 τῶν post συστημάτων addidi   9 καὶ post
γενῶν addidit Marquard   10 ποιητέον conieci: ποιεῖται codd.
περὶ οὗ . . . ὅτι addidi   11 πραγματευτόν Η   12 κατεμεμαθή-
κεισαν Η   15 τιθὲν Β R   16 καθ' αὐτὸ S, ex κατ' αὐτὸ Μ:
καθ' αὑτὸν rell.   17 ἐν om. Η   αὐτῷ] αὐτὸ Η   οὖ om. S
19 εἰρημένην ex εἰρήνην Ma   20 τε post καθόλου add. Η   καὶ
om. R   21 ἐστὶ δίκαιον . . . ἐφ' ὅσον om. R   ἐπὶ om. Η   ἡ
τῶν συστημάτων in ras. Ma   22 διασημαίνει Β sed in marg. σημαίνει   ἡ ante φύσις add. Η   τῆς τῶν post δὲ add. Η   23 ὁμοιό-
τητος Η

καταπύκνωσιν βλέποντας καθάπερ | οἱ ἁρμονικοὶ ἀλλὰ τὴν 25
πρὸς ἄλληλα μελῳδίαν τῶν συστημάτων οἷς ἐπὶ τίνων τόνων
κειμένοις μελῳδεῖσθαι συμβαίνει πρὸς ἄλληλα.   περὶ τούτου
δὲ τοῦ μέρους ⟨ὅτι⟩ ἐπὶ βραχὺ τῶν ἁρμονικῶν ἐνίοις | συμβέ- 30
5 βηκεν εἰρηκέναι κατὰ τύχην, σὺ περὶ τούτου λέγουσιν ἀλλὰ
καταπυκνῶσαι βουλομένοις τὸ διάγραμμα, καθόλου δὲ οὐδενὶ
σχεδὸν ἐν τοῖς ἔμπροσθεν φανερὸν γεγένηται τοῦθ᾽ ἡμῖν,
ἔστι δ᾽ ὡς εἰπεῖν καθόλου τὸ μέρος || τοῦτο τῆς περὶ μετα- 8 ·
βολῆς πραγματείας τὸ συντεῖνον εἰς τὴν περὶ μέλους
10 θεωρίαν.

Τὰ μὲν οὖν τῆς ἁρμονικῆς καλου|μένης ἐπιστήμης μέρη 5
ταῦτά τε καὶ τοσαῦτά ἐστι, τὰς δ᾽ ἀνωτέρω τούτων πραγματείας ἥπερ εἴπομεν ἀρχόμενοι τελειοτέρου τινὸς ὑπολη-
πτέον εἶναι· | περὶ μὲν οὖν ἐκείνων ἐν τοῖς καθήκουσι καιροῖς 10
15 λεκτέον τίνες τ᾽ εἰσὶ καὶ πόσαι καὶ ποία τις ἑκάστη αὐτῶν,
περὶ δὲ τῆς πρώτης νῦν πειρατέον διελθεῖν.

Πρῶτον μὲν οὖν ἁπάντων αὐτῆς τῆς κατὰ τόπον κι-
νήσεως τὰς διαφορὰς | θεωρῆσαι τίνες εἰσὶ πειρατέον. 15
πάσης δὲ φωνῆς δυναμένης κινεῖσθαι τὸν εἰρημένον αὐτὸν
20 τρόπον δύο τινές εἰσιν ἰδέαι κινήσεως, ἥ τε συνεχὴς καὶ ἡ
διαστηματική.   κατὰ μὲν οὖν τὴν συνεχῆ τό|πον τινὰ διε- 20
ξιέναι φαίνεται ἡ φωνὴ τῇ αἰσθήσει οὕτως ὡς ἂν μηδαμοῦ
ἱσταμένη μηδ᾽ ἐπ᾽ αὐτῶν τῶν περάτων κατά γε τὴν τῆς
αἰσθήσεως φαντασίαν, ἀλλὰ φερομένη συνεχῶς μέχρι σιω|-
25 πῆς, κατὰ δὲ τὴν ἑτέραν ἣν ὀνομάζομεν διαστηματικὴν 25

---

1 κατὰ πύκνωσιν B   τὴν πρὸς] πρὸς τὴν H   2 τίνων conieci :
om. H : τῶν rell.   4 ἐνίοις Westphal : ἐνίους codd.   ὅτι addidi
6 περὶ δὲ τοῦ ante καθόλου, ὡς post σχεδὸν add. Marquard   οὐδενὶ
Marquard : οὐδεῖ B R : οὐδεὶς rell.   7 φανερὸν H B R : φανερῶς
M V S, in marg. B   γεγένηται M V S, in marg. B : πεποίηκε H :
πετίγηται supra lin. Mc : πεποίηται B R   12 ἀνωτέρω (ας suprascr.)
B   13 ἥπερ Westphal : εἴπερ codd. : ἐπείπερ Marquard   τελειοτέρου B R : τελεωτέρου rell.   15 τ᾽ om. R   19 τὸν εἰρημένον
Meibom : τῶν εἰρημένων codd.   20 ἰδίαι (ε supra ι secundum
script.) B   21 τὴν ex τὸν Mx : τὸν V B S   25 ἑτέραν] post
ρ ras. M

ἐναντίως φαίνεται κινεῖσθαι· διαβαίνουσα γὰρ ἴστησιν αὐτὴν
ἐπὶ μιᾶς τάσεως εἶτα πάλιν ἐφ᾽ ἑτέρας καὶ τοῦτο ποιοῦσα
30 συνεχῶς—λέγω δὲ | συνεχῶς κατὰ τὸν χρόνον—ὑπερβαί-
νουσα μὲν τοὺς περιεχομένους ὑπὸ τῶν τάσεων τόπους,
ἱσταμένη δ᾽ ἐπ᾽ αὐτῶν τῶν τάσεων καὶ φθεγγομένη ταύ- 5
9 τας μόνον αὐτὰς μελῳδεῖν λέγεται καὶ κινεῖ||σθαι διαστη-
ματικὴν κίνησιν. Ληπτέον δὲ ἑκάτερον τούτων κατὰ τὴν
• τῆς αἰσθήσεως φαντασίαν· πότερον μὲν γὰρ δυνατὸν ἢ
5 ἀδύνατον φωνὴν κινεῖσθαι καὶ πάλιν | ἵστασθαι αὐτὴν ἐπὶ
μιᾶς τάσεως ἑτέρας ἐστὶ σκέψεως καὶ πρὸς τὴν ἐνεστῶσαν 10
πραγματείαν οὐκ ἀναγκαῖον †τὸ δὲ κιθῆσαι τούτων ἑκάτερον†·
10 ὁποτέρως γὰρ ἔχει, τὸ αὐτὸ ποιεῖ πρός γε τὸ χω|ρίσαι τὴν
ἐμμελῆ κίνησιν τῆς φωνῆς ἀπὸ τῶν ἄλλων κινήσεων.
Ἁπλῶς γὰρ ὅταν μὲν οὕτω κινῆται ἡ φωνὴ ὥστε μηδαμοῦ
δοκεῖν ἵστασθαι τῇ ἀκοῇ, συνεχῆ λέγομεν ταύτην τὴν κίνη- 15
15 σιν· ὅταν | δὲ στῆναί που δόξασα εἶτα πάλιν διαβαίνειν
τινὰ τόπον φανῇ καὶ τοῦτο ποιήσασα πάλιν ἐφ᾽ ἑτέρας
τάσεως στῆναι δόξῃ καὶ τοῦτο ἐναλλὰξ ποιεῖν φαινομένη
20 συνεχῶς διατελῇ, δια|στηματικὴν τὴν τοιαύτην κίνησιν λέ-
γομεν. Τὴν μὲν οὖν συνεχῆ λογικὴν εἶναί φαμεν, διαλε- 20
γομένων γὰρ ἡμῶν οὕτως ἡ φωνὴ κινεῖται κατὰ τόπον ὥστε
25 μηδαμοῦ δοκεῖν ἵστασθαι. Κατὰ δὲ | τὴν ἑτέραν ἣν ὀνομά-
ζομεν διαστηματικὴν ἐναντίως πέφυκε γίγνεσθαι· ἀλλὰ γὰρ
ἵστασθαί τε δοκεῖ καὶ πάντες τὸν τοῦτο φαινόμενον ποιεῖν
30 οὐκέτι λέγειν φασὶν ἀλλ᾽ ᾄδειν. Διό|περ ἐν τῷ διαλέγεσθαι 25
φεύγομεν τὸ ἱστάναι τὴν φωνήν, ἂν μὴ διὰ πάθος ποτὲ εἰς

---

1 αὐτὴν Meibom: αὐτὴν codd.   2 ἐφ᾽ ἑκάτερας B in marg.
5 ἐπ᾽] ἐ in ras. Mc: ὑπ᾽ V B R   6 κατ᾽ αὐτὰς B R, Mc (κατ᾽ parvis
litt. supra lin. add.)   7 λοιπτέον H   9 καὶ Marquard: ἢ
codd.   11 τὸ διερευνῆσαι Meibom: τὸ διακρῖναι Marquard   ἑκάτερον om. M, supra lin. add. Mc   12 ὁποτέρως ἂν ἔχῃ, ἔστι πρὸς τὸ
χωρίσαι H   ἔχῃ B   ποιεῖ Marquard: ποιεῖν codd.   14 μὲν
om. M Va   κινεῖται S   δοκεῖν μηδαμῇ H   15 συνεχῇ B
16 τοῦ S   post δόξασα una litt. eras. M   17 ἑτέρας] ἐ in ras. M :
ἑκατέρας V S, B in marg.   18 δόξῃ] ὁ in ras. M   23 πέφυκε]
υκε in ras. M   26 ἵστασθαι H : ἐν τῷ ἱστάναι V, B in marg., S

τοιαύτην κίνησιν ἀναγκασθῶμεν ἐλθεῖν, ἐν δὲ τῷ μελῳδεῖν
τοὐναντίον ποιοῦμεν, τὸ μὲν || γὰρ συνεχὲς φεύγομεν, τὸ 10
δ' ἑστάναι τὴν φωνὴν ὡς μάλιστα διώκομεν. ὅσῳ γὰρ
μᾶλλον ἑκάστην τῶν φωνῶν μίαν τε καὶ ἑστηκυῖαν καὶ τὴν
5 αὐτὴν | ποιήσομεν, τοσούτῳ φαίνεται τῇ αἰσθήσει τὸ μέλος 5
ἀκριβέστερον. Ὅτι μὲν οὖν δύο κινήσεων οὐσῶν κατὰ
τόπον τῆς φωνῆς ἡ μὲν συνεχὴς λογική τίς ἐστιν ἡ δὲ
διαστηματικὴ μελῳδική, | σχεδὸν δῆλον ἐκ τῶν εἰρημένων. 10
    Φανεροῦ δ' ὄντος ὅτι δεῖ τὴν φωνὴν ἐν τῷ μελῳδεῖν τὰς
10 μὲν ἐπιτάσεις τε καὶ ἀνέσεις ἀφανεῖς ποιεῖσθαι τὰς δὲ τά-
σεις αὐτὰς φθεγγομένην | φανερὰς καθιστάναι,—ἐπειδὴ τὸν 15
μὲν τοῦ διαστήματος τόπον ὃν διεξέρχεται ὁτὲ μὲν ἀνιεμένη
ὁτὲ δ' ἐπιτεινομένη λανθάνειν αὐτὴν δεῖ διεξιοῦσαν, τοὺς δὲ
ὁρίζοντας φθόγγους τὰ διαστήμα|τα ἐναργεῖς τε καὶ ἑστηκότας 20
5 ἀποδιδόναι—ὥστ' ἐπεὶ τοῦτ' ἔστι δῆλον λεκτέον ἂν εἴη
περὶ ἐπιτάσεως καὶ ἀνέσεως ἔτι δ' ὀξύτητος καὶ βαρύτητος πρὸς δὲ τούτοις τάσεως. Ἡ μὲν οὖν ἐπίτασίς
ἐστι | κίνησις τῆς φωνῆς συνεχὴς ἐκ βαρυτέρου τόπου εἰς 25
ὀξύτερον, ἡ δ' ἄνεσις ἐξ ὀξυτέρου τόπου εἰς βαρύτερον· ὀξύτης
20 δὲ τὸ γενόμενον διὰ τῆς ἐπιτάσεως, βαρύτης δὲ τὸ γενόμενον
διὰ τῆς ἀνέσεως. | Τάχα οὖν παράδοξον ἂν φαίνοιτο τοῖς ἐλα- 30
φρότερον τὰ τοιαῦτα ἐπισκοπουμένοις τὸ τιθέναι τέτταρα
ταῦτα καὶ μὴ δύο· σχεδὸν γὰρ οἵ γε πολλοὶ ἐπίτασιν μὲν
ὀξύτητι ταὐτὸν λέγουσιν || ἄνεσιν δὲ βαρύτητι, ἴσως οὖν οὐ 11
25 χεῖρον καταμαθεῖν ὅτι συγκεχυμένως πως δοξάζουσι περὶ

1 τοιαύτην corr. ex τὴν S   2 τὸ δ' ἑστάναι ... διώκομεν om. M,
in marg. Mc Vb   3 μὲν post ὅσῳ add. H   ἂν post γὰρ add. B R
5 ποιήσωμεν B R   10 δεστάσεις R   11 αὐτὰς Bellermann,
duce Anonymo (p. 49, sect. 36) : αὐτὴν codd.   φθεγγομένην] λεγομένην B in marg.   14 ἐναργεῖ B   19 ἄνεσις κίνησίς ἐστιν ἐκ
τοῦ ὀξυτέρου H   20 γινομένον B R   post ἐπιτάσεως add. ἀποτέ-
λεσμα B   21 ἐλαφρότερον H : ἐλαφροτέροις rell. : ἐλαφροτέρως Marquard   22 post τέτταρα add. γὰρ M V S   23 πολλοὶ] π in ras. M
24 τῇ ante ὀξύτητι add. H   ταὐτὸν] ταυτὸ (post ὸ una litt. eras.) M
τῇ ante βαρύτητι add. H

5 αὐτῶν. Δεῖ δὲ πειρᾶσθαι κατανοεῖν εἰς αὐτὸ ἀποβλέ|ποντας
τὸ γιγνόμενον τί ποτ' ἐστὶν ὃ ποιοῦμεν ὅταν ἁρμοττόμενοι
τῶν χορδῶν ἐκάστην ἀνιῶμεν ἢ ἐπιτείνωμεν. Δῆλον δὲ τοῖς
γε μὴ παντελῶς ἀπείροις ὀργάνων, ὅτι ἐπιτείνοντες μὲν εἰς |
10 ὀξύτητα τὴν χορδὴν ⟨ἄγομεν ἀνιέντες δ' εἰς βαρύτητα· καθ' 5
ὃν δὲ χρόνον⟩ ἄγομέν τε καὶ μετακινοῦμεν εἰς ὀξύτητα τὴν
χορδήν, οὐκ ἐνδέχεταί που ἤδη εἶναι τήν γε μέλλουσαν ἔσεσθαι ὀξύτητα διὰ τῆς ἐπιτάσεως. τότε γὰρ ἔσται ὀξύτης ὅταν
τῆς ἐπιτάσεως ἀγαγούσης εἰς τὴν προσήκουσαν τάσιν στῇ ἡ |
15 χορδὴ καὶ μηκέτι κινῆται. τοῦτο δ' ἔσται τῆς ἐπιτάσεως ἀπηλ- 10
λαγμένης καὶ μηκέτι οὔσης, οὐ γὰρ ἐνδέχεται κινεῖσθαι ἅμα
20 τὴν χορδὴν καὶ ἑστάναι, ἢν δ' ἡ μὲν ἐπίτασις | κινουμένης τῆς
χορδῆς, ἡ δ' ὀξύτης ἠρεμούσης ἤδη καὶ ἑστηκυίας. Ταὐτὰ δὲ
ἐροῦμεν καὶ περὶ τῆς ἀνέσεώς τε καὶ βαρύτητος πλὴν ἐπὶ τὸν
25 ἐναντίον τόπον. Δῆλον δὲ διὰ τῶν εἰρημένων, ὅτι ἥ τ' ἄνε- 15
σις τῆς βαρύτητος ἕτερόν τί ἐστιν, ὡς τὸ ποιοῦν τοῦ ποιου-
μένου, ἥ τ' ἐπίτασις τῆς ὀξύτητος τὸν αὐτὸν τρόπον. Ὅτι
30 μὲν οὖν ἕτερα ἀλλήλων | ἐστὶν ἐπίτασις μὲν ὀξύτητος ἄνεσις
δὲ βαρύτητος σχεδὸν δῆλον ἐκ τῶν εἰρημένων, ὅτι δὲ καὶ τὸ
τρίτον ὃ δὴ τάσιν ὀνομάζομεν ἕτερόν ἐστιν ἑκάστου τῶν εἰρη- 20
12 μένων, || πειρατέον κατανοῆσαι. Ὁ μὲν οὖν βουλόμεθα λέγειν
τὴν τάσιν σχεδόν ἐστι τοιοῦτον οἷον μονή τις καὶ στάσις τῆς
5 φωνῆς. Μὴ ταραττέτωσαν δ' ἡμᾶς αἱ τῶν εἰς | κινήσεις
ἀγόντων τοὺς φθόγγους δόξαι καὶ καθόλου τὴν φωνὴν κίνησιν
εἶναι φασκόντων, ὡς συμπεσουμένου λέγειν ἡμῖν ὅτι συμ- 25

5 ἄγομεν ... χρόνον restituit Marquard   5, 6 ὀξύτητα τὴν χορδὴν
ἄγομέν τε καὶ μετακινοῦμεν εἰς om. Ma R : in marg. add. Mb : sed
perfod. Mc : praeterea εἰ δ' εἰς ex εἰς Mx : εἰ δ' εἰς V S, B in marg.
7 καὶ ante οὐκ add. R   -γε om. B   9 ἀγαγούσης om. R   ἀγαγούσης
Marquard : ἀγούσης codd.   10 κινεῖται B S   13 ante ταὐτὰ
lac. 5 litt. M : ταῦτα M V B S   14 τὸν ἐναντίον τόπον B : τοῦ
ἐναντίου τόπου R : τῶν ἐναντίων τόπων rell.   17 καὶ ἡ ἐπίτασις H
19 δῆλον post εἰρημένων ponit H   20 τρίτον] πέμπτον Westphal
22 καὶ στάσις] ἱ στ Vb e corr.   23 ταραττέτωσαν] ἐτωσαν in ras.
Mb   τὰς ante κινήσεις add. B R

βήσεταί ποτε τῇ κινήσει μὴ κινεῖσθαι ἀλλ' ἠρεμεῖν τε καὶ
ἑστάναι. | Διαφέρει γὰρ οὐδὲν ἡμῖν τὸ λέγειν ὁμαλότητα   10
κινήσεως ἢ ταυτότητα τὴν τάσιν ἢ εἰ ἄλλο τι τούτων εὑρί-
σκοιτο γνωριμώτερον ὄνομα. οὐδὲν γὰρ ἧττον ἡμεῖς τότε
5 φήσομεν ἑστάναι τὴν φω|νήν, ὅταν ἡμῖν ἡ αἴσθησις αὐτὴν   15
ἀποφήνῃ μήτ' ἐπὶ τὸ ὀξὺ μήτ' ἐπὶ τὸ βαρὺ ὁρμῶσαν, οὐδὲν
ἄλλο ποιοῦντες πλὴν τῷ τοιούτῳ πάθει τῆς φωνῆς τοῦτο τὸ
ὄνομα τιθέμενοι. Φαίνεται δὲ τοῦτο | ποιεῖν ἐν τῷ μελῳδεῖν   20
ἡ φωνή· κινεῖται μὲν γὰρ ἐν τῷ διάστημά τι ποιεῖν, ἵσταται
10 δ' ἐν τῷ φθόγγῳ. Εἰ δὲ κινεῖται μὲν τὴν ὑφ' ἡμῶν λεγομένην
κίνησιν, ἐκείνης τῆς κινήσεως τῆς ὑπ' ἐκείνων λεγομέ|νης   25
τὴν κατὰ τάχος διαφορὰν λαμβανούσης, ἠρεμεῖ δὲ πάλιν αὖ
τὴν ὑφ' ἡμῶν λεγομένην ἠρεμίαν, στάντος τοῦ τάχους καὶ
λαβόντος μίαν τινὰ καὶ τὴν αὐτὴν ἀγωγήν, οὐδὲν ἂν ἡμῖν
15 διαφέροι. | σχεδὸν γὰρ δῆλόν ἐστιν ὅτι ἡμεῖς λέγομεν κίνησίν   30
τε καὶ ἠρεμίαν φωνῆς [καὶ] ὃ ἐκεῖνοι κίνησιν. Ταῦτα μὲν
οὖν ἐνταῦθα ἱκανῶς, ἐν ἄλλοις δὲ ἐπιπλεῖόν τε καὶ σαφέ-
στερον διώρισται. Ἡ δὲ || τάσις ὅτι μὲν οὔτ' ἐπίτασις οὔτ'   13
ἄνεσίς ἐστι παντελῶς δῆλον,—τὴν μὲν γὰρ εἶναί φαμεν
20 ἠρεμίαν φωνῆς, τὰς δ' ἐν τοῖς ἔμπροσθεν εὕρομεν οὔσας
κι|νήσεις τινάς,—ὅτι δὲ καὶ τῶν λοιπῶν, τῆς βαρύτητος καὶ   5
τῆς ὀξύτητος, ἕτερόν ἐστιν ἡ τάσις πειρατέον κατανοῆσαι.
Ὅτι μὲν οὖν ἠρεμεῖν συμβαίνει τῇ φωνῇ καὶ εἰς βαρύτητα
καὶ εἰς ὀξύτητα | ἀφικομένῃ, δῆλον ἐκ τῶν ἔμπροσθεν· ὅτι   10
25 δὲ καὶ τῆς τάσεως ἠρεμίας τινὸς τεθείσης οὐδὲν μᾶλλον
ἐκείνων ἑκατέρᾳ ταὐτὸν τάσις ἐστίν, ἐκ τῶν ῥηθησομένων

3 εἰ om. R   εὑρίσκοι τὸ Β R
rell.   7 ποιοῦντες ex ποιοῦντας Mx   τοῦτο τὸ ὄνομα τιθέμ. ex
τούτω τω (ut vid.) ὀνόματι θέμ. Mb   9 γὰρ om. H   διαστήματι S
12 τὴν] τῆς M   post ἠρεμεῖ ras. M   αὖ τὴν ex αὐτὴν Mb : αὖ
om. H   15 ὅτι conieci: ὃ θ' codd.   ἡμεῖς ex ἱμεῖς Vb   16 καὶ
seclusi   18 ἡ ex τὴν (ut vid.) in ras. Mb   Bellermann: τε
codd.   τάσις ex τάσιν Mb   23 ἠρεμίαν] εἴν in ras. Mx
24 ἀφικομένη Vb, ἀφικο in ras. Mx : ἀφικνουμένη Va Β S : ἀφικομένη R
26 ἑκατέρᾳ conieci: ἑκατέρων codd.

15 ἔσται φανερόν. Δεῖ δὴ καταμανθάνειν | ὅτι τὸ μὲν ἑστάναι
τὴν φωνὴν τὸ μένειν ἐπὶ μιᾶς τάσεώς ἐστι. συμβήσεται
δ' αὐτῇ τοῦτο, ἐάν τ' ἐπὶ βαρύτητος ἐάν τ' ἐπ' ὀξύτητος
ἱστῆται. Εἰ δ' ἡ μὲν τάσις ἐν ἀμφοτέροις ὑπάρξει—καὶ
20 γὰρ ἐπὶ | τῶν βαρέων καὶ ἐπὶ τῶν ὀξέων τὸ ἵστασθαι τὴν 5
φωνὴν ἀναγκαῖον ἦν—, ἡ δ' ὀξύτης μηδέποτε τῇ βαρύτητι
συνυπάρξει μηδ' ἡ βαρύτης τῇ ὀξύτητι, δῆλον ὡς ἕτερόν
25 ἐστιν ἑκατέρου τούτων ἡ τάσις ὡς | [μηδὲν] κοινὸν γιγνό-
μενον ἐν ἀμφοτέροις. Ὅτι μὲν οὖν πέντε ταῦτ' ἐστὶν
ἀλλήλων ἕτερα, τάσις τε καὶ ὀξύτης καὶ βαρύτης πρὸς δὲ 10
30 τούτοις ἄνεσίς τε καὶ ἐπίτασις, σχεδὸν δῆλον ἐκ τῶν | εἰρη-
μένων.

Τούτων δ' ὄντων γνωρίμων ἐχόμενον ἂν εἴη διελθεῖν περὶ
τῆς τοῦ βαρέος τε καὶ ὀξέος διαστάσεως, πότερον
14 ἄπειρος ἐφ' ἑκάτερά ἐστιν ἢ πε||περασμένη. Ὅτι μὲν οὖν 15
εἰς γε τὴν φωνὴν τιθεμένη οὐκ ἔστιν ἄπειρος, οὐ χαλεπὸν
συνιδεῖν. ἁπάσης γὰρ φωνῆς ὀργανικῆς τε καὶ ἀνθρωπικῆς
5 ὡρι|σμένος ἐστί τις τόπος ὃν διεξέρχεται μελῳδοῦσα ὅ τε
μέγιστος καὶ ὁ ἐλάχιστος. οὔτε γὰρ ἐπὶ τὸ μέγα δύναται
ἡ φωνὴ εἰς ἄπειρον αὔξειν τὴν τοῦ βαρέος τε καὶ ὀξέος 20
10 διάστασιν οὔτ' ἐπὶ | τὸ μικρὸν συνάγειν, ἀλλ' ἵσταταί ποτε
ἐφ' ἑκάτερα. Διοριστέον οὖν ἑκάτερον αὐτῶν πρὸς δύο
ποιουμένους τὴν ἀναφοράν, πρός τε τὸ φθεγγόμενον καὶ τὸ
15 κρῖνον· ταῦτα δ' ἐστὶν ἥ τε φωνὴ καὶ ἡ | ἀκοή. ὃ γὰρ
ἀδυνατοῦσιν αὗται ἡ μὲν ποιεῖν ἡ δὲ κρίνειν, τοῦτ' ἔξω 25

2 μέλλον B   3 ἐπ' in ras., erat ἀπ' Ma   4 ἱστῆται M B S:
ἱστῆται Mc Vb R   εἰ δ' ἡ μὲν] ἡ δὲ sed ras. post δὲ M : ἡ δ' εἰ μὲν
Vb : ἡ δ' εἰ μὲν B in marg. : ἡ δ' ἡ μὲν S   8 μηδὲν del. Marquard,
recte   14 διαστάσεως M (?) B : διατάσεως V S R, B in marg.
15 ἑκάτερά Meibom : ἑκάτερας codd.   ἢ ex ἡ Mb : ἡ B   16 γε
conieci : om. H : τε rell.   18 τόπος Meursius : τόνος codd.
20 ἢ ante εἰς add. S   21 διάστασιν] σ ante τ eras. M : διάτασιν
rell.   ἵστασθαί B R   23 διαφορὰν R   πρὸς post καὶ add. H
24 δ' om. B   25 ποιεῖν] εἰν in ras. Mb   ἔξω Bellermann:
ἔξωθεν codd.

106

θετέον τῆς τε χρησίμου καὶ δυνατῆς ἐν φωνῇ γενέσθαι διαστάσεως. Ἐπὶ μὲν οὖν τὸ μικρὸν ἅμα πως ἐοίκασιν ἥ τε
φωνὴ καὶ | ἡ αἴσθησις ἐξαδυνατεῖν· οὔτε γὰρ ἡ φωνὴ διέ- 20
σεως τῆς ἐλαχίστης ἔλαττον ἔτι διάστημα δύναται διασαφεῖν
5 οὐδ' ἡ ἀκοὴ διαισθάνεσθαι ὥστε καὶ ξυνιέναι τί μέρος ἐστὶ
διέσεως εἴτ' ἄλλου τινὸς τῶν γνωρίμων διαστημάτων. | Ἐπὶ 25
δὲ τὸ μέγα τάχ' ἂν δόξειεν ὑπερτείνειν ἡ ἀκοὴ τὴν φωνὴν
οὐ μέντοι γε πολλῷ τινι.   Ἀλλ' οὖν εἴτ' ἐπ' ἀμφότερα δεῖ
ταὐτὸν λαμβάνειν | πέρας τῆς διαστάσεως, εἴς τε τὴν φωνὴν 30
10 καὶ τὴν ἀκοὴν βλέποντας, εἴτ' ἐπὶ μὲν τὸ ἐλάχιστον ταὐτὸν
ἐπὶ δὲ τὸ μέγιστον ἕτερον· ἔσται τι μέγιστον καὶ ἐλάχιστον
μέγεθος τῆς διαστά||σεως ἤτοι κοινὸν τοῦ φθεγγομένου καὶ 15
τοῦ κρίνοντος ἢ ἴδιον ἑκατέρου. Ὅτι μὲν οὖν εἴς τε τὴν
φωνὴν καὶ τὴν ἀκοὴν τεθεῖσα ἡ τοῦ βαρέος τε καὶ ὀξέος
15 δι|άστασις οὐκ εἰς ἄπειρον ἐφ' ἑκάτερα κινηθήσεται, σχεδὸν 5
δῆλον. εἰ δ' αὐτὴ καθ' αὑτὴν νοηθείη ἡ τοῦ μέλους σύστασις, τὴν αὔξησιν εἰς ἄπειρον γίγνεσθαι ⟨εἰ⟩ συμβήσεται
τάχ' ἂν ἄλλος εἴη περὶ τούτων | λόγος, οὐκ ἀναγκαῖος εἰς τὸ 10
παρόν, διόπερ ἐν τοῖς ἔπειτα τοῦτ' ἐπισκέψασθαι πειρατέον.
20   Τούτου δ' ὄντος γνωρίμου λεκτέον περὶ φθόγγου τί
ποτ' ἐστί. | Συντόμως μὲν οὖν εἰπεῖν φωνῆς πτῶσις ἐπὶ μίαν 15
τάσιν ὁ φθόγγος ἐστί· τότε γὰρ φαίνεται φθόγγος εἶναι
τοιοῦτος οἷος εἰς μέλος τάττεσθαι | ἡρμοσμένον, ⟨ὅταν ἡ 20
φωνὴ φανῇ⟩ ἑστάναι ἐπὶ μιᾶς τάσεως. Ὁ μὲν οὖν φθόγγος
25 τοιοῦτος ἐστίν· διάστημα δ' ἐστὶ τὸ ὑπὸ δύο φθόγ|γων 25
ὡρισμένον μὴ τὴν αὐτὴν τάσιν ἐχόντων. Φαίνεται γάρ, ὡς

---

1 διαστάσεως M (σ ante τ eras.), S, B in marg.: διατάσεως R, Vb
fort. e corr., B   5 ἡ om. B   6 εἴτε ante διέσεως parvis litt.
supra lin. add. Mc, in marg. B, R: om. ꝛell.   9 διαστάσεως B S R
12 διαστάσεως] σ ante τ eras. M: διατάσεως B R   13 εἰ (σ
supraser.) τε B   15 εἰς] ἐπ' H   16 νοηθείη] ἀχθείη H   17 εἰ
restituit Bellermann   22 ὁ om. H   ὅρος φθόγγου add. in marg.
Mb Vc   ἐστι τότε γὰρ φαίνεται φθόγγος add. in marg. Ma   23 ὅταν
ἡ φωνὴ φανῇ restituit Meibom   25 ὅρος διαστήματος add. in marg.
Mb Vc

τύπῳ εἰπεῖν, διαφορά τις εἶναι τάσεων τὸ διάστημα καὶ
τόπος δεκτικὸς φθόγγων ὀξυτέρων μὲν τῆς βαρυτέρας τῶν |
30 ὁριζουσῶν τὸ διάστημα τάσεων, βαρυτέρων δὲ τῆς ὀξυτέρας·
διαφορὰ δὲ ἐστὶ τάσεων τὸ μᾶλλον ἢ ἧττον τετάσθαι. Περὶ
μὲν οὖν διαστήματος οὕτως ἄν τις ἀφορίσειε· τὸ δὲ σύ- 5
16 στημα σύνθετόν τι || νοητέον ἐκ πλειόνων ἢ ἑνὸς διαστη-
μάτων. Δεῖ δ' ἕκαστον τούτων εὖ πως ἐκλαμβάνειν
πειρᾶσθαι τὸν ἀκούοντα μὴ παρατηροῦντα τὸν ἀποδιδόμενον
5 λόγον | ἑκάστου αὐτῶν εἴτ' ἐστὶν ἀκριβὴς εἴτε καὶ τυπω-
δέστερος, ἀλλ' αὐτὸν συμπροθυμούμενον κατανοῆσαι καὶ 10
τότε οἰόμενον ἱκανῶς εἰρῆσθαι πρὸς τὸ καταμαθεῖν, ὅταν
10 ἐμβιβάσαι οἷός τε γένηται ὁ | λόγος εἰς τὸ συνιέναι τὸ
λεγόμενον. Χαλεπὸν γὰρ ὑπὲρ πάντων μὲν ἴσως τῶν ἐν
ἀρχῇ λόγον ἀνεπίληπτόν τε καὶ διηκριβωμένην ἑρμηνείαν
15 ἔχοντα ῥηθῆναι, οὐχ ἥκιστα δὲ περὶ τριῶν τούτων, | φθόγγου 15
τε καὶ διαστήματος καὶ συστήματος.

Τούτων δ' οὕτως ὡρισμένων πρῶτον μὲν τὸ διάστημα
20 πειρατέον διε|λεῖν εἰς ὅσας πέφυκε διαιρέσεις διαιρεῖσθαι
χρησίμους, ἔπειτα τὸ σύστημα. Πρώτη μὲν οὖν ἐστι
διαστημάτων διαίρεσις καθ' ἣν μεγέθει ἀλλήλων διαφέρει· | 20
25 δευτέρα δὲ καθ' ἣν τὰ σύμφωνα τῶν διαφώνων· τρίτη δὲ
καθ' ἣν τὰ σύνθετα τῶν ἀσυνθέτων· τετάρτη δ' ἡ κατὰ
30 γένος· | πέμπτη δὲ καθ' ἣν διαφέρει τὰ ῥητὰ τῶν ἀλόγων.
Τὰς δὲ λοιπὰς τῶν διαιρέσεων ὡς οὐ χρησίμους οὔσας εἰς
17 ταύτην τὴν πραγματείαν ἀφετέον τὰ νῦν. || Σύστημα δὲ 25

3 ὁριζόντων R   τό τε διάστημα R   11 οἰόμενοι S   εἰρεῖσθαι
S   12 ἐκβιβάσαι R   γένηται] ηται in ras. Mb   τὸ λεγόμενον]
τὸ: post ὁ ras. M   13 ante μὲν una litt. eras. M   μὲν] εἶναι B R
τῶν] τὸ R : τὸν V B S   τῶν... ἥκιστα δὲ om. H   14 λόγων M
15 φθόγγων R   16 συστήματος] διαστήματος B R   18 διελεῖν V S
sed εῖν Vb in ras. : διελθεῖν M   διαιρέσεις om. B sed in marg. add.
19 χρησίμων H   ἔπειτα in ras. Vb: καὶ ἔτι in ras. Ma
20 διαιρέσεις διαστήματος deinde numeri ἀ. β. κτέ. in marg. Mb
Vc   23 διαφέρει om. H   λόγων B R: ῥητὰ τῶν ἀλόγων in
ras. Mb

συστήματος ταύταις τε διοίσει ταῖς ⟨αὐταῖς⟩ διαφοραῖς πλὴν
μιᾶς—μεγέθει τε γὰρ δῆλον ὡς διαφέρει συστή|ματος σύ- 5
στημα καὶ τῷ [τε] συμφώνους ἢ διαφώνους εἶναι τοὺς ὁρίζοντας
φθόγγους τὸ μέγεθος.   τὴν δὲ τρίτην τῶν ῥηθεισῶν ἐπὶ
5 τῶν τοῦ διαστήματος διαφορῶν ἀδύνατον ὑπάρξαι | συστή- 10
ματι πρὸς σύστημα, δῆλον γὰρ ὡς οὐκ ἐνδέχεται τὰ μὲν
σύνθετα τὰ δ' ἀσύνθετα εἶναι τῶν συστημάτων τοῦτόν γε
τὸν τρόπον ὅνπερ τῶν διαστημάτων τὰ μὲν ἦν σύνθετα τὰ
δ' ἀσύνθετα.   τὴν | δὲ τετάρτην—αὕτη δ' ἦν ἡ κατὰ γένος 15
10 —ἀναγκαῖον καὶ τοῖς συστήμασιν ὑπάρχειν, τὰ μὲν γὰρ
αὐτῶν ἐστὶ διάτονα τὰ δὲ χρωματικὰ τὰ δὲ ἐναρμόνια.
δῆλον δ' ὅτι καὶ ⟨τὴν⟩ πέμπτην, τὰ μὲν | γὰρ αὐτῶν ἀλόγῳ 20
διαστήματι ὥρισται τὰ δὲ ῥητῷ.   Πρὸς δὲ ταύταις τρεῖς
ἐτέρας προσθετέον διαιρέσεις· τήν τ' εἰς συναφὴν καὶ διά-
15 ζευξιν καὶ τὸ συναμφότερον μερίζουσαν τὰ συστήματα· |
⟨πᾶν γὰρ σύστημα⟩ ἀπό τινος μεγέθους ἀρξάμενον ἢ συνημ- 25
μένον ἢ διεζευγμένον ἢ μικτὸν ἐξ ἀμφοτέρων γίγνεται (καὶ
δείκνυται τοῦτο γιγνόμενον ἐν ἐνίοις)· ἔπειτα τήν τ' εἰς
ὑπερβατὸν καὶ συνεχὲς μερίζου|σαν, πᾶν γὰρ σύστημα ἤτοι 30
20 συνεχὲς ἢ ὑπερβατόν ἐστι, τήν τ' εἰς ἁπλοῦν καὶ διπλοῦν
καὶ πολλαπλοῦν διαίρεσιν, πᾶν || γὰρ τὸ λαμβανόμενον 18
σύστημα ἤτοι ἁπλοῦν ἢ διπλοῦν ἢ πολλαπλοῦν ἐστίν.   Τί
δ' ἐστὶ τούτων ἕκαστον ἐν τοῖς ἔπειτα δειχθήσεται. |
Τούτων δ' οὕτως ἀφωρισμένων τε καὶ προδιῃρημένων 5

1 συστήματος διαιρέσεις Mb Vc in marg. ut supra   αὐταῖς restituit
Westphal: ante ταῖς ras. in qua erat ταῖς αὐ M   2 τε in ras. in
qua erat τε δη Ma: δὲ B   γὰρ H: om. rell.   3 καὶ in ras. Ma:
om. rell.   τε seclusit Marquard   4 δὲ in ras. Mb: μέντοι BR
5 διαστήματος Vb B S: συστήματος M R   7 τὰ δ' ἀσύνθετα om. R
εἶναι . . . τὰ δ' ἀσύνθετα om. S   9 τὸ post κατὰ add. H   12 τὴν
restituit Marquard   13 ῥητῷ. Πρὸς δὲ om. B, sed in marg. add.
14 ἐτέρας ante τρεῖς ponit H   εἰς in ras. Mb   16 πᾶν γὰρ
σύστημα restituit Marquard   17 ἢ διεζευγμένον ante ἢ συνημμένον
ponunt codd.: ordinem restituit Marquard   18 τε post εἰς ponit
H: ς in marg. Mb   20 καὶ διπλοῦν om. R: ζ in marg. Mb
22 ἢ διπλοῦν om. B   23 δεχθήσεται S

109

περὶ μέλους ἂν εἴη ἡμῖν πειρατέον ὑποτυπῶσαι τί ποτ'
ἐστὶν ἡ φύσις αὐτοῦ. Ὅτι μὲν οὖν διαστηματικὴν ἐν αὐτῷ
10 δεῖ τὴν τῆς φω|νῆς κίνησιν εἶναι προείρηται, ὥστε τοῦ γε
λογώδους κεχώρισται ταύτῃ τὸ μουσικὸν μέλος· λέγεται
γὰρ δὴ καὶ λογῶδές τι μέλος, τὸ συγκείμενον ἐκ τῶν προσῳ- 5
15 διῶν τῶν ἐν τοῖς ὀνόμασιν· | φυσικὸν γὰρ τὸ ἐπιτείνειν καὶ
ἀνιέναι ἐν τῷ διαλέγεσθαι. Ἐπεὶ δ' οὐ μόνον ἐκ διαστημάτων τε καὶ φθόγγων συνεστάναι δεῖ τὸ ἡρμοσμένον μέλος,
20 ἀλλὰ προσδεῖται συνθέσεώς τινος ποιᾶς | καὶ οὐ τῆς τυχού-
σης—δῆλον γὰρ ὡς τό γ' ἐκ διαστημάτων τε καὶ φθόγγων 10
συνεστάναι κοινόν ἐστιν, ὑπάρχει γὰρ καὶ τῷ ἀναρμόστῳ—,
ὥστ' ἐπειδὴ τοῦθ' οὕτως ἔχει, τὸ μέγιστον μέρος καὶ πλείστην
25 | ἔχον ῥοπὴν εἰς τὴν ὀρθῶς γιγνομένην σύστασιν τοῦ μέλους
(τὸ) περὶ τὴν σύνθεσιν καθόλου καὶ τὴν ταύτης ἰδιότητα
ὑποληπτέον εἶναι. Σχεδὸν δὴ φανερόν, ὅτι τοῦ μὲν ἐπὶ 15
30 τῆς λέξεως γι|γνομένου μέλους τῷ διαστηματικῇ χρῆσθαι τῇ
τῆς φωνῆς κινήσει διοίσει τὸ μουσικὸν μέλος, τοῦ δ' ἀναρ-
μόστου καὶ διημαρτημένου τῇ τῆς συνθέσεως διαφορᾷ τῆς
19 τῶν ἀσυνθέτων || διαστημάτων, περὶ ἧς ἐν τοῖς ἔπειτα
δειχθήσεται τίς ἐστιν αὐτῆς ὁ τρόπος. πλὴν ἐπὶ τοσοῦτόν 20
5 γ' εἰρήσθω καθόλου καὶ νῦν, ὅτι πολλὰς ἔχοντος δια|φορὰς
τοῦ ἡρμοσμένου κατὰ τὴν τῶν διαστημάτων σύνθεσιν, ὅμως
ἔστι τι τοιοῦτον ὃ κατὰ παντὸς ἡρμοσμένου ῥηθήσεται ἕν
τε καὶ ταὐτόν, τοιαύτην ἔχον δύναμιν οἵαν αὐτὴν ἀναιρου-
10 μένην | ἀναιρεῖν τὸ ἡρμοσμένον. ἁπλοῦν δ' ἔσται προϊούσης 25

1 περὶ μέλους in marg. Mb Vc   ἐπιτυπῶσαι R   2 διστηματικὴν
B   3 γε] γ S   4 λέγεται ... μέλος om. B sed in marg. add.
5 δὴ] τὶ S   6 τῶν ἐν τοῖς Meursius : τὸ ἐν τοῖς codd.   7 ἐπεὶ
δ' B R : ἔπειτα rell.   8 συνιστάναι B   9 τύχης R   13 ὀρθῶς
... περὶ τὴν parvis litt. supra lin. Mc, in marg. Vb   14 τὸ restituit
Marquard   καθόλου conieci : κἄπου H : καί που rell.   καὶ seclusit
Bellermann   15 ἐπὶ τῆς λέξεως Bellermann, duce Anonymo
(p. 55) : ἐπιτηδείως codd.   16 διαστηματικῇ χρῆσθαι Meibom :
διαστήματι κεχρῆσθαι codd.   18 διαμαρτημένου B   20 ὁ om. H
21 εἰρείσθω S   24 ταὐτόν] ταὐτὸ (post ὁ litt. eras.) M : ταὐτὸν V :
ταὐτὸ rell.   ἀναιρουμένην om. B

τῆς πραγματείας. Τὸ μὲν οὖν μουσικὸν μέλος ἀπὸ τῶν
ἄλλων οὕτως ἀφωρίσθω. ὑποληπτέον δὲ τὸν εἰρημένον
ἀφορισμὸν τύπῳ εἰ|ρῆσθαι οὕτως ὡς μηδέπω τῶν καθ᾽ ἕκαστα   15
τεθεωρημένων.

5   Ἐχόμενον δ᾽ ἂν εἴη τῶν εἰρημένων τὸ καθόλου λεγόμενον
μέλος διελεῖν εἰς ὅσα φαίνεται γένη διαιρεῖσθαι. Φαί-
νεται | δ᾽ εἰς τρία· πᾶν γὰρ τὸ λαμβανόμενον μέλος τῶν   20
εἰς ταὐτὸ ἡρμοσμένων ἤτοι διάτονόν ἐστιν ἢ χρωματικὸν ἢ
ἐναρμόνιον. Πρῶτον μὲν οὖν καὶ πρεσβύτατον αὐτῶν θετέον
10 τὸ διάτονον, πρῶτον γὰρ | αὐτοῦ ἡ τοῦ ἀνθρώπου φύσις προσ-   25
τυγχάνει, δεύτερον δὲ τὸ χρωματικόν, τρίτον δὲ καὶ ἀνώτατον τὸ ἐναρμόνιον, τελευταίῳ γὰρ αὐτῷ καὶ μόλις μετὰ
πολλοῦ πόνου συνεθίζεται ἡ αἴσθησις· |

Τούτων δ᾽ εἰς τοῦτον τὸν ἀριθμὸν διῃρημένων τῶν δια-   30
15 στηματικῶν διαφορῶν τῆς δευτέρας ῥηθείσης θάτερον μέρος
πειρατέον διασκέψασθαι—ἦν δὲ τὰ μέρη ταῦτα διαφωνία τε
καὶ || συμφωνία—ληπτέον τε τὴν συμφωνίαν εἰς τὴν ἐπί-   20
σκεψιν. Φαίνεται δὲ διάστημα σύμφωνον συμφώνου δια-
φέρειν κατὰ πλείους διαφορὰς ὧν μία | μέν ἐστιν ἡ κατὰ   5
20 μέγεθος, περὶ ἧς ἀφοριστέον ᾗ φαίνεται ἔχειν. Δοκεῖ δὲ
τὸ μὲν ἐλάχιστον τῶν συμφώνων διαστημάτων ὑπ᾽ αὐτῆς
τῆς τοῦ μέλους φύσεως ἀφωρίσθαι, μελῳδεῖται μὲν γὰρ |
τοῦ διὰ τεσσάρων ἐλάττω διαστήματα πολλά, διάφωνα μέν-   10
τοι πάντα. Τὸ μὲν οὖν ἐλάχιστον κατ᾽ αὐτὴν τὴν τῆς φωνῆς

2 ἀφωρίσθω ex ἀφωριείσθω Ma   τὸν] τὸ M (corr. Mc)   3 εἰρῆσθαι ex εἰρήσθω Mc : εἰρεῖσθαι S   ἕκαστον R   6 εἰς om. S
8 ταὐτὸ conieci : τὸ codd.   ἡρμοσμένων conieci : ἡρμοσμένον codd.
τὸ εἰς τὸ ἡρμοσμένον Marquard   10 γὰρ Marquard : τε codd.
ἀνθρώπου] ἀνοῦ S   προστυγχάνει Vb R S : προτυγχάνει rell.
11 νεώτατον H   12 τὸ ἐναρμόνιον ex τὴν ἁρμονίαν Mb   14 δι-
ῃρημένον B   16 σκέψασθαι R   καθ᾽ ἣν τὰ σύμφωνα τῶν
διαφώνων διαφέρει in marg. add. Mb Vc   17 ληπτέον τε] τε om. B :
δὲ S   22 ἀφωρίσθαι ex ἀφωριείσθαι Mb : σ in ras. Vb   μὲν
om. H   24 τὸ om. B : supra lin. add. Mb   τὴν om. B : supra
lin. add. Mb

φύσιν ὥρισται, τὸ δὲ μέγιστον οὕτω μὲν [οὖν] οὐκ ἔοικεν
15 ὁρί|ζεσθαι· φαίνεται γὰρ εἰς ἄπειρον αὔξεσθαι κατά γ᾽ αὐτὴν
τὴν τοῦ μέλους φύσιν καθάπερ καὶ τὸ διάφωνον. παντὸς
γὰρ προστιθεμένου συμφώνου διαστήματος πρὸς τῷ διὰ
20 πασῶν | καὶ μείζονος καὶ ἐλάττονος καὶ ἴσου τὸ ὅλον γίγνε- 5
ται σύμφωνον. Οὕτω μὲν οὖν οὐκ ἔοικεν εἶναί τι μέγιστον
σύμφωνον διάστημα· κατὰ μέντοι τὴν ἡμετέραν χρῆσιν—
25 λέγω δ᾽ ἡμετέραν | τήν τε διὰ τῆς ἀνθρώπου φωνῆς γιγνο-
μένην καὶ τὴν διὰ τῶν ὀργάνων—φαίνεταί τι μέγιστον εἶναι
τῶν συμφώνων. τοῦτο δ᾽ ἐστὶ τὸ διὰ πέντε καὶ τὸ δὶς διὰ 10·
30 πασῶν, τὸ γὰρ τρὶς διὰ | πασῶν οὐκ ἔτι διατείνομεν. Δεῖ
δὲ τὴν διάστασιν ὁρίζειν ἑνός τινος ὀργάνου τόπῳ καὶ πέ-
ρασιν. τάχα γὰρ ὁ τῶν παρθενίων αὐλῶν ὀξύτατος φθόγγος
πρὸς τὸν τῶν ὑπερτελείων βαρύτατον μεῖζον ἂν ποιήσειε
21 τοῦ εἰρημένου τρὶς διὰ πασῶν ‖ διάστημα καὶ κατασπασθείσης 15
γε τῆς σύριγγος ὁ τοῦ συρίττοντος ὀξύτατος πρὸς τὸν τοῦ αὐ-
λοῦντος βαρύτατον μεῖζον ἂν ποιήσειε τοῦ ῥηθέντος διαστή-
5 μα|τος· ταὐτὸν δὲ καὶ παιδὸς φωνὴ μικροῦ πρὸς ἀνδρὸς
φωνὴν πάθοι ἄν. ὅθεν καὶ κατανοεῖται τὰ μεγάλα τῶν
συμφώνων· ἐκ διαφερουσῶν γὰρ ἡλικιῶν καὶ διαφερόντων 20
10 μέτρων τεθεωρήκαμεν, | ὅτι καὶ τὸ τρὶς διὰ πασῶν συμφωνεῖ

---

1 μέγιστον Meibom H: μέγεθος rell.   οὖν seclusit Marquard
2 ὁριεῖσθαι M V S: ὡρίσθαι H   γὰρ supra lin. Mb: δὲ (γὰρ
suprascr.) B a corr. manu: δὲ R   3 διάφωνον ex διάφορον
Mb: δίφωνον B   5 ὅλον] ὅλων S: ὀλίγον R   6 οὖν om. B
10 τοῦτο] τοῦ S   τὸ δὶς] τὸ supra lin. B

δὶς διὰ πασῶν   διὰ ἔ ⎫
     δ   ιϛ   κδ ⎬ in marg. Mb Vc   11 τὸ γὰρ Vb B R S:
     ‾‾‾‾‾‾‾‾ ⎭
     ἐξαπλάσιον

τοῦ γὰρ M (γὰρ in ras. Ma ut vid.): μέχρι γὰρ τοῦ Marquard: γὰρ om. H
ὅρα Πορφύριον ἐν τῷ εἰς ἁρμονικὰ ὑπομνήματι add. in marg. H   οὐκέτι ex
οὖν ἐστι Ma   διατείνωμεν B   12 διάτασιν R   τόπῳ Westphal:
τόπῳ codd.   13 παρθενιῶν M Vb R   παρθ. αὐλ. linea subducta S
14 τὸν om. R   βαρύτατον Marquard: βαρυτάτων codd.   15 τοῦ
R : τοῦτ᾽ rell.   κατασπαθείσης M H   17 ποιήσειε διάστημα τοῦ
τρὶς διὰ πασῶν εἰρημένου διαστήματος H   ῥηθέντος] post ρ ras. M
18 ἡ ante παιδὸς add. et φωνὴ post μικροῦ ponit H

112.

καὶ τὸ τετράκις καὶ τὸ μεῖζον. Ὅτι μὲν οὖν ἐπὶ μὲν τὸ
μικρὸν ἡ τοῦ μέλους φύσις αὐτὴ τὸ διὰ τεσσάρων ἐλάχιστον
ἀποδίδωσι τῶν συμφώνων, ἐπὶ δὲ τὸ μέ|γα τῇ ἡμετέρᾳ πως   15
τὸ μέγιστον ὁρίζεται δυνάμει, σχεδὸν δῆλον ἐκ τῶν εἰρη-
5 μένων· ὅτι δ' ὀκτὼ μεγέθη συμφώνων διαστημάτων συμβαίνει
γίγνεσθαι ῥᾴδιον συνιδεῖν.|

    Τούτων δ' ὄντων γνωρίμων τὸ τονιαῖον διάστημα πει-   20
ρατέον ἀφορίσαι. Ἔστι δὴ τόνος ἡ τῶν πρώτων συμφώνων
κατὰ μέγεθος διαφορά. Διαιρείσθω δ' εἰς τρεῖς διαιρέσεις·
10 μελῳδείσθω γὰρ | αὐτοῦ τό τε ἥμισυ καὶ τὸ τρίτον μέρος καὶ   25
⟨τὸ⟩ τέταρτον· τὰ δὲ τούτων ἐλάττονα διαστήματα πάντα
ἔστω ἀμελῴδητα. Καλείσθω δὲ τὸ μὲν ἐλάχιστον δίεσις
ἐναρμόνιος ἐλαχίστη, τὸ δ' ἐχόμενον | δίεσις χρωματικὴ   30
ἐλαχίστη, τὸ δὲ μέγιστον ἡμιτόνιον.

15   Τούτων δ' οὕτως ἀφωρισμένων τὰς τῶν γενῶν διαφορὰς ὅθεν γίγνονται καὶ ὃν τρόπον πειρατέον καταμαθεῖν.
Δεῖ δὲ || νοῆσαι τῶν συμφώνων διαστημάτων ⟨τὸ⟩ ἐλάχιστον   22
τὸ κατεχόμενον τά γε πλεῖστα ὑπὸ τεττάρων φθόγγων·
ὅθεν δὴ καὶ τὴν προσηγορίαν ὑπὸ τῶν παλαιῶν ἔσχε . . . |
20 [τίνα δὴ τάξιν πλειόνων οὐσῶν νοητέον; ἐν ᾗ ἴσα τά τε   5
κινούμενά εἰσι καὶ τὰ ἠρεμοῦντα ἐν ταῖς τῶν γενῶν διαφοραῖς.
Γίγνεται δ' ἐν τῷ τοιούτῳ οἷον τὸ ἀπὸ μέσης ἐφ' ὑπάτην·
ἐν τούτῳ γὰρ δύο μὲν οἱ πε|ριέχοντες φθόγγοι ἀκίνητοί   10

εἰσιν ἐν ταῖς τῶν γενῶν διαφοραῖς, δύο δ᾽ οἱ περιεχόμενοι
κινοῦνται.] Τοῦτο μὲν οὖν οὕτω κείσθω. τῶν δὲ συγχορ-
δίων πλειόνων τ᾽ οὐσῶν τῶν τὴν εἰρημένην τάξιν τοῦ διὰ |
15 τεσσάρων κατεχουσῶν καὶ ὀνόμασιν ἰδίοις ἑκάστης αὐτῶν
ὡρισμένης, μία τίς ἐστιν ἡ μέσης καὶ λιχανοῦ καὶ παρυπάτης 5
καὶ ὑπάτης σχεδὸν γνωριμωτάτη τοῖς ἀπτομένοις μουσικῆς
20 ἐν ᾗ τὰς | τῶν γενῶν διαφορὰς ἀναγκαῖον ἐπισκέψασθαι
τίνα τρόπον γίγνονται. Ὅτι μὲν οὖν αἱ τῶν κινεῖσθαι
πεφυκότων φθόγγων ἐπιτάσεις τε καὶ ἀνέσεις αἴτιαί εἰσι
25 τῆς τῶν γενῶν διαφορᾶς φανερόν. τίς δ᾽ | ὁ τόπος τῆς 10
κινήσεως ἑκατέρου τῶν φθόγγων τούτων λεκτέον. Λιχανοῦ
μὲν οὖν ἐστὶ τονιαῖος ὁ σύμπας τόπος ἐν ᾧ κινεῖται, οὔτε
30 γὰρ ἔλαττον ἀφίσταται μέσης τονιαίου διαστή|ματος οὔτε
μεῖζον διτόνου. Τούτων δὲ τὸ μὲν ἔλαττον παρὰ μὲν τῶν
ἤδη κατανενοηκότων τὸ διάτονον γένος [οὐχ] ὁμολογεῖται, 15
23 παρὰ δὲ τῶν μήπω συνεωρακότων συγχωροῖτ᾽ ἂν || ἐπα-
χθέντων αὐτῶν· τὸ δὲ μεῖζον οἱ μὲν συγχωροῦσιν οἱ δ᾽ οὔ.
δι᾽ ἣν δὲ γίγνεται τοῦτο αἰτίαν, ἐν τοῖς ἔπειτα ῥηθήσεται.
Ὅτι δ᾽ ἔστι τις μελοποιΐα διτόνου λιχανοῦ δεομένη καὶ οὐχ
5 ἡ φαυλοτάτη γε ἀλλὰ σχεδὸν ἡ καλλίστη, | τοῖς μὲν πολλοῖς 20
τῶν νῦν ἀπτομένων μουσικῆς οὐ πάνυ εὔδηλόν ἐστι, γένοιτο

1 γενῶν] φθόγγων H   2 τοῦτο ex τούτων Mc, duobus punctis
subscr. et ων suprascr. B : τούτων V S   συγχόρδων H   3 τῶν
τὴν] τῶν B in ras. : om. R   4 ὀνόμασιν post ἰδίοις ponit H
5 λίχανος (ut constanter fere) Ma : in λιχανὸς corr. Mc : Va semper
λίχανος : γρ᾽ λιχάνου Vb in marg.   6 καὶ ὑπάτης om. V S   ὑπάτης
in marg. Mc (?)   τοῖς ex τῆς Mb : τῆς R   ἀπτομένης M V R
9 τε om. H   10 τόπος Marquard : τρόπος codd.   11 ἑκάστου H
13 ἀφίσταται Marquard H : ἀφίστασθαι rell. : ἀφίστασθαι φαίνεται
Westphal   14 διτόνου] post ι litt. a eras. τό renovatum
Mb : διατόνου ex διτόνου Vb (ut vid.) : διτονου (a super ι scriptum)
B : διατόνου S   τῶν ἤδη] τῶν ᾗ in ras. Mb   15 δίτονον H
οὐχ seclusi : οὐχ ὁμολογεῖται in ras. Mb   16 παρὰ] περὶ S
συγχοροῖτ᾽ B R   ἐπαχθέντων αὖ in ras. Mb   17 αὐτῷ R
18 τοῦτο post ἔπειτα add. M (eras.), V S, B (suprascr.)   19 διατόνου (duobus punctis sub. α) B   δεομένη] η in ras. Mb   οὐχ
ἡ] οὐχὶ M V S R   20 φαυλότητι B   γε om. H

114

μένταν ἐπαχθεῖσιν αὐτοῖς· τοῖς δὲ συνειθισμένοις τῶν
ἀρ|χαϊκῶν τρόπων τοῖς τε πρώτοις καὶ τοῖς δευτέροις ἱκανῶς 10
δῆλόν ἐστι τὸ λεγόμενον. Οἱ μὲν γὰρ τῇ νῦν κατεχούσῃ
μελοποιίᾳ συνήθεις μόνον ὄντες εἰκότως τὴν δίτονον λιχανὸν
5 ἐξορίζουσι· | συντονωτέραις γὰρ χρῶνται σχεδὸν οἱ πλεῖστοι 15
τῶν νῦν. τούτου δ᾽ αἴτιον τὸ βούλεσθαι γλυκαίνειν ἀεί,
σημεῖον δ᾽ ὅτι τούτου στοχάζονται, μάλιστα μὲν γὰρ καὶ
πλεῖστον χρόνον ἐν τῷ χρώματι δια|τρίβουσιν, ὅταν δ᾽ 20
ἀφίκωνταί ποτε εἰς τὴν ἀρμονίαν, ἐγγὺς τοῦ χρώματος προσ-
10 άγουσι συνεπισπωμένου τοῦ ἤθους. Περὶ τούτων μὲν οὖν
ἐπὶ τοσοῦτον ἀρκείτω· ὁ δὴ τῆς λιχανοῦ τόπος τονιαῖος |
ὑποκείσθω, ὁ δὲ τῆς παρυπάτης διέσεως ἐλαχίστης. οὔτε 25
γὰρ ἐγγυτέρω τῆς ὑπάτης προσέρχεται διέσεως οὔτε πλεῖον
ἀφίσταται ἡμίσεος τόνου. οὐ γὰρ ἐπαλλάττουσιν οἱ τόποι,
15 ἀλλ᾽ ἔστιν αὐτῶν πέρας ἡ | συναφή, ὅταν γὰρ ἐπὶ τὴν αὐτὴν 30
τάσιν ἀφίκωνται ἥ τε παρυπάτη καὶ ἡ λιχανός, ἡ μὲν ἐπιτεινομένη ἡ δ᾽ ἀνιεμένη, πέρας ἔχουσιν οἱ τόποι· καὶ ἔστιν
ὁ μὲν ἐπὶ τὸ βαρὺ παρυπάτης, ὁ δ᾽ ἐπὶ τὸ || ὀξὺ λιχανοῦ. 24
Περὶ μὲν οὖν τῶν ὅλων τόπων λιχανοῦ τε καὶ παρυπάτης
20 οὕτως ὡρίσθω, περὶ δὲ τῶν κατὰ ⟨τὰ⟩ γένη τε καὶ τὰς χρόας
λεκτέον. Τὸ μὲν οὖν διὰ τεσσάρων ὃν τρόπον | ἐξεταστέον, 5
εἴτε μετρεῖταί τινι τῶν ἐλαττόνων διαστημάτων, εἴτε πᾶσίν
ἐστιν ἀσύμμετρον, ἐν τοῖς διὰ συμφωνίας λαμβανομένοις
λέγεται· ὡς φαινομένου δ᾽ [ἐξ] ἐκείνου δύο τόνων καὶ

---

1 ἐπαχθῆσιν H　συνειθισμένοις (ει ex η) Mb : συνηθισμένοις S :
συνεθισμένοις H　4 μόνον post ὄντες ponit H　δίτονον] post ι
litt. eras. M　χαλινὸν sed. in marg. λιχανὸν B　5 ὁρίζουσι
R　συντονοτέραις S　6 ἀεὶ B　10 ἤθους Meibom : ἔθνους H :
ἔθους rell.　11 δὴ Marquard : δὲ codd.　14 ἐπαλλάττουσιν
ex ἐλαττοῦσιν Mc, Vb in marg. cum signo γρ΄, R : ἐλαττοῦσιν Va S B in
marg.　18 λιχανός B R　19 περὶ . . . λιχανοῦ om. M, et καὶ
περὶ τούτων μὲν add. in marg. Mb : eadem Va S, B in marg.: quae in
textu scripta data in B R et Vb in marg. cum signo γρ΄　20 ὡρίσθαι
B sed ω suprascr., M sed ι in ras. Mb : ὁρίσθω Va　τὰ restituit
Marquard　post τε ras. M　22 διαστημάτων om. Va S : add. Vb
in marg.　24 ἐξ del. Marquard　δυοῖν H

10 ἡμί|σεος, κείσθω τοῦτο ἂν εἶναι τὸ μέγεθος. Πυκνὸν δὲ
λεγέσθω τὸ ἐκ δύο διαστημάτων συνεστηκὸς ἃ συντεθέντα
ἔλαττον διάστημα περιέξει τοῦ λειπομένου διαστήματος ἐν
15 τῷ διὰ τεσσάρων. | Τούτων (δ') οὕτως ὡρισμένων πρὸς τῷ
βαρυτέρῳ τῶν μενόντων φθόγγων εἰλήφθω τὸ ἐλάχιστον 5
πυκνόν· τοῦτο δ' ἔσται τὸ ἐκ δύο διέσεων (ἐναρμονίων ἐλα-
χίστων· ἔπειτα δεύτερον πρὸς τῷ αὐτῷ· τοῦτο δὲ ἔσται τὸ
ἐκ δύο διέσεων) χρωματικῶν ἐλαχίστων. ἔσονται δὲ (αἱ)
20 δύο λι|χανοὶ εἰλημμέναι δύο γενῶν βαρύταται, ἡ μὲν ἁρ-
μονίας ἡ δὲ χρώματος. καθόλου γὰρ βαρύταται μὲν αἱ 10
25 ἐναρμόνιοι λιχανοὶ ἦσαν, ἐχόμεναι δ' αἱ χρωματικαί, συν|τον-
ώταται δ' αἱ διάτονοι. Μετὰ ταῦτα τρίτον εἰλήφθω πυκνὸν
πρὸς τῷ αὐτῷ· τέταρτον (δ') εἰλήφθω πυκνὸν τονιαῖον·
πέμπτον δὲ πρὸς τῷ αὐτῷ, τὸ ἐξ ἡμιτονίου καὶ ἡμιολίου
30 διαστή|ματος συνεστηκὸς σύστημα εἰλήφθω· ἕκτον δὲ τὸ 15
ἐξ ἡμιτονίου καὶ τόνου. Αἱ μὲν οὖν τὰ δύο [τὰ] πρῶτα
ληφθέντα πυκνὰ ὁρίζουσαι λιχανοὶ εἴρηνται· ἡ δὲ τὸ τρίτον
25 πυκνὸν ὁρίζουσα || λιχανὸς χρωματικὴ μέν ἐστιν, καλεῖται
δὲ τὸ χρῶμα ἐν ᾧ ἐστὶν ἡμιόλιον. Ἡ δὲ τὸ τέταρτον πυκνὸν
5 ὁρίζουσα λιχανὸς χρωματικὴ μέν ἐστιν, καλεῖται | δὲ τὸ 20
χρῶμα ἐν ᾧ ἐστι τονιαῖον. ἡ δὲ τὸ πέμπτον ληφθὲν σύστημα ὁρίζουσα λιχανός, ὃ μεῖζον ἤδη πυκνοῦ ἦν, ἐπειδήπερ
ἴσα ἐστὶ τὰ δύο τῷ ἑνί, βαρυτάτη διάτονός ἐστιν. ἡ δὲ τὸ
10 ἕκτον ληφθὲν | σύστημα ὁρίζουσα λιχανὸς συντονωτάτη

2 τὸ ex τὰ Mc   δυοῖν H   4 δ' restituit Marquard   5 μενόντων
om. B   6 δυοῖν H   ἐναρμονίων . . . διέσεων] om. M V S : ἐναρμονίων καὶ parvis litt. supra lin. reliquis omissis Mc : ἐναρμονίων τε
καὶ reliquis omissis B R : verba in textu scripta restituit Marquard
8 χρωματικῶν S   αἱ restituit Marquard : δύο δὲ M Va : δύο (δὲ et
αἱ omissis) S : δὲ δύο rell.   9 εἰλημμένων (αι suprascr.) B
11 ἐναρμόνιοι] ἐν supra lin. add., spir. in α eras. Mb : ἁρμόνιοι BMa
συντονώταται ex συντονώτατοι Ma(?) : συντονώτατοι V B : συντονωτατ
δ' αἱ S   13 δ' restituit Marquard   14 ἡμιτόνιον H   16 τὰ
del. Marquard   17 τὸ supra lin. B   19 ἡμιόλιον . . . ἐν ᾧ ἐστι
om. H : ἡμιόλιον . . . χρῶμα om. R   τὸ ante ἡμιόλιον add. M V S
22 δ] ἢ H   μεῖζον Vb S : μείζων M B R   24 σύστημα] σημεῖα R

διάτονός ἐστιν. Ἡ μὲν οὖν βαρυτάτη χρωματικὴ λιχανὸς
τῆς ἐναρμονίου βαρυτάτης ἕκτῳ μέρει τόνου ὀξυτέρα ἐστίν,
ἐπειδήπερ ἡ χρω|ματικὴ δίεσις τῆς ἐναρμονίου διέσεως δω- 15
δεκατημορίῳ τόνου μείζων ἐστί. Δεῖ γὰρ τὸ τοῦ αὐτοῦ
5 τριτημόριον τοῦ τετάρτου μέρους δωδεκατημορίῳ ὑπερέχειν,
αἱ δὲ δύο χρωματικαὶ τῶν δύο | ἐναρμονίων δῆλον ὡς τῷ 20
διπλασίῳ. τοῦτο δὲ ἐστὶν ἐκτημόριον, ἔλαττον διάστημα
τοῦ ἐλαχίστου τῶν μελῳδουμένων. Τὰ δὲ τοιαῦτα ἀμελῴ-
δητά ἐστιν, ἀμελῴδητον γὰρ λέγομεν ὃ μὴ | τάττεται καθ' 25
10 ἑαυτὸ ἐν συστήματι. Ἡ δὲ βαρυτάτη διάτονος τῆς βαρυτάτης χρωματικῆς ἡμιτονίῳ καὶ δωδεκατημορίῳ τόνου ὀξυτέρα
ἐστίν. ἐπὶ μὲν γὰρ τὴν τοῦ ἡμιολίου χρώματος λιχανὸν |
ἡμιτόνιον ἦν ἀπ' αὐτῆς, ἀπὸ δὲ τῆς ἡμιολίου ἐπὶ τὴν ἐναρ- 30
μόνιον δίεσις, ἀπὸ δὲ τῆς ἐναρμονίου ἐπὶ τὴν βαρυτάτην
15 χρωματικὴν ἐκτημόριον, ἀπὸ δὲ τῆς βαρυτάτης χρωματικῆς
ἐπὶ τὴν ἡμιόλιον δωδεκατημόριον τόνου. τὸ || δὲ τεταρτη- 26
μόριον ἐκ τριῶν δωδεκατημορίων σύγκειται, ὥστ' εἶναι φανερόν, ὅτι τὸ εἰρημένον διάστημά ἐστιν ἀπὸ τῆς βαρυτάτης
διατόνου ἐπὶ τὴν | βαρυτάτην χρωματικήν. Ἡ δὲ συντονω- 5
20 τάτη διάτονος τῆς βαρυτάτης διατόνου διέσει ἐστι συντονωτέρα. Ἐκ τούτων δὴ φανεροὶ γίγνονται οἱ τόποι τῶν λιχανῶν
ἑκάστης· ἥ τε γὰρ βαρυ|τέρα τῆς χρωματικῆς πᾶσά ἐστιν 10
ἐναρμόνιος λιχανὸς ἥ τε τῆς διατόνου βαρυτέρα πᾶσά ἐστι

3 δωδεκατημορίου M V S   4 μειζόν Vb : μεῖζον M S   Hoc loco
in marg. M et Va et H multa adscripta sunt, quae videas in Comm.
5 ὑπερέχειν] ν supra lin. add. Mb   6 καὶ post χρωματικαὶ add.
M R Va   8 τῶν ἐλαχίστων H   ἀμελότητα S   10 ἑαυτὸ
ex ἑαυτῶ Mb   τῷ ante συστήματι add. H   11, 12 in marg. Mx Vc
haec: ἡ αἢ ἡ Κ χρῶμα ἐστὶ τὸ δ μετὰ τοῦ ἡ   13 ἡμίτονον H   ἀπ']
ἐπ' R   14 δίεσις ex δίεσιν Mc : δίεσιν V B S   16 δεκατη-
μόριον H   in marg. Mx Vc haec : ἐναρμόν. δίεσις τ⁶ (τόνου ?) τὸ
τέταρτον   17 τριῶν supra lin. Mb   δωδεκατημορίου Ma, sed ον
supra ου scr. Mb   18 τῆς om. Ma : ins. Mb   21 τόποι]
τόνοι B in marg.   22 βαρυτέρα Meibom : βαρυτάτη codd.
23 ἐναρμόνιος] spir. in α eras. ἐν supra lin. add. Mb   ἥ τε]
καὶ ἡ H

⟨χρωματικὴ μέχρι τῆς βαρυτάτης χρωματικῆς ἥ τε τῆς διατόνου συντονωτάτης βαρυτέρα πᾶσά ἐστι⟩ διάτονος μέχρι
τῆς βαρυτάτης διατόνου. Νοητέον γὰρ ἀπείρους τὸν ἀριθμὸν
15 τὰς λιχανούς· οὐ γὰρ | ἂν στήσῃς τὴν φωνὴν τοῦ ἀπο-
δεδειγμένου λιχανῷ τόπου λιχανὸς ἔσται, διάκενον δ' οὐδέν 5
ἐστι τοῦ λιχανοειδοῦς τόπου οὐδὲ τοιοῦτον οἷον μὴ δέχεσθαι
20 λιχανόν. Ὥστ' εἶναι μὴ περὶ μικροῦ τὴν | ἀμφισβήτησιν·
οἱ μὲν γὰρ ἄλλοι διαφέρονται περὶ τοῦ διαστήματος μόνον,
οἷον πότερον δίτονός ἐστιν ἡ λιχανὸς ἢ συντονωτέρα ὡς μιᾶς
25 οὔσης ἐναρμονίου· ἡμεῖς δ' οὐ μόνον πλείους ἐν | ἑκάστῳ 10
γένει φαμὲν εἶναι λιχανοὺς μιᾶς ἀλλὰ καὶ προστίθεμεν ὅτι
ἄπειροί εἰσι τὸν ἀριθμόν. Τὰ μὲν οὖν περὶ τῶν λιχανῶν
οὕτως ἀφωρίσθω· παρυπάτης δὲ δύο εἰσὶ τόποι, ὁ μὲν |
30 κοινὸς τοῦ τε διατόνου καὶ τοῦ χρώματος, ὁ δ' ἕτερος ἴδιος
τῆς ἁρμονίας· κοινωνεῖ γὰρ τὰ δύο γένη τῶν παρυπατῶν. 15
ἐναρμόνιος μὲν οὖν ἐστι παρυπάτη πᾶσα ἡ βαρυτέρα τῆς
27 βαρυτάτης χρωματικῆς, χρωματικὴ δὲ καὶ διάτο||νος ἡ λοιπὴ
πᾶσα μέχρι τῆς ἀφωρισμένης. Τῶν δὲ διαστημάτων τὸ μὲν
ὑπάτης καὶ παρυπάτης τῷ παρυπάτης καὶ λιχανοῦ ἤτοι ἴσον
5 μελῳδεῖται ἢ ἔλατ|τον, τὸ δὲ παρυπάτης καὶ λιχανοῦ τῷ 20
λιχανοῦ καὶ μέσης καὶ ἴσον καὶ ἄνισον ἀμφοτέρως. τούτου
δ' αἴτιον τὸ κοινὰς εἶναι τὰς παρυπάτας τῶν γενῶν, γίγνεται
10 γὰρ ἐμμελὲς τετράχορδον ἐκ παρυ|πάτης τε χρωματικῆς ⟨τῆς⟩
βαρυτάτης καὶ διατόνου λιχανοῦ τῆς συντονωτάτης. Ὁ δὲ

1 χρωματικὴ ... πᾶσά ἐστι restituit Marquard   4 τὰς] τοὺς sed
supra o ras. in qua a fuisse vid. Ma: τοὺς VS, B (sed οὐ in ras. et
a suprascr.)   οὐ ex οὐ Mc: οὐ VS   τοῦ ἀποδεδειγμένου τόπω
λιχάνω Ma, sed ω supra του, ω supra ἀποδεδειγμένου et ου supra λιχανω
add. Mc: τόπω λιχάνω VS: τόπου (ω suprascr.) λιχανοῦ   5 δ']
γὰρ H   8 μόνου H   9 δίτονός Meibom: διάτονός codd.
αὐτῆς post μιᾶς add. R   15 τὰ add. Mx   16 ἐστι] ἔτι B:
ἐστὶ B in marg.   18 τὸ μὲν ... παρυπάτης om. R   20 τὸ]
τῷ S   τῷ λιχανοῦ om. R   21 ἀμφοτέρως Marquard: ἀμφοτέροις
codd.   23 τῆς βαρυτάτης conieci: παρυπάτης codd. (R et B
in marg.): βαρυτέρας τινὸς τῆς ἡμιτονιαίας ante παρυπάτης add.
Marquard

τῆς παρυπάτης τόπος φανερός ἐστι ἐκ τῶν ἔμπροσθεν,
διαιρεθείς τε καὶ συντεθεὶς ὅσος ἐστίν. |

Περὶ δὲ συνεχείας καὶ τοῦ ἐξῆς ἀκριβῶς οὐ πάνυ 15
ῥᾴδιον ἐν ἀρχῇ διορίσαι, τύπῳ δὲ πειρατέον ὑποσημῆναι.
5 Φαίνεται δὲ τοιαύτη τις φύσις εἶναι τοῦ συνεχοῦς ἐν τῇ μελ-
ῳδίᾳ οἵα καὶ ἐν τῇ λέ|ξει περὶ τὴν τῶν γραμμάτων σύν- 20
θεσιν· καὶ γὰρ ἐν τῷ διαλέγεσθαι φύσει ἡ φωνὴ καθ᾽ ἑκάστην
τῶν συλλαβῶν πρῶτόν τι καὶ δεύτερον τῶν γραμμάτων τίθησι
καὶ τρίτον καὶ τέταρτον καὶ κατὰ | τοὺς λοιποὺς ἀριθμοὺς 25
10 ὡσαύτως, οὐ πᾶν μετὰ πᾶν, ἀλλ᾽ ἔστι τοιαύτη τις φυσικὴ
αὔξησις τῆς συνθέσεως.   παραπλησίως δὲ καὶ ἐν τῷ μελ-
ῳδεῖν ἔοικεν ἡ φωνὴ τιθέναι κατὰ συνέχειαν | τά τε διαστή- 30
ματα καὶ τοὺς φθόγγους φυσικήν τινα σύνθεσιν διαφυλάτ-
τουσα, οὐ πᾶν μετὰ πᾶν διάστημα μελῳδοῦσα οὔτ᾽ ἴσον οὔτ᾽
15 ἄνισον.   Ζητητέον δὲ τὸ συνεχὲς οὐχ ὡς οἱ ἀρ||μονικοὶ ἐν 28
ταῖς τῶν διαγραμμάτων καταπυκνώσεσιν ἀποδιδόναι πειρῶν-
ται, τούτους ἀποφαίνοντες τῶν φθόγγων ἐξῆς ἀλλήλων
κεῖσθαι οἷς συμ|βέβηκε τὸ ἐλάχιστον διάστημα διέχειν ἀφ᾽ 5
αὑτῶν.   οὐ γὰρ ὅτι [μὴ] δυνατὸν διέσεις ὀκτὼ καὶ εἴκοσιν
20 ἐξῆς μελῳδῆσαι τῇ φωνῇ ἐστίν, ἀλλὰ τὴν τρίτην δίεσιν
πάντα ποιοῦσα οὐχ οἷα | τέ ἐστι προστιθέναι, ἀλλ᾽ ἐπὶ μὲν 10
τὸ ὀξὺ ἐλάχιστον μελῳδεῖ τὸ λοιπὸν τοῦ διὰ τεσσάρων,—
τὰ δ᾽ ἐλάττω πάντα ἐξαδυνατεῖ—τοῦτο δ᾽ ἐστὶν ἤτοι ὀκτα-
πλάσιον τῆς ἐλαχίστης διέσεως ἢ μικρῷ τινι | παντελῶς καὶ 15

2 συντεθεὶς M V B S: συντιθεὶς R: ἐντεθεὶς Marquard   4 ὑποση-
μεῖναι S   7 ἡ] ᾖ B   φωνῇ B   καθεκάστη H   8 τι] τε
B R   9 λοιποὺς om. H   10 ἀλλ᾽ ἔστι ... συνθέσεως om. M,
in marg. Mc (οι in τοιαύτη in ras.): Vb in marg. sed τοιαύτη et τις om.
τοιαύτη τις] τις αὕτη S   τις om. B   16 γραμμάτων S   17 ἐξῆς
ex ἐξ ἧς Mc: ἐξ ἧς V: ἐφεξῆς H   ἀλλήλων post κεῖσθαι ponit H
19 οὐ γὰρ μόνον τὸ μὴ δύνασθαι δ. ὀ. κ. ἐ. ἐ. μελῳδεῖσθαι τῆς φωνῆς ἐστίν
Marquard   ὅτι conieci: τοῦ codd.   μὴ seclusi   δυνατὸν conieci:
δύνασθαι codd.   διέσις B   20 μελῳδῆσαι conieci: μελῳδεῖσθαι
codd.   24 διέσεως] δι in ras. Mb

ἀμελῳδήτῳ ἔλαττον, ἐπὶ δὲ τὸ βαρὺ τῶν δύο διέσεων τονιαίου
ἔλαττον οὐ δύναται μελῳδεῖν. Οὐ δὴ προσεκτέον εἰ τὸ
20 συνεχὲς ὅτε μὲν ἐξ ἴσων ὅτε δ' ἐξ ἀνίσων γίγνεται, | ἀλλὰ
πρὸς τὴν τῆς μελῳδίας φύσιν πειρατέον βλέπειν κατανοεῖν
τε προθυμούμενον τί μετὰ τί πέφυκεν ἡ φωνὴ διάστημα 5
τιθέναι κατὰ μέλος· εἰ γὰρ μετὰ παρυπάτην καὶ λιχανὸν μὴ |
25 δυνατὸν ἐγγυτέρω μελῳδῆσαι φθόγγον μέσης, αὕτη ἂν εἴη
μετὰ τὴν λιχανόν, εἴτε διπλάσιον εἴτε πολλαπλάσιον διάστημα ὁρίζει ⟨τοῦ⟩ παρυπάτης καὶ λιχανοῦ. Τίνα μὲν οὖν
30 τρόπον τό τε συνεχὲς καὶ | τὸ ἑξῆς δεῖ ζητεῖν, σχεδὸν δῆλον 10
ἐκ τῶν εἰρημένων· πῶς δὲ γίγνεται καὶ τί μετὰ τί διάστημα
29 τίθεταί τε καὶ οὐ τίθεται, ἐν τοῖς || στοιχείοις δειχθήσεται.

Ὑποκείσθω μετὰ τὸ πυκνὸν ἢ τὸ ἄπυκνον τιθέμενον
σύστημα ἐπὶ μὲν τὸ ὀξὺ μὴ τίθεσθαι ἔλαττον διάστημα τοῦ
5 λειπομένου τῆς | πρώτης συμφωνίας, ἐπὶ δὲ τὸ βαρὺ μὴ 15
ἔλαττον τονιαίου· ὑποκείσθω δὲ καὶ τῶν ἑξῆς κειμένων
φθόγγων κατὰ μέλος ἐν ἑκάστῳ γένει ἤτοι τοὺς τετάρτους
10 [τοῖς τέτρασι] διὰ τεττάρων συμ|φωνεῖν ἢ τοὺς πέμπτους
[τοῖς πέντε] διὰ πέντε ἢ ἀμφοτέρως· ᾧ δ' ἂν τῶν φθόγγων
μηδὲν ᾖ τούτων συμβεβηκός, ἐκμελῆ τοῦτον εἶναι πρὸς τοὺς οἷς 20
15 ἀσύμφωνός ἐστιν. Ὑποκείσθω δὲ καὶ | τεττάρων γιγνο-
μένων διαστημάτων ἐν τῷ διὰ πέντε, δύο μὲν ἴσων ὡς ἐπὶ
τὸ πολύ, τῶν τὸ πυκνὸν κατεχόντων, δύο δ' ἀνίσων, τοῦ τε
λειπομένου τῆς πρώτης συμφωνίας καὶ τῆς ὑπεροχῆς ᾗ τὸ
20 διὰ | πέντε τοῦ διὰ τεσσάρων ὑπερέχει, ἐναντίως τίθεσθαι 25

---

1 ἀμελῳδήτῳ] ἡ in ras. Mb   ἔλαττον Meibom : ἐλάττονι MVSR :
ἐλάττωνι B   τονιαίου Meibom : τονιαίων MVR : τονιαῖον BS
2 ἔλαττον supra lin. Mx, om. Va, add. in marg. Vb   δυνατὸν H
δὴ] δὲ H   εἰ conieci : εἰς codd.   7 δυνατὸν om. B : δυνατὴ S, Vb
(sed ἡ in ras.)   9 τοῦ restituit Marquard   12 τε om. H
13 μετὰ conieci : μὲν codd.   τὸ ἄπυκνον ex τὸν πυκνὸν (ut vid.) Mb
14 μὴ τίθεσθαι] μετατίθεσθαι M   15 λοιπομένου H   18 τοῖς
τέτρασι del. Meibom   19 τοῖς πέντε del. Meibom   20 εἶναι
om. H   τοὺς οἷς] τούτοις R   24 λοιπομένου H   ᾗ ex ἢ Mb :
ἢ S   τὸ ex τοῦ Ma (?) S : τὸ Vb cum ras. post ὁ   25 ὑπερέχει
Meibom : ὑπερέχειν codd.

120

πρὸς τοῖς ἴσοις τὰ [δὲ] ἄνισα ἐπί τε τὸ ὀξὺ καὶ τὸ βαρύ.
Ὑποκείσθω δὲ καὶ τοὺς τοῖς ἑξῆς φθόγγοις συμφωνοῦντας
διὰ τῆς αὐτῆς συμ|φωνίας ἑξῆς αὐτοῖς εἶναι. Ἀσύνθετον δὲ 25
ὑποκείσθω ἐν ἑκάστῳ γένει εἶναι διάστημα κατὰ μέλος ὃ ἡ
5 φωνὴ μελῳδοῦσα μὴ δύναται διαιρεῖν εἰς διαστήματα. Ὑπο-
κείσθω δὲ καὶ τῶν συμφώ|νων ἕκαστον μὴ διαιρεῖσθαι εἰς 30
ἀσύνθετα πάντα μεγέθη. Ἀγωγὴ δ' ἔστω ἡ διὰ τῶν ἑξῆς
φθόγγων ⟨ὧν⟩, ἔσωθεν τῶν ἄκρων, [ὧν] ἐν ⟨ἑκάστου⟩ ἑκα-
τέρωθεν ἀσύνθετον κεῖται διάστημα· εὐθεῖα δ' ἡ ἐπὶ τὸ αὐτό.

· · · · · · · · · ·

1 δὲ del. Meibom   τε om. R   τὸ ante βαρύ om. S   2 τοὺς
ex τὸ Mc : τὸ VS   συμφωνοῦντας ex συμφόνου τὰς Mc : συμφόνου
τὰς VS : καὶ τὸ συμφόνου τὰς in marg. B   3 αὐτοῖς Marquard :
αὐτοῖς codd.   4 ante ὃ una litt. eras. M   ἡ supra lin. add. Mx :
om. VS   ἡ ante ἡ add. B   5 φωνὴ] ἡ in ras. Vb   διάστημα
B sed in marg. διαστήματα   7 πάντα supra lin. add. Mc : om. VS
8 ὧν addidi   ἔσωθεν conieci : ἔξωθεν codd.   ἄκρων conieci : ἀρχῶν
codd.   ὧν seclusi : supra lin. B   χῶν ὧν et acc. in ἐν Mc Vb ;
antea in utroque cod. lacuna erat : ἒ S : ἐν rell.   ἑκάστου addidi

ΑΡΙΣΤΟΞΕΝΟΥ ΑΡΜΟΝΙΚΩΝ
ΣΤΟΙΧΕΙΩΝ ΔΕΥΤΕΡΟΝ

30, 10   Βέλτιον ἴσως ἐστὶ τὸ προδι|ελθεῖν τὸν τρόπον τῆς πρα-
γματείας τίς ποτ' ἐστίν, ἵνα προγιγνώσκοντες ὥσπερ ὁδὸν ἦ
βαδιστέον ῥᾴδιον πορευώμεθα εἰδότες τε κατὰ τί μέρος ἐσμὲν 5
15 αὐτῆς | καὶ μὴ λάθωμεν ἡμᾶς αὐτοὺς παρυπολαμβάνοντες τὸ
πρᾶγμα. Καθάπερ Ἀριστοτέλης ἀεὶ διηγεῖτο τοὺς πλείστους
τῶν ἀκουσάντων παρὰ Πλάτωνος τὴν περὶ τἀγαθοῦ ἀκρόασιν
20 παθεῖν. | προσιέναι μὲν γὰρ ἕκαστον ὑπολαμβάνοντα λή-
ψεσθαί τι τῶν νομιζομένων τούτων ἀνθρωπίνων ἀγαθῶν οἷον 10
πλοῦτον ὑγίειαν ἰσχὺν τὸ ὅλον εὐδαιμονίαν τινὰ θαυμαστήν·
25 ὅτε δὲ | φανείησαν οἱ λόγοι περὶ μαθημάτων καὶ ἀριθμῶν
καὶ γεωμετρίας καὶ ἀστρολογίας καὶ τὸ πέρας ὅτι ἀγαθόν
31 ἐστιν ἕν, παντελῶς οἶμαι παράδο||ξόν τι ἐφαίνετο αὐτοῖς·
εἶθ' οἱ μὲν ὑποκατεφρόνουν τοῦ πράγματος οἱ δὲ κατε- 15
μέμφοντο. Τί οὖν τὸ αἴτιον; οὐ προῄδεσαν, ἀλλ' ὥσπερ
5 οἱ ἐριστικοὶ | πρὸς τοὔνομα αὐτὸ ὑποκεχηνότες προσῄεσαν·
εἰ δέ γέ τις οἶμαι προεξετίθει τὸ ὅλον, ἀπεγίνωσκεν ἂν ὁ
μέλλων ἀκούειν ἢ εἴπερ ἤρεσκεν αὐτῷ διέμενεν ἂν ἐν τῇ
10 εἰρημένῃ ὑπολήψει. | Προέλεγε μὲν οὖν καὶ αὐτὸς Ἀριστο- 20

τέλης δι' αὐτὰς ταύτας τὰς αἰτίας, ὡς ἔφη, τοῖς μέλλουσιν
ἀκροᾶσθαι παρ' αὐτοῦ, περὶ τίνων τ' ἐστὶν ἡ πραγματεία καὶ
τίς. Βέλτιον δὲ καὶ ἡμῖν | φαίνεται, καθάπερ εἴπομεν ἐν 15
ἀρχῇ, τὸ προειδέναι. Γίγνεται γὰρ ἐνίοτε ἐφ' ἐκάτερα
5 ἁμαρτία· οἱ μὲν γὰρ μέγα τι ὑπολαμβάνουσιν εἶναι τὸ
μάθημα καὶ ἔσεσθαι ἔνιοι μὲν οὐ μό|νον μουσικοὶ ἀκού- 20
σαντες τὰ ἁρμονικά, ἀλλὰ καὶ βελτίους τὸ ἦθος,—παρακούσαντες τῶν ἐν ταῖς δείξεσι λόγων ὅτι πειρώμεθα ποιεῖν τῶν
μελοποιῶν ἑκάστην καὶ τὸ ὅλον, τῆς μουσικῆς | ὅτι ἡ 25
10 μὲν τοιαύτη βλάπτει τὰ ἤθη ἡ δὲ τοιαύτη ὠφελεῖ, τοῦτο
αὐτὸ παρακούσαντες, τὸ δ' ὅτι καθ' ὅσον μουσικὴ δύναται
ὠφελεῖν οὐδ' ἀκούσαντες ὅλως·—οἱ δὲ πάλιν ὡς οὐδὲν | ἀλλ' 30
ἢ μικρόν τι καὶ βουλόμενοι μὴ εἶναι ἔμπειροι μηδὲ τί ποτ'
ἐστίν. Οὐδέτερον δὲ τούτων ἀληθές ἐστιν, οὔτε γὰρ εὐκατα-
15 φρόνητόν ἐστί τινι ὃς νοῦν ἔχει τὸ μάθημα—δῆλον δ' ἔσται
προϊόν||τος τοῦ λόγου—, οὔτε τηλικοῦτον ὥστ' αὔταρκες 32
εἶναι πρὸς πάντα, καθάπερ οἴονταί τινες. πολλὰ γὰρ δὴ καὶ
ἕτερα ὑπάρχει [ἢ] καθάπερ ἀεὶ λέγεται τῷ | μουσικῷ· μέρος 5
γάρ ἐστιν ἡ ἁρμονικὴ πραγματεία τῆς τοῦ μουσικοῦ ἕξεως,
20 καθάπερ ἥ τε ῥυθμικὴ καὶ ἡ μετρικὴ καὶ ἡ ὀργανική. Λεκτέον
οὖν περὶ αὐτῆς τε καὶ τῶν μερῶν. |

Καθόλου μὲν οὖν νοητέον οὖσαν ἡμῖν τὴν θεωρίαν περὶ 10
μέλους παντὸς πῶς ποτε πέφυκεν ἡ φωνὴ ἐπιτεινομένη καὶ
ἀνιεμένη τιθέναι τὰ διαστήματα. φυσικὴν γὰρ δή τινά 15

1 ἔφη conieci : ἔφην codd.   3 καὶ ἡμῖν] καὶ om. R   6 μὲν
in ras. M: δὲ pro μὲν BR   ἔσεσθαι post μὲν ponit Marquard
ἀκούοντες (σαν suprascr.) B   7 καὶ om. B   παρακούον-
τες B   9 μελωποιῶν S   ἑκάστην καὶ om. R   11 καὶ ante
καθ' ὅσον add. Marquard   12 ἀλλ' ἢ Marquard : ἀλλὰ codd.
13 ἔμπειροι conieci : ἄπειροι codd.   μηδὲ τί ποτ' ἐστίν] μηδέτι
παρέστιν R   14 ἀγνοεῖν πρόσεισι post ποτ' ἐστὶν add. Marquard   δὲ]
γὰρ R   ἀληθές ἐστιν] ἐστιν om. R lac.   15 ἐστί τινι ὃς νοῦν ἔχει
conieci : ἐστιν ὡς νῦν ἔχει codd.   16 λόγου om. R lac.   αὔταρκες
om. R lac.   18 ἢ seclusi   τοῦτο post ἢ add. Westphal   ἀεὶ
om. R   20 καὶ ἡ μετρικὴ om. R   22 οὔσης ἡμῖν τῆς θεωρίας H
24 δή om. B

φαμὲν ἡμεῖς τὴν φωνὴν κίνησιν κινεῖσθαι καὶ οὐχ ὡς ἔτυχε
διάστημα τιθέναι. Καὶ τούτων ἀποδείξεις πειρώμεθα λέγειν
20 ὁμολογουμένας τοῖς φαινομένοις, οὐ κα|θάπερ οἱ ἔμπροσθεν,
οἱ μὲν ἀλλοτριολογοῦντες καὶ τὴν μὲν αἴσθησιν ἐκκλίνοντες
ὡς οὖσαν οὐκ ἀκριβῆ, νοητὰς δὲ κατασκευάζοντες αἰτίας καὶ 5
25 φάσκοντες λόγους τέ τινας ἀριθμῶν εἶναι | καὶ τάχη πρὸς
ἄλληλα ἐν οἷς τό τε ὀξὺ καὶ τὸ βαρὺ γίγνεται, πάντων
ἀλλοτριωτάτους λόγους λέγοντες καὶ ἐναντιωτάτους τοῖς
φαινομένοις· οἱ δ' ἀποθεσπίζοντες ἕκαστα ἄνευ αἰτίας καὶ |
30 ἀποδείξεως οὐδ' αὐτὰ τὰ φαινόμενα καλῶς ἐξηριθμηκότες. 10
Ἡμεῖς δ' ἀρχάς τε πειρώμεθα λαβεῖν φαινομένας ἀπάσας
33 τοῖς ἐμπείροις μουσικῆς καὶ τὰ ἐκ τούτων συμ||βαίνοντα
ἀποδεικνύναι.

Ἔστι δὴ τὸ μὲν ὅλον ἡμῖν ⟨ἡ⟩ θεωρία περὶ μέλους παντὸς
μουσικοῦ τοῦ γιγνομένου ἐν φωνῇ τε καὶ ὀργάνοις. Ἀνάγεται 15
5 δ' ἡ πραγματεία |·εἰς δύο, εἴς τε τὴν ἀκοὴν καὶ εἰς τὴν διά-
νοιαν. τῇ μὲν γὰρ ἀκοῇ κρίνομεν τὰ τῶν διαστημάτων
μεγέθη, τῇ δὲ διανοίᾳ θεωροῦμεν τὰς τῶν ⟨φθόγγων⟩ δυνάμεις.
10 Δεῖ οὖν ἐπεθισθῆναι ἕκαστα | ἀκριβῶς κρίνειν. οὐ γὰρ ἔστιν
ὥσπερ ἐπὶ τῶν διαγραμμάτων εἴθισται λέγεσθαι· ἔστω τοῦτο 20
εὐθεῖα γραμμή,—οὕτω καὶ ἐπὶ τῶν διαστημάτων εἰπόντα
15 ἀπηλλάχθαι [δεῖ]. Ὁ μὲν γὰρ γεωμέτρης | οὐδὲν χρῆται τῇ
τῆς αἰσθήσεως δυνάμει, οὐ γὰρ ἐθίζει τὴν ὄψιν οὔτε τὸ εὐθὺ
οὔτε τὸ περιφερὲς οὔτ' ἄλλο οὐδὲν τῶν τοιούτων οὔτε φαύλως
20 οὔτε εὖ κρίνειν, ἀλλὰ μᾶλλον ὁ τέκτων καὶ | ὁ τορνευτὴς καὶ 25
ἕτεραί τινες τῶν τεχνῶν περὶ ταῦτα πραγματεύονται· τῷ δὲ
μουσικῷ σχεδόν ἐστιν ἀρχῆς ἔχουσα τάξιν ἡ τῆς αἰσθήσεως

1 οὐχ ex οὐκ et ὡς supra lin. M   2 λελέγειν S   5 οὖσαν
post ἀκριβῆ ponit H   οὐκ om. S   καὶ post δὲ add. R   7 τὸ
βαρὺ H : τὸ om. rell.   8 ἐναντιστάτους B   9 ἀποτερπίζοντες H
11 ἀπάσας om. R lac. : ἅπασι H   14 ἡ restituit Marquard   16 τε
om. B   18 τῶν φθόγγων conieci : τούτων codd.   19 ἐπεθισθῆναι]
ἐπεθι in ras. Mb : ἐθισθῆναι R, in marg. B   21 οὕτω] post ω litt.
σ eras. M   22 ἀπηλλαχθῆναι H   δεῖ seclusi   τῇ add. Mb(?)
23 οὔτε τὸ εὐθὺ om. R   27 ἡ supra lin. add. Ma (vel Mb)

124

ἀκρίβεια, οὐ γὰρ ἐνδέχεται φαύλως αἰσθανόμε|νον εὖ λέγειν 25
περὶ τούτων ὧν μηδένα τρόπον αἰσθάνεται. Ἔσται δὲ τοῦτο
φανερὸν ἐπ' αὐτῆς τῆς πραγματείας. Οὐ δεῖ δ' ἀγνοεῖν, ὅτι
ἡ τῆς μουσικῆς ξύνεσις ἅμα μένοντός τινος | καὶ κινουμένου 30
5 ἐστὶ καὶ τοῦτο σχεδὸν διὰ πάσης καὶ κατὰ πᾶν μέρος αὐτῆς,
ὡς εἰπεῖν ἁπλῶς, διατείνειν. Εὐθέως γὰρ τὰς τῶν γενῶν
διαφορὰς αἰσθανόμεθα τοῦ μὲν περιέχοντος μένοντος, τῶν δὲ
μέσων κινουμένων· καὶ πάλιν || ὅταν μένοντος τοῦ μεγέθους 34
τόδε μὲν καλῶμεν ὑπάτην καὶ μέσην, τόδε δὲ παραμέσην καὶ
.10 νήτην, μένοντος [γὰρ] τοῦ μεγέθους συμβαίνει κινεῖσθαι τὰς
τῶν | φθόγγων δυνάμεις· καὶ πάλιν ὅταν τοῦ αὐτοῦ μεγέθους 5
πλείω σχήματα γίγνηται, καθάπερ τοῦ τε διὰ τεσσάρων καὶ
διὰ πέντε καὶ ἑτέρων· ὡσαύτως δὲ καὶ ὅταν τοῦ αὐτοῦ
διαστήματος ποῦ | μὲν τιθεμένου μεταβολὴ γίγνηται, ποῦ δὲ 10
15 μή. Πάλιν ἐν τοῖς περὶ τοὺς ῥυθμοὺς πολλὰ τοιαῦθ' ὁρῶμεν
γιγνόμενα· καὶ γὰρ μένοντος τοῦ λόγου καθ' ὃν διώρισται τὰ
γένη τὰ μεγέθη κινεῖ|ται τῶν ποδῶν διὰ τὴν τῆς ἀγωγῆς 15
δύναμιν, καὶ τῶν μεγεθῶν μενόντων ἀνόμοιοι γίγνονται οἱ
πόδες· καὶ τὸ αὐτὸ μέγεθος πόδα τε δύναται καὶ συζυγίαν·
20 δῆλον δ' ὅτι καὶ ⟨αἱ διαφοραὶ⟩ αἱ τῶν διαιρέσε|ών τε καὶ 20
σχημάτων περὶ μένον τι μέγεθος γίγνονται. καθόλου δ'
εἰπεῖν ἡ μὲν ῥυθμοποιΐα πολλὰς καὶ παντοδαπὰς κινήσεις
κινεῖται, οἱ δὲ πόδες οἷς σημαινόμεθα τοὺς ῥυθμοὺς ἁπλᾶς
τε | καὶ τὰς αὐτὰς ἀεί. Τοιαύτην δ' ἐχούσης φύσιν τῆς 25
25 μουσικῆς ἀναγκαῖον καὶ ἐν τοῖς περὶ τὸ ἡρμοσμένον συνε-

---

1 οὐ Marquard: οὔτε codd.   αἰσθανόμενος B   2 τῶν B: ὃν
in marg.   3 ἐπ'] ἀπ' H   4 μένοντος ex μὲν ὄντος Mc:· μὲν
ὄντος Va B   5 αὐτῆς om. H   10 γὰρ seclusi   συμβαίνει
. . . μεγέθους om. S   12 γίνεται Ma (sed η suprascr. Mc)
V B S   13 διὰ πέντε] διὰ supra lin. add. Mc: om. VS, B
(sed add. in marg.)   14 τοῦ μὲν] ποιοῦμεν H   γίνεται
S R   16 καθ' ὃν ex καθὸ Mc: καθὸ VS B   19 τὸ
αὐτὸ conieci: αὐτὸ τὸ codd.   20 αἱ διαφοραὶ addidi⟨ (διαφοραὶ
post σχημάτων addidit Marquard)   αἱ τῶν] αἱ om. R H   21 περι-
μένοντι B

θισθῆναι τήν τε διάνοιαν καὶ τὴν αἴσθησιν καλῶς κρίνειν τό
30 τε μένον καὶ τὸ κι|νούμενον. Ἁπλῶς μὲν οὖν εἰπεῖν τοιαύτη
τίς ἐστιν ἡ ἁρμονικὴ κληθεῖσα ἐπιστήμη οἵαν διεληλύθαμεν·
συμβέβηκε δ' αὐτὴν διαιρεῖσθαι εἰς ἑπτὰ μέρη. ||
35 Ὧν ἐστὶν ἐν μὲν καὶ πρῶτον τὸ διορίσαι τὰ γένη καὶ 5
ποιῆσαι φανερόν, τίνων ποτὲ μενόντων καὶ τίνων κινουμένων
5 αἱ διαφοραὶ αὗται γίγνονται. Τοῦ|το γὰρ οὐδεὶς πώποτε
διώρισε τρόπον τινὰ εἰκότως· οὐ γὰρ ἐπραγματεύοντο περὶ
τῶν δύο γενῶν, ἀλλὰ περὶ αὐτῆς τῆς ἁρμονίας· οὐ μὴν ἀλλ'
10 οἵ γε διατρίβοντες περὶ τὰ ὄργανα διῃσθάνοντο | μὲν ἑκάστου 10
τῶν γενῶν, αὐτὸ δὲ τὸ πότε ἄρχεται ἐξ ἁρμονίας χρῶμά τι
γίγνεσθαι, οὐδεὶς οὐδ' ἐπέβλεψε πώποτ' αὐτῶν. οὔτε γὰρ
κατὰ πᾶσαν χρόαν ἑκάστου τῶν γενῶν διῃσθάνοντο διὰ τὸ
15 μήτε | πάσης μελοποιίας ἔμπειροι εἶναι μήτε συνειθίσθαι
περὶ τὰς τοιαύτας διαφορὰς ἀκριβολογεῖσθαι· οὔτ' αὐτό 15
πως τοῦτο κατέμαθον ὅτι τόποι τινὲς ἦσαν τῶν κινουμένων
20 φθόγγων ἐν ταῖς | τῶν γενῶν· διαφοραῖς. Δι' ἃς μὲν οὖν
αἰτίας οὐκ ἦν διωρισμένα τὰ γένη πρότερον, σχεδόν εἰσιν αἱ
εἰρημέναι· ὅτι δὲ διοριστέον εἰ μέλλομεν ἀκολουθεῖν ταῖς
25 γιγνομέναις ἐν τοῖς μέλεσι δια|φοραῖς, φανερόν. 20
Πρῶτον μὲν οὖν τῶν μερῶν ἐστὶ τὸ εἰρημένον· δεύτερον
δὲ τὸ περὶ διαστημάτων εἰπεῖν, μηδεμίαν τῶν ὑπαρ-
30 χουσῶν αὐτοῖς διαφορῶν εἰς δύναμιν παραλιμ|πάνοντας.
Σχεδὸν δέ, ὡς ἁπλῶς εἰπεῖν, αἱ πλείους αὐτῶν εἰσὶν ἀθεώ-
ρητοι. οὐ δεῖ δ' ἀγνοεῖν, ὅτι καθ' ἣν ἂν γενώμεθα τῶν 25

---

1 εἰ ante καλῶς et βουλοίμεθα ante κρίνειν add. H   3 κλειθεῖσα B
5 διορίσαι ex διωρίσαι Ma   6 ποτὲ om. R   καὶ Marquard: ἢ
codd.   8 διωρίσαι (e suprascr.) S   10 γε] μὲν H   11 δὲ
in ras. Mb, fuisse vid. μὲν: μέντοι R   12 οὔτε Marquard: οὐδὲ
codd.   15 οὐδ' R   16 κατέμαθον Marquard: κατεμήννον H:
κατεμένονθ' rell.: καταμαθόντες Meibom   ὅτε H   17 ταῖς (ο
suprascr.) B   20 μέλεσι conieci: γένεσι codd.: post τοῖς
dat μελ S sed deletum   21 μὲν om. H   22 ὑπαρχουσῶν
ex ὑπαρχόντων Ma   23 παραλιμπάνονται (ut vid.) B: παραλιμ-
πάνοντες H

ἐκλιμπανουσῶν τε καὶ ἀθεωρήτων διαφορῶν, κατὰ ταύτην
ἀγνοήσομεν || τὰς ἐν τοῖς μελῳδουμένοις διαφοράς.   36

Ἐπεὶ δ' ἐστὶν οὐκ αὐτάρκη τὰ διαστήματα πρὸς τὴν τῶν
φθόγγων διάγνωσιν—πᾶν γάρ, ὡς ἁπλῶς εἰπεῖν, διὰ|στή- 5
5 ματος μέγεθος πλειόνων τινῶν δυνάμεων κοινόν ἐστιν—,
τρίτον ἄν τι μέρος εἴη τῆς ὅλης πραγματείας τὸ περὶ τῶν
φθόγγων εἰπεῖν ὅσοι τ' εἰσὶ καὶ τίνι γνωρίζονται καὶ πό-
τε|ρον τάσεις τινές εἰσιν, ὥσπερ οἱ πολλοὶ ὑπολαμβάνουσιν, 10
ἢ δυνάμεις καὶ αὐτὸ τοῦτο τί ποτ' ἐστὶν ἡ δύναμις. Οὐδὲν
10 γὰρ τῶν τοιούτων διορᾶται καθαρῶς ὑπὸ τῶν τὰ τοιαῦτα
πραγματευομένων. |

Τέταρτον δ' ἂν εἴη μέρος τὰ συστήματα θεωρῆσαι 15
πόσα τ' ἐστὶ καὶ ποῖ' ἄττα καὶ πῶς ἔκ τε τῶν διαστημάτων
καὶ φθόγγων συνεστηκότα. Οὐδέτερον γὰρ τῶν τρόπων
15 τεθεώρηται τὸ μέρος τοῦτο ὑπὸ | τῶν ἔμπροσθεν· οὔτε γὰρ εἰ 20
πάντα τρόπον ἐκ τῶν διαστημάτων συντίθεται τὰ συστήματα
καὶ μηδεμία τῶν συνθέσεων παρὰ φύσιν ἐστὶν ἐπισκέψεως
τετύχηκεν, οὔθ' αἱ διαφοραὶ πᾶσαι τῶν συστημά|των ὑπ' οὐ- 25
δενὸς ἐξηρίθμηνται. Περὶ μὲν γὰρ ἐμμελοῦς ἢ ἐκμελοῦς
20 ἁπλῶς οὐδένα λόγον πεποίηνται οἱ πρὸ ἡμῶν, τῶν δὲ συστη-
μάτων τὰς διαφορὰς οἱ μὲν ὅλως οὐκ ἐπεχείρουν ἐξαριθμεῖν |
—ἀλλὰ περὶ αὐτῶν μόνον τῶν ἑπτὰ ὀκταχόρδων ἃ ἐκάλουν 30
ἁρμονίας τὴν ἐπίσκεψιν ἐποιοῦντο—, οἱ δ' ἐπιχειρήσαντες
οὐδένα τρόπον ἐξηριθμοῦντο, καθάπερ οἱ περὶ Πυθαγόραν
25 τὸν Ζακύνθιον καὶ Ἀγή||νορα τὸν Μιτυληναῖον. Ἔστι 37

---

1 ἐκλιμπανόντων Ma (sed ουσῶν suprascr. Mc) V B S: ἐκλιμπανο-
μένων H   2 ἀγνοήσωμεν M (ut vid.) V B   6 ἔν τι post μέρος
ponit H   7 τίνι ex τίνων corr. S   10 καθαρῶς om. H
12 θεωρεῖσθαι H   14 τῶν ante φθόγγων et συστήματα ante συνεστηκότα add. H   οὐδέτερον] οὐ et έ in ras. Mb   16 συστήματα]
συστή in ras. Mb, fuerat fortasse διαστή   19 μὲν om. H   ἢ H
21 ἀπεχείρουν H   22 μόνων H   ἑπτὰ ὀκταχόρδων Westphal:
ἑπταχόρδων codd., sed in M a poster. manu ex ἑπτὰ χορδῶν factum
23 τὴν om. H   24 τε ante περὶ Πυθαγόραν et οἱ περὶ ante Ἀγήνορα
add. H

δὲ τοιαύτη τις ἡ περὶ τὸ ἐμμελές τε καὶ ἐκμελὲς τάξις
οἵα καὶ ἡ περὶ ⟨τὴν⟩ τῶν γραμμάτων σύνθεσιν ἐν τῷ
5 διαλέγεσθαι· οὐ γὰρ πάν|τα τρόπον ἐκ τῶν αὐτῶν γραμ-
μάτων συντιθεμένη ξυλλαβὴ γίγνεται, ἀλλὰ πὼς μέν, πὼς
δ' οὔ.   5
Πέμπτον δ' ἐστὶ τῶν μερῶν τὸ περὶ τοὺς τόνους ἐφ'·
10 ὧν τιθέμενα τὰ συ|στήματα μελῳδεῖται. Περὶ ὧν οὐδεὶς
οὐδὲν εἴρηκεν, οὔτε τίνα τρόπον ληπτέον οὔτε πρὸς τί βλέποντας τὸν ἀριθμὸν αὐτῶν ἀποδοτέον ἐστίν. ἀλλὰ παντελῶς
15 ἔοικε τῇ τῶν ἡμερῶν ἀγωγῇ τῶν | ἁρμονικῶν ἡ περὶ τῶν τόνων 10
ἀπόδοσις, οἷον ὅταν Κορίνθιοι μὲν δεκάτην ἄγωσιν Ἀθηναῖοι
δὲ πέμπτην ἕτεροι δέ τινες ὀγδόην· οὕτω γὰρ οἱ μὲν τῶν
20 ἁρμονικῶν λέγουσι βαρύτατον μὲν τὸν | ὑποδώριον τῶν
τόνων, ἡμιτονίῳ δὲ ὀξύτερον τούτου τὸν μιξολύδιον, τούτου
δ' ἡμιτονίῳ τὸν δώριον, τοῦ δὲ δωρίου τόνῳ τὸν φρύγιον, 15
25 ὡσαύτως δὲ καὶ τοῦ φρυγίου τὸν λύδιον ἑτέρῳ τόνῳ· ἕτε|ροι
δὲ πρὸς τοῖς εἰρημένοις τὸν ὑποφρύγιον αὐλὸν προστιθέασιν
ἐπὶ τὸ βαρύ, οἱ δὲ αὖ πρὸς τὴν τῶν αὐλῶν τρύπησιν βλέ-
ποντες τρεῖς μὲν τοὺς βαρυτάτους τρισὶ διέσεσιν ἀπ'
30 ἀλλή|λων χωρίζουσιν, τόν τε ὑποφρύγιον καὶ τὸν ὑποδώριον 20
καὶ τὸν δώριον, τὸν δὲ φρύγιον ἀπὸ τοῦ δωρίου τόνῳ, τὸν
δὲ λύδιον ἀπὸ τοῦ φρυγίου πάλιν τρεῖς διέσεις ἀφιστᾶσιν·
ὡσαύτως δὲ καὶ τὸν μιξολύδιον τοῦ λυδίου. Τί δ' ἐστὶ πρὸς
38 ὃ βλέποντες || οὕτω ποιεῖσθαι τὴν διάστασιν τῶν τόνων
προτεθύμηνται, οὐδὲν εἰρήκασιν. Ὅτι δέ ἐστιν ἡ κατα- 25

1 τε om. H   τὸ ante ἐκμελὲς add. H   ἡ supra lin. add. Ma :
om. H   2 τὴν restituit Marquard   σύνθεσιν Meibom : σύνθεσις
codd.   6 τόνους] prior. litt. in ras. Vb (Va fort. τρόπους)   9 ἐστίν
om. H   10 τῇ ... ἀγωγῇ linea subducta S   ἡμερῶν] ἡ in ras.
Mb, erat τῶν μερῶν   περὶ] τῶν B : om. S   11 Κορίνθιοι . . .
ὀγδόην] linea subducta S   13 εἶναι post μὲν add., τὸν ὑποδώριον
om., τὸ ὑποδώριον post τόνων add. H   14 prius τούτου] τούτου Mc R :
τούτων Ma rell.   alterum τούτου] τούτου Mc : τούτων rell.   17 πρὸς
om. H   18 τρίησιν H   19 δὲ post τρισὶ add. V S B   21 καὶ
τὸν δώριον om. R   25 προτεθύμηνται οὐδὲν εἰρήκασιν supra lin.
add. Mb

πύκνωσις ἐκμελὴς καὶ πάντα τρόπον ἄχρηστος, φα|νερὸν ἐπ᾽ 5
αὐτῆς ἔσται τῆς πραγματείας.

Ἐπεὶ δὲ τῶν μελῳδουμένων ἐστὶ τὰ μὲν ἁπλᾶ τὰ δὲ με-
τάβολα, περὶ μεταβολῆς ἂν εἴη λεκτέον, πρῶτον | μὲν αὐτὸ 10
5 τί ποτ᾽ ἐστὶν ἡ μεταβολὴ καὶ πῶς γιγνόμενον—λέγω δ᾽ οἷον
πάθους τίνος συμβαίνοντος ἐν τῇ τῆς μελῳδίας τάξει—,
ἔπειτα πόσαι εἰσὶν αἱ πᾶσαι μεταβολαὶ καὶ κατὰ πόσα |
διαστήματα. Περὶ γὰρ τούτων οὐδεὶς οὐδενὸς εἴρηται λόγος 15
οὔτ᾽ ἀποδεικτικὸς οὔτ᾽ ἀναπόδεικτος.

10 Τελευταῖον δὲ τῶν ⟨μερῶν ἐστι⟩ τὸ περὶ αὐτῆς τῆς με-
λοποιίας. Ἐπεὶ γὰρ ἐν τοῖς αὐτοῖς φθόγ|γοις ἀδιαφόροις 20
οὖσι τὸ καθ᾽ αὑτοὺς πολλαί τε καὶ παντοδαπαὶ μορφαὶ μελῶν
γίγνονται, δῆλον ὅτι παρὰ τὴν χρῆσιν τοῦτο γένοιτ᾽ ἄν.
καλοῦμεν δὲ τοῦτο μελοποιίαν. Ἡ μὲν οὖν περὶ τὸ ἡρμο-
15 σμένον | πραγματεία διὰ τῶν εἰρημένων μερῶν πορευθεῖσα 25
τοιοῦτον λήψεται τέλος.

Ὅτι δ᾽ ἐ⟨στὶ⟩ τὸ ξυνιέναι τῶν μελῳδουμένων τῇ τε ἀκοῇ
καὶ τῇ διανοίᾳ κατὰ πᾶσαν διαφορὰν τοῖς γιγνομέ|νοις παρα- 30
κολουθεῖν ⟨δῆλον⟩—ἐν γενέσει γὰρ δὴ τὸ μέλος, καθάπερ
20 καὶ τὰ λοιπὰ μέρη τῆς μουσικῆς — . . . .
. . . . . ἐκ δύο γὰρ τούτων ἡ τῆς μουσικῆς ξύνεσίς ἐστιν,
αἰσθήσεώς τε καὶ μνήμης· αἰσθάνε||σθαι μὲν γὰρ δεῖ τὸ 39
γιγνόμενον, μνημονεύειν δὲ τὸ γεγονός. κατ᾽ ἄλλον δὲ τρόπον
οὐκ ἔστι τοῖς ἐν τῇ μουσικῇ παρακολουθεῖν.

3 μετάβολα Meibom: ἀμετάβολα codd.   5 λέγω] λέ S   6 τίνος
conieci: τινὸς codd.   7 πᾶσαι post μεταβολαὶ ponunt R H
8 οὐδεὶς post οὐδενὸς ponit H   9 ἀπόδεικτος B   10 μερῶν
ἐστι restituit Meibom: τῶν μερῶν ἐστι om. R: μερῶν ἐστι τὸ om.
rell.   μελοποιίας Meibom H: μελῳδίας rell.   12 τὸ om. H
μορφαὶ om. B, sed a corr. supra lin. add.   μελῶν post γίγνονται
ponit H   13 παρά] πρὸς H   14 μελῳποιίαν S   οὖν] αὖ B
16 τοιοῦτον ex τοιοῦτο Mc: τοιοῦτο VBS   17 ἐστι addidi
ἕκαστον post μελῳδουμένων add. Meibom   18 παρακολουθεῖν
conieci: παρακολουθεῖ codd. (post εἶ ras. M)   19 δῆλον addidi
τὸ supra lin. add. Mb   21 ἐκ δύο . . . μουσικῆς in marg. Mb
22 αἰσθάνεσθαι μὲν] αι μὲν e corr. B   δεῖ ex δὴ Mc: δὴ VBS

MACRAN   K   129

5 Ἃ δέ τινες ποιοῦνται τέλη τῆς | ἁρμονικῆς καλου-
μένης πραγματείας οἱ μὲν τὸ παρασημαίνεσθαι τὰ μέλη
φάσκοντες πέρας εἶναι τοῦ ξυνιέναι τῶν μελῳδουμένων
ἕκαστον, οἱ δὲ τὴν περὶ τοὺς αὐλοὺς θεωρίαν καὶ τὸ
10 ἔχειν | εἰπεῖν τίνα τρόπον ἕκαστα τῶν αὐλουμένων καὶ 5
πόθεν γίγνεται· τὸ δὴ ταῦτα λέγειν παντελῶς ἐστιν ὅλου
τινὸς διημαρτηκότος. Οὐ γὰρ ὅτι πέρας τῆς ἁρμονικῆς
15 ἐπιστήμης ἐστὶν ἡ παρασημ|αντική, ἀλλ' οὐδὲ μέρος οὐ-
δέν, εἰ μὴ καὶ τῆς μετρικῆς τὸ γράψασθαι τῶν μέτρων
ἕκαστον· εἰ δ' ὥσπερ ἐπὶ τούτων οὐκ ἀναγκαῖόν ἐστι 10
τὸν δυνάμενον γράψασθαι τὸ ἰαμβικὸν (μέτρον καὶ εἰδέναι
20 τί ἐστι τὸ ἰαμβικόν), | οὕτως ἔχει καὶ ἐπὶ τῶν μελῳδου-
μένων,—οὐ γὰρ ἀναγκαῖόν ἐστι τὸν γραψάμενον τὸ φρύγιον
μέλος καὶ εἰδέναι τί ἐστι τὸ φρύγιον μέλος—δῆλον ὅτι
25 οὐκ ἂν εἴη τῆς εἰρημένης | ἐπιστήμης πέρας ἡ παρασημ- 15
μαντική. Ὅτι δ' ἀληθῆ τὰ λεγόμενα καὶ ἔστιν ἀναγκαῖον
τῷ παρασημαινομένῳ μόνον τὰ μεγέθη τῶν διαστημάτων
30 διαισθάνεσθαι, φανερὸν γένοιτ' ἂν | ἐπισκοπουμένοις. Ὁ
γὰρ τιθέμενος σημεῖα τῶν διαστημάτων οὐ καθ' ἑκάστην τῶν
ἐνυπαρχουσῶν αὐτοῖς διαφορῶν ἴδιον τίθεται σημεῖον, οἷον 20
40 εἰ τοῦ διὰ τεσσάρων τυγχάνουσιν αἱ δι||αιρέσεις οὖσαι
πλείους ἃς ποιοῦσιν αἱ τῶν γενῶν διαφοραί, ἢ σχήματα
πλείονα ποιεῖ ἡ τῆς τῶν ἀσυνθέτων διαστημάτων τάξεως
5 ἀλλοίωσις· τὸν αὐτὸν δὲ λόγον | καὶ περὶ τῶν δυνάμεων
ἐροῦμεν ἃς αἱ τῶν τετραχόρδων φύσεις ποιοῦσι, τὸ γὰρ 25

3 τοῦ ex τὸ Mb   4 τὴν supra lin. add. Mb   7 διαμαρτη-
κότος B   ἀληθὲς post γὰρ add. H   οὐ post ὅτι add. Mar-
quard˙   9 γράψασθαι] γὰρ ἅψασθαι R   11 τὸν] τὸ M V S
μέτρον . . . ἰαμβικόν restituit Marquard   14 καὶ ἄριστά γε
εἰδέναι in marg. Mc(?) R   καὶ post ἐστι add. H   17 τῷ ex
τὸ Mb   μόνῳ B   20 ὑπαρχουσῶν H : ἐνυπαρχουσῶν ex
ἐνυπαρχόντων Ma   αὐτοῖς supra lin. add. Mc   21 εἰ in ras. Mb
διὰ supra lin. add. Mc : om. V B in marg.   διὰ τεσσάρων] δ' S
23 ἃ post πλείονα add. Marquard   ἢ] ἤ R   συνθέτων B
24 λόγων S

ὑπερβολαίων καὶ νητῶν καὶ μέσων καὶ ὑπατῶν τῷ αὐτῷ γρά-
φεται σημείῳ, τὰς δὲ τῶν δυνάμεων διαφορὰς οὐ διορίζει τὰ |
σημεῖα ⟨ὥστε⟩ μέχρι τῶν μεγεθῶν αὐτῶν κεῖσθαι, πορρωτέρω 10
δὲ μηδέν. Ὅτι δ' οὐδέν ἐστι μέρος τῆς συμπάσης ξυνέσεως τὸ
5 διαισθάνεσθαι τῶν μεγεθῶν αὐτῶν, ἐλέχθη μέν πως καὶ ἐν
ἀρχῇ, ῥᾴδιον | δὲ καὶ ἐκ τῶν ῥηθησομένων συνιδεῖν· οὔτε γὰρ 15
τὰς τῶν τετραχόρδων οὔτε τὰς τῶν φθόγγων δυνάμεις οὔτε τὰς
τῶν γενῶν διαφορὰς οὔτε, ἁπλῶς εἰπεῖν, τὴν τοῦ συνθέτου
καὶ τὴν τοῦ ἀσυν|θέτου διαφορὰν οὔτε τὸ ἁπλοῦν καὶ μετα- 20
10 βολὴν ἔχον οὔτε τοὺς τῶν μελοποιῶν τρόπους οὔτ' ἄλλο
οὐδέν, ὡσαύτως εἰπεῖν, δι' αὐτῶν τῶν μεγεθῶν γίγνεται
γνώριμον. Εἰ μὲν οὖν δι' ἄγνοιαν τὴν ὑπό|ληψιν ταύτην 25
ἐσχήκασιν οἱ καλούμενοι ἁρμονικοί, τὸ μὲν ἦθος οὐκ ἂν εἶεν
ἄτοποι, τὴν δὲ ἄγνοιαν ἰσχυράν τινα καὶ μεγάλην εἶναι παρ'
15 αὐτοῖς ἀναγκαῖον· εἰ δὲ συνορῶντες, ὅτι οὐκ | ἔστι τὸ παρα- 30
σημαίνεσθαι πέρας τῆς εἰρημένης ἐπιστήμης, χαριζόμενοι δὲ
τοῖς ἰδιώταις καὶ πειρώμενοι ἀποδιδόναι ὀφθαλμοειδές τι
ἔργον ταύτην ἐκτεθείκασι τὴν ὑπόληψιν, μεγάλην || ⟨ἂν⟩ 41
αὖθις αὐτῶν ἀτοπίαν τοῦ τρόπου καταγνοίην· πρῶτον μέν,
20 ὅτι κριτὴν οἴονται δεῖν κατασκευάζειν τῶν ἐπιστημῶν τὸν
ἰδιώτην—ἄτοπος γὰρ ἂν | εἴη τὸ αὐτὸ μανθάνων τε καὶ 5
κρίνων ὁ αὐτός—, ἔπειθ' ὅτι ⟨πέρας⟩ τοῦ ξυνιέναι τιθέντες

---

1 ὑπερβολαίων καὶ νητῶν καὶ μέσων καὶ ὑπατῶν conieci   ὑπερβολαίων καὶ νητῶν] τῆς ὑπερβολαίας νήτης H : ὑπερβολαίας νήτης B : ὑπερβολαίας καὶ νήτης R : ὑπερβολαίας rell. (in marg. B)   μέσων
καὶ ὑπατῶν] μέσης καὶ ὑπάτης codd.   2 διορίζει τὰ Marquard :
διορίζεται codd.   3 σημείῳ R   ὥστε restituit Marquard   τὰ κατὰ post γὰρ add. Westphal
6 τοῦ ῥηθησομένου H
8 ὡς ante ἁπλῶς add. H   τὴν R : τὰς rell.   τοῦ συνθέτου
Meibom : τῶν συνθέτων codd.   9 καὶ τῶν ἀσυνθέτων διαφορὰς
H   10 οὔτε a corr. suprascr. B   μελοποιῶν V : μελοποιῶν
rell.   12 γνωρίμων B   δι' ἄγνοιαν] διάνοιαν H   14 δὲ]
δι' H   17 ἰδιόταις S   ἀποδοῦναι H   ὀφθαλμοειδέστι Ma :
accent. acut. supra ε alterum, et τ supra σ add. Mc   18 ἐκτεθήκασι
S   ὑπόλειψιν H   ἂν restituit Marquard   19 καταγνοίην] ν
add. Mb   21 ἰδιότην S   22 πέρας restituit Marquard   τοῦ]
τὸ M V S B : om. R

φανερόν τι ἔργον ὡς οἴονται ἀνάπαλιν τιθέασιν· παντὸς γὰρ
10 ὀφθαλμοφανοῦς ἔργου πέρας ἐστὶν ἡ ξύνεσις. | τὸ γὰρ ἐπι-
στατοῦν πᾶσι καὶ κρῖνον τοῦτ' ἐστι· [ἢ] τὰς ⟨δὲ⟩ χεῖρας ἢ
τὴν φωνὴν ἢ τὸ στόμα ἢ τὸ πνεῦμα [ἢ] ὅστις οἴεται πολύ τι
15 διαφέρειν τῶν ἀψύχων ὀργάνων οὐκ ὀρθῶς διανοεῖται· | εἰ δὲ 5
τὴν ψυχήν που καταδεδυκός ἐστιν ἡ ξύνεσις καὶ μὴ πρόχειρον
μηδὲ τοῖς πολλοῖς φανερόν, καθάπερ αἵ τε χειρουργίαι καὶ
20 τὰ λοιπὰ τῶν τοιούτων, οὐ διὰ τοῦτο ἄλλως ὑπο|ληπτέον
ἔχειν τὰ εἰρημένα. διημαρτηκέναι γὰρ συμβήσεται τἀλη-
θοῦς, ἐὰν τὸ μὲν κρῖνον μήτε πέρας μήτε κύριον ποιῶμεν, τὸ 10
25 δὲ κρινόμενον κύριόν τε καὶ πέρας. Οὐχ ἧττον δέ | ἐστι
ταύτης ἡ περὶ τοὺς αὐλοὺς ὑπόληψις ἄτοπος· μέγιστον
μὲν οὖν καὶ καθόλου μάλιστα ⟨ἄτοπον⟩ τῶν ἁμαρτημάτων
ἐστὶ τὸ εἰς ὄργανον ἀνάγειν τὴν τοῦ ἡρμοσμένου φύσιν· δι'
30 οὐδὲν γὰρ τῶ̈ | τοῖς ὀργάνοις ὑπαρχόντων τοιοῦτόν ἐστι τὸ 15
ἡρμοσμένον οὐδὲ τοιαύτην τάξιν ἔχον. οὐ γάρ, ὅτι ὁ αὐλὸς
τρυπήματά τε καὶ κοιλίας ἔχει καὶ τὰ λοιπὰ τῶν τοιούτων,
42 ὅτι δὲ χειρουργίαν τὴν || μὲν ἀπὸ τῶν χειρῶν τὴν δ' ἀπὸ
τῶν λοιπῶν μερῶν οἷς ἐπιτείνειν τε καὶ ἀνιέναι πέφυκε, διὰ
5 τοῦτο συμφωνεῖ διὰ τεσσάρων ἢ διὰ πέντε ἤτοι διὰ πα|σῶν, 20
ἢ τῶν ἄλλων διαστημάτων ἕκαστον λαμβάνει τὸ προσῆκον
μέγεθος. Πάντων γὰρ τούτων ὑπαρχόντων οὐδὲν ἧττον τὰ
μὲν πλείω διαμαρτάνουσιν οἱ αὐληταὶ τῆς τοῦ ἡρμοσμένου
10 τάξεως, ὀλί|γα δ' ἐστὶν ἃ τυγχάνουσι ποιοῦντες πάντα ταῦτα,
καὶ γὰρ ἀφαιροῦντες καὶ παραβάλλοντες καὶ τῷ πνεύματι 25

3 πᾶσι post ἐπιστατοῦν ponit H   κρίναν H   ἢ seclusi : in ras.
Mb   δὲ addidi   4 ἢ seclusi   ὅστις S B : ὅτις ex εἴ τις (ut
vid.) Mb : ὅ τις cum macula post ὅ V R   5 διαφέρειν Marquard
H : διαφέρει rell.   6 καταδεδυκός Meibom : καταδεδύκός codd.
12 αὐλοὺς Meibom : ἄλλους codd.   13 ἄτοπον restituit Marquard
14 δι' om. H   15 τῶν τοῖς ὀργάνοις in ras. Mb   τὸ om. H
16 τοιαύτην] ταύτην H   17 τὰς ante κοιλίας add. H   18 ὁ
αὐλητὴς ante χειρουργίαν add. Marquard   τὴν μὲν] τὸν μὲν B
20 τὸ ante διὰ τεσσάρων add. H S   τὸ διὰ πέντε ἢ τὸ διὰ πασῶν H
21 λαμβάνῃ R   23 αὐλητal] αὐλοί S   24 ἃ supra lin. add.
Mb   ἐπιτυγχάνουσι B (ου e corr.) R   25 τῷ πνῖ S

132

ἐπιτείνοντες καὶ ἀνιέντες καὶ ταῖς ἄλλαις αἰτίαις ἐνεργοῦντες.
ὥστ᾽ εἶναι | φανερόν, ὅτι οὐδὲν διαφέρει λέγειν τὸ καλῶς ἐν 15
τοῖς αὐλοῖς τοῦ κακῶς· οὐκ ἔδει δὲ τοῦτο συμβαίνειν, εἴπερ
τι ὄφελος ἦν τῆς εἰς ὄργανον τοῦ ἡρμοσμένου ἀναγωγῆς,
5 ἀλλ᾽ ἅμα τ᾽ εἰς | τοὺς αὐλοὺς ἀνῆχθαι τὸ μέλος καὶ εὐθὺς 20
ἀστραβὲς εἶναι καὶ ἀναμάρτητον καὶ ὀρθόν. ἀλλὰ γὰρ οὔτ᾽
αὐλοὶ οὔτε τῶν ἄλλων οὐθὲν ὀργάνων ποτὲ βεβαιώσει τὴν
τοῦ ἡρμοσμένου φύσιν· τάξιν | γάρ τινα καθόλου τῆς φύσεως 25
τοῦ ἡρμοσμένου θαυμαστὴν μεταλαμβάνει τῶν ὀργάνων
10 ἕκαστον ἐφ᾽ ὅσον δύναται, τῆς αἰσθήσεως αὐτοῖς ἐπιστα-
τούσης πρὸς ἣν ἀνάγεται καὶ ταῦτα καὶ τὰ λοιπὰ | τῶν κατὰ 30
μουσικήν. Εἰ ⟨δέ⟩ τις οἴεται, ὅτι τὰ τρυπήματα ὁρᾷ ταὐτὰ
ἑκάστης ἡμέρας ἢ τὰς χορδὰς ἐντεταμένας τὰς αὐτάς, διὰ
τοῦθ᾽ εὑρήσειν τὸ ἡρμοσμένον ἐν αὐτοῖς διαμένον τε καὶ τὴν
15 αὐτὴν τάξιν διασῶζον, παν||τελῶς εὐήθης· ὥσπερ γὰρ ἐν 43
ταῖς χορδαῖς οὐκ ἔστι τὸ ἡρμοσμένον, ἐὰν μή τις αὐτὸ διὰ
τῆς χειρουργίας προσαγαγὼν ἁρμόσηται, οὕτως οὐδὲ ἐν τοῖς |
τρυπήμασιν, ἐὰν μή τις αὐτὸ χειρουργίᾳ προσαγαγὼν ἁρμό- 5
σηται. ὅτι δ᾽ οὐδὲν τῶν ὀργάνων αὐτὸ ἁρμόττεται ἀλλὰ ἡ
20 αἴσθησίς ἐστιν ἡ τούτου κυρία, δῆλον ὅτι οὐδὲ λόγου δεῖται,
φανερὸν γάρ. | Θαυμαστὸν δ᾽ εἰ μηδ᾽ εἰς τὰ τοιαῦτα βλέ- 10
ποντες ἀφίστανται τῆς τοιαύτης ὑπολήψεως ὁρῶντες ὅτι

1 καὶ ἀνιέντες] ἢ ἀνιέντες H   καὶ ταῖς] ἐν ταῖς R   3 κακῶς]
καλῶς B : om. R   τοῦτο] τὸ M R : τοῦ S   4 εἰς ὄργανον τοῦ
ἡρμοσμένου Meibom : εἰς τὸ ἡρμοσμένου ὄργανον codd.   5 μέλος H
6 ἀστραβὲς ex ἀστραβές, deinde 2 litt. eras. Mb : ἀστραβές τε B
7 ἄλλων in ras. Mb   οὐθὲν post ὀργάνων ponit H   8 ἡρμοσμένου
φύσιν. τάξιν γάρ τινα καθόλου τῆς φύσεως τοῦ (ante τοῦ ras.) in marg.
Mb : φύσιν (om. καὶ sed supra lin. add.) γὰρ τῆς καθόλου φύσεως (τῆς
in ras. in qua τινα vel τις erat, ante φύσεως 3 litt. eras.) Vb : item B
sed in marg. τάξιν ut scripturae discrepantia pro φύσιν : τάξιν. καὶ
γὰρ τῆς καθόλου φύσεως S   10 ante ἐφ᾽ 4 litt. eras. M   αὐτοῖς]
αὐτῆς B   ἐπιτατ τούσης R   12 εἰ] εἰς B   δὲ restituit Marquard
(leg. H)   ταῦτα M V B S   13 ἢ om. M V S B   14 τε om. R
15 αὐτὴν om. H   διασώζων Ma : διασῶζον Mb rell.   16 διὰ τῆς
om. R, supra lin. add. Mb   17 χειρουργίᾳ R   ἁρμόσειται (η
suprascr.) B   οὕτως . . . ἁρμόσηται om. H   19 τῶν om. H
20 μυρία (κυ supra μυ scr.) H   οὔτε H   λόγον B H

κινοῦνται οἱ αὐλοὶ καὶ οὐδέποθ' ὡσαύτως ἔχουσιν ἀλλ' ἕκαστα
15 τῶν αὐλουμένων μεταβάλλει | ⟨κατὰ⟩ τὰς αἰτίας ἀφ' ὧν
αὐλεῖται. Σχεδὸν δὴ φανερόν, ὅτι δι' οὐδεμίαν αἰτίαν εἰς
τοὺς αὐλοὺς ἀνακτέον τὸ μέλος, οὔτε γὰρ βεβαιώσει τὴν
τοῦ ἡρμοσμένου τάξιν [τὸ εἰρημένον] ὄργανον οὔτ', εἴ τις | 5
20 ᾠήθη δεῖν εἰς ὄργανόν τι ποιεῖσθαι τὴν ἀναγωγήν, εἰς τοὺς
αὐλοὺς ἦν ποιητέον, ἐπειδὴ μάλιστα πλανᾶται καὶ κατὰ τὴν
αὐλοποιίαν καὶ κατὰ τὴν χειρουργίαν καὶ κατὰ τὴν ἰδίαν
φύσιν. |
25 Ἃ μὲν οὖν προδιέλθοι τις ἂν περὶ τῆς ἁρμονικῆς καλου- 10
μένης πραγματείας σχεδόν ἐστι ταῦτα· μέλλοντας δ' ἐπι-
χειρεῖν τῇ περὶ τὰ στοιχεῖα πραγματείᾳ δεῖ προδιανοηθῆναι
30 τὰ τοι|άδε· ὅτι οὐκ ἐνδέχεται καλῶς αὐτὴν διεξελθεῖν μὴ
προϋπαρξάντων τριῶν τῶν ῥηθησομένων· πρῶτον μὲν αὐτῶν
τῶν φαινομένων καλῶς ληφθέντων, ἔπειτα διορισθέντων ἐν 15
44 αὐτοῖς τῶν || τε προτέρων καὶ τῶν ὑστέρων ὀρθῶς, τρίτον δὲ
τοῦ συμβαίνοντός τε καὶ ὁμολογουμένου κατὰ τρόπον συν-
5 οφθέντος· Ἐπεὶ δὲ πάσης ἐπιστήμης, ἥ τις ἐκ προβλη|μάτων.
πλειόνων συνέστηκεν, ἀρχὰς προσῆκόν ἐστι λαβεῖν ἐξ ὧν
δειχθήσεται τὰ μετὰ τὰς ἀρχάς, ἀναγκαῖον ἂν εἴη λαμβάνειν 20
προσέχοντας δύο τοῖσδε· πρῶτον μὲν ὅπως ἀληθές τε καὶ |
10 φαινόμενον ἕκαστον ἔσται τῶν ἀρχοειδῶν προβλημάτων,
ἔπειθ' ὅπως τοιοῦτον οἷον ἐν πρώτοις ὑπὸ τῆς αἰσθήσεως
συνορᾶσθαι τῶν τῆς ἁρμονικῆς πραγματείας μερῶν· τὸ γάρ
15 πως ἀπαιτοῦν ἀπόδειξιν | οὐκ ἔστιν ἀρχοειδές. Καθόλου 25
δ' ἐν τῷ ἄρχεσθαι παρατηρητέον, ὅπως μήτ' εἰς τὴν
ὑπερορίαν ἐμπίπτωμεν ἀπό τινος φωνῆς ἢ κινήσεως ἀέρος

---

1 post αὐλοὶ unum verbum eras. M　　2 κατὰ restituit Meibom
3 δὴ] δὲ H　　4 μάλος H　　5 τὸ εἰρημένον seclusi　　εἰ om.
M V B S　　6 ἀγωγήν M V S R H　　7 ἦν] ἦν ex ἦν Mb : ἦν
V S B, H (ante εἰς τοὺς)　　8 καὶ κατὰ τὴν χειρουργίαν in marg. Mb
10 προέλθοι B in marg.　　17 τὸν ante τρόπον add. M V S B
συναφθέντος H　　18 ἐπεὶ ex ἐπὶ Mb　　19 προσέχοντα H
24 μέτρων H　　25 πῶς S　　ἀπετοῦν H　　26 τὴν om. V S
27 ἐμπίπτωμεν] lac. πτωμεν R : ἐμπίπτομεν H　　ἢ conieci : ἡ codd.

ἀρχόμενοι, μήτ᾽ αὖ κάμπτοντες ἐντὸς πολ|λὰ τῶν οἰκείων 20
ἀπολιμπάνωμεν . . . .

. . . .

   Τρία γένη τῶν μελῳδουμένων ἐστίν· διάτονον χρῶμα
5 ἁρμονία. αἱ μὲν οὖν διαφοραὶ τούτων ὕστερον ῥηθήσονται·
τοῦτο δ᾽ αὐτὸ ἐκκείσθω, ὅτι πᾶν | μέλος ἔσται ἤτοι διάτονον 25
ἢ χρωματικὸν ἢ ἐναρμόνιον ἢ μικτὸν ἐκ τούτων ἢ κοινὸν
τούτων.

   Δευτέρα δ᾽ ἐστὶ διαίρεσις τῶν διαστημάτων εἶναι τὰ μὲν
10 σύμφωνα τὰ | δὲ διάφωνα. γνωριμώταται μὲν δοκοῦσιν εἶναι 30
αὗται δύο τῶν διαστηματικῶν διαφορῶν, ᾗ τε μεγέθει διαφέρουσιν ἀλλήλων καὶ ᾗ τὰ σύμφωνα τῶν διαφώνων· περιέ-
χεται δ᾽ ἡ ὑστέρα ῥηθεῖσα || διαφορὰ τῇ ·προτέρᾳ, πᾶν γὰρ 45
σύμφωνον παντὸς διαφώνου διαφέρει μεγέθει. Ἐπεὶ δὲ τῶν
15 συμφώνων πλείους εἰσὶ πρὸς ἄλληλα διαφοραί, μία τις ἡ |
γνωριμωτάτη αὐτῶν ἐκκείσθω ⟨πρώτη⟩· αὕτη δ᾽ ἐστὶν ἡ κατὰ 5
μέγεθος. Ἔστω δὴ τῶν συμφώνων ὀκτὼ μεγέθη· ἐλάχιστον
μὲν τὸ διὰ τεσσάρων—συμβαίνει δὲ τοῦτο ⟨αὐτῇ⟩ τῇ τοῦ
⟨μέλους⟩ φύσει ἐλάχιστον εἶναι· σημεῖον δὲ | τὸ μελῳδεῖν 10
20 μὲν ἡμᾶς πολλὰ τοῦ διὰ τεσσάρων ἐλάττω, πάντα μέντοι
διάφωνα—. δεύτερον δὲ τὸ διὰ πέντε, ὅ τι δ᾽ ἂν τούτων
ἀνὰ μέσον ᾖ μέγεθος πᾶν ἔσται διάφωνον. τρίτον ⟨δ᾽⟩ ἐκ
τῶν εἰρημέ|νων συμφώνων σύνθετον τὸ διὰ πασῶν, τὰ δὲ 15

---

4 Mb in marg. ἀρχή Vb in marg. πόσα γένη μελῳδίας ἐστίν ins.
Mb: om. R   5 ἁρμονία] vid. fuisse ἁρμονίαν M   6 μᾶλος H
ἢ τοὶ ex ὃ τε Ma (b?)   7 ἐκ om. M V B R S   9 ἐστὶν post
διαστημάτων ponit H   post ἐστὶ una litt. eras., vid. fuisse ἐστὶν M
12 διαφώνων ex διαφορῶν Ma   13 ἐν ante τῇ add. H   14 παντὸς
om. et μεγέθει ante διαφόνου ponit H   ὅρα Πορφύριον ἐν τῷ εἰς
Ἁρμονικὰ τοῦ Πτολεμαίου ὑπομνήματι in marg. H   16 πρώτη
restituit Marquard, sed ante ἐκκείσθω ponit   18 συμβέβηκε δὴ H
αὐτῇ restituit Westphal   τῇ om. B   τοῦ B : αὐτοῦ M V S R :
αὐτοῦ H   19 μέλους restituit Westphal   20 πολλὰ om. R
22 ἀνὰ μέσων B   ἔσται H : εἶναι rell.   post εἶναι add. λέγομεν
Marquard   δ᾽ restituit Marquard   23 συντεθὲν H

ΑΡΙΣΤΟΞΕΝΟΥ

τούτων ἀνὰ μέσον διάφωνα ἔσται. Ταῦτα μὲν οὖν λέγομεν
ἃ παρὰ τῶν ἔμπροσθεν παρειλήφαμεν, περὶ δὲ τῶν λοιπῶν
20 ἡμῖν αὐτοῖς διοριστέον. | Πρῶτον μὲν οὖν λεκτέον, ὅτι πρὸς
τῷ διὰ πασῶν πᾶν σύμφωνον προστιθέμενον διάστημα τὸ
γιγνόμενον ἐξ αὐτῶν μέγεθος σύμφωνον ποιεῖ. καὶ ἔστιν 5
25 ἴδιον τοῦτο τὸ πάθος τοῦ συμφώνου | τούτου, καὶ γὰρ ἐλάτ-
τονος προστεθέντος καὶ ἴσου καὶ μείζονος τὸ γιγνόμενον ἐκ
τῆς συνθέσεως σύμφωνον γίγνεται· τοῖς δὲ πρώτοις συμ-
φώνοις οὐ συμβαίνει τοῦτο, οὔτε γὰρ τὸ ἴσον ἑκατέρῳ
30 αὐ|τῶν συντεθὲν τὸ ὅλον σύμφωνον ποιεῖ οὔτε τὸ ἐξ ἑκα- 10
τέρου αὐτῶν καὶ τοῦ διὰ πασῶν συγκείμενον, ἀλλ' ἀεὶ
διαφωνήσει τὸ ἐκ τῶν εἰρημένων συμφώνων συγκείμενον.

46   Τόνος δ' ἐστὶν ᾧ τὸ διὰ πέντε || τοῦ διὰ τεσσάρων μεῖζον·
τὸ δὲ διὰ τεσσάρων δύο τόνων καὶ ἡμίσεος. Τῶν δὲ τοῦ
τόνου μερῶν μελῳδεῖται τὸ ἥμισυ, ὃ καλεῖται ἡμιτόνιον, καὶ 15
5 τὸ τρίτον μέρος, | ὃ καλεῖται δίεσις χρωματικὴ ἐλαχίστη,
καὶ τὸ τέταρτον, ὃ καλεῖται δίεσις ἐναρμόνιος ἐλαχίστη·
τούτου δ'. ἔλαττον οὐδὲν μελῳδεῖται διάστημα. Δεῖ δὲ
10 πρῶτον μὲν τοῦτο αὐτὸ μὴ ἀγνοεῖν, ὅτι | πολλοὶ ἤδη διή-
μαρτον ὑπολαβόντες ἡμᾶς λέγειν ὅτι ὁ τόνος εἰς ⟨τρία ἢ⟩ 20
τέσσαρα ἴσα διαιρούμενος μελῳδεῖται. συνέβη δ' αὐτοῖς
τοῦτο παρὰ τὸ μὴ κατανοεῖν ὅτι ἕτερόν ἐστι τό τε λαβεῖν
15 τρίτον μέ|ρος τόνου καὶ τὸ διελόντα εἰς τρία τόνον μελῳδεῖν.
ἔπειτα ἁπλῶς μὲν οὐθὲν ὑπολαμβάνομεν εἶναι διάστημα
ἐλάχιστον.   25

1 ἀνὰ μέσων H   διάφωνα εἶναι λεγόμεν. Ταῦτα μὲν οὖν παρὰ
Marquard (δ. ε. λεγόμενα τ. μ. ο. π. Porphyrius)   ἔσται H : εἶναι
rell.   3 μὲν supra lin. add. Mb   4 τῷ] τὸ S H B in marg.
5 ποιεῖται H   7 μεγέθους post μείζονος add. H   γιγνόμενον
Marquard : λεγόμενον codd. : γενόμενον Porphyrius   9 οὐ supra
lin. add. Mb   πάθος post τοῦτο add. H   11 δὶς τεθέντος post
αὐτῶν add. Meibom   ἀεὶ διαφωνήσει] ἢ διαφώνησις M V B S : ἢ
διαφώνησις R   13 τοῦ] καὶ R   14 ἡμίσεως B H   17 καὶ
... ἐλαχίστη om. H   δ R : om. rell.   20 ὑπολαβόντες ex
ὑπολαβόντας Mb   τρία ἢ restituit Marquard   21 αὐτοῖς post
τοῦτο ponit H   24 ἔπειθ' ἁπλῶς S
136

Αἱ δὲ τῶν γενῶν διαφοραὶ λαμβά|νονται ἐν τετραχόρδῳ 20
τοιούτῳ οἷόν ἐστι τὸ ἀπὸ μέσης ἐφ᾽ ὑπάτην, τῶν μὲν ἄκρων
μενόντων, τῶν δὲ μέσων κινουμένων ὁτὲ μὲν ἀμφοτέρων
ὁτὲ δὲ θατέρου. Ἐπεὶ δ᾽ ἀναγκαῖον τὸν κινού|μενον φθόγ- 25
γον ἐν τόπῳ τινὶ κινεῖσθαι, ληπτέος ἂν εἴη τόπος ὡρισμένος
ἑκατέρου τῶν εἰρημένων φθόγγων. φαί|νεται δὴ συντονω-
τάτη μὲν εἶναι λιχανὸς ἡ τόνον ἀπὸ 'μέσης ἀπέχουσα, |
ποιεῖ δ᾽ αὕτη διάτονον γένος, βαρυτάτη δ᾽ ἡ δίτονον, γίγνεται 30
δ᾽ αὕτη ἐναρμόνιος· ὥστ᾽ εἶναι φανερὸν ἐκ τούτων, ὅτι
10 τονιαῖός ἐστιν ὁ τῆς λιχανοῦ τόπος. τὸ δὲ παρυπάτης ⟨καὶ
ὑπάτης⟩ διάστημα ἔλαττον μὲν ὅτι οὐκ ἂν γένοιτο διέσεως ||
ἐναρμονίου φανερόν, ἐπειδὴ πάντων τῶν μελῳδουμένων 47
ἐλάχιστόν ἐστι δίεσις ἐναρμόνιος· ὅτι δὲ καὶ τοῦτο εἰς τὸ
διπλάσιον αὔξεται, κατανοητέον. ὅταν | γὰρ ἐπὶ τὴν αὐτὴν 5
15 τάσιν ἀφίκωνται ἥ τε λιχανὸς ἀνιεμένη καὶ ἡ παρυπάτη
ἐπιτεινομένη, ὁρίζεσθαι δοκεῖ ἑκατέρας ὁ τόπος. ὥστ᾽ εἶναι
φανερόν, ⟨ὅτι οὐ μείζων διέσεως ἐλαχίστης ἐστὶν ὁ τῆς
παρυπάτης τόπος. Ἤδη δέ τινες θαυμάζουσι πῶς ἐστι
λιχανὸς κινηθέντος ἑνὸς ὅτου | δήποτε τῶν μέσης καὶ λιχανοῦ 10
20 διαστημάτων· διὰ τί γὰρ μέσης μὲν καὶ παραμέσης ἕν ἐστι
διάστημα καὶ πάλιν αὖ μέσης τε καὶ ὑπάτης καὶ τῶν ἄλλων
ὅσοι ⟨μὴ⟩ κι|νοῦνται τῶν φθόγγων, τὰ δὲ μέσης καὶ λιχανοῦ 15
διαστήματα πολλὰ θετέον εἶναι· κρεῖττον γὰρ τῶν φθόγγων

2 τῶν supra lin. add. Mb   3 δὲ supra lin. add. Mb: om. B
δὲ μέσων H : μέσων δὲ rell.   ἀμφοτέρων ex ἀμφοτέρου (ut vid.) Mb
4 ἐπεὶ δ᾽ ἂν M : ἐπειδὰν VBS   5 ληπτέος] τέος corr. Mb
6 ἑκατέρου Marquard : ἑκατέρων codd.   δὴ] μὴ B   8 αὕτη H :
αὐτῇ MVBS : αὐτὴ R   βαρυτάτη δὲ ἡ δῖ in ras. Mb   ἡ om. S
10 καὶ ὑπάτης restituit Marquard   11 ἔλαττον Mc in marg. B :
ἐλάττονι Ma VSB   ὅτι om. R   12 τούτων post πάντων add. H
15 τάσιν] τάξιν H   ἡ παρυπάτη] ὑπαρυπάτη B   16 ὁρίζεσθαι
Marquard : ὁρίσθαι R : ὁρίσθαι in marg. B : ὁριεῖσθαι rell.   ὁ om. H
17 ὅτι . . . θαυμάζουσι restituit Studemund   19 κινιθέντος B :
τεθέντος Marquard   20 παραμέσης ex παραμέσου Mc : παραμέσου
VS : παρὰ μέσου B   21 αὖ ex αὐλοὶ (λοὶ eras.) Mb   καὶ ὑπάτης
om. in marg. B   22 μὴ restituit Meibom   κινοῦνται R : κινοῦσι
ex κεινοῦσι (ut vid.) Mb : κινοῦσι rell.

τὰ ὀνόματα κινεῖν μηκέτι καλοῦντας λιχανοὺς τὰς λοιπάς,
ἐπειδὰν ἡ δίτονος ⟨λιχανὸς⟩ κληθῇ ἢ τῶν ἄλλων μία ἥτις
20 ποτ' οὖν. δεῖν γὰρ | ἑτέρους εἶναι φθόγγους τοὺς τὸ ἕτερον
μέγεθος ὁρίζοντας· ὡσαύτως δὲ δεῖν ἔχειν καὶ τὰ ἀντι-
στρέφοντα. τὰ γὰρ ἴσα τῶν μεγεθῶν τοῖς αὐτοῖς ὀνόμασι 5
25 περιλη|πτέον εἶναι. Πρὸς δὴ ταῦτα τοιοῦτοί τινες ἐλέχθησαν
λόγοι· πρῶτον μὲν ὅτι τὸ ἀξιοῦν τοὺς διαφέροντας ἀλλήλων
φθόγγους ἴδιον μέγεθος ἔχειν διαστήματος μέγα τι κινεῖν
30 ἐστιν· ὁρῶμεν γὰρ | ὅτι νήτη μὲν καὶ μέση παρανήτης καὶ
λιχανοῦ διαφέρει κατὰ τὴν δύναμιν καὶ πάλιν αὖ παρανήτη 10
τε καὶ λιχανὸς τρίτης τε καὶ παρυπάτης, ὡσαύτως δὲ καὶ
48 οὗτοι παραμέσης τε καὶ ὑπάτης—καὶ διὰ ταύτην || τὴν αἰτίαν
ἴδια κεῖται ὀνόματα ἑκάστοις αὐτῶν—, διάστημα δ' αὐτοῖς
πᾶσιν ὑπόκειται ἕν, τὸ διὰ πέντε, ὥσθ' ὅτι μὲν οὐχ οἷόν τ'
5 ἀεὶ τῇ τῶν φθόγγων δια|φορᾷ τὴν τῶν διαστηματικῶν μεγε- 15
θῶν διαφορὰν ἀκολουθεῖν φανερόν. Ὅτι δ' οὐδὲ τοὐναντίον
ἀκολουθεῖν θετέον, κατανοήσειεν ἄν τις ἐκ τῶν ῥηθησομένων.
10 Πρῶτον μὲν οὖν εἰ καὶ καθ' ἑκάστην αὔξησίν τε καὶ ἐλάττωσιν τῶν περὶ τὸ πυκνὸν γιγνομένων ἴδια ζητήσομεν ὀνόματα, δῆλον ὅτι ἀπείρων ὀνομάτων δεησόμεθα, ἐπειδήπερ ὁ 20
49. 7 τῆς λιχανοῦ τόπος εἰς ἀπείρους τέμνεται τομάς. || Ὡς ἀληθῶς
γὰρ τίνι ἄν τις προσθεῖτο τῶν ἀμφισβητούντων περὶ τὰς τῶν
10 γενῶν | χρόας; οὐ γὰρ δὴ πρὸς τὴν αὐτὴν διαίρεσιν βλέ-

1 τὰ add. Mb   2 ἢ] ἢ codd. : ἢ ἡ Marquard   δίττονος R
λιχανὸς addidi : οὕτω Marquard   ἥτις renovat Mb accent. add. Mc :
ἥτις cum ras. supra lin. V   3 δεῖν Marquard : δεῖ codd. .   τὸ om. S
4 δεῖ H   5 γὰρ ἴσα Studemund : πάρισα codd. : δ' ἴσα Marquard
6 τοιοῦτοί] οὗτοί H   ἐλέχθησαν] ἐ in ras. Mc (?)   9 παρανήτης
ex παρανήτην Mb   10 δ' post πάλιν add. H   11 παρυπάτης]
ὑπάτης R   12 ὑπάτης] νήτης H   13 αὐτῶν supra lin. add.
corr. B   14 ἕν, τὸ conieci : ἐν τῷ codd.   15 διαστημάτων H
17 ἀκολουθεῖν θετέον conieci : ἀκολουθητέον codd.   18 εἰ καὶ] καὶ
om. H   ἐλάττοσιν S   19 ζητήσωμεν M V S B   20 δεησόμεθα]
ησό in ras. Vb   21 τέμνεται post τομὰς ponit H   ὡς
ἀληθῶς . . . διαιρέσεων legg. in codd. post διαμένειν in p. 140, l. 1 :
ordinem mutavi   22 προσθεῖτο ex προσθοῖτο Mc : προσθοῖτο V B S
ἀμφισβητούντων (ν suprascr.) B

ποντες πάντες οὔτε τὸ χρῶμα οὔτε τὴν ἁρμονίαν ἁρμοττόνται,
ὥστε τί μᾶλλον τὴν δίτονον λιχανὸν λεκτέον ἢ τὴν μικρῷ
συντονωτέραν; ἁρ|μονία μὲν γὰρ εἶναι τῇ αἰσθήσει κατ’ 15
ἀμφοτέρας τὰς διαιρέσεις φαίνεται, τὰ δὲ μεγέθη τῶν διαστη-
5 μάτων δῆλον ὅτι οὐ ταὐτὰ ἐν ἑκατέρᾳ τῶν διαιρέσεων. |
ἔπειτα πειρώμενοι παρατηρεῖν τό τ’ ἴσον καὶ τὸ ἄνισον ἀπο- 48. 15
βαλοῦμεν τὴν τοῦ ὁμοίου τε καὶ ἀνομοίου διάγνωσιν, ὥστε
μηδὲ πυκνὸν καλεῖν ἔξω ἑνὸς μεγέθους, δῆλον δ’ ὅτι μηδ’
ἁρμονίαν μηδὲ χρῶμα, τόπῳ | γάρ τινι καὶ ταῦτα διώρισται. 20
10 Δῆλον δ’ ὅτι οὐδὲν τούτων ἐστὶ πρὸς τὴν τῆς αἰσθήσεως
φαντασίαν· ἐκείνη μὲν γὰρ εἰς ὁμοιότητα ἑνός τινος εἴδους
βλέπουσα τό τε χρῶμα | λέγει καὶ τὴν ἁρμονίαν ἀλλ’ 25
οὐκ εἰς ἑνός τινος διαστήματος μέγεθος, λέγω δὲ πυκνοῦ
μὲν εἶδος τιθεῖσα ἕως ἂν τὰ δύο διαστήματα τοῦ ἑνὸς
15 ἐλάττω τόπον κατέχῃ—ἐμφαίνεται γὰρ ἐν πᾶσι τοῖς | πυκ- 30
νοῖς πυκνοῦ τινὸς φωνὴ καίπερ ἀνίσων αὐτῶν ὄντων—
χρώματος δὲ εἶδος ἕως ἂν τὸ χρωματικὸν ἦθος ἐμφαίνηται.
ἰδίαν γὰρ δὴ κίνησιν ἕκαστον τῶν γενῶν κινεῖται πρὸς τὴν
αἴσθησιν οὐ || μιᾷ χρώμενον τετραχόρδου διαιρέσει ἀλλὰ 49
20 πολλαῖς. ὥστ’ εἶναι φανερόν, ὅτι κινουμένων τῶν μεγεθῶν
συμβαίνει ⟨μένειν⟩ τὸ γένος, οὐ γὰρ ὁμοίως κινεῖται τῶν
με|γεθῶν κινουμένων μέχρι τινός, ἀλλὰ διαμένει· τούτου δὲ 5

2 post ὥστε add. οὐ πάνυ ῥᾴδιον συνιδεῖν Marquard   δίτονον conieci :
διάτονον codd.   ἢ] ἢ Η   3 ἁρμονίας sed as postea corr. B
4 μεγέθη post διαστημάτων ponit Η   5 ταῦτα M V B S   8 δῆλον
δ’ ὅτι om. et μηθ’ pro μηδ’ scrib. Marquard   δ’ S : om. rell.   11 γὰρ
om. V S   12 βλέπουσα in ras. Ma   13 οὐκ εἰς ἑνὸς renov.
Mb   εἰς om. B   εἰσὶν ὡς R   πυκνοῦμεν B   14 εἶδος in
marg. Mb : εἴδους M V S   post εἶδος add. ὅταν ἡ φωνὴ φανῇ τὰ διαστήματα οὕτω Marquard   τεθεῖσα M V S B   ἕως conieci : ὡς codd.
(δια)στήματα τοῦ erat in ras. deinde renov. Mb   15 κατέχειν
Η   ἐν πᾶσι τοῖς renov. Mb   16 (καί)περ ἀνίσων renov. Mb
17 δὲ εἶδος ἕως conieci : δὲ ἢ διέσεως R : δεῖ διέσεως rell. (διέσεως in
ras. Mb)   ἂν τὸ χρω in ras. Mb   ἐμφαίνηται Marquard : ἐμφαίνεται
codd.   18 ἰδία S   δὴ κίνησιν] δείκνυσιν R   (κιν)εῖται πρὸς τὴν
in ras. Mb   19 μιᾷ] ᾷ in ras. Mb   διαιρέσει ex διαιρεσιν Mb
21 μένειν addidi : ταὐτὸν εἶναι Marquard   οὐ in ras. Mb   22 διαμένει renov. Mb

μένοντος εἰκὸς καὶ τὰς τῶν φθόγγων δυνάμεις διαμένειν. τὸ
20 γὰρ εἶδος τοῦ τετραχόρδου ταὐ|τό, δι᾽ ὅπερ καὶ τοὺς τῶν
διαστημάτων ὅρους ἀναγκαῖον εἰπεῖν τοὺς αὐτούς. Καθόλου
δ᾽ εἰπεῖν, ἕως ἂν μένῃ τὰ τῶν περιεχόντων ὀνόματα καὶ
25 λέγηται αὐτῶν ἡ μὲν ὀξυτέρα μέση ὑπάτη δ᾽ ἡ | βαρυτέρα, 5
διαμενεῖ καὶ τὰ τῶν περιεχομένων ὀνόματα καὶ ῥηθήσεται
αὐτῶν ἡ μὲν ὀξυτέρα λιχανὸς ἡ δὲ βαρυτέρα παρυπάτη, ἀεὶ
γὰρ τοὺς μεταξὺ μέσης τε καὶ ὑπάτης λιχανόν τε καὶ παρ-
30 υπάτην ⟨ἡ⟩ αἴσθη|σις τίθησιν. Τὸ δ᾽ ἀξιοῦν ἢ τὰ ἴσα δια-
στήματα τοῖς αὐτοῖς ὀνόμασιν ὁρίζεσθαι ἢ τὰ ἄνισα ἑτέροις 10
μάχεσθαι τοῖς φαινομένοις ἐστί· τὸ [τε] γὰρ ὑπάτης καὶ
παρυπάτης τῷ παρυπάτης [πλεονάκις ἴσον μελῳδεῖται ἢ]
50 ⟨καὶ⟩ λιχανοῦ || μελῳδεῖται ποτὲ ἴσον ποτὲ ἄνισον· ὅτι δ᾽
οὐκ ἐνδέχεται δύο διαστημάτων ἐξῆς κειμένων τοῖς αὐτοῖς
5 ὀνόμασιν ἑκάτερον αὐτῶν περιέχεσθαι φανερόν, | εἴπερ μὴ 15
μέλλοι ὁ μέσος δύο ἕξειν ὀνόματα. Δῆλον δὲ καὶ ἐπὶ τῶν
ἀνίσων τὸ ἄτοπον· οὐ γὰρ δυνατὸν διαμένοντος τοῦ ἑτέρου
τῶν ὀνομάτων τὸ ἕτερον κινεῖσθαι, πρὸς ἄλληλα γὰρ λέλε-
10 κται· | [ὥσπερ γὰρ ὁ τέταρτος ἀπὸ τῆς μέσης ὑπάτη πρὸς
μέσην λέγεται, οὕτως ὁ ἐχόμενος τῆς μέσης λιχανὸς πρὸς 20
μέσην λέγεται.] Πρὸς μὲν ⟨οὖν ταύτην⟩ τὴν διαπορίαν
τοσαῦτα εἰρήσθω. |

2 γὰρ conieci : δ᾽ codd.   εἶδος ex αἶδος Ma   4 μένει S H
5 λέγηται] γένηται H   ὑπάτη δ᾽ ἡ βαρυτέρα] ὑπάτη in ras. Mb   δὲ
supra lin. add. Mc   ἡ om. M   δ᾽ ἡ om. V S B   ἡ δὲ βαρυτέρα
(omissis ὑπάτη δ᾽ ἡ) R, in marg.   6 διαμενεῖ] διαμένει
codd.   7 λιχανὸς Marquard : μέση codd.   παρυπάτη] ὑπάτη
sed παρ ante ν eras. M : ὑπάτη rell.   9 ἡ restituit Marquard   αἴσθησιν S   10 τοῖς ante ἑτέροις add. H   11 μάχεσθαι] συνέχεσθαι R
ἐστι ante τοῖς φαινομένοις ponit H   τε seclusi   12 πλεονάκις
. . . ἢ del. Meibom   13 καὶ restituit Meibom   ποτε μελῳδεῖται
(β supra ποτε, et α supra μελῳδεῖται scr.) Ma   ποτὲ μὲν ἴσον ποτὲ δὲ
ἄνισον H   14 αὐτοῖς supra lin. add. corr. B   17 τὸ postea
add. Ma (ut vid.)   18 λέγεται H   19 ὥσπερ . . . λιχανὸς πρὸς
μέσην λέγεται seclusit Marquard   ὑπάτης H : ὑπάτη sed ν post η eras.
M : ὑπάτην V B sed ὑπάτη in marg. B   20 λέγεται in ras. Mb : deinde
4 litt. eras. quarum extremae ται fuisse videntur   ante πρὸς μέσην add.
καὶ Mc   21 οὖν ταύτην restituit Marquard   22 τοσαῦτα] ταῦτα H
140

Πυκνὸν δὲ λεγέσθω μέχρι τούτου ἕως ἂν ἐν τετραχόρδῳ 15
διὰ τεσσάρων συμφωνούντων τῶν ἄκρων τὰ δύο διαστήματα
συντεθέντα τοῦ ἑνὸς ἐλάττω τόπον κατέχῃ. Τετραχόρδου
δέ εἰσι δι|αιρέσεις ἐξαίρετοί τε καὶ γνώριμοι αὗται αἵ εἰσω 20
5 εἰς γνώριμα διαιρούμεναι μεγέθη διαστημάτων. Μία μὲν οὖν
⟨τούτων⟩ τῶν διαιρέσεών ἐστιν ἐναρμόνιος ἐν ᾗ τὸ μὲν πυκνὸν
ἡμιτόνιόν ἐστι τὸ | δὲ λοιπὸν δίτονον. τρεῖς δὲ χρωματικαί, 25
ἥ τε τοῦ μαλακοῦ χρώματος καὶ ἡ τοῦ ἡμιολίου καὶ ἡ τοῦ
τονιαίου· μαλακοῦ μὲν οὖν χρώματός ἐστι διαίρεσις ἐν ᾗ τὸ
10 μὲν πυκνὸν ἐκ δύο χρω|ματικῶν διέσεων ἐλαχίστων σύγ- 30
κειται, τὸ δὲ λοιπὸν δύο μέτροις μετρεῖται, ἡμιτονίῳ μὲν
τρίς, χρωματικῇ δὲ διέσει ἅπαξ, ὥστε μετρεῖσθαι τρισὶν
ἡμιτονίοις καὶ τόνου τρίτῳ μέρει ἅπαξ· ἔστι δὲ τῶν χρωμα-
τικῶν πυκνῶν ἐλάχιστον καὶ λιχανὸς αὕτη βαρυτάτη τοῦ ||
15 γένους τούτου. ἡμιολίου δὲ χρώματος διαίρεσίς ἐστιν ἐν 51
ᾗ τό τε πυκνὸν ἡμιόλιόν ἐστι τοῦ [τ′] ἐναρμονίου καὶ τῶν
διέσεων (ἑκατέρα) ἑκατέρας τῶν ἐναρμονίων· ὅτι δ′ ἐστὶ |
μεῖζον τὸ ἡμιόλιον πυκνὸν τοῦ μαλακοῦ, ῥᾴδιον συνιδεῖν, 5
τὸ μὲν γὰρ ἐναρμονίου διέσεως λείπει τόνος εἶναι τὸ δὲ
20 χρωματικῆς. τονιαίου δὲ χρώματος διαίρεσίς ἐστιν ἐν ᾗ
τὸ μὲν πυκνὸν ἐξ ἡμι|τονίων δύο σύγκειται τὸ δὲ λοιπὸν 10
τριημιτόνιόν ἐστιν. Μέχρι μὲν οὖν ταύτης τῆς διαιρέσεως

---

1 ἂν om. R　　3 κατέχῃ ex κατέχει Mb: κατέχει S　　Τετραχόρδου
κ.τ.λ.] in marg. Ὅρα Πτολεμαῖον ἐν Ἁρμονικοῖς H　　4 ante ἐξαίρετοι
una litt. eras. M　　αἵ] καὶ R　　5 εἰ γνώριμά ἐστι τὰ διαιρούμενα
μεγέθη τῶν διαστημάτων H　　διαιρούμενα M V S　　6 τούτων addidi
τῶν om. H　　διαιρέσεων post ἐστι ponit H　　πυκνὸν in ras. Mb: μικρὸν R
7 δίτονον] post ι litt. a eras. M　　8 ἡ τοῦ τονιαίου] ἡ τοῦ supra lin.
add. Mb: ἡμιτονίου R　　9 οὖν om. R　　10 καὶ ante διέσεων
add. R　　12 τρεῖς H　　δὲ add. Mc: om. V B S　　διέσει] ει in
ras. Mb: διέσις Va　　ἅπαξ ὥστε μετρεῖσθαι om. M V B S H　　ὥστε
... ἅπαξ om. R　　τρισὶν ἡμιτονίοις καὶ τόνου τρίτῳ μέρει in marg. Mb
14 πυκνῶν R: πυκνὸν rell.　　λιχανὸς] ος in ras. Mb　　16 τ′
del. Marquard　　ἐναρμονίου] ἐν add. Mb　　17 ἑκατέρα restituit
Marquard (lac. 2 syllab. R)　　19 τόνος post εἶναι ponit H　　20 διαί-
ρεσις] αιρ add. Mx　　in marg. Mb (?) Vc

<table>
<tr><td></td><td>πυκνά</td><td></td><td></td></tr>
<tr><td>ἐναρμον.</td><td>ἐναρμον.</td><td>μαλακ.</td><td>ἡμιολ.</td></tr>
<tr><td>ϛ</td><td></td><td>η</td><td>θ′</td></tr>
</table>

141

ἀμφότεροι κινοῦνται οἱ φθόγγοι, μετὰ ταῦτα δ' ἡ μὲν παρ-
15 υπάτη μένει, διελήλυθε γὰρ τὸν αὑτῆς τόπον, ἡ δὲ | λιχανὸς
κινεῖται δίεσιν ἐναρμόνιον καὶ γίγνεται τὸ λιχανοῦ καὶ
ὑπάτης διάστημα ἴσον τῷ λιχανοῦ καὶ μέσης, ὥστε μηκέτι
γίγνεσθαι πυκνὸν ἐν ταύτῃ τῇ διαιρέσει. συμβαίνει δ' ἅμα 5
20 παύεσθαι τὸ πυ|κνὸν συνιστάμενον ἐν τῇ τῶν τετραχόρδων
διαιρέσει καὶ ἄρχεσθαι γιγνόμενον τὸ διάτονον γένος. Εἰσὶ
δὲ δύο διατόνου διαιρέσεις, ἥ τε τοῦ μαλακοῦ καὶ ἡ τοῦ
25 συντόνου. μαλακοῦ μὲν οὖν ἐστὶ διατόνου διαί|ρεσις ἐν ᾗ
τὸ μὲν ὑπάτης καὶ παρυπάτης ἡμιτονιαῖόν ἐστι, τὸ δὲ παρ- 10
υπάτης καὶ λιχανοῦ τριῶν διέσεων ἐναρμονίων, τὸ δὲ λιχανοῦ
καὶ μέσης πέντε διέσεων· συντόνου δὲ ἐν ᾗ τὸ μὲν ὑπάτης
30 καὶ πα|ρυπάτης ἡμιτονιαῖον, τῶν δὲ λοιπῶν τονιαῖον ἑκάτερόν
ἐστιν. Λιχανοὶ μὲν οὖν εἰσὶν ἕξ, μία ἐναρμόνιος, τρεῖς
52 χρωματικαὶ καὶ δύο διάτονοι, ὅσαι περ αἱ || τῶν τετραχόρδων 15
διαιρέσεις, παρυπάται δὲ δύο ἐλάττους, τῇ γὰρ ἡμιτονιαίᾳ
χρώμεθα πρός τε τὰς διατόνους καὶ πρὸς τὴν τοῦ τονιαίου
5 χρώματος διαίρε|σιν· τεττάρων δ' οὐσῶν παρυπατῶν ἡ μὲν
ἐναρμόνιος ἰδία ἐστὶ τῆς ἁρμονίας, αἱ δὲ τρεῖς κοιναὶ τοῦ
τε διατόνου καὶ τοῦ χρώματος. Τῶν δ' ἐν τῷ τετραχόρδῳ 20
10 διαστημάτων τὸ μὲν ὑπάτης | καὶ παρυπάτης τῷ παρυπάτης
καὶ λιχανοῦ ἢ ἴσον μελῳδεῖται ἢ ἔλαττον, μεῖζον δ' οὐδέποτε. ὅτι μὲν οὖν ἴσον (φανερὸν ἐκ τῆς ἐναρμονίου διαιρέσεως καὶ τῶν χρωματικῶν, ὅτι δ' ἔλαττον ἐκ μὲν τῶν
διατόνων) φανερόν, ἐκ δὲ τῶν χρωματικῶν οὕτως ἄν τις 25
15 κατανοήσειεν, εἰ παρυπάτην | μὲν λάβοι τὴν τοῦ μαλακοῦ

2 αὑτῆς Marquard: αὐτῆς codd.   8 διαίρεσις διατόνου
H   9 οὖν om. R   10 ante ἡμιτονιαῖον 5 fere litt. eras.
(vid. χρῶμα fuisse) M   ἐστι om. R   12 καὶ in marg. Mc: om.
rell.   13 τονιαῖον ex ἡμιτονιαίων Ma   τονιαῖόν post ἑκάτερον
ponit H   14 ἕξ ... τέτταρες in marg. Mb: om. R   15 ὅσαι
ex ὅσα Ma   16 παρυπάται δὲ τέτταρες seclusit Marquard   παρυπάτης B : παρυπα (τ´ suprascr.) S   δυεῖν M : δυοῖν VS   19 ἰδία
H : ἴδιος rell.   21 τῷ παρυπάτης om. R   23 φανερὸν . . .
διατόνων restituit Westphal

χρώματος, λιχανὸν δὲ τὴν ⟨τοῦ⟩ τονιαίου· καὶ γὰρ αἱ τοιαῦται
διαιρέσεις τῶν πυκνῶν ἐμμελεῖς φαίνονται.   τὸ δ' ἐκμελὲς
γένοιτ' ἂν ἐκ τῆς ἐναντίας λήψεως, εἴ | τις παρυπάτην μὲν 20
λάβοι τὴν ἡμιτονιαίαν, λιχανὸν δὲ τὴν τοῦ ἡμιολίου χρώ-
5 ματος, ἢ παρυπάτην μὲν τὴν τοῦ ἡμιολίου, λιχανὸν δὲ τὴν
τοῦ μαλακοῦ χρώματος· ἀνάρμοστοι γὰρ | φαίνονται αἱ 25
τοιαῦται διαιρέσεις.   Τὸ δὲ παρυπάτης καὶ λιχανοῦ ⟨τῷ
λιχανοῦ⟩ καὶ μέσης καὶ ἴσον μελῳδεῖται καὶ ἄνισον ἀμφο-
τέρως· ἴσον μὲν ἐν τῷ συντονωτέρῳ διατόνῳ, ἔλατ|τον δ' 30
10 ἐν πᾶσι τοῖς λοιποῖς, μεῖζον δ' ὅταν ⟨τις⟩ λιχανῷ μὲν τῇ
συντονωτάτῃ τῶν διατόνων, παρυπάτῃ δὲ τῶν βαρυτέρων
τινὶ τῆς ἡμιτονιαίας χρήσηται.

Μετὰ δὲ ταῦτα δεικτέον περὶ τοῦ ἐξῆς ὑποτυπώσαντες
πρῶτον αὐτὸν τὸν || τρόπον καθ' ὃν ἀξιωτέον τὸ ἐξῆς ἀφ- 53
15 ορίζειν. Ἁπλῶς μὲν οὖν εἰπεῖν κατὰ τὴν τοῦ μέλους φύσιν
ζητητέον τὸ ἐξῆς καὶ οὐχ ὡς οἱ εἰς τὴν καταπύκνω|σιν βλέ- 5
ποντες εἰώθασιν ἀποδιδόναι τὸ συνεχές. ἐκεῖνοι μὲν γὰρ
ὀλιγωρεῖν φαίνονται τῆς τοῦ μέλους ἀγωγῆς· φανερὸν δ' ἐκ
τοῦ πλήθους τῶν ἐξῆς τιθεμένων διέσεων, [οὐ γὰρ διὰ
20 τοσούτων | δυνηθείη τις ἂν] μέχρι γὰρ τριῶν ἡ φωνὴ δύναται 10
συνείρειν· ὥστ' εἶναι φανερὸν ὅτι τὸ ἐξῆς οὔτ' ἐν τοῖς
ἐλαχίστοις οὔτ' ἐν τοῖς ἀνίσοις οὔτ' ἐν ⟨τοῖς⟩ ἴσοις ἀεὶ
ζητητέον διαστήμασιν, ἀλλ' ἀκολου|θητέον τῇ φύσει. Τὸν 15

1 τοῦ restituit Marquard   2 ἐμμελεῖς] ἐκμελεῖς H   ἐκμελὲς]
ἐκμελεῖς B: ἐμμελὲς (κ supra prius μ scr.) H   4 ἡμιολίου]
ἡμιολίου M sed post ἡμι una litt. eras., λι in ras. in qua τονιαί fuisse
vid. Mc: ἡμιτονιαίου VSBH   5 ἢ . . . χρώματος om. H   δὲ
add. Mc Vb   7 τῷ λιχανοῦ restituit Meibom   8 μελῳδεῖται
post ἀμφοτέρως ponit H   10 τις addidi   11 βαρυτέρων τινί]
βαρυτόνων παρυπάτη δὲ τῶν βαρυτόνων τινί B: βαρυτέρων in marg. B
12 χρήσηται ex χρήσεται Ma   14 ἀφορίζεσθαι H   16 καὶ οὐχ
ὡς οἱ εἰς τὸ in ras. Mb   17 διδόναι H   19 οὐ . . . ἂν seclusi
ut glossema : οὐ γὰρ ἂν om. codd. praeter
R   τριῶν] τινῶν B   21 συνείρειν ex συνήρειν Ma (?)   οὔτ' ἐν
ex οὔτε Mb   22 τοῖς restituit Marquard   23 ἀκολουθέον H

μὲν οὖν ἀκριβῆ λόγον τοῦ ἑξῆς οὔπω ῥᾴδιον ἀποδοῦναι, ἕως
ἂν αἱ συνθέσεις τῶν διαστημάτων ἀποδοθῶσιν· ὅτι δ' ἐστι
20 τι ἑξῆς καὶ τῷ παντελῶς ἀπείρῳ φανερὸν γένοιτ' ἂν | διὰ
τοιᾶσδέ τινος ἐπαγωγῆς. Πιθανὸν γὰρ τὸ μηδὲν εἶναι
διάστημα ὃ μελῳδοῦντες εἰς ἄπειρα τέμνομεν, ἀλλ' εἶναί 5
τινα μέγιστον ἀριθμὸν εἰς ὃν διαιρεῖται τῶν διαστημάτων
25 ἕκαστον ὑπὸ | τῆς μελῳδίας. Εἰ δὲ τοῦτό φαμεν ἤτοι
πιθανὸν ἢ καὶ ἀναγκαῖον εἶναι, δῆλον ὅτι οἱ ⟨τοῦ⟩ προειρημένου ἀριθμοῦ μέρη περιέχοντες φθόγγοι ἑξῆς ἀλλήλων
ἔχονται. δοκοῦσι δ' εἶναι ⟨τοιούτων⟩ τῶν φθόγγων καὶ | 10
30 οὗτοι οἷς τυγχάνομεν ἐκ παλαιοῦ χρώμενοι οἷον ἡ νήτη
⟨καὶ⟩ ἡ παρανήτη καὶ οἱ τούτοις συνεχεῖς.

Ἐχόμενον δ' ἂν εἴη τὸ ἀφορίσαι τὸ πρῶτον καὶ ἀναγκαι-
54 ότατον τῶν συντεινόν||των πρὸς τὰς ἐμμελεῖς συνθέσεις τῶν
διαστημάτων. Ἐν παντὶ δὲ γένει ἀπὸ παντὸς φθόγγου διὰ 15
5 τῶν ἑξῆς τὸ μέλος ἀγόμενον καὶ ἐπὶ τὸ βαρὺ καὶ ἐπὶ τὸ | ὀξὺ
ἢ τὸν τέταρτον τῶν ἑξῆς διὰ τεσσάρων ἢ τὸν πέμπτον διὰ
πέντε σύμφωνον λαμβανέτω, ᾧ δ' ἂν μηδέτερα τούτων συμ-
βαίνῃ, ἐκμελὴς ἔστω οὗτος πρὸς ἅπαντας οἷς συμβέβηκεν |
10 ἀσυμφώνῳ εἶναι κατὰ τοὺς εἰρημένους ἀριθμούς. Οὐ δεῖ 20
δ' ἀγνοεῖν, ὅτι οὐκ ἔστιν αὔταρκες τὸ εἰρημένον πρὸς τὸ
ἐμμελῶς συγκεῖσθαι τὰ συστήματα ἐκ τῶν διαστημάτων·
15 οὐδὲν γὰρ κωλύει συμφω|νούντων τῶν φθόγγων κατὰ τοὺς
εἰρημένους ἀριθμοὺς ἐκμελῶς τὰ συστήματα συνεστάναι,

3 τῷ add. Mb : om. R   φανερὸν] ανερον S   5 τέμνωμεν H
6 ὃν] ὁ S   8 πυθανὸν H   τοῦ restituit Marquard   προειρημένου
ἀριθμοῦ Marquard : προειρημένοι (προειρη in ras. Mb) ἀριθμοὶ M V S B :
(οἱ)γε εἰρημένοι ἀριθμοὶ R   10 τοιούτων restituit Marquard   11 ἡ
νήτη Westphal : ἤν τε H : ἤν rell.   12 καὶ add. Marquard   ἡ
παρανήτη H (coni. Marquard) : τῇ παρανήτῃ rell.   οἱ τούτοις συνεχεῖς
R : ἡ τούτοις συνεχής rell.   16 τῶν] τὸν H   17 τὸν ... τὸν]
τὸ ... τὸ H   τῶν Marquard : τῷ codd.   18 σύμφωνον S
λαμβανέτω conieci : λαμβάνεται codd.   μηδέτερον Meibom   συμβαίνει H   19 ἐκμελὴς (ἐκ in ras.) Mb : ἐμμελὴς in marg. B   οὗτως
H   οἷς H : ἐν οἷς rell.   20 ἀσυμφώνοις H   δεῖ H : om. rell.
22 συγκεῖσθαι] κινεῖσθαι R   23 κωλύοι S   συμφώνων ὄντων H
24 ἐκμελῶς (ἐκ in ras.) Mb : ἐμμελῶς R   συνεστάναι H : συνιστάναι rell.

ἀλλὰ τούτου μὴ ὑπάρχοντος οὐδὲν ἔτι γίγνεται τῶν λοιπῶν
ὄφελος. θετέον οὖν τοῦτο πρῶτον εἰς | ἀρχῆς τάξιν οὗ 20
μὴ ὑπάρχοντος ἀναιρεῖται τὸ ἡρμοσμένον. Ὅμοιον δ᾽ ἐστὶ
τούτῳ τρόπον τινὰ καὶ ⟨τὸ⟩ περὶ τὰς τῶν τετραχόρδων πρὸς
5 ἄλληλα θέσεις· δεῖ γὰρ τοῖς τοῦ αὐτοῦ συστήματος | τετρα- 25
χόρδοις ἐσομένοις δυοῖν θάτερον ὑπάρχειν, ἢ γὰρ συμφωνεῖν
πρὸς ἄλληλα, ὥσθ᾽ ἕκαστον ἑκάστῳ σύμφωνον εἶναι καθ᾽
ἣν δήποτε τῶν συμφωνιῶν, ⟨ἢ⟩ πρὸς τὸ αὐτὸ συμφωνεῖν μὴ
ἐπὶ τὸν | αὐτὸν τόπον συνεχῆ ὄντα ᾧ συμφωνεῖ ἑκάτερον 30
10 αὐτῶν. Ἔστι δ᾽ οὐδὲ τοῦτο αὔταρκες πρὸς τὸ εἶναι τοῦ
αὐτοῦ συστήματος τὰ τετράχορδα, προσδεῖται γάρ τινων καὶ
ἑτέρων περὶ ὧν ἐν τοῖς ἔπειτα ῥη‖θήσεται, ἀλλ᾽ ἄνευ γε 55
τούτου πάντα γίγνεται τὰ λοιπὰ ἄχρηστα.

Ἐπεὶ δὲ τῶν διαστηματικῶν μεγεθῶν τὰ μὲν τῶν συμφώ-
15 νων ἤτοι ὅλως οὐκ | ἔχειν δοκεῖ τόπον ἀλλ᾽ ἑνὶ μεγέθει 5
ὡρίσθαι, ἢ παντελῶς ἀκαριαῖόν τινα, τὰ δὲ τῶν διαφώνων
πολλῷ ἧττον τοῦτο πέπονθε καὶ διὰ ταύτας τὰς αἰτίας πολὺ
μᾶλλον τοῖς τῶν συμφώνων μεγέθεσι πι|στεύει ἢ αἴσθησις 10
ἢ τοῖς τῶν διαφώνων· ἀκριβεστάτη δ᾽ ἂν εἴη διαφώνου
20 διαστήματος λῆψις ἡ διὰ συμφωνίας. Ἐὰν μὲν οὖν προσ-
ταχθῇ πρὸς τῷ δοθέντι φθόγγῳ λαβεῖν ἐπὶ τὸ βαρὺ τὸ |
διάφωνον οἷον δίτονον ἢ ἄλλο τι τῶν δυνατῶν ληφθῆναι 15
διὰ συμφωνίας, ἐπὶ τὸ ὀξὺ ἀπὸ τοῦ δοθέντος φθόγγου λη-

1 οὐδὲν om. R   2 ὄφελος S   4 τὸ restituit Meibom
περὶ τὰς] τὰς περὶ M V B S   6 δυσὶ M V B S   ἢ] ἤτοι H
7 ὥσθ᾽ ex δθ᾽ Mx : δθ᾽ V B   8 ἢ restituit Meibom   μὴ om. et
τῷ αὐτῷ τόπῳ scrib. Marquard   9 ᾧ] τῷ H   13 ἄχριστα H
14 διαστημάτων B   συμφώνων Meibom : συμφωνιῶν codd.   15 ὅλως]
ὅλ in ras. Vb: ἄλλως M : ἁπλῶς Marquard   δοκεῖν in marg. B
ἑνὶ conieci : ἐν codd. : ἢ εἰ Marquard   16 ὡρίσθαι conieci : ὥρισται
codd.   διαφόνων S   17-19 πόλλῳ . . . διαφόνων om. R   19 τοῖς
ex τας vel ταις in ras. Mb   δ᾽ del. Marquard   20 ἢ in ras. Mb
22 δίτονον] δί in ras. Mb. fuisse vid. τι vel τε : οἷον τε τονον in marg.
B   23 ἐπὶ δὲ τὸ punctis post ἐπὶ V : δὲ scripsisse vid. Mb, eras.
Mc (?) : ἐπὶ δὲ τὸ S, B (sed punctis in marg. additis)

πτέον τὸ διὰ τεσσάρων; εἶτ' ἐπὶ τὸ βαρὺ τὸ διὰ πέντε, εἶτα
20 πάλιν ἐπὶ τὸ | ὀξὺ τὸ διὰ τεσσάρων, εἶτ' ἐπὶ τὸ βαρὺ τὸ
διὰ πέντε. καὶ οὕτως ἔσται τὸ δίτονον ἀπὸ τοῦ ληφθέντος
φθόγγου εἰλημμένον τὸ ἐπὶ τὸ βαρύ. ἐὰν δ' ἐπὶ τοὐναντίον
25 προσταχθῇ λαβεῖν τὸ διάφω|νον; ἐναντίως ποιητέον τὴν τῶν 5
συμφώνων λῆψιν. Γίγνεται δὲ καὶ ἐὰν ἀπὸ συμφώνου
διαστήματος τὸ διάφωνον ἀφαιρεθῇ διὰ συμφωνίας καὶ τὸ
30 λοιπὸν διὰ συμφωνίας εἰλημμένον· ἀφαιρείσθω | γὰρ τὸ
δίτονον ἀπὸ τοῦ διὰ τεσσάρων ⟨διὰ⟩ συμφωνίας· δῆλον δὴ
ὅτι οἱ τὴν ὑπεροχὴν περιέχοντες ᾗ τὸ διὰ τεσσάρων ὑπερέχει 10
τοῦ διτόνου διὰ συμφωνίας ἔσονται πρὸς ἀλλήλους εἰλημ-
56 μένοι· ὑπάρ||χουσι μὲν γὰρ οἱ τοῦ διὰ τεσσάρων ὅροι σύμ-
φωνοι· ἀπὸ δὲ τοῦ ὀξυτέρου αὐτῶν λαμβάνεται φθόγγος
σύμφωνος ἐπὶ τὸ ὀξὺ διὰ τεσσάρων, ἀπὸ δὲ τοῦ λη|φθέντος
5 ἕτερος ἐπὶ τὸ βαρὺ διὰ πέντε; (εἶτα πάλιν ἐπὶ τὸ ὀξὺ διὰ 15
τεσσάρων,) εἶτ' ἀπὸ τούτου ἕτερος ἐπὶ τὸ βαρὺ διὰ πέντε.
καὶ πέπτωκε τὸ τελευταῖον σύμφωνον ἐπὶ τὸν ὀξύτερον τῶν
10 ⟨τὴν⟩ ὑπεροχὴν ὁριζόντων; ὥστ' εἶναι φα|νερόν, ὅτι, ἐὰν ἀπὸ
συμφώνου διάφωνον ἀφαιρεθῇ διὰ συμφωνίας; ἔσται καὶ
τὸ λοιπὸν διὰ συμφωνίας εἰλημμένον.   20

Πότερον δ' ὀρθῶς ὑπόκειται τὸ διὰ τεσσάρων ἐν ἀρχῇ
15 δύο τόνων καὶ ἡμί|σεος, κατὰ τόνδε τὸν τρόπον ἐξετάσειεν
ἄν τις ἀκριβέστατα· εἰλήφθω γὰρ τὸ διὰ τεσσάρων καὶ πρὸς
ἑκατέρῳ τῶν ὅρων ἀφορίσθω δίτονον διὰ συμφωνίας. δῆλον
20 δὴ ὅτι ἀναγκαῖον τὰς | ὑπεροχὰς ἴσας εἶναι, ἐπειδήπερ καὶ 25

1 εἶτα] εἴτε H 2 ἐτ' ἐπὶ B : εἶτ' ἐπὶ in marg. B : εἴ τ' ἐπὶ S   τὸ
διὰ πέντε] τὸ supra lin. add. Mb   4 φθόγγος M V S   τὸ del. Meibom
7 ante ἀφαιρεθῇ una litt. eras. M : αι in ras. Mc : ε in ras. Mb
8 ἀφηρείσθω M V S : ἀφηρήσθω B R   9 τοῦ] τῆς H   διὰ restituit
Marquard   11 διτόνου] post ι litt. a eras. M : διατόνου B   12 γὰρ
om. B   ὅροι] οι in ras. Mb : ὀρθοὶ R, B in marg.   15 εἶτα . . .
τεσσάρων restituit Meibom   17 τὸν Meibom : τὸ codd.   18 τὴν
restituit Meibom   19 συμφώνους H   διάφωνον] δια in ras. Mb
24 δίτονον Meibom : σύμφωνον codd.

146

ἴσα ἀπ' ἴσων ἀφῄρηται. μετὰ δὲ τοῦτο τῷ τὸ ὀξύτερον δίτονον ἐπὶ τὸ βαρὺ ὁρίζοντι διὰ τεσσάρων εἰλήφθω ἐπὶ τὸ
ὀξύ, τῷ δὲ τὸ βαρύτερον δίτονον ἐπὶ τὸ | ὀξὺ ὁρίζοντι 25
εἰλήφθω ἕτερον διὰ τεσσάρων ἐπὶ τὸ βαρύ. φανερὸν δὴ
5 ὅτι πρὸς ἑκατέρῳ τῶν ὁριζόντων τὸ γεγονὸς σύστημα δύο
συνεχεῖς ἔσονται κείμεναι ὑπεροχαὶ ἃς ἀναγκαῖον | ἴσας 30
εἶναι διὰ τὰ ἔμπροσθεν εἰρημένα. Τούτων δ' οὕτω προκατε-
σκευασμένων τοὺς ἄκρους τῶν ὡρισμένων φθόγγων ἐπὶ τὴν
αἴσθησιν ἐπανακτέον· εἰ μὲν οὖν φανήσονται διάφωνοι,
10 δῆλον ὅτι οὐκ ἔσται τὸ διὰ τεσσάρων δύο τό||νων καὶ ἡμίσεος, 57
εἰ δὲ συμφωνήσουσι διὰ πέντε [τέσσαρα,] δῆλον ὅτι δύο
τόνων καὶ ἡμίσεος ἔσται τὸ διὰ τεσσάρων. ὁ μὲν γὰρ
βαρύτατος τῶν εἰλημμένων | φθόγγων διὰ τεσσάρων ἡρμόσθη 5
σύμφωνον τῷ τὸ βαρύτερον δίτονον ἐπὶ τὸ ὀξὺ ὁρίζοντι,
15 τὸν δ' ὀξύτατον τῶν εἰλημμένων φθόγγων διὰ πέντε συμ-
βέβηκε συμφωνεῖν τῷ βαρυτάτῳ, ὥστε | τῆς ὑπεροχῆς 10
οὔσης τονιαίας τε καὶ εἰς ἴσα διῃρημένης ὧν ἑκάτερον ἡμιτό-
νιόν τε καὶ ὑπεροχὴ [μὲν] τοῦ διὰ τεσσάρων ἐστὶν ὑπὲρ τὸ
δίτονον, δῆλον ὅτι πέντε ἡμιτονίων συμβαίνει τὸ διὰ τεσ-
20 σάρων | εἶναι. Ὅτι δ' οἱ τοῦ ληφθέντος συστήματος ἄκροι 15
οὐ συμφωνήσουσιν ἄλλην συμφωνίαν ἢ τὴν διὰ πέντε, ῥάδιον
συνιδεῖν· πρῶτον μὲν οὖν ὅτι τὴν διὰ τεσσάρων οὐ συμ-
φωνοῦσι κατανοητέον, | ἐπειδήπερ πρὸς τῷ ληφθέντι ἐξ 20
ἀρχῆς διὰ τεσσάρων ὑπεροχὴ πρόσκειται ἐφ' ἑκάτερα· ἔπειθ'
25 ὅτι τὴν διὰ πασῶν οὐκ ἐνδέχεται συμφωνίαν δεικτέον. τὸ

---

3 τὸ βαρύτερον] τὸ om. R   βαρύτερον Va R : βαρύτονον M Vb S B
διάτονον R   4 ἕτερον H : ἕτερος rell.   6 κείμεναι conieci : καὶ μὴ
ἓν αἱ codd. : καὶ μὴ μία αἱ Marquard   7 προκατασκευασμένων B :
προσκατεσκευασμένων H   8 ὁριζόντων M (sed ζόντ in ras. Mc) R H :
ὁρισμῶν Va : ὡρισμένων Vb rell.   10 δηδηλονότι B   11 συμφω-
νήσωσι M   τέσσαρα del. Marquard   15 δ'] τέσσαρα M V S B :
τέταρτον R   16 συφωνεῖν S   17 διῃρημένης ex διῃρημένην
Mc : διῃρημένην V B S   18 μὲν seclusit Marquard   19 ἡμιτονιαίων H   τεσσάρων Meibom : πέντε codd.   20 οἱ] ἢ S
25 δεικτέον Marquard : λεκτέον codd.

·γὰρ ἐκ τῶν ὑπεροχῶν γιγνόμενον μέγεθος ἔλαττόν ἐστι
25 διτόνου, ἐλάττονι | γὰρ ὑπερέχει τὸ διὰ τεσσάρων ἢ τόνῳ
τοῦ διτόνου· συγχωρεῖται ⟨γὰρ⟩ παρὰ πάντων τὸ διὰ τεσ-
σάρων μεῖζον μὲν εἶναι δύο τόνων ἔλαττον δὲ τριῶν, ὥστε |
30 πᾶν τὸ προσκείμενον τῷ διὰ τεσσάρων ἔλαττόν ἐστι τοῦ διὰ 5
πέντε· φανερὸν ⟨δὴ⟩ ὅτι τὸ συγκείμενον ἐξ αὐτῶν οὐκ ἂν
εἴη διὰ πασῶν. εἰ δὲ συμφωνοῦσιν οἱ ἄκροι τῶν ληφθέντων
58 φθόγγων μείζω μὲν || συμφωνίαν τῆς διὰ τεσσάρων ἐλάττω
δὲ τῆς διὰ πασῶν, ἀναγκαῖον αὐτοὺς διὰ πέντε σύμφωνεῖν·
τοῦτο γάρ ἐστι μόνον μέγεθος σύμφωνον μεταξὺ τοῦ διὰ | 10
5 τεσσάρων καὶ τοῦ διὰ πασῶν.

2 διτόνου] post ι una litt. eras. M   ἐλάττονι] ἔλαττον R   ὑπάρχει H
3 δίτονου ex διττόνου M c: διττόνου S   ἀλλὰ ante συγχωρεῖται ins.
Marquard   γὰρ addidi   5 τῷ] τὸ M V B S   6 δὴ restituit
Marquard : δὲ H : om. rell.   10 τούτου H   σύμφωνον] inter ν
et o una litt. et in ω acc. eras. M   τε post μεταξὺ τοῦ add. H

ΑΡΙΣΤΟΞΕΝΟΥ ΑΡΜΟΝΙΚΩΝ
ΣΤΟΙΧΕΙΩΝ Γ´

Τὰ ἐξῆς τετράχορδα ἢ συν|ῆπται ἢ διέζευκται· καλείσθω 15
δὲ συναφὴ μὲν ὅταν δύο τετραχόρδων ἐξῆς μελῳδουμένων
ὁμοίων κατὰ σχῆμα φθόγγος ᾖ ἀνὰ μέσον κοινός, διάζευξις |
δ' ὅταν δύο τετραχόρδων ἐξῆς μελῳδουμένων ὁμοίων κατὰ 20
5 σχῆμα τόνος ᾖ ἀνὰ μέσον. Ὅτι δ' ἀναγκαῖον ἕτερον πότερον
συμβαίνειν τοῖς ἐξῆς τετραχόρδοις, φανερὸν ἐκ τῶν ὑποκει-
μένων· | οἱ μὲν γὰρ τέταρτοι τῶν ἐξῆς διὰ τεσσάρων συμφω- 25
νοῦντες συναφὴν ποιήσουσιν, οἱ δὲ || πέμπτοι διὰ πέντε 59
διάζευξιν. δεῖ δ' ἕτερον πότερον τούτων ὑπάρχειν τοῖς
1 φθόγγοις, ὥστε καὶ τοῖς ἐξῆς τετραχόρδοις ἀναγκαῖον ἕτερον
τῶν εἰρημένων ὑπάρ|χειν. 5

Ἤδη δέ τις ἠπόρησε τῶν ἀκουόντων περὶ τοῦ ἐξῆς· πρῶτον
μὲν καθόλου τί ποτ' ἐστὶ τὸ ἐξῆς, ἔπειτα πότερον κατὰ ἕνα
μόνον γίγνεται τρόπον ἢ κατὰ πλείους, τρί|τον δ' εἰ ἴσως 10
15 ἀμφότερα ταῦτ' ἐστὶν ἐξῆς τά τε συνημμένα καὶ τὰ διεζευγμένα. Πρὸς δὴ ταῦτα τοιοῦτοί τινες ἐλέγοντο λόγοι·
καθόλου ταῦτα εἶναι συστήματα συνεχῆ ὧν οἱ ὅροι ἤτοι ἐξῆς

2-4 ὅταν . . . ὅταν δύο] erat ὅ τε, τ' ἀν supra lin. add., τε corr. in δύο,
et τε inscr., reliqua in marg. Mc : om. V B, R (sed 'postea alieno loco
interponuntur' v. Herwerden)   2-5 ὅτε pro ὅταν δύο leg., ἐξῆς
. . . σχῆμα om. S   5 πότερον om. H   7 τέταρτοι B : δ rell.
συμφώνων ὄντες H   9 δεῖ Meibom : τί codd.   12 τάδε post
ἐξῆς add. H   14 μόνον Mc (supra lin.), R H : ὅρον M B S   τρόπον]
τρόπ e corr. V   κατὰ om. H   δ' εἰ Marquard : δὲ codd.
16 δὴ H : δὲ rell.   τοιοῦτόν B   17 συστήματα ex συστήμα
Mb

15 εἰσὶν ἢ | ἐπαλλάττουσιν. τοῦ δ' ἑξῆς δύο τρόποι εἰσί, καὶ
ὁ μὲν ⟨καθ' ὃν τῷ τοῦ ὀξυτέρου συστήματος βαρυτέρῳ ὅρῳ
κοινός ἐστιν ὁ τοῦ βαρυτέρου συστήματος ὅρος⟩ ὀξύτερος, ὁ
δ' ἕτερος καθ' ὃν ὁ τοῦ ὀξυτέρου συστήματος βαρύτερος ὅρος
ἑξῆς ἐστὶ τῷ τοῦ βαρυτέρου συστήματος ὀξυτέρῳ ὅρῳ. κατὰ 5
20 μὲν οὖν τὸν | πρότερον τῶν τρόπων τόπου τέ τινος κοινωνεῖ
τὰ τῶν ἑξῆς τετραχόρδων συστήματα καὶ ὁμοιά ἐστιν ἐξ
ἀνάγκης, κατὰ δὲ τὸν ἕτερον κεχώρισται ἀπ' ἀλλήλων καὶ
25 ὅμοια δύναται γί|γνεσθαι τὰ εἴδη τῶν τετραχόρδων· τοῦτο δὲ
γίγνεται τόνου ἀνὰ μέσον τεθέντος, ἄλλως δ' οὔ, ὥστε δύο 10
τετράχορδα ὅμοια τοιαῦτα συμβαίνειν ἑξῆς ἀλλήλων εἶναι
30 ὧν ἤτοι τόνος ἀνὰ | μέσον ἐστὶν ἢ οἱ ὅροι ἐπαλλάττουσιν.
ὥστε τὰ ἑξῆς τετράχορδα ὅμοια ὄντα ἢ συνημμένα ἀναγκαῖον
εἶναι ἢ διεζευγμένα. Φαμὲν δὲ δεῖν τῶν ἑξῆς τετραχόρδων
60 ἤτοι ἁπλῶς μηδὲν εἶ||ναι ἀνὰ μέσον τετράχορδον ἢ μὴ 15
ἀνόμοιον. τῶν μὲν οὖν ὁμοίων κατ' εἶδος τετραχόρδων οὐ
τίθεται ἀνόμοιον ἀνὰ μέσον τετράχορδον, τῶν δ' ἀνομοίων
5 μὲν | ἑξῆς δ' οὐδὲν τίθεσθαι δυνατὸν ἀνὰ μέσον τετράχορδον.
Ἐκ δὲ τῶν εἰρημένων φανερὸν ὅτι τὰ ὅμοια κατ' εἶδος
τετράχορδα κατὰ δύο τρόπους τοὺς εἰρημένους ἑξῆς ἀλλήλων 20
τεθήσεται. |
10 Ἀσύνθετον δ' ἐστὶ διάστημα τὸ ὑπὸ τῶν ἑξῆς φθόγγων
περιεχόμενον. εἰ γὰρ ἑξῆς οἱ περιέχοντες, οὐδεὶς ἐκλιμπάνει,
μὴ ἐκλιμπάνων δ' οὐκ ἐμπεσεῖται, μὴ ἐμπίπτων δ' οὐ διαι-
15 ρήσει, ὁ δὲ μὴ διαίρεσιν ἔχει οὐδὲ σύνθεσιν | ἕξει· πᾶν γὰρ 25

1 εἰσὶν in ras. Ma : om. V B S   ἐπαλλάττουσιν ex ἐπελαττοῦσιν Mb
(ut vid.)   2 καθ' ... ὅρος restituit Meibom   3 ὀξύτερον B
4 ὀξυτέρου om. B   6 τρόπων Marquard : ὁρῶν B : ὁρῶν rell.
κοινωνοῦσιν H   7 ὁμοιά Meibom : ἀνόμοια codd.   ἐστιν om. H
11 ante ὅμοια 2 litt. eras. M   τοιαῦτα Marquard : ταῦτα codd.
συμβαίνει B   13 ἢ] ἤτοι H   15 ἢ μὴ Meibom : εἰ μὴ εἰ μὴ B :
εἰ μὴ rell.   16 ἀνόμοιον Meibom : ὅμοιον codd.   17 τίθεσθαι H
ἀνόμοιον Meibom : ὅμοιον codd.   17 τῶν δ' ... τετράχορδον
om. R   18 τίθεσθαι ex τίθεται Mc : τίθεται rell.   19 δὲ] δὴ H
22 διαστήματα R   25 διαίρεσιν ex διαίρησιν vel vice versa M
ἕξει] ἐξ B

τὸ σύνθετον ἔκ τινων μερῶν ἐστὶ σύνθετον εἰς ἅπερ καὶ
διαιρετόν. Γίγνεται δὲ καὶ περὶ τοῦτο τὸ πρόβλημα πλάνη
διὰ τὴν τῶν μεγεθῶν κοινότητα τοιάδε τις· θαυμάζουσι γὰρ |
πῶς ποτε τὸ δίτονον ἀσύνθετον ὅ γ᾽ ἐστὶ δυνατὸν διελεῖν εἰς 20
5 τόνους ἢ πῶς πάλιν ποτ᾽ ἐστὶν ὁ τόνος ἀσύνθετος ὄν γ᾽ ἐστὶ
δυνατὸν εἰς δύο ἡμιτόνια διελεῖν· τὸν αὐτὸν δὲ λόγον λέγουσι
καὶ | περὶ τοῦ ἡμιτονίου. Γίγνεται δ᾽ αὐτοῖς ἡ ἄγνοια παρὰ 25
τὸ μὴ συνορᾶν ὅτι τῶν διαστηματικῶν μεγεθῶν ἔνια κοινὰ
τυγχάνει ὄντα συνθέτου τε καὶ ἀσυνθέτου διαστήματος· διὰ
10 γὰρ ταύτην τὴν | αἰτίαν οὐ μεγέθει διαστήματος τὸ ἀσύνθετον 30
ἀλλὰ τοῖς περιέχουσι φθόγγοις ἀφώρισται. τὸ γὰρ δίτονον
ὅταν μὲν ὁρίζωσι μέση καὶ λιχανός, ἀσύνθετόν ἐστιν, ὅταν
δὲ μέση καὶ παρυπάτη, σύν||θετον· δι᾽ ὅπερ φαμὲν οὐκ ἐν 61
τοῖς μεγέθεσι τῶν διαστημάτων εἶναι τὸ ἀσύνθετον ἀλλ᾽ ἐν
15 τοῖς περιέχουσι φθόγγοις. |

Ἐν δὲ ταῖς τῶν γενῶν διαφοραῖς τὰ τοῦ διὰ τεσσάρων μέρη 5
μόνα κινεῖται, [τὸ δ᾽ ἴδιον τῆς διαζεύξεως ἀκίνητόν ἐστιν.]
πᾶν μὲν γὰρ διῄρητο τὸ ἡρμοσμένον εἰς συναφήν τε καὶ
διάζευξιν, ὅ γε συνέστηκεν | ἐκ πλειόνων ἢ ἑνὸς τετραχόρδου. 10
20 Ἀλλ᾽ ἡ μὲν συναφὴ ἐκ (τῶν τοῦ διὰ) τεσσάρων μερῶν
μόνων [ἀσυνθέτων] σύγκειται, ὥστ᾽ ἐξ ἀνάγκης ἕν γε ταύτῃ
τὰ τοῦ διὰ τεσσάρων μόνα μέρη κινηθήσεται· ἡ δὲ διάζευξις |
ἴδιον ἔχει παρὰ ταῦτα τὸν τόνον. ἐὰν οὖν δειχθῇ τὸ ἴδιον 15

1 post καὶ ras. M   2 ἀδιαίρετον V S   δὲ Marquard : δὴ codd.
4 πώποτε H   ἀσύνθετ ον Ma, sed ον supra θετ et acc. et spir. add.
Mc   δ γ᾽ conieci : om. V S B : ὄν rell.   5 πῶς post πάλιν
ponit H   πάλιν] ιν ras. in Mc : πάλαι V S   6 ἐστὶν post δυνατὸν
ponit H   δὲ Marquard : δὴ S : δὲ δὴ rell.   12 ὁρίζουσι B
13 post σύνθετον in unc. quad. ἀλλ᾽ ἐν τοῖς περιέχουσι φθόγγοις S
17 τὸ δ᾽ . . . ἐστιν seclusi   19 post Marquard ʻ post ὃ una litt.
eras. quae ν fuisse vid. M᾽ : sed ego quidem γε fuisse suspicor.
Quod si legitur, tum certe verborum translatione nulla opus est :
neque, si omittitur, ordinem librorum mutare velim   verba ὃ . . .
τετραχόρδου post ἡρμοσμένον ponit Meibom   20 τῶν τοῦ διὰ addidit
Westphal   21 μόνον H   ἀσυνθέτων seclusi   23 ἔχει
Meibom : ἔχοι codd.   παρὰ ταῦτα] παρὰ post ταῦτα eras. et supra
lin. add. Mc   ταῦτα παρὰ V B S   τὸ supra lin. add. Mb (?)

τῆς διαζεύξεως μὴ κινούμενον ἐν ταῖς τῶν γενῶν διαφοραῖς,
δῆλον ὅτι λείπεται ἐν αὐτοῖς τοῖς τοῦ διὰ τεσσάρων μέρεσι
20 τὴν κίνησιν εἶναι. Ἔστι δ' ὁ | μὲν βαρύτερος τῶν ⟨τὸν⟩
τόνον περιεχόντων ὀξύτερος τῶν τὸ τετράχορδον περιεχόντων
τὸ βαρύτερον τῶν ἐν τῇ διαζεύξει κειμένων· [ὁμοίως δ'] ἦν 5
⟨δ'⟩ [καὶ] οὗτος ἀκίνητος ἐν ταῖς τῶν γενῶν διαφοραῖς· ὁ δ' |
25 ὀξύτερος τῶν ⟨τὸν⟩ τόνον περιεχόντων βαρύτερος τῶν τὸ
τετράχορδον περιεχόντων τὸ ὀξύτερον τῶν ἐν τῇ διαζεύξει
κειμένων· ὁμοίως δ' ἦν καὶ οὗτος ἀκίνητος ἐν ταῖς τῶν γενῶν
30 διαφοραῖς. Ὥστ' ἐπειδὴ | φανερὸν ὅτι οἱ τὸν τόνον περιέ- 10
χοντες ἀκίνητοί εἰσιν ἐν ταῖς τῶν γενῶν διαφοραῖς, δῆλον ὅτι
λείποιτ' ἂν αὐτὰ τὰ τοῦ διὰ τεσσάρων μέρη μόνα κινεῖσθαι
ἐν ταῖς εἰρημέναις διαφοραῖς. ||

62 Ἐν ἑκάστῳ δὲ γένει τοσαῦτά ἐστιν ἀσύνθετα ⟨τὰ⟩ πλεῖστα
ὅσα ἐν τῷ διὰ πέντε. Πᾶν μὲν γὰρ γένος ἤτοι ἐν συναφῇ 15
5 μελῳδεῖται ἢ ἐν διαζεύξει, καθάπερ | ἔμπροσθεν εἴρηται.
δέδεικται δ' ἡ μὲν συναφὴ ἐκ τῶν τοῦ διὰ τεσσάρων μερῶν
μόνων συγκειμένη, ἡ δὲ διάζευξις ἐν προστιθεῖσα τὸ ἴδιον
10 διάστημα, τοῦτο δ' ἐστὶν ὁ τόνος· προστεθέντος δὲ | τοῦ
τόνου πρὸς τὰ τοῦ διὰ τεσσάρων μέρη τὸ διὰ πέντε συμ- 20
πληροῦται. Ὥστ' εἶναι φανερὸν ὅτι, ἐπειδήπερ οὐδὲν τῶν
γενῶν ἐνδέχεται κατὰ μίαν χρόαν λαμβανόμενον ἐκ πλειόνων
15 ἀσυνθέτων συντε|θῆναι τῶν ἐν τῷ διὰ πέντε ὄντων, [δῆλον

2 τοῖς om. VBS · 3 τὸν restituit Marquard   4 τόνων
BR ·   5 περιεχόντων post βαρύτερον ponit H   ὁμοίως δ' et καὶ
seclusit, et δ' addidit Westphal   7 τὸν restituit Marquard
βαρύτερος . . . περιεχόντων in marg. Mc: om. VB : τόνον περιεχόντων
τὸ τὸ βαρύτερον ὀξύτερον τῶν ἐν τῇ δ. S   8 περιεχόντων
post τὸ ὀξύτερον ponit H   ὀξύτερον ex βαρύτερον Mb : βαρύτερον B
10-13 ὥστ' . . . εἰρημέναις διαφοραῖς om. R   10 ὅτι supra lin. add.
Mc: om. VBS   12 λείποιτ'] εἴποιτ' R   κινεῖται B   14 τὰ
addidi   16 ἔμπροσθεν om., et πρότερον post εἴρηται add. H
18 μόνων Meibom : μόνῃ codd.   ἐν προστιθεῖσα conieci: ἔμπροσθεν
τεθεῖσα codd. : προστιθεῖσα Marquard   22 λαμβάνομεν B in
marg.   23 ἐν τῷ ex ἐκ τῶν M : ἐκ τῶν VSB   δῆλον ὅτι seclusit
Marquard

ὅτι] ἐν ἑκάστῳ γένει τοσαῦτα ἔσται τὰ πλεῖστα ἀσύνθετα ὅσα
ἐν τῷ διὰ πέντε.

    Ταράττειν δ᾽ εἴωθεν ἐνίους καὶ ἐν τούτῳ τῷ προβλήματι
πῶς τὰ πλεῖστα | προστίθεται καὶ διὰ τί οὐχ ἁπλῶς δείκνυται, 20
5 ὅτι ἐκ τοσούτων ἀσυνθέτων ἕκαστον τῶν γενῶν συνέστηκεν
ὅσα ἐστὶν ἐν τῷ διὰ πέντε.   Πρὸς οὓς ταῦτα λέγεται, ὅτι
ἐξ ἐλαττόνων ἀσυνθέτων ἔσται ποθ᾽ ἕκα|στον τῶν γενῶν 25
συγκείμενον ἐκ πλειόνων δ᾽ οὐδέποτε.   Διὰ ταύτην δὲ τὴν
αἰτίαν τοῦτο αὐτὸ πρῶτον ἀποδείκνυται, ὅτι οὐκ ἐνδέχεται ἐκ
10 πλειόνων ἀσυνθέτων συντεθῆναι τῶν γε|νῶν ἕκαστον ἢ ὅσα ἐν 30
τῷ διὰ πέντε τυγχάνει ὄντα.   ὅτι δὲ καὶ ἐξ ἐλαττόνων ποτὲ
συντεθήσεται ἕκαστον αὐτῶν, ἐν τοῖς ἔπειτα δείκνυται.

    Πυκνὸν δὲ πρὸς πυκνῷ οὐ μελῳδεῖ||ται οὔθ᾽ ὅλον οὔτε 63
μέρος αὐτοῦ.   Συμβήσεται γὰρ μήτε τοὺς τετάρτους τῷ διὰ
15 τεσσάρων συμφωνεῖν μήτε τοὺς πέμπτους τῷ διὰ πέντε· οἱ
δὲ οὕτω κείμενοι | τῶν φθόγγων ἐκμελεῖς ἦσαν.   τῶν δὲ τὸ 5
δίτονον περιεχόντων ὁ μὲν βαρύτερος ὀξύτατός ἐστι πυκνοῦ
ὁ δ᾽ ὀξύτερος βαρύτατος· ἀναγκαῖον γὰρ ἐν τῇ συναφῇ τῶν
πυκνῶν διὰ τεσσάρων συμ|φωνούντων ἀνὰ μέσον αὐτῶν 10
20 κεῖσθαι τὸ δίτονον, ὡσαύτως δὲ καὶ τῶν διτόνων διὰ
τεσσάρων συμφωνούντων ἀναγκαῖον ἐν μέσῳ κεῖσθαι τὸ

1 συνθετά R   ὅσα ἐν τῷ om. R   3 εἴωθεν] γ postea add. M
4 πῶς in marg. Mb   5 συγκείμενόν ἐστιν ante ἕκαστον add., et
συνέστηκεν om. H   7 ἔσται ποθ᾽ om. R: ἔσται ποθ᾽ ἕκαστον om. V
ἐστὶ post γενῶν add. R, Mc (supra lin.) · post γενῶν add. συνεστηκὸς
ὅσα ἐστὶν ἐν τῷ διὰ πέντε. πρὸς οὓς λέγεται ὅτι ἐξ ἐλαττόνων ἀσυνθέτων
τῶν γενῶν S B Vb in marg., nisi quod συνεστηκός om. Vb, τῶν γενῶν
om. Vb, τῶν om. S   10 ἢ eras. M : om. V S B H   14 τετάρτους
Marquard : δ᾽ in marg. Mc, S : om. Va : τέσσαρας rell.   τῷ] τὸ H :
post τω litt. γ eras. M : τῶν V B   15 πέμπτους Marquard : πέντε
codd.   τῷ add. Mc : om. V S   οἱ δὲ] οὐδ᾽ H   16 post
οὕτω litt. σ eras. M   ἐκμελεῖς ex ἐμμελεῖς Mc : ἐμμελεῖς V B S
17 βαρύτερος Marquard : βαρύτατος codd.   ὀξύτατος . . . βαρύτατος
om. R   18 βαρύτερος B, sed in marg. βαρύτατος   20 κεῖσθαι
om., et εἶναι post δίτονον add. H   τὸ] τὸν V S   δὲ om. S   post
καὶ add. ἐν τῇ συναφῇ in marg. Mc, τῇ συναφῇ R   τὸ ante διὰ τεσσάρων
add. H   21 post τὸ litt. γ eras. M : τὸν V S B

15 πυκνόν· τούτων δ' οὕτως ἐχόντων ἀναγκαῖον | ἐναλλὰξ τό τε
πυκνὸν καὶ τὸ δίτονον κεῖσθαι, ὥστε δῆλον ὅτι ὁ μὲν βαρύτερος τῶν περιεχόντων τὸ δίτονον ὀξύτατος ἔσται τοῦ ἐπὶ τὸ
20 βαρὺ κειμένου πυκνοῦ, ὁ δ' ὀξύτερος τοῦ ἐπὶ τὸ ὀξὺ | κειμένου
πυκνοῦ βαρύτατος· οἱ δὲ τὸν τόνον περιέχοντες ἀμφότεροι 5
εἰσι πυκνοῦ βαρύτατοι, τίθεται γὰρ ὁ τόνος ἐν τῇ διαζεύξει
μεταξὺ τοιούτων τετραχόρδων ἃ οἱ περιέχοντες βαρύτατοί
25 εἰσι | πυκνοῦ· ὑπὸ τούτων δὲ καὶ ὁ τόνος περιέχεται. ὁ μὲν
γὰρ βαρύτερος τῶν ⟨τὸν⟩ τόνον περιεχόντων ὀξύτερός ἐστι τῶν
τὸ βαρύτερον τῶν τετραχόρδων περιεχόντων, ὁ δὲ ὀξύτερος 10
30 τῶν ⟨τὸν⟩ τόνον περιεχόντων βα|ρύτερός ἐστι τῶν τὸ ὀξύτερον
τῶν τετραχόρδων περιεχόντων, ὥστ' εἶναι δῆλον ὅτι οἱ τὸν
τόνον περιέχοντες βαρύτατοι ἔσονται πυκνοῦ.

64   Δύο δὲ δίτονα ἐξῆς οὐ τεθήσεται. Τιθέ||σθω γάρ· ἀκο-
λουθήσει δὴ τῷ μὲν ὀξυτέρῳ διτόνῳ πυκνὸν ἐπὶ τὸ βαρύ, 15
ὀξύτατος γὰρ ἦν πυκνοῦ ὁ ἐπὶ τὸ βαρὺ ὁρίζων τὸ δίτονον·
5 τῷ δὲ βαρυτέρῳ δι|τόνῳ ἐπὶ τὸ ὀξὺ ἀκολουθήσει πυκνόν,
βαρύτατος γὰρ ἦν πυκνοῦ ὁ ἐπὶ τὸ ὀξὺ ὁρίζων τὸ δίτονον.
Τούτου δὲ συμβαίνοντος δύο πυκνὰ ἐξῆς τεθήσεται· τούτου
10 δὲ ἐκμελοῦς ὄντος ἐκμελὲς ἔσται | καὶ τὰ δύο δίτονα ἐξῆς 20
τίθεσθαι.

    Ἐν ἁρμονίᾳ δὲ καὶ χρώματι δύο τονιαῖα ἐξῆς οὐ τεθήσεται.
Τιθέσθω γὰρ ἐπὶ τὸ ὀξὺ πρῶτον· ἀναγκαῖον δὴ εἴπερ ἐστὶν

1 ἐναλλάξ] acc. add. et postea 2 litt. eras. Mc : ἐναλλάξαι VBS (sed
ἐναλλάξ in marg. B)   2 βαρύτερος Marquard : βαρύτατος codd.
4 τοῦ ἐπὶ τὸ ὀξὺ κειμένου πυκνοῦ in marg. Mc : om. VSB   5 πυκνοῦ
om. R   βαρύτατος Marquard : βαρύτερος codd.   οἱ] ὁ B
7 τοιοῦτον B   ἃ Ma, sed ὧν suprascr. Mc : ὧν R   περιέχοντες
ex περισχόντες Mc   9 βαρύτερος Marquard : βαρύτατος codd.
τὸν restituit Marquard   τόνων R   περιεχόντων om. R   10 τὸ
supra lin. add. B : om. S   βαρύτερον Marquard : βαρύτατον codd.
τῶν τετραχόρδων] τῶν supra lin. add. Mx : om. VS   11 τὸν
restituit Marquard (legit H)   12 τῶν τετ.] τῶν supra lin. add.
Mx : om. Va S   14 δίτονα] post ι litt. a eras. M : διάτονα VBS
18 διορίζων R   20 ἐκμελέσθαι supra ε acc. eras., τ suprascr. et
in marg. ἐκμελὲς ἔσται add. Mc : ἐκμελὲς ἔσται (ἐς ἔστ e corr.) Vb
καὶ om. H   διάτονα MVS   22 ἐναρμόνια S   23 δὴ] δὲ VSB

ἐμμελὴς ὁ τὸν προστεθέντα τόνον | ὁρίζων φθόγγος ἐπὶ τὸ 15
ὀξὺ συμφωνεῖν ἤτοι τῷ τετάρτῳ τῶν ἑξῆς διὰ τεσσάρων ἢ
τῷ πέμπτῳ διὰ πέντε· μηδετέρου (δὲ) τούτων αὐτῷ συμ-
βαίνοντος ἀναγκαῖον ἐκμελῆ εἶναι.　ὅτι δ’ οὐ συμ|βήσεται 20
5 φανερόν· ἐναρμόνιος μὲν γὰρ οὖσα ἡ λιχανὸς τέσσαρας
τόνους ἀπὸ τοῦ προσληφθέντος ἀφέξει φθόγγος τέταρτος ὤν,
χρωματικὴ δ’ εἴτε μαλακοῦ χρώματος εἴθ’ ἡμιολίου μεῖ|ζον 25
ἀφέξει διάστημα τοῦ διὰ πέντε, τονιαίου δὲ γενομένη διὰ
πέντε συμφωνήσει τῷ προσληφθέντι φθόγγῳ.　οὐκ ἔδει δέ
10 γε, ἀλλὰ ἤτοι τὸν τέταρτον διὰ τεσσάρων συμφωνεῖν ἢ τὸν
πέμπτον διὰ πέν|τε.　Τούτων δ’ οὐδέτερον γίγνεται, ὥστε 30
φανερόν, ὅτι ἐκμελὴς ἔσται ὁ τὸν προσληφθέντα τόνον ὁρίζων
φθόγγος ἐπὶ τὸ ὀξύ.　Ἐπὶ δὲ τὸ βαρὺ τιθέμενον τὸ δεύτερον
τονιαῖον διάτονον ποιήσει τὸ || γένος, ὥστε δῆλον ὅτι ἐν 65
15 ἁρμονίᾳ καὶ χρώματι οὐ τεθήσεται δύο τονιαῖα ἑξῆς.　Ἐν
διατόνῳ δὲ τρία τονιαῖα ἑξῆς τεθήσεται, πλείω ·δ’ οὔ· ὁ γὰρ
τὸ τέταρτον | τονιαῖον ὁρίζων φθόγγος οὔτε τῷ τετάρτῳ διὰ 5
τεσσάρων οὔτε τῷ πέμπτῳ διὰ πέντε συμφωνήσει.

　　Ἐν τῷ αὐτῷ δὲ γένει τούτῳ δύο ἡμιτονιαῖα ἑξῆς οὐ τε-
20 θήσεται.　Τιθέσθω γὰρ | πρῶτον ἐπὶ τὸ βαρὺ τοῦ ὑπάρχον- 10
τος ἡμιτονίου τὸ προστεθὲν ἡμιτόνιον· συμβαίνει δὴ τὸν
ὁρίζοντα φθόγγον τὸ προστεθὲν ἡμιτόνιον μήτε τῷ τετάρτῳ
διὰ τεσσάρων συμφωνεῖν μήτε τῷ πέμ|πτῳ διὰ πέντε.　οὕτω 15

---

1 ἐμμελὴς ex ἐκμελὴς Mc: ἐκμελὴς V S, B (sed in marg. ἐμμελὴς)
3 τῶν ante διὰ πέντε add. R　　μηδ’ ἑτέρω τούτο ex μηδ’ ἑτέρω τούτω
M : μηδ’ ἑτέρῳ τούτῳ V S B　　δὲ restituit Marquard　　αὐτῶν ex
αὐτῷ Mc　　αὐτῷ post συμβαίνοντος ponit H　　6 ἀφέξει B (sed
ἀφέξει in marg.)　　10 ἀλλ’ ἤτοι ex ἄλλα τοι deinde 2 litt. eras. Mc :
ἀλλὰ τοιοῦτο V B S : ἀλλὰ τὸν in marg. B　　τέταρτον] δ’ S　　11 δὲ
in marg. Mc : om. V B S　　13 ἐπὶ τὸ ὀξὺ ἐπὶ τὸ ὀξὺ (cum punctis
sub ἐπὶ τὸ ὀξὺ altero) B　　δεύτερον τονιαῖον Ma, sed β supra δεύτερον
et α supra τονιαῖον add. Mc　　17 τὸ om. H　　19 ἡμιτονιαῖα]
τονιαῖα V S B et Ma, sed ημι supra lin. add. Mc　　τίθεται in marg.
B, R　　21 ἡμιτοναίου B　　δὴ H: δὲ rell.　　22 τὸ
supra lin. add. Mc: om. V B S　　23 συμφωνεῖν post διὰ πέντε
ponit H

μὲν οὖν ἐκμελὴς ἔσται τοῦ ἡμιτονιαίου ἡ θέσις. ἐὰν δ᾽ ἐπὶ
τὸ ὀξὺ τεθῇ τοῦ ὑπάρχοντος, χρῶμα ἔσται, ὥστε δῆλον ὅτι
ἐν διατόνῳ δύο ἡμιτονιαῖα οὐ τεθήσεται ἑξῆς.—Ποῖα μὲν |
20 οὖν τῶν ἀσυνθέτων δύναται ἴσα ἑξῆς τίθεσθαι καὶ πόσα τὸν
ἀριθμὸν καὶ ποῖα τοὐναντίον πέπονθεν ἁπλῶς οὐ δυνάμενα 5
τίθεσθαι ἴσα ὄντα ἑξῆς, δέδεικται· περὶ δὲ τῶν ἀνίσων νῦν
λεκτέον. |
25   Πυκνὸν μὲν οὖν πρὸς διτόνῳ καὶ ἐπὶ τὸ βαρὺ καὶ ἐπὶ τὸ
ὀξὺ τίθεται. Δέδεικται γὰρ ἐν τῇ συναφῇ ἐναλλὰξ τιθέμενα
ταῦτα τὰ διαστήματα, ὥστε δῆλον ὅτι ἑκάτερον ἑκατέρου 10
30 καὶ ἐπὶ τὸ βαρὺ καὶ | ἐπὶ τὸ ὀξὺ τεθήσεται.

     Τόνος δὲ πρὸς διτόνῳ ἐπὶ τὸ ὀξὺ μόνον τίθεται. Τι-
θέσθω γὰρ ἐπὶ τὸ βαρύ· συμβήσεται δὴ πίπτειν ἐπὶ τὴν
·66 αὐτὴν τάσιν ὀξύτα||τόν τε πυκνοῦ καὶ βαρύτατον, ὁ μὲν γὰρ
τὸ δίτονον ἐπὶ τὸ βαρὺ ὁρίζων ὀξύτατος ἦν πυκνοῦ, ὁ δὲ τὸν 15
5 τόνον ἐπὶ τὸ ὀξὺ βαρύτατος. τούτων δὲ πιπτόντων | ἐπὶ
. τὴν αὐτὴν τάσιν ἀναγκαῖον δύο πυκνὰ τίθεσθαι. τούτου δ᾽
ἐκμελοῦς ὄντος ἀναγκαῖον καὶ τόνον ἐπὶ τὸ βαρὺ διτονιαίου
ἐκμελῆ εἶναι.

10   Τόνος δὲ πρὸς πυκνῷ ἐπὶ τὸ βαρὺ | μόνον τίθεται. Τι- 20
θέσθω γὰρ ἐπὶ τοὐναντίον· συμβήσεται δὴ τὸ αὐτὸ πάλιν
ἀδύνατον, ἐπὶ γὰρ τὴν αὐτὴν τάσιν ὀξύτατός τε πυκνοῦ
πεσεῖται καὶ βαρύτατος, ὥστε δύο πυκνὰ τίθεσθαι ἑξῆς.
15 τού|του δ᾽ ὄντος ἐκμελοῦς ἀναγκαῖον καὶ τὴν τόνου θέσιν
τὴν ἐπὶ τὸ ὀξὺ τοῦ πυκνοῦ ἐκμελῆ εἶναι.   · 25

1 ἐμμελὴς M V B   τοῦ ἡμιτονιαίου post ἡ ponit H   5 δυνάμενα
M H : δυνάμεθα rell.   6 δὲ om. R   8 τὸ βαρὺ] τὸ supra lin.
add Mc(?): om. S   καὶ ἐπὶ τὸ βαρὺ post καὶ ἐπὶ τὸ ὀξὺ ponit H
10 ὅτι H : om. rell.   12 τῷ ante διτόνῳ add. R   13 τὸ om. B
συμβήσεται] βήσεται in ras. Ma   15 ὁρίζω S   17 αὐτὴν supra
lin. add. B   πυκνὰ B   18 τόνον Meibom : τοῦτον codd.
διτονιαίου ἐκμελῆ ex διτοναῖον ἐκμελὴς Mc : διτοναῖον ἐκμελὴς V S B
21 ἐπὶ supra lin. add. B   τὸ αὐτὸ post πάλιν ponit H   22 αὐτὴν
in marg. add. B   πεσεῖται post βαρύτατος ponit H   24 τόνον
Meibom : τούτου codd.

Ἐν διατόνῳ δὲ τόνου ἐφ᾽ ἑκάτερα ἡμιτόνιον οὐ μελῳδεῖται.
Συμβήσεται γὰρ | μήτε τοὺς τετάρτους τῶν ἑξῆς διὰ τεσσάρων 20
συμφωνεῖν μήτε τοὺς πέμπτους διὰ πέντε.   Δύο δὲ τόνων
ἢ τριῶν ἡμιτόνιον ἐφ᾽ ἑκάτερα μελῳδεῖται· συμφωνήσουσι
5 γὰρ ἢ οἱ τέταρτοι διὰ τεσσά|ρων ἢ οἱ πέμπτοι διὰ πέντε.   25
    [Ἀπὸ ἡμιτονίου μὲν ἐπὶ τὸ ὀξὺ δύο ὁδοὶ καὶ ἐπὶ τὸ βαρὺ
δύο,] ἀπὸ δὲ τοῦ διτόνου δύο μὲν ἐπὶ τὸ ὀξύ, μία δ᾽ ἐπὶ τὸ
βαρύ.   Δέδεικται γὰρ ἐπὶ μὲν τὸ | ὀξὺ πυκνὸν τεθειμένον 30
καὶ τόνος, πλείους δὲ τούτων οὐκ ἔσονται ὁδοὶ ἀπὸ τοῦ
10 εἰρημένου διαστήματος ἐπὶ τὸ ὀξύ· [ἐπὶ δὲ τὸ βαρὺ πυκνὸν
μόνον,] λείπεται μὲν γὰρ τῶν ἀσυνθέτων τὸ δίτονον μόνον· ||
δύο δὲ δίτονα ἑξῆς οὐκέτι τίθεται.   ὥστε δῆλον ὅτι δύο μόναι 67
ὁδοὶ ἔσονται ἀπὸ τοῦ διτόνου ἐπὶ τὸ ὀξύ· ἐπὶ δὲ τὸ βαρὺ μία·
δέδεικται γάρ, ὅτι οὔτε δίτονον | πρὸς διτόνῳ τεθήσεται οὔτε 5
15 τόνος ἐπὶ τὸ βαρὺ διτόνου, ὥστε λείπεται τὸ πυκνόν.   φανερὸν
δὴ ὅτι ἀπὸ διτόνου ἐπὶ μὲν τὸ ὀξὺ δύο ὁδοί, ἡ μὲν ἐπὶ τὸν τόνον
ἡ δ᾽ ἐπὶ τὸ πυκνόν, ἐπὶ δὲ τὸ βαρὺ μία, ἡ ἐπὶ | τὸ πυκνόν.   10
    Ἀπὸ πυκνοῦ δ᾽ ἐναντίως ἐπὶ μὲν τὸ βαρὺ δύο ὁδοί, ἐπὶ
δὲ τὸ ὀξὺ μία.   Δέδεικται γὰρ ἀπὸ πυκνοῦ ἐπὶ τὸ βαρὺ δί-
20 τονον τεθειμένον καὶ τόνος· τρίτη δ᾽ οὐκ | ἔσται ὁδός, 15
λείπεται μὲν γὰρ τῶν ἀσυνθέτων τὸ πυκνόν, δύο δὲ πυκνὰ
ἑξῆς οὐ τίθεται, ὥστε δῆλον ὅτι μόναι δύο ὁδοὶ ἔσονται ἀπὸ

1 διατόνου M V B S   τόνου Meibom: τόνῳ codd.   2 συμβήσεται
Marquard: συμπεσεῖται codd.   3 συμφωνεῖν in marg. add. B   τῶν
ἑξῆς post πέμπτους add. H   5 prius ἢ] ἤτοι H   διὰ τεσσάρων ex
διὰ τετάρτου Mc: διὰ τετάρτου V S B   6 Ἀπὸ ... δύο seclusi
μὲν] οὐ μὲν S   δύο ὁδοὶ ex δύο δ᾽ οἱ Mc: δύο δ᾽ οἱ V S B   καὶ in
marg. Mc   καὶ ἐπὶ τὸ βαρὺ ... μία δ᾽ om. V S B   7 ἀπὸ δὲ τοῦ
διτόνου ... ἐπὶ τὸ βαρὺ in marg. Mc   8 διὸ ante δέδεικται add.
Vb S B   γὰρ add. Mc: om. V S B   τεθειμένον] τέθηται R:
τιθέμενον H   10 ἐπὶ ... μόνον supra lin. in marg. superiori
add. Mc: om. V B S   11 δίτονον (post ι litt. α eras.) M: διάτονον V B S   13 al ante ὁδοὶ add. H   14 ὅτι οὔτε] ὅτι
οὐδὲν H: ὅτι οὐδὲ M V B S   15 φανερὸν δὴ Marquard: εὗρον
δὲ codd.   17 μίαν M V B S   19 πυκνοῦ ex ὀξὺ Mc: ὀξὺ V B S
20 τιθέμενον H   22 οὐ τίθεται ... βαρύ. ἐπὶ om. R   δύο post
ὁδοὶ ponit S   ὁδοὶ post ἔσονται ponit H

πυκνοῦ ἐπὶ τὸ βαρύ. ἐπὶ δὲ τὸ ὀξὺ μία ⟨ἡ⟩ ἐπὶ τὸ δίτονον·
20 οὔτε γὰρ | πυκνὸν πρὸς πυκνῷ τίθεται οὔτε τόνος ἐπὶ τὸ
ὀξὺ πυκνοῦ, ὥστε λείπεται τὸ δίτονον. Φανερὸν δὴ ὅτι ἀπὸ
πυκνοῦ ἐπὶ μὲν τὸ βαρὺ δύο ὁδοί, ἥ τε ἐπὶ ⟨τὸν⟩ τόνον καὶ
25 ἡ ἐπὶ τὸ δίτονον, ἐπὶ δὲ τὸ ὀξὺ μία, | ἡ ἐπὶ τὸ δίτονον.

'Απὸ δὲ τόνου μία ἐφ' ἑκάτερα ὁδός, ἐπὶ μὲν τὸ βαρὺ
ἐπὶ τὸ δίτονον ἐπὶ δὲ τὸ ὀξὺ ἐπὶ τὸ πυκνόν. 'Επὶ μὲν
30 τὸ βαρὺ δέδεικται ὅτι οὔτε τόνος τίθεται | οὔτε πυκνόν,
ὥστε λείπεται τὸ δίτονον· ἐπὶ δὲ τὸ ὀξὺ δέδεικται ὅτι οὔτε
τόνος τίθεται οὔτε δίτονον, ὥστε λείπεται τὸ πυκνόν. Φανε- 10
ρὸν δὴ ὅτι ἀπὸ τόνου μία ἐφ' ἑκάτερα ὁδός, ἐπὶ μὲν τὸ βαρὺ
68 ἐπὶ τὸ δίτονον, ‖ ἐπὶ δὲ τὸ ὀξὺ ἐπὶ τὸ πυκνόν.

'Ομοίως δ' ἕξει καὶ ἐπὶ τῶν χρωμάτων πλὴν τό γε μέσης
5 καὶ λιχανοῦ διάστημα μεταλαμβάνεται ἀντὶ διτόνου τὸ | γι-
γνόμενον καθ' ἑκάστην χρόαν κατὰ τὸ τοῦ πυκνοῦ μέγεθος. 15
'Ομοίως δ' ἕξει καὶ ἐπὶ τῶν διατόνων· ἀπὸ γὰρ τοῦ κοινοῦ
τόνου τῶν γενῶν μία ἔσται ἐφ' ἑκάτερα ὁδός, ἐπὶ μὲν τὸ
10 βαρὺ ἐπὶ τὸ μέσης καὶ λιχανοῦ | διάστημα ὅ τι ἄν ποτε
τυγχάνῃ ὂν καθ' ἑκάστην χρόαν τῶν διατόνων, ἐπὶ δὲ τὸ ὀξὺ
ἐπὶ τὸ παραμέσης καὶ τρίτης.   20

Ἤδη δέ τισι καὶ τοῦτο τὸ πρόβλημα παρέσχε πλάνην·
15 θαυμάζουσι γὰρ | πῶς οὐχὶ τοὐναντίον συμβαίνει· ἄπειροι
γάρ τινες αὐτοῖς φαίνονται εἶναι ὁδοὶ ἐφ' ἑκάτερα τοῦ τόνου,
ἐπειδήπερ τοῦ τε μέσης καὶ λιχανοῦ διαστήματος ἄπειρα

---

1 τὸ ὀξὺ] τοῦ ὀξὺ S   ἡ restituit Westphal   δὲ ante τὸ δίτονον
add. R   2 ὅτε τόνος in marg. B   3 δὴ Marquard : δὲ codd.
4-6 πυκνοῦ . . . ἀπὸ δὲ om. H   4 τὸν restituit Marquard   5 ἡ
om. B   ἐπὶ δὲ δίτονον R   ἐπὶ δὲ . . . δίτονον in marg. add. Mc Vb
(nisi quod ἡ om. Mc)   ἡ om. R   6 ἀπὸ δὲ τόνου μία add.
in marg. Mc Vb: om. VS   7-12 ἐπὶ μὲν . . . πυκνόν om. H
8 πυκνόν] δίτονον R   10 τίθεται om. R   post τίθεται 10 litt. eras.
M   λέλειπται R   11 δὴ] δὲ M V S B   14 διτόνου] δὲ
τόνου R   15 κατὰ R : καὶ rell.   18 τὸ supra lin. add. Mc:
om. V S B   μέσης καὶ om. R   καὶ supra lin. add. Mc : om.
V B S   19 τυγχάνει B S   διτόνων B   20 διάστημα post
τρίτης add. H   24 τε om. S

μεγέθη φαίνονται εἶναι τοῦ τε πυκνοῦ | ὡσαύτως. Πρὸς δὴ 20
ταῦτα πρῶτον μὲν τοῦτ' ἐλέχθη, ὅτι οὐδὲν μᾶλλον ἐπὶ τούτου τοῦ προβλήματος ἐπιβλέψειεν ἄν τις τοῦτο ἢ ἐπὶ τῶν
προτέρων. δῆλον γὰρ ὅτι καὶ τῶν ἀπὸ τοῦ πυκνοῦ τὴν
5 ἑτέ|ραν τῶν ὁδῶν ἄπειρα μεγέθη συμβήσεται λαμβάνειν καὶ 25
τῶν ἀπὸ τοῦ διτόνου [δ'] ὡσαύτως [ὡς]· τό τε γὰρ τοιοῦτον
διάστημα οἷον τὸ μέσης καὶ λιχανοῦ ἄπειρα λαμβάνει μεγέθη
τό τε τοιοῦτον οἷον | τὸ πυκνὸν ταὐτὸ πάσχει πάθος τῷ 30
ἔμπροσθεν εἰρημένῳ διαστήματι, ἀλλ' ὅμως οὐδὲν ἧττον ἀπό
10 τε τοῦ πυκνοῦ δύο γίγνονται ὁδοὶ ἐπὶ τὸ βαρὺ καὶ ἀπὸ τοῦ
διτόνου ἐπὶ τὸ ὀξύ, ὡσαύτως δὲ καὶ ἀπὸ τοῦ τόνου μία
γίγνεται ἐφ' ἑκάτερα ὁδός. || Καθ' ἑκάστην γὰρ χρόαν ἐφ' 69
ἑκάστου γένους ληπτέον ἐστὶ τὰς ὁδούς· δεῖ γὰρ ἕκαστον
τῶν ἐν τῇ μουσικῇ καθ' ὃ πεπέρασται κατὰ τοῦτο τιθέναι
15 τε καὶ τάττειν εἰς | τὰς ἐπιστήμας, ᾗ δ' ἄπειρόν ἐστιν ἐᾶν. 5
κατὰ μὲν οὖν τὰ μεγέθη τῶν διαστημάτων καὶ τὰς τῶν
φθόγγων τάσεις ἄπειρά πως φαίνεται εἶναι τὰ περὶ μέλος,
κατὰ δὲ τὰς δυνάμεις καὶ κατὰ τὰ εἴδη | καὶ κατὰ τὰς θέσεις 10
πεπερασμένα τε καὶ τεταγμένα. Εὐθέως οὖν ἀπὸ τοῦ
20 πυκνοῦ αἱ ὁδοὶ ἐπὶ τὸ βαρὺ τῇ τε δυνάμει καὶ τοῖς εἴδεσιν
ὡρισμέναι τ' εἰσὶ καὶ δύο μόνον τὸν ἀριθμόν, ἡ μὲν | γὰρ 15
κατὰ τόνον εἰς διάζευξιν ἄγει τὸ τοῦ συστήματος εἶδος, ἡ
δὲ κατὰ θάτερον διάστημα, ὅ τι δήποτ' ἔχει μέγεθος, εἰς
συναφήν. δῆλον δ' ἐκ τούτων ὅτι καὶ ἀπὸ τοῦ τόνου μία
25 τ' | ἔσται ἐφ' ἑκάτερα ὁδὸς καὶ ἑνὸς εἴδους συστήματος 20
αἰτίαι αἱ συναμφότεραι ὁδοί, τῆς διαζεύξεως. Ὅτι δ' ἄν

2 ἐλέχθη] ante χ litt. γ eras. M: ἐλέγχθη VB   6 δ' del.
Marquard   ὡς del. Meibom   7 λαμβάνειν μεγέθει H   8 ταῦτὸ
in marg. B, R: αὐτὸ rell.   10 τε Marquard: δὲ codd.   11 τοῦ
om. H   12 γίνεται (ινε in ras.) M   13 δεῖ γὰρ ἕκαστον
Meibom: διὰ γὰρ ἑκάστου codd.   14 ante καθ' ras. M   πεπέρασται
(πε in ras., fuisse vid. καθάπερ πέρασται) M: πεπέραται R: πεπεράσθαι H
15 τε Marquard: γε codd.   ᾗ conieci: εἰ codd.   20 αἱ ὁδοὶ Marquard: ὁδοὶ αἱ codd.   21 μόνον Meibom: τόνοι codd.   γὰρ om. S
25 τ'] τις R   26 συναμφότεραι (οι suprascr.) H: συναμφότεροι M V B S

τις μὴ κατὰ μίαν χρόαν ἑνὸς γένους ἐπιχειρῇ τὰς ἀπὸ τῶν
25 διαστημάτων ὁδοὺς ἐπισκο|πεῖν ἀλλ᾽ ἅμα κατὰ πάσας ἁπάν-
των τῶν γενῶν εἰς ἀπειρίαν ἐμπεσεῖται, φανερὸν ἔκ τε τῶν
εἰρημένων καὶ ἐξ αὐτοῦ τοῦ πράγματος.

30 Ἐν χρώματι δὲ καὶ ἁρμονίᾳ πᾶς | φθόγγος πυκνοῦ μετ- 5
έχει. Πᾶς μὲν γὰρ φθόγγος ἐν τοῖς εἰρημένοις γένεσιν
ἤτοι πυκνοῦ μέρος ὁρίζει ἢ τόνον ἤ τι τοιοῦτον οἷον τὸ
70 μέσης καὶ λιχανοῦ διάστημα. οἱ μὲν οὖν || τὰ τοῦ πυκνοῦ
μέρη ὁρίζοντες οὐδὲν δέονται λόγου, φανεροὶ γάρ εἰσι
πυκνοῦ μετέχοντες· οἱ δὲ τὸν τόνον περιέχοντες ἐδείχθησαν 10
5 ἔμπροσθεν πυκνοῦ | βαρύτατοι ὄντες ἀμφότεροι· τῶν δὲ
τὸ λοιπὸν διάστημα περιεχόντων ὁ μὲν βαρύτερος ὀξύτατος
ἐδείχθη πυκνοῦ ὁ δ᾽ ὀξύτερος βαρύτατος. Ὥστ᾽ ἐπειδὴ
10 τοσαῦτα μέν ἐστι μόνα τὰ ἀσύν|θετα, ἕκαστον δ᾽ αὐτῶν
ὑπὸ τοιούτων φθόγγων περιέχεται ὧν ἑκάτερος πυκνοῦ μετ- 15
έχει, δῆλον ὅτι πᾶς φθόγγος ἐν ἁρμονίᾳ καὶ χρώματι πυκνοῦ
μετέχει. |

15 Ὅτι δὲ τῶν ἐν πυκνῷ κειμένων φθόγγων τρεῖς εἰσι
χῶραι, ῥᾴδιον συνιδεῖν, ἐπειδήπερ πρὸς πυκνῷ οὔτε πυκνὸν
τίθεται οὔτε πυκνοῦ μέρος. δῆλον γὰρ ὅτι διὰ ταύτην τὴν 20
20 αἰτίαν οὐκ ἔσονται | πλείους τῶν εἰρημένων χῶραι φθόγγων.

Ὅτι δὲ ἀπὸ μόνου τοῦ βαρυτάτου δύο ὁδοί εἰσιν ἐφ᾽
ἑκάτερα, ἀπὸ δὲ τῶν λοιπῶν μία ὁδὸς ἐφ᾽ ἑκάτερα, δεικτέον.
25 ἦν δὲ δεδειγμένον ἐν τοῖς ἔμπροσθεν, ὅτι | (ἀπὸ πυκνοῦ ἐπὶ
τὸ βαρὺ δύο ὁδοί εἰσιν, ἡ μὲν ἐπὶ τὸν τόνον ἡ δ᾽ ἐπὶ τὸ 25

---

1 ἐπιχειρῇ ex ἐπιχειρεῖ Mc (?): ἐπιχειρεῖ rell.   7 πυκνοῦ μέρος]
πυκνούμενος V S in marg. B   ἤ τι] ἤτοι R   9 ὁρίζοντες Marquard : διορίζοντες codd.   δέονται post λόγου ponit H   10 τόνον]
τόπον R   11 τοῦ ante πυκνοῦ add. R   12 τὸ supra lin. add.
Mc: om. V B S   λοιπῶν S   βαρύτερος Marquard : βαρύτατος codd.
ὀξύτατος in marg. add. B   13 ὁ δ᾽ add. Mc: om. V B S   ὀξύτερος
Marquard: ὀξύτατος codd.   14 ἀσύνθετα R : σύνθετα rell.   15 ὧν]
τῶν B   μετέχεις S, B (sed μετέχει in marg.)   16 δῆλον . . .
μετέχει in marg. Mc Vb   20 γὰρ om. H   21 χῶραι post
φθόγγων ponit H   24 δὲ supra lin. add. Mc: om. V B S   ἀπὸ
. . . δὲ τὸ restituit Marquard

δίτονον. ἔστι δὲ τὸ) ἀπὸ πυκνοῦ δύο ὁδοὺς εἶναι τὸ αὐτὸ
τῷ ἀπὸ τοῦ βαρυτάτου τῶν ἐν τῷ πυκνῷ κειμένων δύο ὁδοὺς
ἐπὶ τὸ βαρὺ εἶναι, οὗτος γάρ ἐστιν ὁ περαίνων τὸ πυκνόν·
ἐδέδεικτο οὖν ὅτι ἀπὸ διτόνου ἐπὶ τὸ ὀξὺ | δύο ὁδοί εἰσιν, 30
5 ἡ μὲν ἐπὶ τὸν τόνον ἡ δ᾽ ἐπὶ τὸ πυκνόν· ἔστι δὲ τὸ ἀπὸ
διτόνου δύο ὁδοὺς εἶναι τὸ αὐτὸ τῷ ἀπὸ τοῦ ὀξυτέρου τῶν
τὸ δίτονον ὁριζόντων δύο ὁδοὺς ἐπὶ τὸ ὀξὺ εἶναι, οὗτος γάρ
ἐστιν ὁ ὁρίζων τὸ || δίτονον ⟨ἐπὶ τὸ ὀξύ. δῆλον δ᾽ ὅτι 71
ὁ αὐτὸς τὸ δίτονον ἐπὶ τὸ ὀξὺ ὁρίζων καὶ ὁ τὸ πυκνὸν ἐπὶ
10 τὸ βαρὺ) βαρύτατος ὢν πυκνοῦ, ἐδέδεικτο γὰρ καὶ τοῦτο.
ὥστ᾽ εἶναι δῆλον, ὅτι ἀπὸ τοῦ εἰρημένου φθόγγου δύο ὁδοὶ
ἐφ᾽ ἑκάτερα ἔσονται. |

Ὅτι δ᾽ ἀπὸ τοῦ ὀξυτάτου μία ὁδὸς ἐφ᾽ ἑκάτερα, δεικτέον. 5
Ἐδέδεικτο δ᾽ ὅτι ἀπὸ πυκνοῦ ἐπὶ τὸ ὀξὺ μία ὁδός ἐστιν,
15 οὐδὲν δὲ διαφέρει λέγειν ἀπὸ πυκνοῦ μίαν ὁδὸν εἶναι ἐπὶ
τὸ ὀξὺ ἢ ἀπὸ | τοῦ περαίνοντος αὐτὸ φθόγγου διὰ τὴν εἰρη- 10
μένην αἰτίαν ἐπὶ τῶν ἔμπροσθεν. δέδεικται δ᾽ ὅτι καὶ ἀπὸ
διτόνου μία ὁδός ἐστιν ἐπὶ τὸ βαρύ, οὐδὲν δὲ διαφέρει
λέγειν ἀπὸ διτόνου μίαν ὁδὸν εἶναι ἐπὶ | τὸ βαρὺ ἢ ἀπὸ τοῦ 15
20 ὁρίζοντος αὐτὸ φθόγγου διὰ τὴν προειρημένην αἰτίαν· δῆλον
δὲ ὅτι καὶ ὁ αὐτός ἐστι φθόγγος ὅ τε τὸ δίτονον ἐπὶ τὸ
βαρὺ ὁρίζων καὶ ὁ τὸ πυκνὸν ἐπὶ τὸ ὀξὺ ὀξύτατος ὢν
πυ|κνοῦ. Ὥστ᾽ εἶναι φανερὸν ἐκ τούτων, ὅτι μία ὁδὸς ἐφ᾽ 20
ἑκάτερα ἔσται [ἐπὶ] τοῦ εἰρημένου φθόγγου.

25 Ὅτι δὲ καὶ ἀπὸ τοῦ μέσου μία ὁδὸς ἐφ᾽ ἑκάτερα ἔσται,

---

1 ἐπὶ τὸ βαρὺ post ὁδοὺς add. H   2 βαρυτάτου τῶν ex βαρὺ
τούτων Mc : βαρὺ τούτων VSB   3 ὁ περαίνων (αι in ras., fuisse
vid. ε et supra lin. ras.) M : ὅπερ ἐνῶν VS, B (sed αίνων in marg.)
4 ἐδέδεικνειτο B, sed in marg. ἐδέδεικτο   δύο post ὁδοὶ ponit B
5 τὸ ἀπὸ R : τὰ ἀπὸ rell.   6 διτόνου Meibom : τόνου codd.   τοῦ
om. R   7 οὗτος] υτ in ras. Ma   8 ἐπὶ . . . βαρὺ restituit
Marquard   10 καὶ supra lin. add. corr. B   15 τοῦ ante πυκνοῦ
add. H   19 τοῦ ante διτόνου add. R   21 ὁ αὐτός] ὁ om. M V
S B   τε] τι R   22 ὁ om. M V B R   24 ἐπὶ seclusi : δεικτέον
ἐπὶ eras. S : ἀπὸ Marquard   ἐπὶ . . . ἔσται om. R

25 δεικτέον. Ἐπεὶ τοίνυν | ἀναγκαῖον μὲν τῶν τριῶν ἀσυν-
θέτων ἔν τι ⟨πρὸς⟩ τῷ εἰρημένῳ φθόγγῳ τίθεσθαι, ὑπάρχει
δὲ αὐτοῦ κειμένη δίεσις ἐφ’ ἑκάτερα, δῆλον ὅτι οὔτε δίτονον
30 τεθήσεται πρὸς αὐτῷ κατ’ οὐδέτερον τῶν τόπων | οὔτε
τόνος. διτόνου γὰρ οὕτω τιθεμένου ἤτοι βαρύτατος πυκνοῦ 5
ἢ ὀξύτατος πεσεῖται ἐπὶ τὴν αὐτὴν τάσιν τῷ εἰρημένῳ
φθόγγῳ μέσῳ ὄντι πυκνοῦ, ὥστε γίγνεσθαι τρεῖς διέσεις ἐξῆς
72 ὁποτέρως ἂν τεθῇ τὸ δίτονον τῶν τόπων· τόνου ⟨δὲ⟩
τεθειμένου τὸ αὐτὸ συμβήσεται, βαρύτατος γὰρ πυκνοῦ
πεσεῖται ἐπὶ τὴν αὐτὴν τάσιν μέσῳ πυκνοῦ, ὥστε τρεῖς 10
5 δι|έσεις ἐξῆς τίθεσθαι. τούτων δ’ ἐκμελῶν ὄντων δῆλον
ὅτι μία ὁδὸς ἐφ’ ἑκάτερα ἔσται ἀπὸ τοῦ εἰρημένου φθόγγου.
Ὅτι μὲν οὖν ἀπὸ ⟨τοῦ βαρυτάτου⟩ τῶν φθόγγων τῶν ἐν
10 πυκνῷ κειμένων δύο ἐφ’ ἑκά|τερα ἔσονται ὁδοὶ ἀπὸ δὲ τῶν
λοιπῶν ἑκατέρου μία ἐφ’ ἑκάτερα ἔσται ὁδός, φανερόν.   15
Ὅτι δ’ οὐ τεθήσονται δύο φθόγγοι ἀνόμοιοι κατὰ τὴν
15 τοῦ πυκνοῦ μετοχὴν | ἐπὶ τὴν αὐτὴν τάσιν ἐμμελῶς, δει-
κτέον. Τιθέσθω γὰρ πρῶτον ὅ τ’ ὀξύτατος καὶ ὁ βαρύτατος
ἐπὶ τὴν αὐτὴν τάσιν· συμβήσεται δὴ τούτου γιγνομένου
20 δύο πυκνὰ ἐξῆς τίθεσθαι. τούτου δ’ ἐκμελοῦς | ὄντος ἐκμελὲς 20
τὸ πίπτειν ⟨ἐπὶ τὴν αὐτὴν τάσιν τοὺς κατὰ ταύτην
τὴν διαφορὰν ἀνομοίους⟩ ἐν πυκνῷ φθόγγους. Δῆλον
δ’ ὅτι οὐδ’ οἱ κατὰ τὴν λειπομένην διαφορὰν ἀνόμοιοι φθόγγοι

2 ἔν] ἓν S   πρὸς restituit Meibom   4 αὐτῷ Meibom H : αὐτὸ
rell.   τόπων conieci : τρόπων codd.   εἰρημένων ante τρόπων add.
H   5 τόνος διτόνου. οὕτω γὰρ M V S B, nisi quod διατόνου (cum
duobus punctis sub α) B   6 τῷ εἰρημένῳ φθόγγῳ Meibom, et μέσῳ
Marquard : τῶν εἰρημένων μέσον codd.   8 τῶν τόπων
conieci : τῷ τόπῳ codd.   δὲ coniecit Meibom   ἐπὶ δὲ ante τῷ, et
αὐτῷ ante τόπῳ add. Marquard   10 αὐτὴν . . . ὥστε om. R
μέσῳ Meibom : μέσον codd.   ὥστε Marquard : ὡς codd.   11 ἐξῆς
τίθεσθαι] γίνεσθαι ἐξῆς H   δ’ Marquard : δὴ codd.   12 μία supra
lin. add. corr. B   13 τοῦ βαρυτάτου restituit Meibom   15 ἔσται
ante ἐφ’ ἑκάτερα ponit H   18 τιθέσθω . . . τὴν αὐτὴν τάσιν in
marg. S   ὁ (ante βαρύτατος) H : om. rell.   20 ἐκμελὲς] ἐμμελὲς
M V B   21 ἐπὶ τὴν . . . ἀνομοίους addidi   23 δ’ om. B   ἀνόμοιοι Marquard : ὅμοιοι codd.

161

τῆς αὐτῆς τάσεως ἐμμελῶς κοινωνήσουσι· τρεῖς γὰρ ἀναγκαῖον
τί|θεσθαι διέσεις ἐξῆς, ἐάν τε βαρύτατος ἐάν τ᾽ ὀξύτατος 25
τῷ μέσῳ τῆς αὐτῆς μετάσχῃ τάσεως.

- Ὅτι δὲ τὸ διάτονον σύγκειται ἤτοι ἐκ δυοῖν ἢ τριῶν ἢ
5 τεσσάρων ἀσυν|θέτων, δεικτέον. Ὅτι μὲν οὖν ἐκ τοσούτων 30
πλείστων ἀσυνθέτων ἕκαστον τῶν γενῶν συνεστηκός ἐστιν
(ὅσα) ἐν τῷ διὰ πέντε, δέδεικται πρότερον· ἔστι δὲ ταῦ||τα 73
τέσσαρα τὸν ἀριθμόν. ἐὰν οὖν τῶν τεσσάρων τὰ μὲν τρία
ἴσα γένηται τὸ δὲ ⟨τέταρτον⟩ ἄνισον—⟨τοῦτο δὲ⟩ γίγνεται
10 ἐν τῷ συντονωτάτῳ διατόνῳ—, δύο ἔσται μεγέθη μόνα ἐξ
ὧν τὸ | διάτονον συνεστηκὸς ἔσται· ἐὰν δὲ τὰ μὲν δύο ἴσα 5
τὰ δὲ δύο ἄνισα τῆς παρυπάτης ἐπὶ τὸ βαρὺ κινηθείσης,
τρία ἔσται μεγέθη ἐξ ὧν τὸ διάτονον γένος συνεστηκὸς
ἔσται, τό τ᾽ ἔλαττον ἡμιτο|νίου καὶ τόνος καὶ τὸ μεῖζον 10
15 τόνου· ἐὰν δὲ πάντα τὰ τοῦ διὰ πέντε μεγέθη ἄνισα γένηται,
τέσσαρα ἔσται μεγέθη ⟨ἐξ ὧν⟩ τὸ εἰρημένον γένος ἔσται
συνεστηκός. Ὥστ᾽ εἶναι φανερὸν ὅτι τὸ διάτονον | ἤτοι 15
ἐκ δυοῖν ἢ τριῶν ἢ τεσσάρων ἀσυνθέτων σύγκειται.

Ὅτι δὲ ⟨τὸ⟩ χρῶμα καὶ ἡ ἁρμονία ἤτοι ἐκ τριῶν ἢ ἐκ
20 τεσσάρων σύγκειται, δεικτέον. Ὄντων δὲ τῶν μὲν ⟨τοῦ⟩
διὰ πέντε ἀσυν|θέτων τεσσάρων τὸν ἀριθμὸν ἐὰν μὲν τὰ 20
τοῦ πυκνοῦ μέρη ἴσα ᾖ, τρία ἔσται μεγέθη ἐξ ὧν τὰ εἰρημένα γένη συνεστηκότα ἔσται, τό τε τοῦ πυκνοῦ μέρος ὅ
τι ἂν ᾖ καὶ τόνος καὶ τὸ τοιοῦτον οἷον μέσης καὶ | λιχανοῦ 25
25 διάστημα. ἐὰν δὲ τὰ τοῦ πυκνοῦ μέρη ἄνισα ᾖ, τέσσαρα

---

1 κοινήσουσι B   3 τάσεως in marg. B: στάσεως rell.   4 ἤτοι]
ἢ τὸ H   δυοῖν ἢ τριῶν Meibom: τριῶν ἢ δυοῖν codd.   5 ἀσύνθετον
M V B S   6 ἀσύνθετον H   7 ὅσα restituit Meibom   9 τὸ
δὲ τέταρτον ἄνισον—τοῦτο δὲ γίγνεται Marquard: τὸ δὲ ἴσον γένηται
codd. (nisi quod γένηται om. H)   10 διατόνῳ om. R   14 ἡμιτόνιον
M V B S   16 μεγέθει H   ἐξ ὧν restituit Meursius   18 δυοῖν
Marquard: δύο codd.   19 τὸ restituit Marquard   ἐκ ante τεσσάρων
om. V B S   20 δὲ] μὲν οὖν H   τοῦ restituit Marquard   21 τὸν
corr. ex τω S   22, 23 μέρη . . . πυκνοῦ om. R   22 ᾖ] ἢ B
23 συνεστηκότα Meibom: συνεστηκός codd.   μέρους M V B S
24 τὸ ante τόνος add. V S

ἔσται μεγέθη ἐξ ὧν τὰ εἰρημένα γένη συνεστηκότα ἔσται,
ἐλάχιστον μὲν τὸ τοιοῦτον οἷον τὸ ὑπάτης καὶ παρυπάτης,
30 δεύτερον δ' οἷον τὸ παρυπάτης καὶ λιχανοῦ, τρίτον δὲ τό|νος,
τέταρτον δὲ τὸ τοιοῦτον οἷον τὸ μέσης καὶ λιχανοῦ.

Ἤδη δέ τις ἠπόρησε διὰ τί οὐκ ἂν καὶ ταῦτα τὰ γένη 5
74 ἐκ δύο ἀσυνθέτων || εἴη συνεστηκότα ὥσπερ καὶ τὸ διάτονον.
Φανερὸν δὴ τίς ἐστι παντελῶς καὶ ἐπιπολῆς ἡ αἰτία τοῦ
5 μὴ γίγνεσθαι τοῦτο· τρία γὰρ ἀσύνθετα ἴσα ἐξῆς ἐν ἁρμο|νίᾳ
μὲν καὶ χρώματι οὐ τίθεται, ἐν διατόνῳ δὲ τίθεται. διὰ
ταύτην δὴ τὴν αἰτίαν τὸ διάτονον μόνον ἐκ δύο ἀσυνθέτων 10
συντίθεταί ποτε.

10 Μετὰ δὲ ταῦτα λεκτέον τί ἐστι καὶ | ποία τις ἡ κατ'
εἶδος διαφορά—διαφέρει δ' ἡμῖν οὐδὲν εἶδος λέγειν ἢ σχῆμα,
φέρομεν γὰρ ἀμφότερα τὰ ὀνόματα ταῦτα ἐπὶ τὸ αὐτό.
15 Γίγνεται δ' ὅταν τοῦ αὐτοῦ μεγέθους ἐκ τῶν αὐτῶν ἀ|συν- 15
θέτων συγκειμένου μεγέθει καὶ ἀριθμῷ ἡ τάξις αὐτῶν
ἀλλοίωσιν λάβῃ. Τούτου δ' οὕτως ἀφωρισμένου τοῦ διὰ
τεσσάρων ὅτι τρία εἴδη, δεικτέον. πρῶτον μὲν οὖν οὐ τὸ
20 πυκνὸν ἐπὶ τὸ | βαρύ, δεύτερον δ' οὗ δίεσις ἐφ' ἑκάτερα
τοῦ διτόνου κεῖται, τρίτον δ' οὗ τὸ πυκνὸν ἐπὶ τὸ ὀξὺ τοῦ 20
διτόνου. ὅτι δ' οὐκ ἐνδέχεται πλεοναχῶς τεθῆναι τὰ τοῦ
25 διὰ τεσσάρων μέρη πρὸς ἄλληλα ἢ | τοσαυταχῶς, ῥᾴδιον
συνιδεῖν. . . . .

1 ἔσται om. H   συνεστηκὸς M R   7 δὴ] δ' εἰ S   ἐπὶ πολλῆς
V B S R   8 verba ἐν ἁρμονίᾳ et quae sequuntur omnia in marg.
add. Mc: in V scripta sunt a Vb vel manu diversa a Va, paullo
iuniore   ἐναρμόνια S   9 οὐ ante τίθεται prius om., et οὐ ante
τίθεται alterum add. H   9-11 διὰ . . . ποτε om. H   10 τὸ
διάτονον om. R   μόνον ἐκ δύο Marquard: ἐκ δύο μόνων codd.
12 τί M B R: τίς V S   ἐστι om. V   13 ἡμῖν post οὐδὲν ponit H
15 ἀσυνθέτων ex ἀσυνθέτου corr. V: ἀσυνθέτου S   16 συγκειμένου
H S: συγκειμένων M R, V (ex συγκειμένου corr.)   καὶ ante μεγέθει
add. M V B S H   17 ἀλύωσιν B   ἀλλοίωσιν post λάβῃ ponit H
τοῦ δ' οὕτως, sed τοῦ et οὗ in ras. corr. V   ἀφορισμένον H : ἀφορισμένου
B   18 εἴδη] ἤδη B   οὗ] οὐ S   19 οὗ] οὐ S   20 οὗ] οὐ S
22 τεσσάρων] τετάρτου V B

THE ELEMENTS OF HARMONY
BY ARISTOXENUS

BOOK I[1]

THE branch of study which bears the name of Harmonic I. 11 is to be regarded as one of the several divisions or special sciences embraced by the general science that concerns itself with Melody. Among these special sciences Harmonic occupies a primary and fundamental position; its subject matter consists of the fundamental principles — all that relates to the theory of scales and keys; and this once mastered, our knowledge of the science fulfils every just requirement, because it is in such a mastery that its aim consists. In advancing to the profounder speculations 2 which confront us when scales and keys are enlisted in the service of poetry, we pass from the study under consideration to the all-embracing science of music, of which Harmonic is but one part among many. The possession of this greater science constitutes the musician.

The early students of Harmonic contented themselves, as a matter of fact, with being students of *Harmonic* in the literal sense of the term; for they investigated the *enharmonic* scale alone, without devoting any consideration to the other genera. This may be inferred from the fact that the tables of scales presented by them are always of enharmonic scales, never in one solitary instance of diatonic or chromatic; and that too, although these very tables in which they con-

[1] The references throughout the translation are to Meibom's edition.

fined themselves to the enumeration of enharmonic octave scales nevertheless exhibited the complete system of musical intervals. Nor is this the sole mark of their imperfect treatment. In addition to ignoring diatonic and chromatic scales they did not even attempt to observe the various magnitudes and figures in the enharmonic as well as in the other genera. Confining themselves to what is but the third part of that complete system, they selected for exclusive treatment a single magnitude in that third part, namely, the Octave. Again, their mode of treating even branches of the study to which they did apply themselves was imperfect. This has been clearly illustrated in a former work in which we examined the views put forward by the students of Harmonic; but it will be brought into a still clearer light by an enumeration of the various subdivisions of this science, and a description of the sphere of each. We 3 shall find that they have been in part ignored, in part inadequately treated; and while substantiating our accusations we shall at the same time acquire a general conception of the nature of our subject.

The preliminary step towards a scientific investigation of music is to adjust our different notions of change of voice, meaning thereby change in the position of the voice. Of this change there are more forms than one, as it is found both in speaking and in singing; for in each of these there is a *high* and *low*, and a change that results in the contrast of high and low is a change of position. Yet although this movement between high and low of the voice in speaking differs specifically from the same movement in singing, no authority has hitherto supplied a careful determination of the difference, and that despite the fact that without such a determination the definition of a note becomes a task very difficult of accomplishment. Yet we are bound to accomplish it with some degree of accuracy, if we wish to avoid the blunder of Lasus and some of the school of Epigonus, who attribute *breadth* to notes. A careful definition will ensure us increased correctness in discussing many of the problems which will afterwards encounter us. Furthermore, it is essential to a clear comprehension of these points that we differentiate distinctly between tension and relaxation, height and depth, and pitch—conceptions not as yet adequately discussed, but either ignored or confused. This done, we shall then be confronted by the question whether distance on the line of pitch can be indefinitely extended or diminished, and if so, from what point of view. Our next task will be a discussion of intervals in general, followed by a classification of them according to every principle of division of which they admit ; after which our attention will be engaged by a consideration of the scale in general, and a presentation of the various natural classes of scales. We must then indicate in outline the nature of *musical* melody—*musical*, because of melody there are several kinds, and tuneful melody—that which is employed in musical expression—is only one class among many. And as the method by which one is led to a true conception of this latter involves the differentiation of it from the other kinds of melody, it will scarcely be possible to avoid touching on these other kinds, to some extent at least. When we have thus defined musical melody as far as it can be done by a general outline before the consideration of details, we must divide the general class, breaking it up into as many species as it may appear to contain. After this division we must consider the nature and origin of continuity or consecution in scales. Our next point will be to set forth the differences of the musical genera which manifest themselves in the variable notes, as well as to give an account of the loci of variation of these variable notes. Hitherto these questions have been absolutely ignored, and in dealing with them we shall be compelled to break new ground, as there is in existence no previous treatment of them worth mentioning.

5 Intervals, first simple and then compound, will next occupy our attention. In dealing with compound intervals, which as a matter of fact are in a sense scales as well, we shall find it necessary to make some remarks on the synthesis of simple intervals. Most students of Harmonic, as we perceived in a previous work, have failed even to notice that a treatment of this subject was required. Eratocles and his school have contented themselves with remarking that there are two possible melodic progressions starting from the interval of the Fourth, both upwards and downwards. They do not definitely state whether the law holds good from whatever interval of the Fourth the melody starts; they assign no reason for their law; they do not inquire how other intervals are synthesized—whether there is a fixed principle that determines the synthesis of any given interval with any other, and under what circumstances scales do and do not arise from the syntheses, or whether this matter is incapable of determination. On these points we find no statements made by any writer, with or without demonstration; the result being that although as a matter of fact there is a marvellous orderliness in the constitution of melody, music has yet been condemned, through the fault of those who have meddled with the subject, as falling into the opposite defect. The truth is that of all the objects to which the five senses apply not one other is characterized by an orderliness so extensive and so perfect. Abundant evidence for this statement will be forthcoming throughout our investigation of our subject, to the enumeration of the parts of which we must now return.

6 Our presentation of the various methods in which simple intervals may be collocated will be followed by a discussion of the resulting scales (including the Perfect Scale) in which

we will deduce the number and character of the scales from
the intervals, and will exhibit the several magnitudes of scales
as well as the different figures, collocations, and positions possible in each magnitude ; our aim being that no principle of
concrete melody, whether magnitude, or figure, or collocation, or position shall lack demonstration. This part of our
study has been left untouched by all our predecessors with the
exception of Eratocles, who attempted a partial enumeration
without demonstration. How worthless his statements are,
and how completely he failed even in perception of the facts,
we have already dwelt upon, when this very subject was the
matter of our inquiry. As we then observed all the scales
with the exception of one have been completely passed over ;
and of that one scale Eratocles merely endeavoured to
enumerate the figures of one magnitude, namely the octave,
empirically determining their number, without any attempt
at demonstration, by the recurrence of the intervals. He
failed to observe that unless there be previous demonstration
of the figures of the Fifth and Fourth, as well as of the laws
of their melodious collocation, such an empirical process
will give us not seven figures, but many multiples of seven.
Further discussion here is rendered unnecessary by our
previous demonstration of these facts ; and we may now 7
resume our sketch of the divisions of our subject.

When the scales in each genus have been enumerated in
accordance with the several variations just mentioned, we
must blend the scales and repeat the process of enumeration. The necessity for this investigation has escaped most
students ; nay, they have not so much as mastered the true
conception of ' blending.'

Notes form the next subject for inquiry, inasmuch as
intervals do not suffice for their determination.

Again, every scale when sung or played is located in
a certain region of the voice ; and although this location

induces no difference in the scale regarded in itself, it im-
parts to the melody employing that scale no common—nay
rather perhaps its most striking characteristic. Hence he
who would deal with the science before us must treat of the
$\sqrt{}$ 'region of the voice' in general and in detail so far as is
reasonable ; in other words so far as the nature of the scales
themselves prescribes. And in dealing with the affinity
between scales and regions of the voice, and with keys, we
must not follow the Harmonists in their endeavour at compression, but aim rather at the intermodulation of scales, by
considering in what keys the various scales must be set so
as to admit of intermodulation. We have shown in a previous
work that, though as a matter of fact some of the Harmonists
have touched on this branch of our subject in a purely
accidental way, in connexion with their endeavour to exhibit
a close-packed scheme of scales, yet there has been no
general treatment of it by a single writer belonging to this
8 school. This position of our subject may broadly be
described as the part of the science of modulation concerned with melody.

We have now set forth the nature and number of the
parts of Harmonic. Any investigations that would carry us
further must, as we remarked at the outset, be regarded
as belonging to a more advanced science. Postponing
accordingly to the proper occasion the consideration of
these, their number, and their several natures, it now
devolves upon us to give an account of the primary science
itself.

Our first problem consists in ascertaining the various
species of motion. Every voice is capable of change of
position, and this change may be either continuous or by
intervals. In continuous change of position the voice
seems to the senses to traverse a certain space in such a
manner that it does not become stationary at any point, not

even at the extremities of its progress—such at least is the evidence of our sense-perception—but passes on into silence with unbroken continuity. In the other species which we designate motion by intervals, the process seems to be of exactly the opposite nature: the voice in its progress stations itself at a certain pitch, and then again at another, pursuing this process continuously—continuously, that is, in time. As it leaps the distances contained between the successive points of pitch, while it is stationary at, and produces sounds upon, the points themselves, it is said to sing only the latter, and to move by intervals. Both these descriptions must of course be regarded in the 9 light of sensuous cognition. Whether voice can really move or not, and whether it can become stationary at a given point of pitch, are questions beyond the scope of the present inquiry, which does not demand the raising of this problem. For whatever the answer may be, it does not affect the distinction between the melodious motion of the voice and its other motions. Disregarding all such difficulties, we describe the motion of the voice as continuous when it moves in such a way as to seem to the ear not to become stationary at any point of pitch; but when the reverse is the case—when the voice seems to the ear first to come to a standstill on a point of pitch, then to leap over a certain space, and, having done so, to come to a standstill on a second point, and to repeat this alternating process continuously—the motion of the voice under these circumstances we describe as motion by intervals. Continuous motion we call the motion of speech, as in speaking the voice moves without ever seeming to come to a standstill. The reverse is the case with the other motion, which we designate motion by intervals: in that the voice does seem to become stationary, and when employing this motion one is always said not to speak but to sing. Hence

in ordinary conversation we avoid bringing the voice to a
standstill, unless occasionally forced by strong feeling to
resort to such a motion·; whereas in singing we act in
10 precisely the opposite way, avoiding continuous motion and
making the voice become, as far as possible, absolutely
stationary. The more we succeed in rendering each of our
voice-utterances one, stationary, and identical, the more
correct does the singing appear to the ear. To conclude,
enough has been said to show that there are two species of
the voice's motion, and that one is continuous and employed
in speaking, while one proceeds by intervals and is
employed in singing.

It is evident that the voice must in singing produce the
tensions and relaxations inaudibly, and that the points of
pitch alone must be audibly enunciated. This is clear from
the fact that the voice must pass imperceptibly through the
compass of the interval which it traverses in ascending or
descending, while the notes that bound the intervals must
be audible and stationary. Hence it is needful to discuss
tension and relaxation, and in addition height and depth of
pitch, and finally pitch in general.

Tension is the continuous transition of the voice from a
lower position to a higher, **relaxation** that from a higher to
a lower. **Height of pitch** is the result of tension, **depth**
the result of relaxation. On a superficial consideration of
these questions it might appear surprising that we distinguish
four phenomena here instead of two, and in fact it is usual
to identify height of pitch with tension, and depth of pitch
11 with relaxation. Hence we may perhaps with advantage
observe that the usual view implies a confusion of thought.
In doing so we must endeavour to understand, by observing
the phenomenon itself, what precisely takes place when in
tuning we tighten a string or relax it. All who possess even
a slight acquaintance with instruments are aware that in

172

producing tension we raise the string to a higher pitch, and that in relaxing it we lower its pitch. Now, while we are thus raising the pitch of the string, it is obvious that the height of pitch which is to result from the process cannot yet be in existence. Height of pitch will only result when the string becomes stationary and ceases to change, after having been brought by the process of tension to the point of pitch required; in other words, when the tension has ceased and no longer exists. For it is impossible that a string should be at the same moment in motion and at rest; and as we have seen, tension takes place when the string is in motion, height of pitch when it is quiescent and stationary. The same remarks will apply to relaxation and depth of pitch, except that these are concerned with change in the opposite direction and its result. It is evident, then, that relaxation and depth of pitch, tension and height of pitch, must not be identified, but stand to one another in the relation of cause and effect. It remains to show that the term pitch also connotes a quite distinct conception.

By the term pitch we mean to indicate a certain per- 12 sistence, as it were, or stationary position of the voice. And let us not be alarmed by the theory which reduces notes to motions and asserts sound in general to be a motion, as though our definition involved the proposition that under certain circumstances motion will, instead of moving, be stationary and at rest. The definition of pitch as a certain condition of motion—call it 'equability' or 'identity,' or by any more enlightening term you can find— will not affect our position. We shall none the less describe the voice as stationary when our senses assure us that it is neither ascending nor descending, simply fixing on this term as descriptive of such a state of the voice without any further implications. To proceed, then, the voice appears to act thus in singing; it moves in making an interval, it is stationary on the note. Now if we use the term 'motion' and say 'the voice moves' in cases where, according to the physical theory, it undergoes a change in the rate of motion; and if, again, we use the term 'rest' and say 'the voice rests' in cases where this change in the rate of motion has ceased, and the motion has become uniform, our musical theory is not thereby affected. For it is plain enough that the term 'motion' in the physical sense covers both 'motion' and 'rest' in the sense in which we employ them. Sufficient has been said on this point here; elsewhere it has been treated more fully and clearly.

13   To resume; it now being clear that pitch is distinct from tension or relaxation, the former being, as we say, a rest of the voice, the latter, as we have seen, motions, our next task is to understand that it is distinct from the remaining phenomena of height and depth of pitch. Now, our previous observations have shown that the voice is, as a matter of fact, in a state of rest after a transition to height or depth; yet the following considerations will make it clear that pitch, though a rest of the voice, is a phenomenon distinct from both. We must understand that for the voice to be stationary means its remaining at one pitch; and this will happen equally whether it becomes stationary at a high pitch or a low. If pitch, then, be met in high notes as well as low notes—and the voice, as we have shown, must of necessity be capable of becoming stationary on both alike— it follows that, inasmuch as height and depth are absolutely incompatible, pitch, which is a phenomenon common to both, must be distinct from one and the other alike. Enough has now been said to show that pitch, height and depth of pitch, and tension and relaxation of pitch are five conceptions which do not admit of any identification *inter se.*

The next point for our consideration is whether distance on the line of pitch admits of infinite extension or diminu-

174

tion. There is no difficulty in seeing that if we refer solely **14**
to musical sounds, such infinite extension and diminution
are impossible. For every musical instrument and for every
human voice there is a maximum compass which they
cannot exceed, and a minimum interval, less than which
they cannot produce. No organ of sound can indefinitely
enlarge its range or indefinitely reduce its intervals : in both
cases it reaches a limit. Each of these limits must be
determined by a reference to that which produces the sound
and to that which discriminates it—the voice, namely, and
the ear. What the voice cannot produce and the ear
cannot discriminate must be excluded from the available
and practically possible range of musical sound. In the
progress *in parvitatem* the voice and the ear seem to fail at
the same point. The voice cannot differentiate, nor can
the ear discriminate, any interval smaller than the smallest
diesis, so as to determine what fraction it is of a diesis or of
any other of the known intervals. In the progress *in
magnitudinem* the power of the ear may perhaps be considered to stretch beyond that of the voice, though to no
very great distance. In any case, whether we are to assume
the same limit for voice and ear in both directions, or
whether we are to suppose it to be the same in the progress
in parvitatem but different in the progress *in magnitudinem*,
the fact remains that there is a maximum and minimum
limit of distance on the line of pitch, either common to **15**
voice and ear, or peculiar to each. It is clear, then, that
distance of high and low on the line of pitch, regarded in
relation to voice and ear, is incapable of infinite extension or
infinitesimal diminution. Whether, regarding the constitution
of melody in the abstract, we are bound to admit such an
infinite progress, is a question demanding a different method
of reasoning not required for our present purpose, and we
shall accordingly reserve its discussion for a later occasion.

The question of distance on the line of pitch being disposed of, we shall proceed to define a note. Briefly, it is the incidence of the voice upon one point of pitch. Whenever the voice is heard to remain stationary on one pitch, we have a note qualified to take a place in a melody.

An interval, on the other hand, is the distance bounded by two notes which have not the same pitch. For, roughly speaking, an interval is a difference between points of pitch, a space potentially admitting notes higher than the lower of the two points of pitch which bound the interval, and lower than the higher of them. A difference between points of pitch depends on degrees of tension.

16   A scale, again, is to be regarded as the compound of two or more intervals. Here we would ask our hearers to receive these definitions in the right spirit, not with jealous scrutiny of the degree of their exactness. We would ask him to aid us with his intelligent sympathy, and to consider our definition sufficiently instructive when it puts him in the way of understanding the thing defined. To supply a definition which affords an unexceptionable and exhaustive analysis is a difficult task in the case of all fundamental motions, and by no means least difficult in the case of the note, the interval, and the scale.

We must now endeavour to classify first intervals and then scales according to all those principles of division that are of practical use. The first classification of intervals distinguishes them by their compass, the second regards them as concordant or discordant, the third as simple or compound, the fourth divides them according to the musical genus, the fifth as rational or irrational. As all other classifications are of no practical use, let us disregard them for the present.

17   In scales will be found, with one exception, all the dis-

tinctions which we have met in intervals. It is obvious
that scales may differ both in compass and owing to the
fact that the notes bounding that compass may be either
concordant or discordant. The third, however, of the distinctions mentioned in the case of intervals cannot exist
in the case of scales. Evidently we cannot have simple
and compound scales, at least not in the same way as we
had simple and compound intervals. The fourth distinction—that according to genera—must also exist in the
case of scales, some of them being diatonic, some chromatic,
and some enharmonic. It is obvious that they also admit
the fifth principle of division: some are bounded by a
rational, and some by an irrational, interval. To these four
there must be added **three other classifications.** First,
there is that into the conjunct scales, the disjunct scales,
and the scales that are a combination of both ; every scale,
provided it is of a certain compass, becomes either conjunct
or disjunct, or else combines both these qualities—for cases
are to be seen where the latter process takes place. There
is, secondly, the division into transilient and continuous,
every scale belonging to one category or the other ; and
finally, that into single, double, and multiple, as all without 18
exception admit of classification under these heads. An
explanation of each of these terms will be given in the
sequel.

Starting from these definitions and classifications we
must seek to indicate in outline the nature of melody. We
have already observed that here the motion of the voice
must be by intervals ; herein, then, lies the distinction
between the melody of music and of speech—for there is
also a kind of melody in speech which depends upon the
accents of words, as the voice in speaking rises and sinks
by a natural law. Again, melody which accords with
the laws of harmony is not constituted by intervals and

notes alone. Collocation upon a definite principle is also indispensable, it being obvious that intervals and notes are equally constituents of melody which violates the laws of harmony. It follows that the most important and significant factor in the right constitution of melody is the principle of collocation in general as well as its special laws. We see, then, that musical melody differs from the melody of speech, on the one hand, in employing motion by intervals, and from faulty melody, on the other hand, melody which violates the laws of harmony, by the different 19 manner in which it collocates the simple intervals. What this manner is will be shown in the sequel; for the present it will suffice to insist on the fact that, though melody which accords with the laws of harmony admits of many variations in collocating the intervals, there is yet one invariable attribute that can be predicated of every such melody, of so great importance that with its removal the harmony disappears. A full explanation will be given in the course of the treatise. For the present we content ourselves with this definition of musical melody in contradistinction to the other species, but it must be understood that we have supplied a mere outline without as yet reviewing the details.

Our next step will be to enumerate the **genera** into which melody in general may be divided. These are apparently three in number. Any melody we take that is harmonized on one principle is diatonic or chromatic or enharmonic. Of these genera the diatonic must be granted to be the first and oldest, inasmuch as mankind lights upon it before the others; the chromatic comes next. The enharmonic is the third and most recondite; and it is only at a late stage, and with great labour and difficulty, that the ear becomes accustomed to it.

We shall now return to the second of the distinctions in intervals previously enumerated, and shall proceed to

178

examine one of the two classes there contrasted. These
classes consist, as was remarked, of concords and discords, 20
and it is the former that we shall now take for consideration.
We shall endeavour to establish the facts with regard to one
of the many points in which concords differ, namely respect
of compass. The nature of melody in the abstract determines which concord has the least compass. Though many
smaller intervals than the Fourth occur in melody, they are
without exception discords. But while the least concordant
interval is thus determined, we find no similar determination
for the greatest; for as far at any rate as the nature of
melody in the abstract is concerned, concords seem capable
of infinite extension just as much as discords. If we add
to an octave any concord, whether greater than, equal to,
or less than, an octave, the sum is a concord. From this
point of view, then, there is no maximum concord. If,
however, we regard our practical capacities—in other words,
the capacities of the human voice and of instruments—there
is apparently such a maximum, the interval, namely, composed of two octaves and a Fifth. The compass of three
octaves is, as a matter of fact, beyond our reach. We must
of course determine the compass of the maximum concord
by the pitch and limits of some *one* instrument. For
doubtless we should find an interval greater than the above-
mentioned three octaves between the highest note of the
soprano clarinet, and the lowest note of the bass clarinet;
and again between the highest note of a clarinet player 21
performing with the speaker open, and the lowest note of
a clarinet player performing with the speaker closed. A
similar relation, too, would be found to exist between the
voices of a child and a man. It is, indeed, from cases
such as these that we come to know the large concords.
For it is from voices of different ages, and instruments of
different measurements that we have learned that the interval

of three octaves, of four octaves, and even greater intervals than these are concordant. Our conclusion then is that, while the smallest concord is given by the nature of abstract melody, the greatest is only determined by our capabilities.

That the concordant intervals are eight in number will be readily admitted. . . .

The determination of the interval of a tone is our next task. A tone is the difference in compass between the first two concords, and may be divided by three lowest denominators, as melody admits of half tones, thirds of tones, and quarter-tones, while undeniably rejecting any interval less than these. Let us designate the smallest of these intervals the smallest enharmonic diesis, the next the smallest chromatic diesis, and the greatest a semitone.

Let us now set ourselves to consider the origin and 22 nature of the differences of the genera. Our attention must be directed to the smallest of the concords, that of which the compass is usually occupied by four notes— whence its ancient name. [Now since in such an interval the notes may be arranged in many different orders, what order are we to choose for consideration? One in which the fixed notes and the notes that change with the variation in genus are equal in number. An example of the order required will be found in the interval between the Mese and the Hypate: here, while the two intermediate notes vary, the two extremes are left unchanged by genus-variation.] Let this then be granted. Further, while there are several groups of notes which fill this scheme of the Fourth, each distinguished by its own special nomenclature, there is one which, as being more familiar than any other to the student of music, may be selected as that wherein we shall consider how variation of genus makes its appearance. It consists of the Mese, Lichanus, Parhypate, and Hypate.

THE ELEMENTS OF HARMONY

That variation of genus arises through the raising and lowering of the movable notes is obvious; but the locus of the variation of these notes requires discussion. The locus of the variation of the Lichanus is a tone, for this note is never nearer the Mese than the interval of a tone, and never further from it than the interval of two tones. The lesser of these extreme intervals is recognized as legitimate by those who have grasped the principle of the Diatonic Genus, and those who have not yet mastered it 23 can be led by particular instances to the same admission. The greater of these extreme intervals, on the other hand, finds no such universal acceptance; but the reason for this must be postponed to the sequel. That there is a style of composition which demands a Lichanus at a distance of two tones from the Mese, and that far from being contemptible it is perhaps the noblest of all styles—this is a truth which is indeed far from patent to most musical students of to-day, though it would become so if they were led to the apprehension of it by the aid of concrete examples. But to any one who possesses an adequate acquaintance with the first and second styles of ancient music, it is an indisputable truth. Theorists who are only familiar with the style of composition now in vogue naturally exclude the two-tone Lichanus, the prevailing tendency being to the use of the higher Lichani. The ground of this fashion lies in the perpetual striving after sweetness, attested by the fact that time and attention are mostly devoted to chromatic music, and that when the enharmonic is introduced, it is approximated to the chromatic, while the ethical character of the music suffers a corresponding deflection. Without carrying this line of thought any further, we shall assume the locus of the Lichanus to be a tone, and that of the Parhypate to be the smallest diesis, as the latter note is never nearer to the

Hypate than a diesis, and never further from it than a semitone. For the loci do not overlap; their point of contact serves as a limit to both of them. The point of pitch upon which the Parhypate in its ascent meets the Lichanus in its descent supplies a boundary to the loci, 24 the lower locus being that of the Parhypate, the higher that of the Lichanus.

Having thus determined the total loci of the Lichanus and Parhypate, we shall now proceed to ascertain their loci as qualified by genus and *shade*. The proper method of investigating whether the Fourth can be expressed in terms of any lower intervals, or whether it is incommensurable with them all, is given in my chapter on 'Intervals ascertained by the principle of Concord.' Here we shall assume that its apparent value is correct, and that it consists of two and a half tones. Again, we shall apply the term Pycnum [1] to the combination of two intervals, the sum of which is less than the complement that makes up the Fourth. Let us now, starting from the lower of the two fixed notes, take the least Pycnum: it will consist of the two least enharmonic dieses; while a second Pycnum, taken from the same note, will consist of two of the least chromatic dieses. This gives the two lowest Lichani of two genera— the enharmonic and the chromatic; the enharmonic Lichani being in general, as we saw, the lowest, the chromatic coming next, and the diatonic being the highest. Again, let a third Pycnum be taken, still from the same note; then a fourth, which is equal to a tone; then fifthly, from the same note, let there be taken a scale consisting of a tone and a quarter; then a sixth scale consisting of a tone and a half. We have already mentioned the Lichani bounding 25 the first and the second Pycna; that bounding the third is chromatic, and the special chroma to which it belongs is

[1] i. e. 'close,' 'compressed.'

THE ELEMENTS OF HARMONY

called the *Hemiolic*. The Lichanus bounding the fourth
Pycnum is also chromatic, and the special class to which it
belongs is called the *Tonic* Chromatic. The fifth scale is
too great for a Pycnum, for here the sum of the intervals
between the Hypate and Parhypate and between the Parhypate and the Lichanus is equal to the interval between
the Lichanus and the Mese. The Lichanus bounding this
scale is the lowest diatonic. The sixth scale we assumed is
bounded by the highest diatonic Lichanus. Thus the
lowest chromatic Lichanus is one-sixth of a tone higher
than the lowest enharmonic; since the chromatic diesis
is greater than the enharmonic by one-twelfth of a tone—
the third of a quantity being one-twelfth greater than the
fourth—and similarly the two chromatic dieses exceed the
two enharmonic by double that quantity, namely one-sixth
—an interval smaller than the smallest admitted in melody.
Such intervals are not melodic elements, or in other words
cannot take an independent place in a scale. Again, the
lowest diatonic Lichanus is seven-twelfths of a tone higher
than the lowest chromatic; for from the former to the
Lichanus of the hemiolic chroma is half a tone; from this
Lichanus to the enharmonic is a diesis; from the enharmonic Lichanus to the lowest chromatic is one-sixth of
a tone; while from the lowest chromatic to that of the
hemiolic chroma is one-twelfth of a tone. But as a quarter **26**
consists of three-twelfths, it is clear that there is the interval
just mentioned between the lowest diatonic and the lowest
chromatic Lichanus. The highest diatonic Lichanus is
higher than the lowest diatonic by a diesis. These considerations show the locus of each of the Lichani. Every
Lichanus below the chromatic is enharmonic, every Lichanus
below the diatonic is chromatic down to the lowest chromatic, and every Lichanus lower than the highest diatonic is
diatonic down to the lowest diatonic. For we must regard

the Lichani as infinite in number. Let the voice become
stationary at any point in the locus of the Lichanus here
demonstrated, and the result is a Lichanus. In the locus
of the Lichanus there is no empty space—no space incapable
of admitting a Lichanus. The point we are discussing is
one of no little importance. Other musicians only dispute
as to the position of the Lichanus—whether, for instance,
the Lichanus in the enharmonic species is two tones removed from the Mese or holds a higher position, thus
assuming but one enharmonic Lichanus; we, on the other
hand, not only assert that there is a plurality of Lichani
in each class, but even declare that their number is infinite.

Passing from the Lichani we find but two loci for the
Parhypate, one common to the diatonic and chromatic
genus and one peculiar to the enharmonic. For two of the
genera have the Parhypate in common. Every Parhy-
27 pate lower than the lowest chromatic is enharmonic; every
other down to this point of limitation is chromatic *and*
diatonic. As regards the intervals, while that between the
Hypate and Parhypate is either equal to or less than that
between the Parhypate and the Lichanus, the latter may
be less than, equal to, or greater than that between the
Lichanus and the Mese, the reason being that the two
genera have their Parhypate in common. We can have
a melodious tetrachord with the lowest chromatic Parhypate
and the highest diatonic Lichanus. Enough has now been
said to show how great is the locus of the Parhypate both
in respect of its subdivisions and when regarded as a
whole.

Of continuity and consecution it would be no easy task
to give accurate definitions at the outset, but a few rough
indications must be offered. Continuity in melody seems
in its nature to correspond to that continuity in speech which

is observable in the collocation of the letters. In speaking, the voice by a natural law places one letter first in each syllable, another second, another third, another fourth, and so on. This is done in no random order : rather, the growth of the whole from the parts follows a natural law. Similarly in singing, the voice seems to arrange its intervals and notes on a principle of continuity, observing a natural law of collocation, and not placing any interval at random after any other, whether equal or unequal. In inquiring into 28 continuity we must avoid the example set by the Harmonists in their condensed diagrams, where they mark as consecutive notes those that are separated from one another by the smallest interval. For so far is the voice from being able to produce twenty-eight consecutive dieses, that it can by no effort produce three dieses in succession. If ascending after two dieses, it can produce nothing less than the complement of the Fourth, and that is either eight times the smallest diesis, or falls short of it only by a minute and unmelodic interval. If descending, it cannot after the two dieses introduce any interval less than a tone. It is not, then, in the mere equality or inequality of successive intervals that we must seek the clue to the principle of continuity. We must direct our eyes to the natural laws of melody and endeavour to discover what intervals the voice is by nature capable of placing in succession in a melodic series. For if after the Parhypate and the Lichanus the voice can produce no note nearer than the Mese, then the Mese is the next note to the Lichanus, whether the interval between them be twice or several times that between the Lichanus and the Parhypate. The proper method of investigating continuity is now clear ; but how it arises, and what intervals do and do not form a succession, are questions 29 which will be treated in the *Elements*.

We shall here assume that, having posited a Pycnum or

185

a scale that is not a Pycnum, the smallest interval that can succeed in the ascending scale is the complement of the interval of the Fourth, and that the smallest similarly in the descending scale is a tone. We shall assume that if a series of notes be arranged in proper melodic continuity in any genus, any note in that series will either form with the fourth from it in order the concord of the Fourth, or with the fifth from it in order the concord of the Fifth, while possibly forming both. A note that answers to none of these tests cannot belong to the same melodic series as those with which it makes no concord. Further, we shall assume that whereas there are four intervals contained in the interval of the Fifth, two of which are usually equal, viz. those constituting the Pycnum, and two unequal—one the complement of the first concord, the other the excess of the interval of the Fifth over that of the Fourth, the unequal intervals which succeed the equal intervals do so in different order according as we ascend or descend the scale. We shall assume too that notes which form respectively the same concord with consecutive notes are themselves consecutive; that in each genus a simple melodic interval is one which the voice cannot divide in a melodic progression; that not all the magnitudes into which a concord can be divided are simple; that a sequence is a progression by consecutive notes, each of which, between the first and last, is preceded and succeeded by a simple interval; and that a direct sequence is one that maintains the same direction throughout.

BOOK II

IT will be well perhaps to review in anticipation the course 30. 10
of our study; thus a foreknowledge of the road that we must
travel will enable us to recognize each stage as we reach it,
and so lighten the toil of the journey; nor shall we be
harbouring unknown to ourselves a false conception of our
subject. (Such was the condition, as Aristotle used often to
relate, of most of the audience that attended Plato's lectures
on the Good. They came, he used to say, every one of
them, in the conviction that they would get from the
lectures some one or other of the things that the world calls
good; riches or health, or strength, in fine, some extraordinary gift of fortune. But when they found that Plato's
reasonings were of sciences and numbers, and geometry,
and astronomy, and of good and unity as predicates of the
finite, methinks their disenchantment was complete. The 31
result was that some of them sneered at the thing, while
others vilified it. Now to what was all this trouble due?
To the fact that they had not waited to inform themselves
of the nature of the subject, but after the manner of the sect
of word-catchers had flocked round open-mouthed, attracted
by the mere title ' good ' in itself.)

But if a general exposition of the subject had been given
in advance, the intending pupil would either have abandoned
his intention or if he was pleased with the exposition, would
have remained in the said conviction to the end. (It was
for these very reasons, as he told us, that Aristotle himself
used to give his intending pupils a preparatory statement of

187

the subject and method of his course of study. And we agree with him in thinking, as we said at the beginning, that such prior information is desirable. For mistakes are often made in both directions. Some consider Harmonic a sublime science, and expect a course of it to make them musicians; nay some even conceive it will exalt their moral nature. This mistake is due to their having run away with such phrases in our preamble as ' we aim at the construction of every style of melody,' and with our general statement ' one class of musical art is hurtful to the moral character, another improves it '; while they missed completely our qualification of this statement, ' in so far as musical art can improve the moral character.' Then on the other hand there are persons who regard Harmonic as quite a thing of no importance, and actually prefer to remain totally un-acquainted even with its nature and aim. Neither of these views is correct. On the one hand the science is no proper object of contempt to the man of intelligence—this we shall

32 see as the discussion progresses; nor on the other hand has it the quality of all-sufficiency, as some imagine. To be a musician, as we are always insisting, implies much more than a knowledge of Harmonic, which is only one part of the musician's equipment, on the same level as the sciences of Rhythm, of Metre, of Instruments.

We shall now proceed to the consideration of Harmonic and its parts. It is to be observed that in general the subject of our study is the question, In melody of every kind what are the natural laws according to which the voice in ascending or descending places the intervals? For we hold that the voice follows a natural law in its motion, and does not place the intervals at random. And of our answers we endeavour to supply proofs that will be in agreement with the phenomena—in this unlike our predecessors. For some of these introduced extraneous reasoning, and rejecting the senses as inaccurate fabricated rational principles, asserting that height and depth of pitch consist in certain numerical ratios and relative rates of vibration—a theory utterly extraneous to the subject and quite at variance with the phenomena; while others, dispensing with reason and demonstration, confined themselves to isolated dogmatic statements, not being successful either in their enumeration of the mere phenomena. It is our endeavour that the principles which we assume shall without exception be evident to those who understand music, and that we 33 shall advance to our conclusions by strict demonstration.

Our subject-matter then being all melody, whether vocal or instrumental, our method rests in the last resort on an appeal to the two faculties of hearing and intellect. By the former we judge the magnitudes of the intervals, by the latter we contemplate the functions of the notes. We must therefore accustom ourselves to an accurate discrimination of particulars. It is usual in geometrical constructions to use such a phrase as ' Let this be a straight line'; but one must not be content with such language of assumption in the case of intervals. The geometrician makes no use of his faculty of sense-perception. He does not in any degree train his sight to discriminate the straight line, the circle, or any other figure, such training belonging rather to the practice of the carpenter, the turner, or some other such handicraftsman. But for the student of musical science accuracy of sense-perception is a fundamental requirement. For if his sense-perception is deficient, it is impossible for him to deal successfully with those questions that lie outside the sphere of sense-perception altogether. This will become clear in the course of our investigation. And we must bear in mind that musical cognition implies the simultaneous cognition of a permanent and of a changeable element, and that this applies without limitation or qualification to every

branch of music. To begin with, our perception of the differences of the genera is dependent on the permanence of the containing, and the variation of the intermediate,
34 notes. Again, while the magnitude remains constant, we distinguish the interval between Hypate and Mese from that between Paramese and Nete; here, then, the magnitude is permanent, while the functions of the notes change; similarly, when there are several figures of the same magnitude, as of the Fourth, or Fifth, or any other; similarly, when the same interval leads or does not lead to modulation, according to its position. Again, in matters of rhythm we find many similar examples. Without any change in the characteristic proportion constituting any one genus of rhythm, the lengths of the feet vary in obedience to the general rate of movement; and while the magnitudes are constant, the quality of the feet undergoes a change; and the same magnitude serves as a foot, and as a combination of feet. Plainly, too, unless there was a permanent quantum to deal with there could be no distinctions as to the methods of dividing it and arranging its parts. And in general, while rhythmical composition employs a rich variety of movements, the movements of the feet by which we note the rhythms are always simple and the same. Such, then, being the nature of music, we must in matters of harmony also accustom both ear and intellect to a correct judgement of the permanent and changeable element alike.

These remarks have exhibited the general character of the science called Harmonic; and of this science there are,
35 as a fact, seven parts. Of these one and the first is to define the **genera,** and to show what are the permanent and what are the changeable elements presupposed by this distinction. None of our predecessors have drawn this distinction at all; nor is this to be wondered at. For they confined their attention to the Enharmonic genus, to the

neglect of the other two. Students of instruments, it is true, could not fail to distinguish each genus by ear, but none of them reflected even on the question, At what point does the Enharmonic begin to pass into the Chromatic? For their ability to discriminate each genus extended not to all the *shades*, inasmuch as they were not acquainted with all styles of musical composition or trained to exercise a nice discrimination in such distinctions ; nor did they even observe that there were certain loci of the notes that alter their position with the change of genus. These reasons sufficiently explain why the genera have not as yet been definitely distinguished; but it is evident that we must supply this deficiency if we are to follow the differences that present themselves in works of musical composition.

Such is the first branch of Harmonic. In the second we shall deal with **intervals**, omitting, to the best of our ability, none of the distinctions to be found in them. The majority of these, one might say, have as yet escaped observation. But we must bear in mind that wherever we come upon a distinction which has been overlooked, and not scientifically considered, we shall there fail to recognize the distinctions **36** in works of melodic composition.

Again, since intervals are not in themselves sufficient to distinguish notes—for every magnitude, without qualification, that an interval can possess is common to several musical functions—the third part of our science will deal with **notes**, their number, and the means of recognizing them; and will consider the question whether they are certain points of pitch, as is vulgarly supposed, or whether they are musical functions, and also what is the meaning of a musical 'function.' Not one of these questions is clearly conceived by students of the subject.

The fourth part will consider **scales**, firstly as to their number and nature, secondly as to the manner of their

construction from intervals and notes. Our predecessors
have not regarded this part of the subject in either of these
respects. On the one hand, no attention has been devoted
to the questions whether intervals are collocated in any
order to produce scales, or whether some collocations may
not transgress a natural law. On the other hand, the distinctions in scales have not been completely enumerated by
any of them. As to the first point, our forerunners simply
ignored the distinction between 'melodious' and 'unmelodious'; as to the second, they either made no attempt
at all at enumeration of scale-distinctions, confining their
attention to the seven octave scales which they called
Harmonies; or if they made the attempt, they fell very
short of completeness, like the school of Pythagoras of
37 Zacynthus, and Agenor of Mitylene. The order that distinguishes the melodious from the unmelodious resembles
that which we find in the collocation of letters in language.
For it is not every collocation but only certain collocations
of any given letters that will produce a syllable.

The fifth part of our science deals with the keys in which
the scales are placed for the purposes of melody. No explanation has yet been offered of the manner in which those keys
are to be found, or of the principle by which one must be
guided in enunciating their number. The account of the
keys given by the Harmonists closely resembles the observance of the days according to which, for example, the tenth
day of the month at Corinth is the fifth at Athens, and the
eighth somewhere else. Just in the same way, some of
the Harmonists hold that the Hypodorian is the lowest
of the keys; that half a tone above lies the Mixolydian;
half a tone higher again the Dorian; a tone above the
Dorian the Phrygian; likewise a tone above the Phrygian the
Lydian. The number is sometimes increased by the addition of the Hypophrygian clarinet at the bottom of the list.

Others, again, having regard to the boring of finger-holes
on the flutes, assume intervals of three quarter-tones between
the three lowest keys, the Hypophrygian, the Hypodorian,
and the Dorian; a tone between the Dorian and Phrygian;
three quarter-tones again between the Phrygian and Lydian,
and the same distance between the Lydian and Mixolydian.
But they have not informed us on what principle they have 38
persuaded themselves to this location of the keys. And
that the close packing of small intervals is unmelodious and
of no practical value whatsoever will be clear in the course
of our discussion.

Again, since some melodies are simple, and others contain
a modulation, we must treat of modulation, considering
first the nature of modulation in the abstract, and how it
arises, or in other words, to what modification in the melodic
order it owes its existence; secondly, how many modulations
there are in all, and at what intervals they occur. On these
questions we find no statements by our predecessors with
or without proof.

The last section of our science is concerned with the
actual construction of melody. For since in the same
notes, indifferent in themselves, we have the choice of
numerous melodic forms of every character, it is evident
that here we have the practical question of the employment
of the notes; and this is what we mean by the construction
of melody. The science of harmony having traversed the
said sections will find its consummation here.

It is plain that the apprehension of a melody consists in
noting with both ear and intellect every distinction as it
arises in the successive sounds—successive, for melody,
like all branches of music, consists in a successive production. For the apprehension of music depends on these
two faculties, sense-perception and memory; for we must 39
perceive the sound that is present, and remember that which

is past. In no other way can we follow the phenomena of music.

Now some find the goal of the science called Harmonic in the notation of melodies, declaring this to be the ultimate limit of the apprehension of any given melody. Others again find it in the knowledge of clarinets, and in the ability to tell the manner of production of, and the agencies employed in, any piece rendered on the clarinet.

Such views are conclusive evidence of an utter misconception. So far is notation from being the perfection of Harmonic science that it is not even a part of it, any more than the marking of any particular metre is a part of metrical science. As in the latter case one might very well mark the scheme of the iambic metre without understanding its essence, so it is with melody also; if a man notes down the Phrygian scale it does not follow that he must know the essence of the Phrygian scale. Plainly then notation is not the ultimate limit of our science.

That the premises of our argument are true, and that the faculty of musical notation argues nothing beyond a discernment of the size of intervals, will be clear on consideration. In the use of signs for the intervals no peculiar mark is employed to denote all their individual distinctions, 40 such as the several methods of dividing the Fourth, which depend on the differences of genera, or the several figures of the same interval which result from a variation in the disposition of the simple intervals. It is the same with the musical functions proper to the natures of the different tetrachords; the same notation is employed for the tetrachords Hyperbolaeôn, Netôn, Mesôn, and Hypatôn. Thus the signs fail to distinguish the functional differences, and consequently indicate the magnitudes of the intervals, and nothing more. But that the mere sense-discrimination of magnitudes is no part of the general comprehension of music was stated in the introduction, and the following considerations will make it patent. Mere knowledge of magnitudes does not enlighten one as to the functions of the tetrachords, or of the notes, or the differences of the genera or, briefly, the difference of simple and compound intervals, or the distinction between modulating and non-modulating scales, or the modes of melodic construction, or indeed anything else of the kind.

Now if the Harmonists, as they are called, have in their ignorance seriously entertained this view, while there is nothing preposterous in their motives, their ignorance must be profound and invincible. But if, being aware that notation is not the final goal of Harmonic, they have propounded this view merely through the desire to please amateurs, and to represent as the perfection of the science a certain visible activity, their motives deserve condemnation 41 as very preposterous indeed. In the first place they would constitute the amateur judge of the sciences—and it is preposterous that the same person should be learner and judge of the same thing ; in the second place, they reverse the proper order in their fancy of representing a visible activity as the consummation of intellectual apprehension ; for, as a fact, the ultimate factor in every visible activity is the intellectual process. For this latter is the presiding and determining principle ; and as for the hands, voice, mouth, or breath—it is an error to suppose that they are very much more than inanimate instruments. And if this intellectual activity is something hidden deep down in the soul, and is not palpable or apparent to the ordinary man, as the operations of the hand and the like are apparent, we must not on that account alter our views. We shall be sure to miss the truth unless we place the supreme and ultimate, not in the thing determined, but in the activity that determines.

No less preposterous is the above-mentioned theory

concerning clarinets. Nay, rather there is no error so
fatal and so preposterous as to base the natural laws of
harmony on any instrument. The essence and order of
harmony depend not upon any of the properties of instruments. It is not because the clarinet has finger-holes and
42 bores, and the like, nor is it because it submits to certain
operations of the hands and of the other parts naturally
adapted to raise and lower the pitch, that the Fourth, and
the Fifth, and the Octave are concords, or that each of the
other intervals possesses its proper magnitude. For even
with all these conditions present, players on the clarinet
fail for the most part to attain the exact order of melody;
and whatever small success attends them is due to the
employment of agencies external to the instrument, as in
the well-known expedients of drawing the two clarinets
apart, and bringing them alongside, and of raising and
lowering the pitch by changing the pressure of the breath.
Plainly, then, one is as much justified in attributing their
failures as their success to the essential nature of the
clarinet. But this would not have been so if there was
anything gained by basing harmony on the nature of an
instrument. In that case, as an immediate consequence of
tracing melody up to its original in the nature of the
clarinet, we should have found it there fixed, unerring, and
correct. But as a fact neither clarinets nor any other
instrument will supply a foundation for the principles of
harmony. There is a certain marvellous order which
belongs to the nature of harmony in general; in this order
every instrument, to the best of its ability, participates
under the direction of that faculty of sense-perception on
which they, as well as everything else in music, finally
depend. To suppose, because one sees day by day the
finger-holes the same and the strings at the same tension,
that one will find in these harmony with its permanence

and eternally immutable order—this is sheer folly. For 43
as there is no harmony in the strings save that which the
cunning of the hand confers upon them, so is there none in
the finger-holes save what has been introduced by the same
agency. That no instrument is self-tuned, and that the
harmonizing of it is the prerogative of the sense-perception
is obvious, and requires no proof. It is strange that the
supporters of this absurd theory can cling to it in face of the
fact that clarinets are perpetually in a state of change; and
of course what is played on the instrument varies with the
variation in the agencies employed in its production. It is
surely clear then that on no consideration can melody be
based on clarinets; for, firstly, an instrument will not supply
a foundation for the order of harmony, and secondly, even
if it were supposed that harmony should be based on some
instrument, the choice should not have fallen on the clarinet,
an instrument especially liable to aberrations, resulting from
the manufacture and manipulation of it, and from its own
peculiar nature.

This will suffice as an introductory account of Harmonic
science; but as we prepare ourselves to enter upon the
study of the *Elements* we must at the outset attend to the
following considerations. Our exposition cannot be a successful one unless three conditions be fulfilled. Firstly,
the phenomena themselves must be correctly observed;
secondly, what is prior and what is derivative in them must 44
be properly discriminated; thirdly, our conclusions and
inferences must follow legitimately from the premises. And
as in every science that consists of several propositions the
proper course is to find certain principles from which to
deduce the dependent truths, we must be guided in our
selection of principles by two considerations. Firstly, every
proposition that is to serve as a principle must be true and
evident; secondly, it must be such as to be accepted by the

sense-perception as one of the primary truths of Harmonic science. For what requires demonstration cannot stand as a fundamental principle ; and in general we must be watchful in determining our highest principles, lest on the one hand we let ourselves be dragged outside the proper track of our science by beginning with sound in general regarded as air-vibration, or on the other hand turn short of the flag and abandon much of what truly belongs to Harmonic.

There are three genera of melodies ; Diatonic, Chromatic, and Enharmonic. The differences between them will be stated hereafter ; this we may lay down, that every melody must be Diatonic, or Chromatic, or Enharmonic, or blended of these kinds, or composed of what they have in common.

The second classification of intervals is into concords and discords. The two most familiar distinctions in intervals are difference of magnitude, and difference between concords and discords ; and the latter of these is embraced by the former, since every concord differs from every discord in magnitude. Now there being many distinctions among
45 concords, let us first treat of the most familiar of them, namely, difference of magnitude. We assume then eight magnitudes of concords ; the smallest, the Fourth—determined as smallest by the abstract nature of melody ; for while we can produce several smaller intervals, they are all discords ; the next smallest, the Fifth, all intervals between the Fourth and Fifth being discords ; the third smallest, the sum of the first two, that is the Octave, all intervals between the Fifth and the Octave being discords. So far we have been stating what we have learned from our predecessors ; henceforth we must arrive at our conclusions unaided.

In the first place then we shall assert that if any concord be added to the octave the sum is a concord. This property is peculiar to the octave. For if to an octave be added any concord, whether less than, equal to, or greater than itself, the sum is a concord. But this is not the case with the two smallest concords. For the doubling of a Fourth or Fifth does not produce a concord; nor does the addition to either one of them of the concord compounded of the octave and that one; but the sum of such concords will always be a discord.

A tone is the excess of the Fifth over the Fourth; the 46 Fourth consists of two tones and a half. The following fractions of a tone occur in melody: the half, called a semitone; the third, called the smallest Chromatic diesis; the quarter, called the smallest Enharmonic diesis. No smaller interval than the last exists in melody. Here we have two cautions for our hearers; firstly, many have misunderstood us to say that melody admits the division of the tone into three or four equal parts. This misunderstanding is due to their not observing that to employ the third part of a tone is a very different thing from dividing a tone into three parts and singing all three. Secondly, from an abstract point of view, no doubt, we regard no interval as the smallest possible.

The differences of the genera are found in such a tetrachord as that from Mese to Hypate, where the extremes are fixed, while one or both of the means vary. As the variable note must move in a certain locus, we must ascertain the limits of the locus of each of these intermediate notes. The highest Lichanus is that which is a tone removed from the Mese. It constitutes the genus Diatonic. The lowest is that which is two tones below the Mese; this is Enharmonic. The locus of the Lichanus is thus seen to be a tone. The interval between the Parhypate and Hypate cannot, plainly, be less than an enharmonic diesis, for this latter is 47 the minimum melodic distance. It is to be observed also that it can only be extended to twice that distance; for when the Lichanus in its descent, and the Parhypate in its ascent reach the same pitch, the locus of each note finds its limit. Thus it is seen that the locus of the Parhypate is not greater than the smallest diesis.

· This proposition has afforded some students great perplexity. ' If,' they ask in surprise; ' the interval between the Mese and the Lichanus (assuming it to be any *one* of the above-mentioned intervals) be increased or diminished, how can the note bounding the new interval be a Lichanus? There is admittedly but one interval between the Mese and Paramese, and again between the Mese and Hypate, and in fact between any pair of the permanent notes. Why then should we admit a plurality of intervals between the Mese and the Lichanus? Surely it would be better to change the names of the notes ; and restricting the term Lichanus to any one of them, the two-tone or any other, to employ other designations for the rest. For notes that bound unequal magnitudes must be different notes. And one · might add that the converse is equally valid, namely, that the boundaries of equal magnitudes must have the same designations.' To these objections the following reply was given. In the first place, to postulate that a difference in notes necessarily implies a difference in the magnitudes bounded by them is a startling innovation. We see that the Nete and Mese differ in function from the Paranete and Lichanus, and the Paranete and Lichanus again from the Trite and Parhypate, and these latter again from the Paramese and Hypate ; and 48 for this reason each pair has names of its own, though the contained interval is in every case a Fifth. Thus it is seen that a difference in the contained intervals is not necessarily implied by a difference of notes.

That the converse implication is equally inadmissible will appear from the following remarks. In the first place, if we seek particular designations to suit every increase and decrease in the intervals of the Pycnum, we shall evidently

need an infinite vocabulary, since the locus of the Lichanus
is infinitely divisible.   For as a matter of fact, to which of 49. 7
the disputants as to the *shades* of the genera should we give ͵
our adherence ?   Every one is not guided by the same divisions in harmonizing the chromatic or enharmonic scale.
Why then should the term Lichanus be applied to the two-
tone Lichanus rather than to one slightly higher ?   Whichever division be employed, the ear equally recognizes an
enharmonic genus; yet it is plain that the magnitudes of
the intervals are different in the two divisions.   In the 48. 15
second place, if we have eyes exclusively for equality and
inequality we shall miss the distinction between the like
and unlike.   Thus we shall have to restrict the term Pycnum
to one particular magnitude; as likewise evidently the
terms Enharmonic and Chromatic ; for they too are determined not to a point but to a locus.   But it is evident that
such a restriction is not in accordance with the mode in
which sense forms its representations.   It is by considering
the common qualities found in some one class, not the
magnitude of some one interval, that sense employs such
terms as Pycnum, Chromatic, Enharmonic.   That is to say,
it constitutes a class Pycnum to embrace every case in
which the two intervals occupy a smaller space than the
one ; for in all Pycna, though they are unequal in size, there
is evident to the ear the sound of a certain compression.
Likewise it constitutes a class Chromatic to embrace all
cases in which the Chromatic character is apparent.   For
the ear detects a motion peculiar to each of the genera,
though each genus employs not one but many divisions of 49
the tetrachord.   Thus it is clear that, while the magnitudes
change, the genus may remain unaltered, for up to a certain
point changes in the magnitudes do not involve a change of
genus.   And if the genus remains the same, it is reasonable
to suppose that the functions of the notes may be permanent

also. For the species of the tetrachord is the same, and for this reason we must hold that the boundaries of the intervals are the same notes. In general, as long as the names of the extreme notes remain the same, the higher being called Mese, and the lower Hypate, so long will the names of the intermediate notes also remain the same, the higher being called Lichanus, and the lower Parhypate. For the notes between the Mese and Hypate are always stamped by the ear as Lichanus and Parhypate. To demand that all notes bounding equal intervals should have the same names, or that all notes bounding unequal intervals should have different names, is to join battle with the evidence of the senses. For in melody we make the interval between the Hypate and Parhypate sometimes equal and sometimes 50 unequal to that between the Parhypate and Lichanus. Now in the case of two equal consecutive intervals it is impossible that the notes bounding each of them should be designated by the same terms, unless the middle note is to have two names. The absurdity is also evident when the above-mentioned intervals are unequal. For it is impossible that one of any pair of such names should change while the other remains the same; since the names have meaning only in their relation to one another. So much for this objection.

The term Pycnum we shall employ in all cases when, in a tetrachord whose extremes form a Fourth, the sum of two of the intervals occupies a lesser space than the third. There are certain divisions of the tetrachord which stand out from the rest as familiar, because the magnitudes of the intervals in them are familiar. Of these divisions, one is Enharmonic, in which the Pycnum is a semitone, and its complement two tones; three are Chromatic, namely, the *Soft*, the *Hemiolic*, and the *Tonic* Chromatic. The division of the Soft Chromatic is that in which the Pycnum consists

of two of the smallest Chromatic dieses, while its complement is expressed in terms of two quanta, namely, a
semitone taken thrice, and a Chromatic diesis taken once,
so that the sum of it amounts to three semitones and the
third of a tone. This is the smallest of the Chromatic
Pycna and its Lichanus is the lowest in this genus. The
division of the Hemiolic Chromatic is that in which the 51
Pycnum is one and a half times the Enharmonic Pycnum,
and each Diesis one and a half times an Enharmonic
diesis. . It is manifest that the Hemiolic Pycnum is greater
than the Soft, since the former is less than a tone by an
Enharmonic diesis, the latter by a Chromatic diesis. The
division of the Tonic Chromatic is that in which the Pycnum consists of two semitones, and its complement of a tone
and a half. Up to this point both the inner notes vary;
but now the Parhypate, having traversed the whole of its
locus, remains at rest, while the Lichanus moves an enharmonic diesis. Thus the interval between the Lichanus
and Hypate becomes equal to that between the Lichanus
and Mese, so that the Pycnum does not occur in this
division as in the preceding. The disappearance of the
Pycnum in the division of the tetrachord is coincident with
the first appearance of the Diatonic genus. There are two
divisions of the Diatonic genus, the Soft and the Sharp
Diatonic. The division of the Soft Diatonic is that in
which the interval between the Hypate and Parhypate is
a semitone, that between the Parhypate and Lichanus three
Enharmonic dieses, that between the Lichanus and Mese
five dieses. The division of the Sharp Diatonic is that in
which the interval between the Hypate and Parhypate is
a semitone, while each of the remaining intervals is a tone.
. Thus, while we have six Lichani, as there are six divisions 52
of the tetrachord, one enharmonic, three chromatic, and
two diatonic, we have but four Parhypatae, that is, two

less than the divisions of the tetrachord. For the semitone
Parhypate is employed for both diatonic divisions, and for
the Tonic Chromatic. Thus, of the four Parhypatae, one
is peculiar to the Enharmonic genus, while the Diatonic
and Chromatic between them employ three. Of the intervals in the tetrachord, that between the Hypate and
Parhypate may be equal to that between the Parhypate
and Lichanus, or less than it, but never greater. That it
may be equal is evident from the Enharmonic and Chromatic division of the tetrachord; that it may be less is
evident from the Diatonic scales, and also may be ascertained in the Chromatic by taking a Parhypate of the Soft,
and a Lichanus of the Tonic Chromatic; for such divisions
of the Pycnum sound melodious. But to adopt the opposite
order produces an unmelodious result; for instance, to take
the semitone Parhypate, and the Lichanus of the Hemiolic
Chromatic, or the Parhypate of the Hemiolic, and the
Lichanus of the Soft Chromatic. Such divisions produce
an inharmonious effect. On the other hand, the interval
between the Parhypate and Lichanus may be equal to,
greater than, or less than that between the Lichanus and
Mese. It is equal in the Sharp Diatonic, less in all the
other *shades*, and greater when we employ as Lichanus
the highest of the Diatonic Lichani, and as Parhypate any
one lower than that of the semitone.

We shall next proceed to explain, beginning with a general
53 indication, the method by which we should expect to determine the nature of continuity. To put it generally, in
investigating continuity the laws of melody must be our
guide, nor must we imitate those who shape their account
of continuity with a view to the massing of small intervals. Such theorists plainly disregard the natural sequence
of melody, as appears from the number of dieses that
they place in succession; for the voice's power of con-

necting dieses stops short of three. Thus it appears that continuity must not be sought in the smallest intervals, nor in equal nor in unequal intervals; we must rather follow the guidance of natural laws. Now, though it were no easy matter at present to offer an accurate exposition of continuity before we have explained the collocation of intervals, yet the veriest novice can see from the following reasoning that there is such a thing as continuity. It will be admitted that there is no interval which can be divided *ad infinitum* in melody, and that the natural laws of melody assign a maximum number of fractions to every interval. Assuming that this will be, or rather must be, admitted, we necessarily infer that the notes containing fractions of the said number are consecutive. To this class belong the notes which, as a matter of fact, have been in use from the earliest times, as for instance the Nete, the Paranete, and those that follow them.

Our next duty will be to determine the first and most indispensable condition of the melodious collocation of intervals. Whatever be the genus, from whatever note one 54 starts, if the melody moves in continuous progression either upwards or downwards, the fourth note in order from any note must form with it the concord of the Fourth, or the fifth note in order from it the concord of the Fifth. Any note that answers neither of these tests must be regarded as out of tune in relation to those notes with which it fails to form the above-mentioned concords. It must be observed, however, that the above rule is not all-sufficient for the melodious construction of scales from intervals. It is quite possible that the notes of a scale might form the above-mentioned concords with one another, and yet that the scale might be unmelodiously constructed. But if this condition be not fulfilled, all else is useless. Let us assume this then as a fundamental principle, the violation of which is destructive of harmony. A law, in some respects similar, holds with regard to the relative position of tetrachords. If any two tetrachords are to belong to the same scale, one or other of the following conditions must be fulfilled; either they must be in concord with each other, the notes of one forming some concord or other with the corresponding notes of the other, or they must both be in concord with a third tetrachord, with which they are alike continuous but in opposite directions. This, in itself, is not sufficient to constitute tetrachords of the same scale: certain other conditions must be satisfied, 55 of which we shall speak hereafter. But the absence of the condition renders the rest useless.

When we consider the magnitudes of intervals, we find that while the concords either have no locus of variation, and are definitely determined to one magnitude, or have an inappreciable locus, this definiteness is to be found in a much lesser degree in discords. For this reason, the ear is much more assured of the magnitudes of the concords than of the discords. It follows that the most accurate method of ascertaining a discord is by the principle of concordance. If then a certain note be given, and it be required to find a certain discord below it, such as the ditone (or any other that can be ascertained by the method of concordance), one should take the Fourth above the given note, then descend a Fifth, then ascend a Fourth again, and finally descend another Fifth. Thus, the interval of two tones below the given note will have been ascertained. If it be required to ascertain the discord in the other direction, the concords must be taken in the other direction. Also, if a discord be subtracted from a concord by the method of concordance, the remaining discord is thereby ascertained on the same principle. For, subtract the ditone from the Fourth on the principle of concordance, and it is evident that the notes bounding the excess of the latter over the former will have been found on the same principle. For the bounding notes of the Fourth are con- **56** cords to begin with; and from the higher of these a concord is taken, namely, the Fourth above; from the note thus found another, namely, the Fifth below; from this again. a Fourth above, and finally from this a Fifth below; and the last concord alights on the higher of the notes bounding the excess of the Fourth over the Ditone. Thus it appears that if a discord be subtracted from a concord by the method of concordance the complement also will have been thereby ascertained on the same principle.

The surest method of verifying our original assumption that the Fourth consists of two and a half tones is the following. Let us take such an interval, and let us find the discord of two tones above its lower note, and the same discord below its higher note. Evidently the complements will be equal, since they are remainders obtained by subtracting equals from equals. Next let us take the Fourth above the lower note of the higher ditone, and the Fourth below the higher note of the lower ditone. It will be seen that adjacent to each of the extreme notes of the scale thus obtained there will be two complements in juxtaposition, which must be equal for the reasons already given. This construction completed, we must refer the extreme notes thus determined to the judgement of the ear. If they prove discordant, plainly the Fourth will not be composed **57** of two and a half tones; and just as plainly it will be so composed, if they form a Fifth. For the lowest of the assumed notes is, by construction, a Fourth of the higher boundary of the lower ditone; and it has now turned out that the highest of the assumed notes forms with the lowest of them the concord of the Fifth. Now as the excess of the latter interval over the former is a tone, and as it is

here divided into two equal parts; and as each of these
equal parts which is thus proved to be a semitone is at
the same time the excess of the Fourth over a ditone,
it follows that the Fourth is composed of five semitones.
It will be readily seen that the extremes of our scale
cannot form any concord except a Fifth. They cannot
form a Fourth; for there is here, besides the original Fourth,
an additional complement at each extremity. They cannot
form an octave; for the sum of the complements is less
than two tones, since the excess of the Fourth over the
ditone is less than a tone (for it is universally admitted
that the Fourth is greater than two tones and less than
three); consequently, the whole of what is here added to
the Fourth is less than a Fifth; plainly then their sum
cannot be an octave. But if the concord formed by the
58 extreme notes of our construction is greater than a Fourth,
and less than an octave, it must be a Fifth; for this is
the only concordant magnitude between the Fourth and
Octave.

BOOK III

Successive Tetrachords are either Conjunct or Disjunct.

WE shall employ the term conjunction when two succes- 58. 15
sive tetrachords, similar in figure, have a common note ; the
term disjunction, when two successive tetrachords similar in
figure are separated by the interval of a tone. That successive
tetrachords must be related in either of these ways, is evident
from our axioms. For a series, in which each note forms
a Fourth with the fourth note in order from it, will constitute
conjunct tetrachords; while disjunct tetrachords result, when 59
each note forms a Fifth with the fifth from it. Now as all
successions of notes must fulfil one or other of these conditions, so all successive similar tetrachords must be either
conjunct or disjunct.

Difficulties have been raised by some of my hearers on
the question of succession. It has been asked, Firstly,
what is succession in general? Secondly, does it appear in
one form only, or in several? Thirdly, are conjunct and
disjunct tetrachords equally successive? To these questions
the following answers have been given. In general, scales
are continuous, whose boundaries either are successive or
coincide. There are two forms of succession in scales ; in
the one, the upper boundary of the lower scale coincides
with the lower boundary of the upper scale ; in the other,
the lower boundary of the higher scale is in the line of
succession with the higher boundary of the lower scale. In
the first of these forms, the scales of the successive tetrachords have a certain space in common, and are necessarily

similar in figure. In the other form, they are separated
from one another, and the species of the tetrachords may
be similar, only on condition, however, that the separating
interval is one tone. Thus we are led to conclude that two
similar tetrachords are successive, if they are either separated
by a tone, or if their boundaries coincide. Consequently
similar successive tetrachords are either conjunct or disjunct.

We also assert that two successive tetrachords either
60 must be separated by no tetrachord whatsoever, or must not
be separated by a tetrachord dissimilar to themselves.
Tetrachords similar in species cannot be separated by a
dissimilar tetrachord, and dissimilar but successive tetrachords cannot be separated by any tetrachord whatsoever.
Hence we see that tetrachords similar in species can be
arranged in succession in the two forms above mentioned.

The interval contained by successive notes is simple.

For if the containing notes are successive, no note is
wanting; if none is wanting, none will intrude; if none
intrudes, none will divide the interval. But that which
excludes division excludes composition. For every composite is composed of certain parts into which it is divisible.

The above proposition is often the object of perplexity
on account of the ambiguous character of the intervallic
magnitudes. 'How,' it is asked in surprise, 'can the ditone
possibly be simple, seeing that it can be divided into tones?
Or, how again is it possible for the tone to be simple seeing
that it can be divided into two semitones?' And the same
point is raised about the semitone.

This perplexity arises from the failure to observe that
some intervallic magnitudes are common to simple and
compound intervals. For this reason the simplicity of an
interval is determined not by its magnitude, but the relations
of the notes that bound it. The ditone is simple when

210

bounded by the Mese and Lichanus; when bounded by the Mese and Parhypate, it is compound. This is why we 61 assert that simplicity does not depend on the sizes of the intervals, but on the containing notes.

In variations of genus, it is only the parts of the Fourth that undergo change.

All harmonious scales consisting of more than one tetrachord were divided into conjunct and disjunct. But conjunct scales are composed of the simple parts of the Fourth alone, so that here at least it will be the parts of the Fourth alone that will undergo change. Again, disjunct scales comprise besides these parts of the Fourth a tone peculiar to disjunction. If then it be proved that this particular tone does not alter with variation of genus, evidently the change can affect only the parts of the Fourth. Now the lower of the notes containing the tone is the higher of the notes containing the lower of the disjunct tetrachords; as such we have seen that it is immovable in the changes of the genera. Again, the higher of the notes bounding the tone is the lower of the notes bounding the higher of the disjunct tetrachords; it likewise, as we have seen, remains constant through change of genus. Since therefore, it appears that the notes containing the tone do not vary with a change of genus, the necessary conclusion is that it is only the parts of the Fourth that participate in that change.

Every Genus comprises at most as many simple intervals 62 *as are contained in the Fifth.*

The scale of every genus, as we have already stated, takes the form of conjunction or disjunction. Now it has been shown that the conjunct scale consists merely of the parts of the Fourth, while the disjunct scale adds a single interval peculiar to itself, namely the tone. But the addition of this tone to the parts of the Fourth completes the interval of the Fifth. Since therefore it appears that no scale of any genus taken in the one *shading* is composed of more simple intervals than those in the Fifth, it follows that every genus comprises at most as many simple intervals as are contained in the Fifth.

In this proposition the addition of the words 'at the most' sometimes proves a stumbling-block. 'Why not,' it is asked, 'show without qualification that each genus is composed of as many simple intervals as are contained in the Fifth?' The answer to this is that in certain circumstances each of the genera will comprise fewer intervals than exist in the Fifth, but never will comprise more. This is the reason that we prove first that no genus can be constituted of more simple intervals than there are in the Fifth; that every genus will sometimes be composed of fewer, is shown in the sequel.

63   *A Pycnum cannot be followed by a Pycnum or by part of a Pycnum.*

For the result of such a succession will be that neither the fourth notes in order from one another will form Fourths, nor the fifth notes in order from one another Fifths. But we have already seen that such an order of notes is unmelodious.

The lower of the notes containing the ditone is the highest note of a Pycnum, and the higher of the notes containing the ditone is the lowest note of a Pycnum.

For as the Pycna in conjunct tetrachords form Fourths with one another, the ditone must lie between them; similarly since the ditones form Fourths with one another, the Pycnum must lie between them. It follows that the Pycnum and the ditone must succeed one another alternately. Therefore it is evident that of the notes containing the ditone, the lower will be the highest note of the Pycnum below, and the higher will be the lowest note of the Pycnum above.

The notes containing the tone are both the lowest notes of a Pycnum.

For in disjunction the tone is placed between tetrachords the boundaries of which are the lowest notes of a Pycnum ; and it is by these notes that the tone is contained. For the lower of the notes containing the tone is the higher of those containing the lower tetrachord ;. and the higher of those containing the tone is the lower of those containing the higher tetrachord. Therefore it is evident that the notes containing the tone will be the lowest notes of a Pycnum.

A succession of two Ditones is forbidden.   **64**

Suppose such a succession ; then the higher ditone will be followed by a Pycnum below, and the lower ditone will be followed by a Pycnum above, for we saw that the note that forms the upper boundary of the ditone is the lowest note of a Pycnum. The result will be a succession of two Pycna ; and as this has been proved unmelodious, the succession of two ditones must be equally so.

In Enharmonic and Chromatic scales a succession of two tones is not allowed. Suppose such a succession, first in the ascending scale ; now if the note that forms the upper boundary of the added tone is musically correct, it must form either a Fourth with the fourth note in order from it, or a Fifth with the fifth in order ; if neither of these conditions is satisfied, it must be unmelodious. But that neither of them will be satisfied, is clear. · For if it be Enharmonic, the Lichanus, which is the fourth note in order from the added note, will be four tones removed from it. If it be Chromatic, whether of the Soft or Hemiolic colour, the Lichanus will be further removed than a Fifth ; and if it be of the Tonic Chromatic, the Lichanus will form a Fifth with the added note. But this does not satisfy our law which demands that either the fourth note should form a Fourth, or the fifth a Fifth. Neither condition is here fulfilled. It follows that the note constituting the upper boundary of the added tone will be unmelodious.

Again, if the second tone be added below it will render
65 the genus Diatonic. Therefore it is evident that in the Enharmonic and Chromatic genera a succession of two tones is impossible.

In the Diatonic genus three consecutive tones are permitted; but no more. For let the contrary be supposed; then the note bounding the fourth tone will not form a Fourth with the fourth note from it, nor a Fifth with the fifth.

In the same genus a succession of two semitones is not allowed. For first suppose the second semitone to be added below the semitone already present. The result is that the note bounding the added semitone neither makes a Fourth with the fourth note from it, nor a Fifth with the fifth. The introduction, then, of the semitone here will be unmelodious. But if it be added above the semitone already present, the genus will be Chromatic. Thus it is clear that in a Diatonic scale the succession of two semitones is impossible.

It has now been shown which of the simple intervals can be repeated in immediate succession, and how often they can be repeated; and which of them on the contrary it is absolutely impossible to repeat at all. We shall now speak of the collocation of unequal intervals.

A ditone may be succeeded either above or below by a Pycnum. For it has been proved that in conjunct tetrachords these intervals follow alternately. Therefore each can succeed the other either in an ascending or descending order.

A ditone can be followed by a tone in the ascending scale only. For suppose such a succession in the descending
66 order. The result will be that the highest and the lowest note of a Pycnum will fall on the same pitch. For we saw

that the note that forms the lower boundary of the ditone was the highest note of a Pycnum, and that the note that forms the upper boundary of the tone was the lowest note of a Pycnum. But if these notes fall on the one pitch, it follows that there is a succession of two Pycna. As this latter succession is unmelodious, a tone immediately below a ditone must be equally so.

A tone can be followed by a Pycnum in the descending order only. For suppose such a succession in the opposite order ; the same impossibility will be found to result again. The highest and lowest note of a Pycnum will fall on the same pitch, and consequently there will be a succession of two Pycna. This latter being unmelodious, the position of the tone above the Pycnum must be equally so.

In the Diatonic genus, a tone cannot be both preceded and succeeded by a semitone. For the consequence would be that neither the fourth notes in order from one another would form a Fourth, nor the fifth a Fifth.

A pair of tones, or a group of three tones may be both preceded and succeeded by a semitone ; for either the fourth notes from one another will form a Fourth, or the fifth a Fifth.

From the ditone there are two possible progressions upwards, one only downwards. For it has been proved that the ditone can be followed in the ascending scale by either a Pycnum or a tone. But more progressions upwards from the said interval there cannot be. For the only other simple interval left is the ditone, and two consecutive ditones are forbidden. In the descending order there is 67 but one progression from the ditone. For it has been proved that a ditone cannot lie next a ditone, and that a tone cannot succeed a ditone in the descending order. Consequently the progression to the Pycnum alone remains. It is clear then that from the ditone there are two possible progressions upwards, one to the tone, and one to the Pycnum ; and one possible progression downwards, to the Pycnum.

From the Pycnum, on the contrary, there are two possible progressions downwards, and one upwards. For it has been proved that in the descending scale a Pycnum can be followed by a ditone, or a tone. A third progression there cannot be. For the only remaining simple interval is the Pycnum, and a succession of two Pycna is forbidden. It follows that there are only two possible progressions from a Pycnum downwards. Upwards there is but one, to the ditone. For a Pycnum cannot adjoin a Pycnum, nor can a tone succeed the Pycnum in the ascending scale; therefore the ditone alone remains. It is evident then that from the Pycnum there are two possible progressions downwards, one to the tone, and one to the ditone; and one possible progression upwards, to the ditone.

From the tone there is but one progression in either direction: downwards to the ditone, upwards to the Pycnum. It has been shown that in the descending scale the tone cannot be followed by a tone or by a Pycnum. Therefore the ditone alone remains. And it has been shown that in the ascending scale the tone cannot be followed by a tone or a ditone. Therefore the Pycnum alone remains. It follows that from the tone there is but one possible pro-
68 gression in either direction, downwards to the ditone, and upwards to the Pycnum.

The same law can be applied to the Chromatic scales, except of course that one must substitute for the ditone the interval between the Mese and Lichanus, which varies, according to the particular *shade*, with the size of the Pycnum.

The same law will also hold good of the Diatonic scales. From the tone common to the genera there is one possible progression in either direction; downwards to the interval between the Mese and Lichanus, whatever it may happen to be in any particular *shade* of the Diatonic scales; upwards to the interval between the Paramese and Trite.

Some persons have been much perplexed by this proposition. They are surprised that we do not arrive at quite a contrary conclusion; for they think that the progressions in either direction from the tone are innumerable, since there are innumerable possible magnitudes of the interval between the Mese and Lichanus, and of the Pycnum as well. To this objection we offered the following answer. To begin with, the same observation might be made equally well in the other cases we have considered. Evidently one of the two descending progressions from the Pycnum admits of innumerable possible magnitudes; likewise one of the two ascending progressions from the ditone. For such an interval as that between the Mese and Lichanus admits of innumerable magnitudes, and the same may be said of such an interval as the Pycnum. Nevertheless there are but two progressions from the Pycnum downwards, and two from the ditone upwards; and similarly one from the tone in either direction. For the progressions must be 69 ascertained in accordance with one individual *shade* in one particular genus. In making any musical phenomenon the object of scientific knowledge, its definite side should be insisted on, its indefinite features left in the background. Now in respect of the sizes of intervals and the pitch of notes, the phenomena of melody are indefinite, while in respect of functions, common qualities, and orders of arrangement, they are definite and determined. To take the first example that occurs, the progressions downwards from the Pycnum are in function and character determined as two in number. The first proceeds by the tone and brings the scale into the disjunct class; the second pro-

ceeding by the other interval (whatever its size may be)
brings the scale into the conjunct class. Hence we see also
that there is but one possible progression in either direction
from the tone, and that both these progressions alike
produce but one class of scale—the disjunct. But it is
quite plain from these observations, and from the nature
of the facts, that if one seek to discover the possible progressions by considering not one *shade* of one genus at
a time, but all *shades* and all genera together, one will
come upon an infinity of them.

*In the Chromatic and Enharmonic scales every note partici-
pates in the Pycnum.* For every note in the said genera is
the boundary either of a part of the Pycnum, or of the tone,
or of an interval such as that between the Mese and Licha-
70 nus. The case of notes that bound the parts of the Pycnum
requires no proof; it is immediately evident that they participate in the Pycnum. And we proved already that the notes
containing the tone are both the lowest notes of a Pycnum;
we showed also that the lower of the notes containing the
remaining interval was the highest of a Pycnum, and the
higher of them the lowest of a Pycnum. Now as these are
the only simple intervals, and each of them is contained by
notes both of which participate in the Pycnum, it follows
that every note in the Chromatic and Enharmonic genus
participates in the Pycnum.

One will readily see *that the positions of the notes situated
in the Pycnum are three in number,* since, as we know, a
Pycnum cannot be followed by another Pycnum or part of
one. For it is evident in consequence of this latter law,
that the number of the said notes is so limited.

*It is required to prove that from the lowest only of the notes
in a Pycnum there are two possible progressions in either
direction, while from the others there is but one.* It has
already been proved that from the Pycnum there are two

218

progressions downwards, one to the tone, and one to the ditone. But to prove that there are two progressions downwards from the Pycnum is the same as proving that there are two progressions downwards from the lowest of the notes situated in the Pycnum; for this note marks the limit of the Pycnum. Again, it was proved that from the ditone there are two progressions upwards. But to say that there are two progressions upwards from the ditone is the same as saying that there are two progressions upwards from the higher of the notes bounding the ditone. For this note marks the upper boundary of the ditone. But it 71 is clear that the same note which forms the upper boundary of the ditone also forms the lower boundary of the Pycnum; being the lowest note of a Pycnum (for this too was proved). Hence it is evident that from this note there are two possible progressions in either direction.

It is required to prove that from the highest note of a Pycnum there is but one progression in either direction. It was proved that from a Pycnum there is but one progression upwards. But to say that there is one progression upwards from the Pycnum is (for the reason given in the former proposition) the same as saying that there is but one from the note limiting it.

Again, it was proved that from the ditone there is but one progression downwards : but to say that there is but one progression downwards from the ditone is (for the reason given) the same as saying that there is but one from the note bounding it. But it is evident that the note which bounds the ditone below is at the same time the upper boundary of the Pycnum; being the highest note of a Pycnum. It is plain, then, that from the given note there is but one possible progression in either direction.

It is required to prove, that from the middle note of a Pycnum there is but one progression in either direction. Now since the given note must be adjoined by some one or other of the three simple intervals, and there lies already a diesis on each side of it, plainly it cannot be adjoined on either side by either a ditone or a tone. For suppose a ditone to adjoin it; then either the lowest or the highest note of a Pycnum will fall on the same pitch as the given note, which is the middle note of a Pycnum; consequently there will be a succession of three dieses, no matter on 72 which side the ditone be located. Again, suppose a tone to adjoin the given note; we shall have the same result. The lowest note of a Pycnum will fall on the same pitch as the middle note of a Pycnum, so that we shall again have three dieses in succession. But this succession is unmelodious; therefore it follows that there is but one possible progression from the given note in either direction.

It has now been shown that from the lowest of the notes of a Pycnum there are two possible progressions in either direction; while from the others in either direction there is but one.

It is required to prove that two notes that occupy dissimilar positions in the Pycnum cannot fall on the same pitch without violating the nature of melody. Suppose, firstly, that the highest and lowest note of a Pycnum fall on the same pitch. The result will be two consecutive Pycna, and as this is unmelodious, it must be equally unmelodious that notes dissimilar in the Pycnum in the manner of the assumed notes should fall upon the same pitch.

Again, it is evident that the notes also that are dissimilar in the other possible manner cannot have a common pitch. For if the highest or lowest note of a Pycnum coincide in pitch with a middle note, there necessarily results a succession of three dieses.

It is required to prove that the Diatonic genus is composed of two or of three or of four simple quanta. It has been

already shown that each genus comprises at most as many
simple intervals as there are in the Fifth. These are four **73**
in number. If then three of those four become equal,
leaving but one odd,—as happens in the Sharp Diatonic—
there will be only two different quanta in the Diatonic
scale. Again, if two become equal and two remain unequal,
which will result from the lowering of the Parhypate, there
will be three quanta constituting the Diatonic scale, namely,
an interval less than a semitone, a tone, and an interval
greater than a tone. Again, if all the parts of the Fifth
become unequal, there will be four quanta comprised in the
genus in question.

It is clear then that the Diatonic genus is composed of
two or of three or of four simple quanta.

*It is required to prove that the Chromatic and Enharmonic
genera are composed of three or four simple quanta.* The
simple intervals of the Fifth being four in number, if the
parts of the Pycnum are equal, the genera in question will
comprise those quanta, namely, the half of the Pycnum,
whatever its size may be, the tone, and an interval such as
that between the Mese and Lichanus. If on the other
hand the parts of the Pycnum are unequal, the said
genera will be composed of four quanta, the least, an
interval such as that between the Hypate and Parhypate,
the next smallest one such as that between the Parhypate and Lichanus, the third smallest a tone, and the
largest an interval such as that between the Mese and
Lichanus.

On this point the difficulty has been raised, How is it
that all the genera cannot be composed of two simple **74**
quanta, as is the case with the Diatonic? We can now
see the complete and obvious explanation of the difference.
Three equal simple intervals cannot occur in succession
in the Enharmonic and Chromatic genera ; in the Diatonic

they can. That is the reason that the last-named genus is sometimes composed of only two simple quanta.

Passing from this subject we shall proceed to consider the meaning and nature of difference of species. We shall use the terms 'species' and 'figure' indifferently, applying both to the same phenomenon. Such a difference arises when the order of the simple parts of a certain whole is altered, while both the number and magnitude of those parts remain the same. Proceeding from this definition we have to show that there are three species of the Fourth. Firstly, there is that in which the Pycnum lies at the bottom; secondly, that in which a diesis lies on each side of the ditone; thirdly, that in which the Pycnum is above the ditone. It will be readily seen that there are no other possible relative positions of the parts of the Fourth.

NOTES

[The references in these notes are to the pages and lines of the present edition.]

Page 95, line 3. The term μέλος signifies a song, and as such includes the words, the melody proper, i. e. the alternation of higher and lower pitch, and the rhythm. But as the second of these factors is evidently that which is characteristic of song, it came to appropriate to itself the term μέλος. Then τέλειον μέλος was used in the wider sense. Cp. Anonymus, § 29, Τέλειον δὲ μέλος ἐστὶ τὸ συγκείμενον ἔκ τε λέξεως καὶ μέλους καὶ ῥυθμοῦ. See also Aristides Quintilianus (ed. Meibom, p. 6, line 18). μέλος then in the narrower sense signifies in Aristoxenus that moment of music which consists in the employment of higher and lower notes, always with the implication that the complete series of compossible higher and lower notes is determined by a natural law. This quality of μέλος by which it is obedient to a law, or rather the embodiment of a law, is called τὸ ἡρμοσμένον : and consequently all true melody is an ἡρμοσμένον μέλος. Thus for the Greeks Harmony is the law of Melody. ἡ μουσική on the other hand is a term of very wide signification. Aristides Quintilianus (ed. Meibom, pp. 7, 8) gives the following analysis of it—

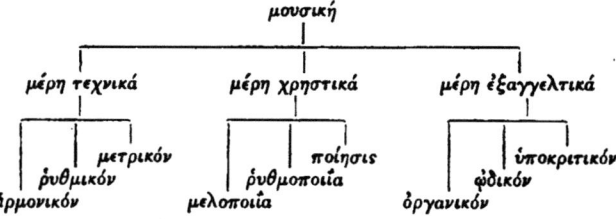

Now in which sense is the term μέλους used in the passage

before us? Marquard supposes in the general sense of the object-matter of μουσική. (In support of this view he might have quoted Anonymus, § 29, Μουσική ἐστιν ἐπιστήμη θεωρητικὴ καὶ πρακτικὴ μέλους τελείου τε καὶ ὀργανικοῦ.) But this is not in accordance with Aristoxenus' use, and probably Westphal is right in interpreting it in its close and strict meaning. If so, what are the other sciences of it besides ἁρμονική? Westphal replies, μελοποιία, ὀργανική, ᾠδική (i.e. the sciences of composition, of instrumental music, of singing).

l. 4. μίαν τινὰ αὐτῶν ὑπολαβεῖν δεῖ κ.τ.λ.— The construction of this sentence is δεῖ ὑπολαβεῖν τὴν ἁρμονικὴν καλουμένην πραγματείαν εἶναι μίαν τινὰ αὐτῶν (i. e. τῶν ἰδεῶν), τῇ τε τάξει πρώτην οὖσαν, κ.τ.λ.

Marquard and Westphal construe δεῖ ὑπολαβεῖν μίαν τινὰ αὐτῶν, τὴν ἁρμονικὴν καλουμένην, εἶναι πραγματείαν τῇ τε τάξει πρώτην οὖσαν, κ.τ.λ., and translate 'we must regard one of them, namely Harmonic, as primary.' But the Greek for 'to be a good man' is not εἶναι ἀνὴρ ἀγαθὸς ὤν.

τὴν ἁρμονικήν. The English word 'Harmony' in no wise corresponds to the Greek ἁρμονία. This latter properly signifies an adjustment or fitting together of parts. Hence, by being transferred from the method to the concrete object which embodies it, it is used to connote (a) a scale or system as a whole whose parts have been adjusted in their proper relations, (b) the enharmonic scale, because in that genus three notes of the Tetrachord are fitted most closely to one another, that is, placed at the smallest possible intervals. The term ἁρμονική signifies then the science of scales, that is the science by which we constitute a system of related and compossible notes. Harmony in the modern sense of the word was in its infancy among the ancient Greeks.

l. 6. τυγχάνει γὰρ οὖσα τῶν πρώτων θεωρητική· ταῦτα δ' ἐστὶν ὅσα. The MSS reading is here plainly ungrammatical. If we retain πρώτη τῶν θεωρητικῶν, we must change ταῦτα to ταύτης, 'to this science belong,' &c. [cp. l. 12, οὐκέτι ταύτης ἐστίν]. But I prefer to read as above with Westphal, in which case of course ταῦτα refers to τὰ πρῶτα. Cp. Anonymus (a mere echo of Aristoxenus), § 31, πρωτεῦον δὲ μέρος τῆς μουσικῆς ἡ ἁρμονική ἐστι· τὰ γὰρ ἐν μουσικῇ πρῶτα αὕτη θεωρεῖ. Also § 19, τῶν δὲ τῆς μουσικῆς μερῶν κυριώτατόν ἐστι καὶ πρῶτον τὸ ἁρμονικόν· τῶν γὰρ πρώτων μουσικῆς πέφυκε θεωρητική. Cp. also l. 14 of this page, δι' ὧν πάντα θεωρεῖται τὰ κατὰ μουσικήν.

For the relation between Harmonic and Music, cp. Plutarch *de Musica*, 1142 F, φανερὸν δ' ἂν γένοιτο, εἴ τις ἑκάστην ἐξετάζοιτο τῶν ἐπιστημῶν, τίνος ἐστὶ θεωρητική· δῆλον γὰρ ὅτι ἡ μὲν ἁρμονικὴ γενῶν τε τῶν τοῦ ἡρμοσμένου καὶ διαστημάτων καὶ συστημάτων καὶ φθόγγων καὶ τόνων καὶ μεταβολῶν συστηματικῶν ἐστι γνωστική· πορρωτέρω δ' οὐκέτι ταύτῃ προελθεῖν οἷόν τε. ὥστ' οὐδὲ ζητεῖν παρὰ ταύτης τὸ διαγνῶναι δύνασθαι, πότερον οἰκείως εἴληφεν ὁ ποιητὴς . . . τὸν Ὑποδώριον τόνον ἐπὶ τὴν ἀρχὴν ἢ τὸν Μιξολύδιόν τε καὶ Δώριον ἐπὶ τὴν ἔκβασιν ἢ τὸν Ὑποφρύγιόν τε καὶ Φρύγιον ἐπὶ τὴν μέσην.

l. 16. The point of the passage lies in the possible ambiguity of the term ἁρμονικός, which properly signifying 'concerned with scales' [cp. ἁρμονική = science of scales] might also mean 'concerned with the enharmonic scale.' Cp. note on l. 4.

P. 96, l. 2. καί τοι τὰ διαγράμματά γ' αὐτῶν. See end of note on p. 101, l. 1.

l. 4. περὶ δὲ τῶν ἄλλων μεγεθῶν τε καὶ σχημάτων. I have changed the MSS reading γενῶν to μεγεθῶν for three reasons: (1) quite sufficient stress has been laid on the early theorists' omission of the Chromatic and Diatonic genera, and further reference to it is not required; (2) a reference to their omission of 'other magnitudes' is required in view of what follows (cp. l. 7); (3) the close connexion of γενῶν and σχημάτων by τε καί would make it necessary to supply the qualification ἐν αὐτῷ τε τῷ γένει τούτῳ καὶ τοῖς λοιποῖς with both, which is obviously impossible.

σχῆμα, which we shall translate by 'Figure,' signifies the arrangement or order of the parts of a whole, and two things differ in σχῆμα if they have the same parts, but these parts are arranged in a different order. Thus the scale from C to c and the scale from B to b on the white notes of the piano are composed of the same intervals, five tones and two semitones, but they differ in σχῆμα or the arrangement of those intervals.

l. 6. ἀποτεμνόμενοι . . . τὸ διὰ πασῶν. By the phrase τὸ τρίτον μέρος τῆς ὅλης μελῳδίας is meant the Enharmonic genus, just as a few lines above τὴν πᾶσαν τῆς μελῳδίας τάξιν means the Enharmonic, Chromatic, and Diatonic Genera.

Hence the MSS reading ἕν τι γένος μέγεθος δέ is untenable. What is the τρίτον μέρος of μελῳδία from which the Harmonists can be said to have selected one genus? According to Marquard ἁρμονία (in the sense of 'melodic element in music'). But even granting that μελῳδία here means music in general, and that music in general may be divided into ἁρμονία, ῥυθμός, and λόγος, could this division have been so universally familiar that Aristoxenus would presuppose it, and employ the phrase τρίτον μέρος without explanation?

I omit γένος and δέ. The former might easily be inserted by an ignorant scribe, who not understanding τοῦ τρίτου μέρους missed the necessary reference to the enharmonic genus. The intrusion of γένος naturally entailed the addition of δέ.

l. 11. An unknown polemic.

l. 18. φωνῆς. The term φωνή in Aristoxenus comprehends the human voice, and the sounds of instruments. See Aristotle, de Anima, 420 b, ἡ δὲ φωνὴ ψόφος τίς ἐστιν ἐμψύχου· τῶν γὰρ ἀψύχων οὐθὲν φωνεῖ, ἀλλὰ καθ' ὁμοιότητα λέγεται φωνεῖν, οἷον αὐλὸς καὶ λύρα καὶ ὅσα ἄλλα τῶν ἀψύχων ἀπότασιν ἔχει καὶ μέλος καὶ διάλεκτον.

P. 97, l. 2. I read ἐπιμελὲς for ἐπιμελῶς of the MSS which (1) gives a weak construction to γεγένηται, and (2) requires, as Marquard saw, the διορισθέντος of l. 4 to be supplemented by an adverb.

l. 6. Λάσος. Lasus of Hermione, the well-known dithyrambic poet, and teacher of Pindar. Suidas credits him with the authorship of the earliest work on the theory of Music. See Suidas s. v.; Athenaeus x, 455 c and xiv, 624 c; Herodotus vii. 6; Plutarch, de Musica, 1141 B–C.

Ἐπιγονείων. Disciples of Epigonus of Ambracia, a famous musical performer. See Athenaeus iv, 183 d and xiv, 637 f.

l. 7. πλάτος. The spatial image, under which Aristoxenus represents the pitch relations of notes, is that of an indefinite line x–y

on which the several notes appear as points *a b c d* [cp. Nicomachus (ed. Meibom, p. 24, l. 21), φθόγγος ἐστὶ φωνὴ ἄτομος, οἷον μονὰς κατ᾽ ἀκοήν], and the intervals as the one-dimension spaces between them. The obvious objection to this conception is that it attributes quantity and so reality to the spaces between the notes, while it denies it to the notes themselves, whereas our senses tell us that the notes are the realities, and the intervals only their relations. This objection lies at the basis of the contending theory, here quoted by Aristoxenus, which assigns to notes a certain quantity or 'breadth.'

l. 16. ἢ πῇ μὲν πῇ δ᾽ οὔ. For Aristoxenus' answer to the question see p. 107, ll. 13-19.

l. 17. I conjecture λεκτέον for δίκαιον of the MSS. Cf. note on p. 143, l. 13.

l. 19. Probably Marquard's διελθόντα is correct. διελόντα is not objectionable in itself (cp. p. 98, l. 5, p. 108, l. 18, &c.) ; but if we retain it, the passage lacks any reference to the *general* treatment of the scale.

l. 22. πλείους εἰσὶ φύσεις μέλους. See p. 110.

P. 98, l. 9. The meaningless αὐτῆς of the MSS may have been interpolated to produce a show of connexion between this paragraph and the preceding.

l. 17. οἷς ἅμα . . . συμβαίνει.

The distance between *e* and *a*, regarded as a whole, is an interval ; regarded as a series of smaller distances, between *e* and *f, f* and *g, g* and *a*, it is a scale.

l. 21. Of Eratocles nothing is known beyond what we learn from Aristoxenus himself.

l. 22. ὅτι ἀπὸ . . . μέλος. That is, one has a choice between conjunction and disjunction.

At the point  the ascending melodic progression

diverges into 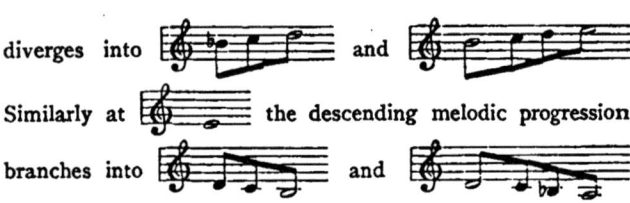 and

Similarly at the descending melodic progression

branches into and

l. 23. εἰ ἀπὸ παντὸς . . . γίγνεται. Evidently the law only holds of those Fourths of which the boundaries are fixed notes. If we take the Fourth  there is but one method of completing the melodic progression in each direction; thus—

P. 99, l. 12. For the Perfect System or Scale see Introduction A § 29.

l. 14. κατὰ σύνθεσιν, 'in respect of the method of their composition,' according as that may be by conjunction, disjunction, or a combination of both these methods. See Introduction A *passim.*

l. 15. κατὰ σχῆμα. Cp. note on p. 96, l. 4.

H probably supplies the true reading here. Marquard inserts καὶ κατὰ θέσιν on account of μήτε θέσις in l. 17. But the latter words (which do not appear in H) are probably a dittograph to μήτε σύνθεσις. Though θέσις does not occur as a technical term in Aristoxenus, it might conceivably mean 'key' on the analogy of τίθεσθαι (see e. g. p. 128, l. 7); but key-distinctions belong to a later part of the subject (p. 100, ll. 14–20) and are out of place here, Aristoxenus being well aware that such distinctions are not essentially scale-distinctions (see p. 100, l. 16).

l. 25. ἀναποδείκτως . . . γίγνεσθαι δείκνυται. Eratocles, according to the criticism of Aristoxenus, would seem to have presupposed the constitution of the octave scale

and to have arrived at the enumeration of its Figures by showing

that after proceeding through the various arrangements to be
obtained by beginning successively with *e, f, g, a, b, c, d,* one is
brought back again to the first Figure with which one started.
Against this superficial empiricism Aristoxenus very justly
urges that the Figures of the Fourth and Fifth and the laws of
their collocation must be demonstrated prior to the enumeration
of the Figures of the Octave. Otherwise we are not justified in
limiting these Figures to seven. Why, for example, should we
not admit the Figure

Here we have a scale that is illegitimate though it consists of
five tones and two semitones, because it violates the law of the
Figures of the Fourth and Fifth and their collocation.

P. 100, l. 10. Several words must have been lost here
the substance of which I have supplied. Aristoxenus is evidently insisting that the enumeration of the scales cannot be
complete unless account be taken of the scales of mixed
genus: therefore after the number of possible scales in each
genus has been ascertained, we must, he tells us, mix genera
and repeat the process of enumeration. But what is the sense
of giving as a reason for the necessity of this process the fact
that 'they,' whoever 'they' may be, 'had not even perceived
what mixture is'?

l. 17. Marquard inserts τοῦ τόπου before αὑτοῦ and translates
'though the space is in itself homogeneous.' Westphal rightly
reads with the MSS and understands αὑτοῦ as equal to τοῦ
συστήματος.

l. 22. The question here raised is one of great importance.
Are there any affinities between scales and keys? By scales we
mean so many series of notes in which abstraction is made of
pitch and regard is had solely to the order of intervals. By
keys we mean so many series of notes, in which the intervals
and their order are identical, while each series is situated at
a different pitch from every other.

See Introduction A, § 22.

P. 101, l. 1. Aristoxenus here contrasts two principles by

which one might be guided in determining the relative positions of the keys proper to the several scales. One is the false principle of καταπύκνωσις, or 'close-packing' of intervals; the other the true principle of the possibility of intermodulation. To understand the difference between these principles let us take the seven modes or scales of Table 20 in Introduction A, in the Enharmonic forms as follows:

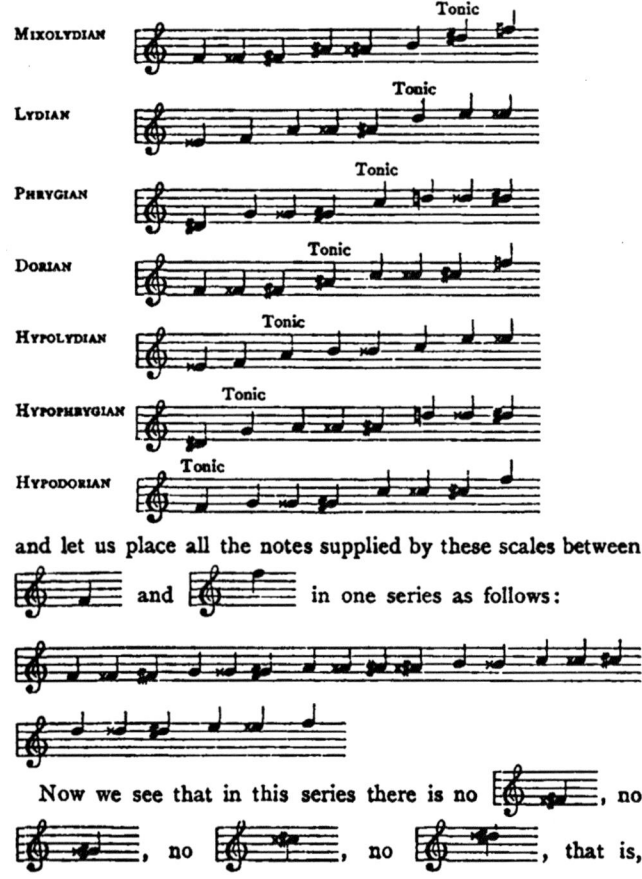

and let us place all the notes supplied by these scales between

and in one series as follows:

Now we see that in this series there is no , no

, no , no , that is,

there are several intervals of a semitone which are not divided into their apparently possible quarter-tones. At the same time it is evident that the tonics of these keys are so related to one another that it will be possible to pass directly or indirectly from any one to any other. (See note on p. 129, l. 4.)

Once more let us again take the same seven enharmonic modes, but changing the keys let us arrange them as follows:

Writing in one series all the notes of these keys between and we obtain the following result:

Here we have an unbroken series of the absolutely smallest intervals (i.e. quarter-tones); but the keys are so related to one another, their tonics being spaced by the interval of three

231

ARISTOXENUS

quarter-tones, that a modulation from one to another of them is impossible. (See note on p. 129, l. 4.)

The first of the above sets of scales is arranged on the principle of possible intermodulation; the second on the principle of καταπύκνωσις, or arrangement at the closest possible intervals. It is obvious that the former is the true principle of music. The unbroken series of small intervals may satisfy the eye, but to use the words of Aristoxenus [p. 129, l. 1] it is ἐκμελὴς καὶ πάντα τρόπον ἄχρηστος, that is, at variance with the nature of melody which forbids a succession of more than two quarter-tones; and of no practical value, because the only object in a relative determination of keys is to render inter-modulation possible.

We can now understand the statement of Aristoxenus [p. 96, l. 2] that the tables of the early harmonists, though only constructed with a view to the Enharmonic Genus, exhibited the whole melodic system. In such a series as that last given all the chromatic and diatonic scales are *implicitly* presented. [It is however possible that ἐδήλου in this passage may signify 'professed to exhibit.']

l. 2. I read τίνων for MSS τῶν.

l. 3. περὶ τούτου . . . τοῦθ᾽ ἡμῖν. I have corrected the readings of the MSS by inserting ὅτι before ἐπὶ βραχύ. Then ὅτι ἐνίοις συμβέβηκεν περὶ τούτου τοῦ μέρους εἰρηκέναι, οὐδενὶ δὲ συμβέβηκεν καθόλου εἰρηκέναι is the subject of φανερὸν γεγένηται.

l. 7. πεπίγηται of Mc. for πεποίηται is an interesting example of a mistake arising from dictation. Such mistakes are frequent in the MSS of Aristoxenus. Compare p. 144, l. 12 ἡ τούτοις συνεχής for οἱ τούτοις συνεχεῖς, p. 139, l. 18 δείκνυσιν (in R) for δὴ κίνησιν, p. 139, l. 13 εἰσὶν ὡς (in R) for εἰς ἑνός, p. 137, l. 15 ὑπαρυπάτη (in B) for ἡ παρυπάτη; also such spellings as ἀπετοῦν, ἀλύωσιν, πικνά, ἄχριστα, εἰρείσθω, for ἀπαιτοῦν, ἀλλοίωσιν, πυκνά, ἄχρηστα, εἰρήσθω, and the constant confusion of subjunctive and indicative forms.

P. 102, l. 8. πότερον...ἐστὶ σκέψεως. See Introduction B § 2. Aristoxenus is not concerned with the truth or falsity of the physical theory of sound.

l. 11. τὸ δὲ κινῆσαι τούτων ἑκάτερον. The true reading here

NOTES

is hard to conjecture. Marquard's first idea was to omit δέ and understand κινῆσαι in the sense of 'to raise or moot a question'; but he afterwards abandoned this view on the ground that κινεῖν occurring so often in the same passage in the technical sense of 'motion' could not in this one case bear a different meaning. [On this point Mr. Goligher aptly cites Berkeley's *Principles of Human Knowledge*, § 77 : 'If what you mean by the word matter be only the unknown support of unknown qualities, it is no matter whether there is such a thing or no, since it in no way concerns us.'] His final conjecture is δια-κρῖναι for δὲ κινῆσαι, and he gives as the meaning of the passage 'for the purposes of the present argument it is not necessary to decide this question.' But this is, I think, quite untenable. Even if we grant that 'it is not necessary to discriminate each of these things' is a possible expression of the meaning 'it is not necessary to decide for either of these alternatives,' yet it is clear from l. 7 that ἑκάτερον τούτων must here mean 'each of these phenomena,' namely, the two kinds of voice-motion. Once we admit this, we must reject τὸ διακρῖναι; for it is obviously false to say that 'the discrimination of these phenomena from one another is unnecessary for our argument.'

I believe the true reading to be τοῦ διευκρινῆσαι (or some such word) τούτων ἑκάτερον, where τοῦ διευκρινῆσαι is the genitive of the material after τὴν ἐνεστῶσαν πραγματείαν : and the meaning to be 'the question of the objective possibility of rest and motion of the voice belongs to a different sphere of speculation, and is irrelevant to our present purpose, which is to discriminate each of these two phenomena from the other.'

l. 26. διὰ πάθος. As in the case of impassioned recitation. Cp. Aristides Quintilianus (ed. Meibom, p. 7, l. 23), ἡ μὲν οὖν συν-εχής (κίνησις) ἐστιν, ᾗ διαλεγόμεθα· μέση δέ, ᾗ τὰς τῶν ποιημάτων ἀναγνώσεις ποιούμεθα· διαστηματικὴ δὲ ἡ κατὰ μέσον τῶν ἁπλῶν φωνῶν ποσὰ ποιουμένη διαστήματα καὶ μονάς, ᾗ τις καὶ μελῳδικὴ καλεῖται.

P. 103, ll. 1–6. As the monotone of declamation is a license of speech, so is the *tremolo* a license of music; and the use of either, if not justified by the presence of an exceptional emotion, is a sin against nature.

ARISTOXENUS

l. 3. Probably ὅσῳ γὰρ ἂν ... ποιήσωμεν, the reading of B and R, is right.

l. 16. ἐπίτασις and ἄνεσις signify the *processes*, not the *states*, of tension and relaxation. Though properly applying only to strings, they are used metaphorically of the human voice and the sounds of wind-instruments.

P. 104, l. 14. ἐπὶ τὸν ἐναντίον τόπον, the reading of B, is undoubtedly right. Cp. p. 145, l. 9; also the phrases ἐπὶ τὸ ὀξύ, ἐπὶ τὸ βαρύ.

l. 20. τρίτον. Westphal's conjecture of πέμπτον is, I think, unnecessary, in spite of p. 106, l. 9. For the purposes of the argument ἐπίτασις and ἄνεσις may be regarded as subdivisions of one conception, and similarly ὀξύτης and βαρύτης.

l. 23. μὴ ταραττέτωσαν κ.τ.λ. Aristoxenus very rightly insists that the validity of his distinction is not injured by the fact that it is verbally incompatible with the theory of the Physicists. When he speaks of motion and rest of the voice, he refers to certain phenomena which *the ear* distinguishes as motion and rest, though this distinction may directly contradict the ultimate nature of these phenomena as apprehended by the intellect. Thus, when the Physicist presses upon him the theory that all sound is vibration or motion, and urges that motion at rest is a contradiction, he replies: 'According to the evidence of the ear (which, for my purposes, is the final test of truth) the voice is at rest in cases where, according to your theory of objective facts, the rate of its vibration is constant; consequently, to distinguish the phenomena before us, we may employ the language of the ear just as well as the language of physics.'

P. 105, l. 15. The MSS read here ὅ θ' ἡμεῖς λέγομεν κίνησίν τε καὶ ἠρεμίαν φωνῆς καὶ ὃ ἐκεῖνοι κίνησιν which is translated 'it is fairly evident what we mean by rest and motion of the voice, and what they mean by motion.' But this is unsatisfactory, not only on account of the weakness of the conclusion thus drawn, but also because ὅ θ' ... κίνησιν being a relative sentence and not an indirect question, the correct translation would be 'the thing to which we give the name of rest and motion of the voice is a fairly patent thing, as is also the thing to which they give the name of motion,' which does not give the required meaning.

P. 107, l. 3. διέσεως τῆς ἐλαχίστης. That is a quarter-tone. Aristoxenus uses διεσις for any interval less than a semitone.

l. 5. ὥστε καὶ ξυνιέναι κ.τ.λ. Aristoxenus does not mean that we cannot hear any interval smaller than a quarter-tone, but that though we may be conscious of such a smaller interval, we can have no perception of it as a musical entity, since we cannot estimate its magnitude in reference to other musical intervals.

P. 108, l. 21. καθ' ἣν τὰ σύμφωνα τῶν διαφώνων. The only concords recognized by Greek theorists are the Fourth; the Fifth; the Octave; the sum of two or more Octaves: the sum of one or more Octaves and a Fourth; the sum of one or more Octaves and a Fifth.

In his note on this passage Marquard has collected several definitions of concords and discords.

According to Gaudentius [ed. Meibom, p. 11, l. 17] σύμφωνοι δὲ ὧν ἅμα κρουομένων ἢ αὐλουμένων ἀεὶ τὸ μέλος τοῦ βαρυτέρου πρὸς τὸ ὀξὺ καὶ τοῦ ὀξυτέρου πρὸς τὸ βαρὺ τὸ αὐτὸ ᾖ ... διάφωνοι δὲ ὧν ἅμα κρουομένων ἢ αὐλουμένων οὐδέν τι φαίνεται τοῦ μέλους εἶναι τοῦ βαρυτέρου πρὸς τὸ ὀξὺ ἢ τοῦ ὀξυτέρου πρὸς τὸ βαρὺ τὸ αὐτό.

'The nature of concordant sounds is that when they are struck or blown simultaneously, the melodic relation of the lower note to the higher is identity, as likewise the relation of the higher to the lower; but when discordant sounds are struck or blown together, there seems to be nothing of identity in the relation of the lower note to the higher, or of the higher to the lower.' [Practically the same definition is given by Aristides Quintilianus (ed. Meibom, p. 12, l. 21), and Bacchius (ed. Meibom, p. 2, l. 28).]

Marquard professes himself unable to find any meaning in this definition. The language is certainly not happy; but I think the sense is clear enough. If two sounds are discordant, when they are sounded together, the particular character of each will stand out unreconciled against the other; that is, the relation of the higher to the lower or of the lower to the higher will not be one of identity in which differences are sunk. On the other hand, when concordant sounds are heard together, the resulting impression is that of the reconciliation of differences, the merging of particular natures in an identical whole. This is well illustrated by the concord called the Octave, where the relation of identity is so predominant that we regard the notes of it as the one note repeated at different heights of pitch.

According to the *Isagoge* (ed. Meibom, p. 8, l. 24) ἔστι δὲ συμφωνία μὲν κρᾶσις δύο φθόγγων ὀξυτέρου καὶ βαρυτέρου· διαφωνία δὲ τοὐναντίον δύο φθόγγων ἀμιξία ὥστε μὴ κραθῆναι, ἀλλὰ τραχυνθῆναι τὴν ἀκοήν. 'Concord is the blending of two notes, a higher and a lower ; discord, on the contrary, is the refusal of two notes to combine, with the result that they do not blend but grate on the ear.' The same conception is more clearly expressed in the definition quoted by Porphyrius :—συμφωνία δ' ἐστὶ δυοῖν φθόγγων ὀξύτητι καὶ βαρύτητι διαφερόντων κατὰ τὸ αὐτὸ πτῶσις καὶ κρᾶσις· δεῖ γὰρ τοὺς φθόγγους συγκρουσθέντας ἔν τι ἕτερον εἶδος φθόγγου ἀποτελεῖν παρ' ἐκείνους ἐξ ὧν φθόγγων ἡ συμφωνία γέγονεν. 'Concord is the coincidence and blending of two notes of different pitch, for the notes when struck together must result in a single species of sound distinct from the notes which have given birth to the concord.'

The following definition of Adrastus is quoted by Theo. Smyrn., p. 80, and Porphyrius, p. 270, συμφωνοῦσι δὲ φθόγγοι πρὸς ἀλλήλους ὧν θατέρου κρουσθέντος ἐπί τινος ὀργάνου τῶν ἐντατῶν καὶ ὁ λοιπὸς κατά τινα οἰκειότητα καὶ συμπάθειαν συνηχῇ· κατὰ τὸ αὐτὸ δὲ ἅμα ἀμφοτέρων κρουσθέντων λεία καὶ προσηνὴς ἐκ τῆς κράσεως ἐξακούεται φωνή. 'Notes are in concord with one another when upon the one being struck upon a stringed instrument, the other sounds along with it by affinity and sympathy ; and when the two being struck simultaneously one hears, in consequence of the blending, a smooth and sweet sound.'

Most philosophic of all is Aristotle's definition in *Problems* xix, 38, συμφωνίᾳ δὲ χαίρομεν ὅτι κρᾶσίς ἐστι λόγον ἐχόντων ἐναντίων πρὸς ἄλληλα. ὁ μὲν οὖν λόγος τάξις, ὃ ἦν φύσει ἡδύ. 'The reason that we take pleasure in concord is that it is a blending of opposites that have a relation to one another. Now relation is order and we saw that order naturally gave pleasure.' Cp. also Aristotle περὶ αἰσθήσεως καὶ αἰσθητῶν c. 3, p. 439[b], τὰ μὲν γὰρ ἐν ἀριθμοῖς εὐλογίστοις χρώματα, καθάπερ ἐκεῖ τὰς

236

συμφωνίας, τὰ ἥδιστα τῶν χρωμάτων εἶναι δοκοῦντα. 'The most agreeable colours, like concords, depend upon the easily calculable relations of their ingredients.'

Later theorists introduced παράφωνος as an intermediate term between σύμφωνος and διάφωνος. According to Gaudentius [ed. Meibom, p. 11, l. 30], παράφωνοι δὲ οἱ μέσοι μὲν συμφώνου καὶ διαφώνου· ἐν δὲ τῇ κρούσει φαινόμενοι σύμφωνοι, ὥσπερ ἐπὶ τριῶν τόνων φαίνεται, ἀπὸ παρυπάτης μέσων ἐπὶ παραμέσην, καὶ ἐπὶ δύο τόνων, ἀπὸ μέσων διατόνου ἐπὶ παραμέσην. 'Paraphone sounds stand midway between concords and discords; when struck' [this probably means 'when not prolonged by voice or wind instrument, but sounded momentarily on strings'] 'they give the impression of concord; such an impression we receive in the case of the interval of three tones between the Parhypate Mesôn and the Paramese; and in the case of the interval of two tones between the Lichanus' [the term 'Diatonus' is sometimes used for Lichanus] 'Mesôn and the Paramese.'

The term ὁμόφωνοι is applied to notes which differ in function, but coincide in pitch. Thus the Dominant of the key of *D* and the Subdominant of the key of *E* fall alike on *A*. See Aristides Quintilianus, ed. Meibom, p. 12, l. 25.

l. 22. τὰ σύνθετα τῶν ἀσυνθέτων. Aristoxenus means by a simple interval one that is contained by two notes between which none can be inserted *in the particular scale to which they belong.*

Thus in the enharmonic scale, the interval between *f* and *a* is simple, because *in this scale* no note can occur between them; but in the diatonic scale the interval between *f* and *a* is compound, because in this scale *g* occurs between them. Thus the same μέγεθος or *magnitude f-a*, which as a μέγεθος is of course composite [the simple 'magnitude of music being a quarter-tone], may sometimes be occupied by a simple, sometimes by a composite *interval.*

l. 23. καθ' ἣν διαφέρει τὰ ῥητὰ τῶν ἀλόγων. This διαφορά is not without difficulty. The terms ῥητά and ἄλογα naturally apply to quanta *in relation to one another.* 4 is ἄλογον in relation to 7, the area of a square in relation to that of a circle. But where

237

in the case of an interval are the two quanta the relation between which constitutes it rational or irrational? Not inside the interval, for Aristoxenus, as we have already seen, has nothing to do with the Pythagorean view of intervals as numerical relations. An interval then must be rational or irrational in virtue of the relation it bears to some quantum outside itself. Marquard supposes this quantum to be the twelfth of a tone because that is the smallest measure used by Aristoxenus in calculating the comparative sizes of intervals. (See p. 117, ll. 1–19.) But this supposition, as we shall presently see, is directly forbidden by Aristoxenus himself. The true explanation is supplied by the following interesting passage from the *Elements of Rhythm* (Aristoxenus, ed. Marquard, p. 413, 29):—

Ὥρισται δὲ τῶν ποδῶν ἕκαστος ἤτοι λόγῳ τινὶ ἢ ἀλογίᾳ τοιαύτῃ, ἥτις δύο λόγων γνωρίμων τῇ αἰσθήσει ἀνὰ μέσον ἔσται. Γένοιτο δ' ἂν τὸ εἰρημένον ὧδε καταφανές· εἰ ληφθείησαν δύο πόδες, ὁ μὲν ἴσον τὸ ἄνω τῷ κάτω ἔχων καὶ δίσημον ἑκάτερον, ὁ δὲ τὸ μὲν κάτω δίσημον, τὸ δὲ ἄνω ἥμισυ, τρίτος δέ τις ληφθείη ποὺς παρὰ τούτους, τὴν μὲν βάσιν ἴσην ἂν τοῖς ἀμφοτέροις ἔχων, τὴν δὲ ἄρσιν μέσον μέγεθος ἔχουσαν τῶν ἄρσεων. Ὁ γὰρ τοιοῦτος ποὺς ἄλογον μὲν ἕξει τὸ ἄνω πρὸς τὸ κάτω· ἔσται δ' ἡ ἀλογία μεταξὺ δύο λόγων γνωρίμων τῇ αἰσθήσει, τοῦ τε ἴσου καὶ τοῦ διπλασίου. . . .

Δεῖ δὲ μηδ' ἐνταῦθα διαμαρτεῖν, ἀγνοηθέντος τοῦ τε ῥητοῦ καὶ τοῦ ἀλόγου, τίνα τρόπον ἐν τοῖς περὶ τοὺς ῥυθμοὺς λαμβάνεται. Ὥσπερ οὖν ἐν τοῖς διαστηματικοῖς στοιχείοις τὸ μὲν κατὰ μέλος ῥητὸν ἐλήφθη, ὃ πρῶτον μέν ἐστι μελῳδούμενον, ἔπειτα γνώριμον κατὰ μέγεθος, ἤτοι ὡς τά τε σύμφωνα καὶ ὁ τόνος, ἢ ὡς τὰ τούτοις σύμμετρα, τὸ δὲ κατὰ τοὺς τῶν ἀριθμῶν μόνον λόγους ῥητόν, ᾧ συνέβαινεν ἀμελῳδήτῳ εἶναι· οὕτω καὶ ἐν τοῖς ῥυθμοῖς ὑποληπτέον ἔχειν τό τε ῥητὸν καὶ τὸ ἄλογον. Τὸ μὲν γὰρ κατὰ τὴν τοῦ ῥυθμοῦ φύσιν λαμβάνεται ῥητόν, τὸ δὲ κατὰ τοὺς τῶν ἀριθμῶν μόνον λόγους. Τὸ μὲν οὖν ἐν ῥυθμῷ λαμβανόμενον ῥητὸν χρόνου μέγεθος πρῶτον μὲν δεῖ τῶν πιπτόντων εἰς τὴν ῥυθμοποιίαν εἶναι, ἔπειτα τοῦ ποδὸς ἐν ᾧ τέτακται μέρος εἶναι ῥητόν· τὸ δὲ κατὰ τοὺς τῶν ἀριθμῶν λόγους λαμβανόμενον ῥητὸν τοιοῦτόν τι δεῖ νοεῖν οἷον ἐν τοῖς διαστηματικοῖς τὸ δωδεκατημόριον τοῦ τόνου καὶ εἴ τι τοιοῦτον ἄλλο ἐν ταῖς τῶν διαστημάτων παραλλαγαῖς λαμβάνεται. Φανερὸν δὲ διὰ τῶν εἰρημένων, ὅτι ἡ μέση ληφθεῖσα τῶν ἄρσεων οὐκ ἔσται σύμμετρος τῇ βάσει· οὐδὲν γὰρ αὐτῶν μέτρον ἐστὶ κοινὸν

238

ἔνρυθμον. 'Every foot is determined either by a ratio (between its accented and unaccented parts) or by an irrational relation such as lies midway between two ratios familiar to sense. This statement may be illustrated as follows: take two feet, one of which has the accented and unaccented parts equal, each of them consisting of two minims of time, while the other has its accented part equal to two minims, but its unaccented only half that length.' [Assuming the minim to be, what it once was, the sign of the shortest possible musical time, the first of these feet would be of the form | 𝄽 𝄽 |, the second of the form | 𝄽 𝄽 |.] 'Now take a third foot besides, having its accented part equal to the accented part of either of the first two, but its unaccented, a mean in size between their unaccented parts.' [Its form will be | 𝄽 𝄽 . |.] 'In such a foot the relation between the accented and unaccented parts will be irrational, and will lie between two ratios familiar to sense, the equal,' [𝄽 : 𝄽] 'and the double' [𝄽 : 𝄽] ... 'Nor must we be led astray here by ignorance of the principle on which the conceptions "rational" and "irrational" are determined in matters of rhythm. In the *Elements of Intervals* we assumed on the one hand a "rational in respect of melody" which is firstly something that can be sung, and secondly, something whose size is well known, either [directly] as the concords and the tone, or else [indirectly] as the intervals commensurate with these; and on the other hand, a "rational in respect of numerical ratios," which, as a fact, was something that could not be sung. A similar view must be taken in the case of rhythm, and we must distinguish the rational in respect of the natural laws of rhythm from the rational in respect of numerical ratios only. According to the first reference, a rational time-length is one which, firstly, can be introduced into rhythmical composition, and secondly, is a rational fraction of the foot in which it is placed. According to the second reference, it must be conceived as something in the sphere of rhythm corresponding to the twelfth of a tone in the sphere of melody, or to any other similar quantum assumed in the comparative measurement of intervals. It is

clear from these remarks that the mean between the two un-
accented parts will not be commensurate with the accented
part; for they have no common measure with a rhythmical
existence.'

We see here that the reason why the foot | ♩ ♩. | is
irrational is, that though ♩. is a possible rhythmical element,
and though the relation of ♩. to ♩ is known as that of 3 to 4,
yet the length ♩. , while mathematically commensurate with
♩, is rhythmically incommensurate. *For their common measure,
being half the minimum time length, has no existence in the
practice of rhythm.*

The case is similar with regard to Melody. If any interval
can be sung; if its length be readily cognisable, either immediately as a concord or tone, or because it is commensurate
with one of these, *the common measure being an actual melodic
interval*, then it is ῥητόν. If these conditions be not fulfilled, it
is ἄλογον. Thus a twelfth of a tone is not a rational interval
in respect of melody, because it cannot be sung; neither is the
interval of three sevenths of a tone rational; because though it
can be sung, and though its length can be mathematically
expressed in relation to a tone, yet the common measure of
it and of a tone is one seventh of the latter; which is not an
actual melodic interval.

l. 24. τὰς δὲ λοιπὰς κ.τ.λ. Cp. Aristides Quintilianus [Mei-
bom, p. 14, l. 10], ἔτι δ' αὐτῶν ἃ μέν ἐστιν ἄρτια, ἃ δὲ περιττά.
ἄρτια μὲν τὰ εἰς ἴσα διαιρούμενα, ὡς ἡμιτόνιον καὶ τόνος· περιττὰ
δὲ τὰ εἰς ἄνισα· ὡς αἱ γ̄ διέσεις καὶ πέντε καὶ ζ, and [Meibom, p. 14,
l. 20], ἔτι τῶν διαστημάτων ἃ μέν ἐστιν ἀραιὰ ἃ δὲ πυκνά· πυκνὰ μὲν
τὰ ἐλάχιστα ὡς αἱ διέσεις, ἀραιὰ δὲ τὰ μέγιστα ὡς τὸ διὰ τεσσάρων.

P. 109, l. 7. τοῦτόν γε τὸν τρόπον κ.τ.λ. Aristoxenus implies
by this reservation the possibility of dividing scales into those
which are composed *of other scales* (as for instance an octave,
which is a compound of a Fourth and a Fifth), and those which
are not so composed, as for instance . But
even this last scale, though it cannot be analysed *into other
scales*, is composed of certain parts, namely intervals, and so can
hardly be called simple.

l. 16. ἀπό τινος μεγέθους. The meaning is, 'Every scale from a certain magnitude upward.' Evidently a scale of a Fourth or any smaller scale *need* not exhibit either conjunction or disjunction.

l. 18. τοῦτο. 'This phenomenon of the blending of conjunction and disjunction.'

ἐν ἐνίοις, i.e. συστήμασιν. See Introduction A, § 20.

l. 19. The term ὑπερβατόν signifies that the scale skips certain notes which would naturally belong to it by the laws of continuity or sequence. See Introduction A, § 26.

l. 20. ἁπλοῦν καὶ διπλοῦν κ.τ.λ. Cp. Aristides Quintilianus [ed. Meibom, p. 16, l. 2], καὶ τὰ μὲν ἁπλᾶ ἃ καθ᾽ ἕνα τρόπον ἔκκειται, τὰ δὲ οὐχ ἁπλᾶ ἃ κατὰ πλειόνων τρόπων πλοκὴν γίνεται. 'Single scales are those that are composed in one mode; manifold scales those that are based on a complex of several modes.'

Cp. also *Isagoge* [ed. Meibom, p. 18, l. 20], τῇ δὲ τοῦ ἀμεταβόλου καὶ ἐμμεταβόλου διοίσει καθ᾽ ἣν διαφέρει τὰ ἁπλᾶ συστήματα τῶν μὴ ἁπλῶν· ἁπλᾶ μὲν οὖν ἐστι τὰ πρὸς μίαν μέσην ἡρμοσμένα, διπλᾶ δὲ τὰ πρὸς δύο, τριπλᾶ δὲ τὰ πρὸς τρεῖς, πολλαπλάσια δὲ τὰ πρὸς πλείονας. 'The difference between the modulating and non-modulating scale will be the difference between single scales and those that are not single. Single scales are those that are tuned to one Mese, double those that are tuned to two, triple those that are tuned to three, multiple those that are tuned to several.'

The distinctions here referred to we have already considered in our comparison of the three ancient Harmonies [Introduction A, § 14]. The Mixolydian scale on the old reading of it [Introduction A, § 20] was a σύστημα διπλοῦν.

Cp. p. 131, ll. 9-10 where Aristoxenus contrasts ἁπλοῦν and μεταβολὴν ἔχον.

P. 110, l. 5. λογῶδές τι μέλος. For the relation between Greek speech and Greek song, see Mr. Monro's *Modes of Ancient Greek Music*, § 37.

l. 14. I read καθόλου for καί που. Some such word is called for by the following ἰδιότητα.

l. 21. ὅτι πολλὰς ... ἕν τε καὶ ταὐτὸν κ.τ.λ. Aristoxenus means that in spite of the great variety of forms that consecution adopts, there underlies this variety one immutable law, which decides in any case whether any given sounds may or may not succeed one another.

P. 111, l. 7. τῶν εἰς ταὐτὸ ἡρμοσμένων is my suggestion for the impossible τῶν εἰς τὸ ἡρμοσμένον of the MSS. Aristoxenus is obliged to add this qualifying phrase to show that his division of the μέλος is not inconsistent with mixture of genus. Thus the meaning is 'every melody that observes *one* genus throughout falls into one of the three classes of diatonic, chromatic, and enharmonic.'

l. 8. ἤτοι διάτονόν ἐστιν ἢ χρωματικὸν κ.τ.λ. Aristides Quintilianus (ed. Meibom, p. 18, l. 19), gives the following derivations of these names: Enharmonic, ἀπὸ τοῦ συνηρμόσθαι, i. e. from the close fitting of intervals exhibited in its Pycnum; Diatonic, ἐπειδὴ σφοδρότερον ἡ φωνὴ κατ' αὐτὸ διατείνεται (διάτονος is to διατείνω as σύντονος to συντείνω); Chromatic, ὡς γὰρ τὸ μεταξὺ λευκοῦ καὶ μέλανος χρῶμα καλεῖται· οὕτω καὶ τὸ διὰ μέσων ἀμφοῖν θεωρούμενον χρῶμα προσείρηται.

Cp. Nicomachus (ed. Meibom, p. 25, l. 32), καὶ ἐκ τούτου γε διατονικὸν καλεῖται, ἐκ τοῦ προχωρεῖν διὰ τῶν τόνων αὐτὸ μονώτατον τῶν ἄλλων. (p. 26, l. 27), ὥστ' ἀντικεῖσθαι τὸ ἐναρμόνιον τῷ διατόνῳ· μέσον δ' αὐτῶν ὑπάρχειν τὸ χρωματικόν. μικρὸν γὰρ παρέτρεψεν, ἐν μόνον ἡμιτόνιον ἀπὸ τοῦ διατονικοῦ· ἔνθεν δὲ καὶ χρῶμα ἔχειν λέγομεν τοὺς εὐτρέπτους ἀνθρώπους.

Cp. also the interpolated passage in Aristides Quintilianus (Meibom, p. 111, l. 8), χρωματικὸν δὲ καλεῖται παρὰ τὸ χρώζειν αὐτὸ τὰ λοιπὰ διαστήματα, μὴ δεῖσθαι δέ τινος ἐκείνων. [According to Bellermann (*Anonymi Scriptio*, p. 59) χρώζειν τὰ λοιπὰ διαστήματα = attingere cetera genera; the μὴ δεῖσθαι δέ τινος ἐκείνων is unintelligible] . . . τὸ δ' ἐναρμόνιον διὰ τὸ ἐν τῇ τοῦ διηρμοσμένου τελείᾳ διαστάσει λαμβάνεσθαι· οὐ γὰρ διτόνου πλέον, οὔτε διέσεως ἔλαττον ἐνδέχεται (MSS ἐδέχετο) κατὰ αἴσθησιν λαβεῖν τὰ διαστήματα i. e. the Enharmonic genus derives its name from the fact that it uses to the full the liberty of variation permitted by the laws of Harmony. It uses quarter-tones, than which there is no smaller, and ditones, than which there is no greater (simple) interval.

l. 11. If ἀνώτατον be correct, it means 'highest' in the process of development and so furthest from the state of nature. But νεώτατον, the reading of H, is very tempting.

242

NOTES

l. 24. τὸ μὲν ἐλάχιστον. The Greeks did not recognize the Greater or Lesser Thirds as concords.

P. 112, l. 11. τὸ γὰρ τρὶς κ.τ.λ. Marquard reads μέχρι γὰρ τοῦ. I prefer to read τὸ γάρ with VbBRS, and am quite willing to construe it either as a direct accusative after διατείνομεν (just as we can say 'to stretch an interval' as well as 'to stretch the voice'), or as an accusative of length with διατείνομεν used in a neuter sense.

l. 13. αὐλῶν. For a full description of the αὐλός the reader is referred to the exhaustive article of Mr. A. A. Howard, in Vol. IV of the *Harvard Studies in Classical Philology*. A few general remarks will suffice here.

The term αὐλός commonly denotes a reed instrument of cylindrical bore; whether the reed was double-tongued as in the oboe, or single as in the clarinet, or whether both these forms of mouthpiece were employed, there is no conclusive evidence to prove. The musician generally performed on a pair of these instruments simultaneously, playing the melody on one, and an accompaniment (which in Greek music was higher than the melody), on the other. These double pipes were divided according to their pitch into five classes, παρθένιοι, παιδικοί, κιθαριστήριοι, τέλειοι, and ὑπερτέλειοι, corresponding closely to the soprano, alto, tenor, baritone, and bass ranges of the voice.

l. 15. κατασπασθείσης γε τῆς σύριγγος. According to the ingenious theory of Mr. Howard (see last note), the term σύριγξ, which commonly signifies a pan's-pipe, was used to denote a hole near the mouthpiece of the αὐλός, like the 'speaker' of the clarinet, the opening of which facilitated the production of the harmonies by the performer. The passages which he quotes on the matter are the following :—

(1) Aristotle (*de audib.* p. 804 a), διὸ καὶ τῶν ἀνδρῶν εἰσὶ παχύτεραι καὶ τῶν τελείων αὐλῶν, καὶ μᾶλλον ὅταν πληρώσῃ τις αὐτοὺς τοῦ πνεύματος· φανερὸν δ' ἐστίν· καὶ γὰρ ἂν πιέσῃ τις τὰ ζεύγη (i. e. 'if one squeezes the reed between the lips or teeth') μᾶλλον ὀξυτέρα ἡ φωνὴ γίγνεται καὶ λεπτοτέρα, κἂν κατασπάσῃ τις τὰς σύριγγας, κἂν δὲ ἐπιλάβῃ, παμπλείων ὁ ὄγκος γίγνεται τῆς φωνῆς διὰ τὸ πλῆθος τοῦ πνεύματος καθάπερ καὶ ἀπὸ τῶν παχυτέρων χορδῶν.

From this passage, as from the passage of Aristoxenus before us, it is evident that the effect of the operation κατασπᾶν τὴν σύριγγα was to raise the pitch of the instrument.

(2) Plutarch (*non posse suaviter*, p. 1096 a), διὰ τί τῶν ἴσων αὐλῶν ὁ στενώτερος ⟨ὀξύτερον, ὁ δ' εὐρύτερος⟩ βαρύτερον φθέγγεται· καὶ διὰ τί τῆς σύριγγος ἀνασπωμένης πᾶσιν ὀξύνεται τοῖς φθόγγοις, κλινομένης δὲ πάλιν βαρύνει (read βαρύνεται) καὶ συναχθεὶς πρὸς τὸν ἕτερον ⟨βαρύτερον⟩, διαχθεὶς δὲ ὀξύτερον ἠχεῖ; From this passage we learn that the effect of the operation ἀνασπᾶν τὴν σύριγγα was to raise all the tones of the instrument.

(3) *Anecdota Graeca Oxoniensia*, Vol. II, p. 409, (σῦριγξ) σημαίνει τὴν ὀπὴν τῶν μουσικῶν αὐλῶν.

(4) Plutarch (*de Musica*, p. 1138 a), Αὐτίκα Τηλεφάνης ὁ Μεγαρικὸς οὕτως ἐπολέμησε ταῖς σύριγξιν, ὥστε τοὺς αὐλοποιοὺς οὐδ' ἐπιθεῖναι πώποτε εἴασεν ἐπὶ τοὺς αὐλούς, ἀλλὰ καὶ τοῦ Πυθικοῦ ἀγῶνος μάλιστα διὰ ταῦτ' ἀπέστη.

[Mr. Howard gathers from this passage that Telephanes as a virtuoso objected to mechanical shifts such as the σῦριγξ which brought elaborate execution within the reach of poor performers. I am rather disposed to think from the context that this musician was a lover of the simplicity and reserve of ancient art, and resisted innovations in the direction of complexity.]

The only difficulty offered by these passages is in the apparently indifferent use of ἀνασπᾶν and κατασπᾶν to signify the same operation (or operations with the same effect). Mr. Howard thinks that the σῦριγξ might have been covered when not in use by a sliding band, which in some instruments was pushed up to open the hole, and in other cases pulled down for the same purpose. I might suggest that possibly ἀνασπᾶν and κατασπᾶν in these passages are not direct opposites; that κατασπᾶν may be used in its primary sense of 'to draw down,' and ἀνασπᾶν in its secondary sense of 'to open' (being answered in (2) by κλίνειν, 'to shut').

Von Jan supposes (*Phil.* XXXVIII, p. 382), that the σῦριγξ was a joint at the lower end of the αὐλός which could be detached from it. But this view, as Mr. Howard points out, does violence to the passage of Aristoxenus before us, as may

NOTES

be seen from his own explanation of it. 'Der Theil also, auf welchem man nach Abnahme der Syrinx weiter blasen kann, heisst selbst Syrinx, und das Blasen darauf συρίττειν.'

P. 113, l. 5. ὀκτώ is the excellent emendation of Westphal for ἐκ τῶν of the MSS. The eight concordant intervals are, The Fourth : The Fifth : The Octave : The Fourth and an Octave : The Fifth and an Octave : The interval of Two Octaves : The Fourth and Two Octaves : The Fifth and Two Octaves.

ll. 7-12. For Aristoxenus the Concords are the *elements* of intervals, and from them are derived directly or indirectly, by processes of addition and subtraction, all the discordant intervals. Even the quarter-tone must be thus ascertained: From a Fifth subtract a Fourth, and divide the result into four equal parts. The latter part of this construction is unsatisfactory, for how is the ear to assure itself of the equality of those parts? It could apparently do so only by such an *immediate* recognition of the interval in question as would render any *method* of ascertaining it nugatory.

l. 8. The contrast between the Pythagorean and Aristoxenian views of musical science comes out strongly in the definitions of a tone. For the Pythagoreans a tone is the difference between two sounds whose rates of vibration stand in the relation 8 : 9 ; for the school of Aristoxenus, the difference between a Fourth and a Fifth. The latter explain the phenomena of music by reducing these to more immediately known *musical* phenomena, the former by reducing them to their mathematical antecedents.

τῶν πρώτων συμφώνων. That is, the Fourth and Fifth.

l. 18. For καλούμενον τά τε πλεῖστα of the MSS I read κατεχόμενον τά γε πλεῖστα. If καλούμενον be retained it necessitates the insertion of the phrase διὰ τεσσάρων, to give it a meaning ; similarly, ὑπὸ τεσσάρων φθόγγων, being left without any construction, calls for some such word as κατεχόμενον.

τά γε πλεῖστα. Usually, not always; see note on p. 115, l. 1.

l. 20. τίνα δὴ τάξιν . . . κινοῦνται. This is undoubtedly, as Westphal has pointed out, a marginal scholium that has crept into the text and displaced the conclusion of the preceding sentence. Observe the use of εἰσι instead of ἐστι.

l. 21. For the meaning of the terms 'variable' and 'fixed' notes, see Introduction A, § 8.

P. 114, l. 14. τούτων δὲ τὸ μὲν ἔλαττον κ.τ.λ. According to Marquard's explanation (accepted by Westphal) of this difficult sentence, τὸ ἔλαττον and τὸ μεῖζον are used by brachylogy for τὸ 'οὐκ ἔλαττον ἀφίσταται,' and τὸ 'οὐ μεῖζον ἀφίσταται,' and thus repeat the ἔλαττον and μεῖζον of the preceding sentence. Against this it may be urged that the brachylogy is a very violent one ; and also that on this interpretation the latter clause of the sentence implies that the existence of a Lichanus further than two tones from the Mese was a matter of dispute. But of such a Lichanus we have no evidence. Mr. Monro would avoid the latter difficulty by supposing τὸ μεῖζον to be used illogically in the sense of 'the question of the greater limit.'

I consider that the misinterpretation of this passage is due to the natural but false assumption that τὸ ἔλαττον refers to the ἔλαττον of the preceding sentence. On my view τούτων = τούτων τῶν διαστημάτων = τοῦ τονιαίου διαστήματος καὶ τοῦ διτόνου : the genitive is a partitive one ; τὸ ἔλαττον τούτων (τῶν διαστημάτων) and τὸ μεῖζον τούτων mean respectively the tone interval and the ditone interval. The general object of the sentence beginning at τούτων is to justify not the smallness but the largeness of the localization of the Lichanus. In fact Aristoxenus would say, 'The interval between the Lichanus and Mese cannot be less than one tone or greater than two tones. The lesser of these distances (which I have assigned as the minimum limit of the space between the Lichanus and Mese), is found in the Diatonic genus, and is consequently of unquestionable legitimacy ; the greater of these distances (which I have assigned as the maximum limit of the space between the Lichanus and Mese) is admissible, though often disputed in the present day, and was the distinguishing feature of the Ancient Enharmonic music.'

l. 15. οὐχ is plainly wrong, as is seen from the following συγχωροῖτ' ἄν.

l. 16. ἐπαχθέντων. ἐπάγειν means to lead one on to the recognition of a general principle through the consideration of particular cases. Hence ἐπαγωγή = induction.

P. 115, l. 1. τῶν ἀρχαϊκῶν τρόπων τοῖς τε πρώτοις καὶ τοῖς δευτέροις.

Besides the enharmonic scale of the form
there was another enharmonic scale (commonly called after its
inventor Olympus), of the form which in-
troduced but one note of division into the tetrachord. It is
possible, as Marquard thinks, that these two scales are here
referred to as the earlier and later of the ancient modes ; but
the phrase is a strange one.

l. 3. οἱ μὲν γὰρ κ.τ.λ. Aristoxenus here records the fact,
familiar to us from other sources, of the gradual extinction of
the old enharmonic music. The intervals it employed were so
fine and required such delicacy of ear and voice, that it can
never have been popular. But, as we saw in the Introduction A,
§ 6, the cause which not only accounts for but justifies its
abandonment is the necessarily imperfect determination of its
intervals. Aristoxenus himself was quite aware of this deficiency,
though not alive to the seriousness of it. In a passage quoted
by Plutarch (*de Musica*, cap. 38, 1145 B), after assigning as one
cause of the disuse of the enharmonic music the difficulty of
hearing such a small interval as a quarter-tone, he proceeds to
suggest another explanation, εἶτα καὶ τὸ μὴ δύνασθαι ληφθῆναι διὰ
συμφωνίας τὸ μέγεθος καθάπερ τό τε ἡμιτόνιον καὶ τὸν τόνον καὶ τὰ
λοιπὰ δὲ τῶν τοιούτων διαστημάτων. ' Besides, there is the fact that
the magnitude of this interval (i. e. the quarter-tone) cannot be
determined by concord, as can the semitone, the tone, and the
like.' For this important principle of the determination of
discordant intervals by concord, see pp. 145, 146.

l. 6. γλυκαίνειν. Anonymus (§ 26) contrasts the Diatonic
genus as ' ἀνδρικώτερον . . . καὶ αὐστηρότερον ' with the Chromatic
as ' ἥδιστόν τε καὶ γοερώτατον.'

l. 20. The subdivisions of the genus are called χρόαι or
' shades.' See note on p. 116, l. 4.

P. 116, l. 1. For convenience, the word Pycnum will be
retained in the translation to denote the sum of the two small
intervals of the tetrachord, when that sum is less than the
remainder of the Fourth. For the meaning of the term see
p. 139, ll. 29–30.

In the Enharmonic tetrachord [♪ musical notation: *Pycnum*] the sum of the intervals between *e* and *xe*, and between *e* and *f* is a Pycnum, because it is less than the interval between *f* and *a*.

For the same reasons in the Chromatic [♪ musical notation: *Pycnum*] tetrachord the sum of the intervals between *e* and *f*, and *f* and ♯*f* is a Pycnum.

But in the Diatonic tetrachord [♪ musical notation] there is no Pycnum, for the sum of the intervals between *e* and *f*, and *f* and *g* is greater than that between *g* and *a*.

l. 4. τούτων δ' οὕτως κ.τ.λ. We have already seen that the Greeks recognize three genera, differentiated by the magnitudes of the intervals into which they divide the tetrachord; and we have given as the plan of the Enharmonic, quarter-tone, quarter-tone, ditone; of the Chromatic, semitone, semitone, tone and a-half; of the Diatonic, semitone, tone, tone. But it will immediately be asked, 'Are not other divisions intermediate between these equally permissible? Why not for instance divide your tetrachord into third of a tone, third of a tone, eleven-sixths of a tone? Or into five-twelfths of a tone, semitone, nineteen-twelfths of a tone?' Certainly, Aristoxenus replies, the possible divisions of the tetrachord, the possible locations of the Parhypate and Lichanus, are as infinite as the points of space. But the ear ignoring the mathematical differences attends to the common features in the impressions which these divisions make upon it, and constitutes accordingly three genera, the Enharmonic, Chromatic, and Diatonic, subdividing the latter two again into χρόαι, that is colours or shades of distinction; the Chromatic into the Soft, the Hemiolic and the Tonic; the Diatonic into the lower or Flat, and the Sharp or higher. It is evident then that each of these subclasses covers many differences of numerical division; but one division is taken by Aristoxenus as typical of each.

The exact proportions of these typical divisions are exhibited

248

in the following table in which the tetrachord is in each case represented by a line divided into thirty equal parts, each part consequently being the twelfth of a tone. The places of the Parhypate are definitely marked as they are given in pp. 141, 142; in this present passage their positions are less accurately stated.

TABLE OF THE GENERA AND SHADES.

$\frac{1}{}$ = one-twelfth of a tone.

$\frac{1 \ 2 \ 3}{}$ = a quarter-tone, or the least Enharmonic diesis.

$\frac{1 \ 2 \ 3 \ 4}{}$ = a third of a tone, or the least Chromatic diesis.

$\frac{1 \ 2 \ 3 \ 4 \ 5 \ 6}{}$ = a semitone.

$\frac{1 \ 2 \ 3 \ 4 \ 5 \ 6 \ 7 \ 8 \ 9 \ 10 \ 11 \ 12}{}$ = a tone.

ENHARMONIC

Parhypate   Lichanus

CHROMATIC (SOFT)

Parhypate   Lichanus

CHROMATIC (HEMIOLIC)

Parhypate   Lichanus

CHROMATIC (TONIC)

Parhypate   Lichanus

DIATONIC (FLAT)

Parhypate   Lichanus

DIATONIC (SHARP)

Parhypate   Lichanus

l. 19. τὸ χρῶμα, 'the particular species of chromatic.' ἡμι-όλιον, 'in the ratio of three to two'; because this was the relation between the Pycnum of the Hemiolic Chromatic and the Pycnum of the Enharmonic scale (9 and 6 respectively in the above table).

P. 117, l. 4. δεῖ γὰρ κ.τ.λ. These words are followed in some of the MSS by a detailed proof of the fact that the third of any quantity exceeds the fourth of the same quantity by a twelfth. It runs as follows: ἐπειδήπερ ὁ τόνος ἐν μὲν χρώματι εἰς τρία διαιρεῖται, τὸ δὲ τριτημόριον καλεῖται χρωματικὴ δίεσις· ἐν ἁρμονίᾳ δὲ εἰς δ̄ (τέσσαρα M) διαιρεῖται, τὸ δὲ τεταρτημόριον (δ̄ μόριον M) καλεῖται ἁρμονικὴ δίεσις, τὸ οὖν τριτήμοριον (γ̄ μόριον M) τοῦ αὐτοῦ καὶ ἑνὸς τοῦ τεταρτημορίου (δ̄ μορίου? M) τοῦ αὐτοῦ δωδεκάτῳ ὑπερέχει). οἷον ὡς ἐπὶ τοῦ ῑβ. ἂν διέλω τὸν ῑβ εἰς γ̄. δ̄. καὶ πάλιν τὸν αὐτὸν ῑβ εἰς δ̄.δ̄ (δ̄. γ̄. restituit Marquard), ἐν μὲν τῇ εἰς γ̄. δ̄. διαιρέσει γίνονται τέσσαρες τριάδες, ἐν δὲ τῇ εἰς δ̄. δ̄. (δ̄. γ̄. restituit Marquard) τρεῖς τετράδες. ὑπερέχει οὖν ἡ δ̄ τῆς γ̄. δ̄. (γ̄ restituit Marquard) τὸ τριτημόριον τοῦ τεταρτημορίου μονάδι, ὅπερ ἐστὶ τοῦ ὅλου δωδέκατον. Marquard very properly relegated this gloss to the Critical Commentary.

P. 118, l. 3. ἀπείρους τὸν ἀριθμόν. Aristoxenus means of course not that there can be more than one Lichanus in any one scale, but that, given any note and its Fourth above as boundaries, one can constitute an infinite number of scales differentiated by the positions of their variable notes, that is of their Lichani and Parhypatae.

l. 15. Marquard, followed by Westphal, changes the order of the sentences here and reads κοινωνεῖ γὰρ τὰ δύο γένη τῶν παρυπατῶν—ὁ δ᾽ ἕτερος ἴδιος τῆς ἁρμονίας, on the ground that the former sentence gives the explanation of ὁ μὲν κοινὸς τοῦ τε διατόνου καὶ τοῦ χρώματος and so must immediately follow it. But the MSS order is correct. κοινωνεῖ γὰρ κ.τ.λ. explains not the phrase ὁ μὲν κοινὸς κ.τ.λ., but the principal sentence παρυπάτης δὲ δύο εἰσὶ τόποι, and ὁ μὲν κοινὸς ... τῆς ἁρμονίας is a parenthesis. The sense is, 'The loci of the Parhypate are not three, like those of the Lichanus, but two (one common to two genera, and one particular); for the Chromatic and Diatonic have their Parhypatae in common.'

For τὰ δύο γένη compare p. 126, l. 8, οὐ γὰρ ἐπραγματεύοντο περὶ τῶν δύο γενῶν, ἀλλὰ περὶ αὐτῆς τῆς ἁρμονίας.

NOTES

l. 17. χρωματικὴ δὲ κ.τ.λ. There are two loci of the Parhypate; the line 4 in the above table, which is peculiar to the
Enharmonic genus, and the line consisting of 5 and 6 which
is common to the Chromatic and Diatonic. The meaning of
this last assertion is that the Diatonic and Chromatic genera
borrow one another's Parhypatae, so that you may melodiously
combine in a tetrachord any Parhypate in 5 and 6 with any
Lichanus in the lines from 8 to 18 inclusive *with this important
exception however that the lowest interval of the tetrachord must
never be greater than the one above it.* See Introduction A, § 7.

ll. 18–21. Of this most important law Aristoxenus offers no
proof beyond an appeal to the ear—γίγνεται γὰρ ἐμμελὲς τετράχορδον κ.τ.λ.

l. 21. ἄνισον ἀμφοτέρως, 'unequal in both ways' that is 'greater
and less.'

ll. 23, 24. The substitution of παρυπάτης τε χρωματικῆς τῆς βαρυτάτης for the παρυπάτης τε χρωματικῆς παρυπάτης of the MSS
completely restores the sense. Aristoxenus proves his statements that the Chromatic and Diatonic genera borrow each
other's Parhypatae by appealing to the extreme case. A melodious tetrachord is obtained from the combination of the *lowest*
Chromatic Parhypate, and the *highest* Diatonic Lichanus.

P. 119, l. 2. I retain συντεθείς the reading of M V B R S.
Aristoxenus means that he has exhibited the extent of the locus
of the Parhypate, both as divided into the loci peculiar to
certain genera and colours, and as a whole embracing all those
divisions. In p. 115, l. 19, he says that having determined the loci
as wholes (τῶν ὅλων τόπων) he must proceed to determine their
divisions according to genus and colour. Here he sums up his
account of the locus of the Parhypate by stating that he has
dealt with it from both these points of view.

Marquard, followed by Westphal, reads ἐντεθείς, and translates, 'The locus of the Parhypate is clear (from the above
remarks) as to its division and its place of insertion.' But this
translation conveniently ignores the words ὅσος ἐστίν, which
show that the *size* of the locus is what is here considered ; and
the space of a locus is not affected by its place.

l. 15. Aristoxenus here returns to his criticism of the method

251

of καταπύκνωσις (cp. note on p. 101, l. 1), and shows that it
supplies a false conception of musical continuity or sequence;
in other words, that it gives a false answer to the question,
'Starting from a given note, how are we to determine what
is the next note to it above or below?' For it ignores the
δύναμις of the given note, that is, its function in the system
of which it is a member; and regarding it merely as a point
of pitch, it declares that the next note to it is that point of
pitch which is separated from it by the smallest possible interval.
But Aristoxenus sees that though there may be a certain truth
in this answer from the point of view of Physics, it is musically
absurd. Let us take the note *f*, and ask what is the next note
above it. But for the purposes of music *f* is nothing except
as a member of a system or scale, and the question of the next
note to it is meaningless until its function in a scale is determined. Let us then restate our question thus: 'what is the next
note above an *f* which is the second passing note in an enharmonic scale ascending from *e*?' Now the answer to this cannot
be x*f*, as the theory of καταπύκνωσις would lead us to believe;
for that would imply the possibility of singing three quarter-
tones one after the other; whereas it is a law of the voice, and
consequently a law of music, that only two dieses can occur in
succession. In fact, the theory of καταπύκνωσις in its complete
application would imply the possibility of singing in succession
as many quarter-tones as are contained in the whole compass
of the scale.

l. 19. οὐχ ὅτι like οὐχ ὅπως is an elliptical phrase signifying
'not to speak of,' and is used for οὐ μόνον οὐ. Cp. p. 130, l. 7,
οὐ γὰρ ὅτι πέρας τῆς ἁρμονικῆς. The corruption of the MSS
reading here might be traced through the following stages; the
insertion of οὐ after ὅτι by a scribe who, ignorant of the ellipse,
felt the want of a negative; the misreading of ὅτι οὐ as τοῦ;
the consequent change of δυνατόν to δύνασθαι to supply an
infinitive for the article, the addition of μή to supply the place
of the lost οὐ; the change of μελῳδῆσαι to μελῳδεῖσθαι to explain
τῇ φωνῇ, the true construction of which had been hidden by
the corruption of δυνατόν.

διέσεις ὀκτὼ καὶ εἴκοσιν. Why twenty-eight quarter-tones

and not rather twenty-four, seeing that there are six tones in an octave? Because some scales, such as the Dorian, consisted of seven tones. See Introduction A, § 20.

l. 24. ἢ μικρῷ κ.τ.λ. This seems to be a somewhat contemptuous reference of Aristoxenus to the fact that in strict mathematical accuracy a Fourth is not quite two tones and a half. As we have often seen already, Aristoxenus is concerned with musical phenomena with a view to their artistic use, not their physical investigation.

P. 120, l. 2. οὐ δὴ προσεκτέον εἰ. Marquard retains the reading of the MSS and translates 'Nicht also ist für die Aufeinanderfolge darauf zu sehen, wann sie aus gleichen, wann aber aus ungleichen entsteht.' But ὅτε is relative usually, demonstrative sometimes; but never interrogative.

The general meaning of the passage is clear. The nature of melodic consecution, Aristoxenus would say, cannot be expressed by any law enjoining a succession of so many equal or so many unequal intervals. Thus, we cannot say, 'Two equal intervals must be followed by two unequal,' for while this rule is fulfilled by the Enharmonic scale, it is violated by the Diatonic, which has three tones in succession. Nor can we say 'three equal intervals may follow one another'; for while this is possible in the Diatonic genus, it is impossible in the Enharmonic. [Cp. p. 143, ll. 21–23.] Translate, 'We must not fix our attention on the fact that in certain cases,' &c.

l. 13. I read μετά for μέν of the MSS. μέν is out of place, as there is no antithesis between this assumption and the following; and some preposition is required to give a construction to τὸ πυκνὸν . . . σύστημα.

l. 16. ὑποκείσθω δὲ καὶ τῶν ἑξῆς κ.τ.λ. Here Aristoxenus states for the first time his fundamental law of continuity; that if a series of notes be continuous, any note in that series will form either a Fourth with the fourth note in order from it above or below, or a Fifth with the fifth note in order from it above or below, or will fulfil both these conditions.

Thus

is a legitimately continuous scale. *A*, though it does not form a Fourth with *c*, forms a Fifth with *e*; *B*, though it does not form a Fifth with ×*e*, forms a Fourth with *e*; ×B does not form a Fifth with *f*, but forms a Fourth with ×*e*; *c* does not form a Fifth with *a*, but forms a Fourth with *f*; *e* forms a Fourth with *a* and a Fifth with *b*; and so on.

On the other hand,

is not a legitimate scale; for *b* forms neither a Fourth with ♭*e* nor a Fifth with *f*.

l. 22. ὡς ἐπὶ τὸ πολύ i.e. in the Enharmonic and Chromatic scales, but not in the Diatonic.

l. 25. ἐναντίως τίθεσθαι κ.τ.λ., τὰ δύο ἴσα are the two equal intervals of the Pycnum: τὰ δύο ἄνισα are (1) the complement of the Fourth and (2) the disjunctive tone. Now in the scale descending from the Pycnum

the disjunctive tone lies next the Pycnum, and the complement of the Fourth second from it; while in the scale ascending from the Pycnum

we find the complement of the Fourth next the Pycnum, and the disjunctive tone second from it.

P. 121, l. 5. Every compound interval can be analysed into simple intervals but not into simple magnitudes. Thus, a Fourth

254

in the Enharmonic scale is analysed into quarter-tone, quarter-tone, ditone. Now quarter-tones are simple intervals and simple magnitudes at the same time; for quite apart from any consideration of systems or scales, no smaller musical magnitude than a quarter-tone exists for ear or voice. But the ditone though a simple interval in this scale, since the voice in this scale cannot divide it, is not by any means a simple magnitude. For if we abstract rom consideration of systems and scales, a ditone as a space is obviously reducible to two tones, and even farther.

l. 7. This passage is quite corrupt in the MSS. I read ἄκρων for ἀρχῶν, ἔν for ἐν, and ἔσωθεν for ἔξωθεν; insert ὧν after φθόγγων, and omit it after ἄκρων, and insert ἐκάστου before ἐκατέρωθεν.

It must be remembered that οἱ ἐξῆς φθόγγοι are not necessarily consecutive or *immediately successive* notes; the phrase applies equally to notes that are *in the same line of succession* even if at a distance from one another. Thus, in our major scale of C, the notes D, A, B, are ἐξῆς, because members of the same legitimate scale. Now an ἀγωγή is a sequence of consecutive or immediately successive notes, and this could not be expressed by saying merely that it proceeds διὰ τῶν ἐξῆς φθόγγων. The further necessary qualification is given by the following words: the successive notes must be separated from one another by simple intervals; must, in other words, be the nearest possible notes to one another in their scale.

Direct sequence is a species of sequence in general. Thus

is a sequence, but not direct;

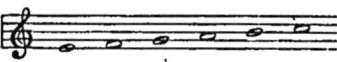

is a direct sequence.

ἔσωθεν τῶν ἄκρων means 'within the extremes,' that is 'between the first and last notes.' The first note of a sequence is not preceded, the last note not succeeded, by a simple interval. [Mr. Monro would retain ἔξωθεν in the sense of 'except.']

P. 122, l. 10. τούτων. For οὗτος in the sense of *iste,* cp. p. 132, l. 24.

l. 13. There may be an allusion here to such a doctrine as we find in the *Philebus*, or possibly τὸ πέρας may be an accusative in apposition to the following sentence, and mean 'as the sum or final conclusion of the matter.' In the latter case I should prefer to read τἀγαθόν.

l. 20. Marquard quite unnecessarily reads εἰλημμένη for εἰρημένη, and gives the following reason for the change ; 'Kann man denn eine prior opinio griechisch einfach eine εἰρημένη ὑπόληψις nennen, wenn vorher von einem Aussprechen gar keine Rede gewesen ist?' ἡ εἰρημένη ὑπόληψις refers back to ὑπολαμβάνοντα of l. 9.

P. 123, l. 1. ὡς ἔφη. The MSS read ὡς ἔφην which Marquard retains, translating 'aus den genannten Gründen.' But ὡς ἔφην is not the same as ἃς εἶπον, and must refer, not to αὐτὰς ταύτας τὰς αἰτίας, but to δι' αὐτὰς ταύτας τὰς αἰτίας προέλεγε 'Αριστοτέλης, and Aristoxenus has not said *that*.

l. 11. Marquard ruins the sense of this passage by his insertion of καί between ὅτι and καθ' ὅσον, and his mistranslation of οὐδ' ἀκούσαντες ὅλως—'das aber, dass die Musik und in wie weit sie nützen kann, verstehn sie gar nicht.' The sentence τὸ δ' ὅτι . . . ὠφελεῖν is elliptical. The complete statement which Aristoxenus had made was ὅτι ἡ μὲν τοιαύτη μουσικὴ βλάπτει ἡ δὲ τοιαύτη ὠφελεῖ, καθ' ὅσον μουσικὴ δύναται ὠφελεῖν. The careless listeners just caught the first part of the statement ὅτι ἡ μὲν . . . τοιαύτη ὠφελεῖ : the concluding qualification ὅτι [ἡ μὲν . . . τοιαύτη ὠφελεῖ] καθ' ὅσον μουσικὴ δύναται ὠφελεῖν escaped their ears altogether. In such a sentence as this ὅτι serves the same purpose as inverted commas in English.

Westphal rewrites the whole sentence and destroys its meaning.

l. 13. I read ἔμπειροι for ἄπειροι. If ἄπειροι be retained we must suppose a deficiency in the MSS. Marquard supplies it by inserting ἀγνοεῖν πρόσεισιν after ἐστίν. As he translates 'kommen aber herzu,' it would seem that he has confused the forms of εἰμί and εἶμι.

l. 15. ὡς νῦν ἔχει of the MSS is meaningless. The present

256

condition of the science has nothing to do with the argument.

l. 18. *ὑπάρχει καθάπερ ἀεὶ λέγεται.* Marquard retaining the *ἤ* of the MSS translates 'many other things are indispensable to the musician than those that are constantly said to be so'; but both the grammar and sense of this sentence are doubtful. Is there any evidence or any likelihood that there was a *perpetual* misunderstanding of the qualification of a musician? Would not *πολλὰ ἕτερα ἤ* mean 'many things different from' rather than 'many things in addition to'? And why not *ἕτερα ἤ ἅ* rather than *ἕτερα ἤ καθάπερ. καθάπερ ἀεὶ λέγεται*, if we omit the *ἤ*, means 'as we consistently assert' [see, for example, p. 95, ll. 13-15]. For a similar use of the present passive of *λέγω*, cp. p. 130, l. 16, *ὅτι δ' ἀληθῆ τὰ λεγόμενα*, 'that our assertion is true'; also p. 153, l. 6. Westphal secures the right sense by the clumsy insertion of *τοῦτο* after *ἤ*.

P. 124, l. 2. In this paragraph Aristoxenus defines his position in relation to the question What is the foundation of musical science? On the one hand, he rejects the intellectual or mathematical theory of the Pythagoreans on the ground that the principles, from which they seek to deduce the facts of music, lie outside the sphere of music altogether, and fail to account for those facts. On the other hand, he rejects equally the blind empiricism which takes the single facts and registers them without any attempt to ensure completeness, or ascertain the general law. See Introduction B, § 2.

l. 17. Let us suppose that as we are listening to a passage of music in the diatonic scale

the voice passes from ![music] to ![music] ; to apprehend this musical phenomenon, what faculties must we employ? In the first place we obviously require our sense of hearing to tell us that a semitone has been sung; but that is not enough. We require our intellect also to form a conception of the system in which the *e* and *f* occur, and to identify their functions in it; so that the phenomenon before us may be for us something quite distinct from the passage from

to ▓▓ in the enharmonic scale

l. 18. τῶν φθόγγων. τούτων of the MSS is wrong. The διαστήματα Aristóxenus always regards as mere distances; functions he attributes only to the notes. Cp. p. 127, l. 3, οὐκ αὐτάρκη τὰ διαστήματα κ.τ.λ.

δυνάμεις. δύναμις signifies the function which a note discharges in relation to the other notes of a scale. Thus in modern music the δύναμις of *b* is that of a leading note in the key of *c*, that of a dominant in the key of *e*, that of a tonic in the key of *b*.

P. 124, l. 22-P. 125, l. 2. Marquard and Westphal have completely missed the meaning of this passage. τῷ μουσικῷ is not the musician in the sense of the musical artist; nor is Aristoxenus labouring at the obvious fact that keenness of sense is a *sine qua non* of artists in general as distinguished from students of science. τῷ μουσικῷ is the student of musical science; and the point to which Aristoxenus would draw our attention is that Music presents us with a *science* for which accuracy of sense is indispensable. In this respect musical and geometrical science differ from one another. The propositions of Geometry are deduced from principles which, though possibly in the last resort principles of sight in the sense that without sight we never could have conceived them, are yet so abstract and fundamental that their acceptance accompanies the lowest use of that faculty. But the principles of musical science rest, not on the presuppositions of hearing in general, but on the evidence of the developed and cultivated ear. That a straight line is the shortest distance between two points may be a principle of sight in the sense that 'straight,' 'distance,' 'two,' &c. are phenomena of sight; but it does not require sharp eyes to apprehend it. On the other hand Aristoxenus' proof of the magnitude of the Fourth [pp. 146-147] depends on an appeal to the ear, by no means universal, that can distinguish a concord from a discord.

P. 125, l. 6. From consideration of the faculties Aristoxenus turns to the object matter which those faculties are to apprehend. Of this object matter he finds the all-pervading characteristic to be identity under difference, the co-existence of a permanent and a changeable element; and cites in support of his statement several cases which may be made clearer by the following illustrations:

(1) l. 7. [εὐθέως γὰρ κ.τ.λ.].

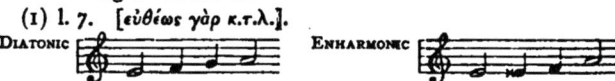

Here we have as permanent element the relation between the fixed notes; as changeable the position of the intermediate notes.

(2) l. 8. [πάλιν ὅταν μένοντος κ.τ.λ.].

Compare the interval between *E* and *A*, and the interval between *b* and *e*. Here we have as permanent the magnitude of the intervals (a Fourth); as variable the δύναμις of the notes containing the interval.

(3) l. 11. [καὶ πάλιν ὅταν τοῦ αὐτοῦ μεγέθους κ.τ.λ.].

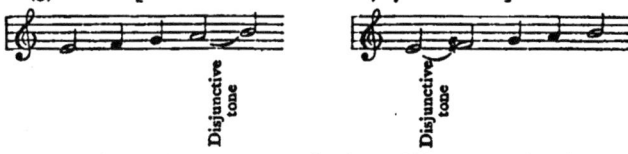

Here we have the same magnitude, a Fifth, appearing in two different figures, that is with its intervals arranged in different orders.

(4) l. 13. [ὡσαύτως δὲ καὶ ὅταν κ.τ.λ.].

In the two scales

and

compare the tetrachord between *b* and *e* in the former, with that between *a* and *d* in the latter. Here we have as permanent the size and figure of the interval; as variable the function of the tetrachord which in one case is modulating, in the other, not modulating.

(5) l. 16. [καὶ γὰρ μένοντος τοῦ λόγου κ.τ.λ.].

Compare the three following feet or bars :

τὸ δακτυλικὸν γένος, τὸ ἐν τῷ ἴσῳ λόγῳ
ἐν ὀκτασήμῳ μεγέθει (taking the crotchet as the unit).
ἐν ἑξασήμῳ μεγέθει.
ἐν τετρασήμῳ μεγέθει.

In these three we have as permanent the Dactylic character with its ratio of equality between the arsis and thesis; while the lengths of the feet differ, their difference being due to the different rate of movement.

(6) l. 18. [καὶ τῶν μεγεθῶν μενόντων κ.τ.λ.].

Compare the two following bars or feet :

τὸ δακτυλικὸν γένος τὸ ἐν τῷ ἴσῳ λόγῳ
τὸ ἰαμβικὸν γένος τὸ ἐν τῷ διπλασίῳ λόγῳ
ἐν ἑξασήμῳ μεγέθει.

Here we have the μέγεθος permanent, six crotchets; but the genus varies, the first being 'dactylic' with the arsis equal to the thesis, the second being 'iambic' with the arsis double the thesis.

(7) l. 19. [καὶ τὸ αὐτὸ μέγεθος πόδα κ.τ.λ.].

Compare (*a*) and (*b*).

(*a*)   (*b*)

Here the same quantity, eight crotchets, appears in (*a*) as a single foot, in (*b*) as a pair of feet.

(8) l. 20. [αἱ διαφοραὶ . . . διαιρέσεων].

The same magnitude, say | ||◁|| | may be divided into two

semibreves, or four minims, or one semibreve and two minims, or eight crotchets, or one semibreve, one minim, and two crotchets, &c.

(9) l. 20. [αἱ διαφοραὶ . . . σχημάτων].

Let us suppose a certain magnitude, say of three crotchets divided into a minim and a crotchet, these parts may be arranged in the order ♩ ♩ or in the order ♩ ♩.

(10) l. 21. [καθόλου δ' εἰπεῖν κ.τ.λ.].

In general, rhythmical science reduces the infinite variety and multiplicity of verse to combinations of a few primary elements, namely feet.

l. 10. The omission of γάρ, suggested to me by Mr. Bury, restores the construction of this sentence.

P. 126, l. 20. I have changed the MSS γένεσι to μέλεσι. The corruption might easily be explained both *e rei materia* and also through the proximity of γιγνομέναις. For the plural of μέλος used of the concrete, cp. p. 130, l. 2.

γένεσι is plainly wrong. 'That we must distinguish the genera if we are to follow the distinctions that occur in the genera' is an absurd tautology. A comparison with p. 126, l. 25, οὐ δεῖ δ' ἀγνοεῖν κ.τ.λ. makes clear the meaning of Aristoxenus' warning :—'if we neglect the scientific determination of any difference, we shall fail to detect the concrete cases of that difference which meet us in any musical composition.'

[Since writing this note I have discovered, in collating the Selden MS, the letters μελ crossed out before γένεσι.]

P. 127, l. 3. ἐπεὶ δ' ἐστὶν οὐκ κ.τ.λ. For example, part of the connotation of the terms Mese and Hypate is that they are the upper and lower boundaries of a Fourth; but more is required to determine the conception of these notes ; for the same might be predicated of the Nete and Paramese.

l. 8. See Introduction B, § 2.

l. 14. οὐδέτερον . . . τῶν τρόπων. One method is to exhaust the acts by a faithful enumeration ; the other is to deduce the facts from the principle on which they depend.

l. 24. Pythagoras of Zacynthus was the inventor of a stringed instrument called the τρίπους. See Athenaeus, xiv, 637.

ARISTOXENUS

l. 25. Agenor of Mitylene is quite unknown. See Porphyry, p. 189.

P. 128, l. 6. πέμπτον δ' ἐστὶ κ.τ.λ. On the whole paragraph cp. Introduction A, §§ 22–26, where I have explained also the uncertainty as to the key of the Mixolydian mode.

l. 19. τρισὶ διέσεσιν. The separation of keys by intervals of three quarter-tones would be an application of the principle of καταπύκνωσις. Cp. note on p. 101, l. 1.

P. 129, l. 4. μεταβολῆς. The modulation with which Aristoxenus is here primarily concerned is the μεταβολὴ συστηματική which is thus defined by Bacchius [ed. Meibom, p. 14, l. 1], ὅταν ἐκ τοῦ ὑποκειμένου συστήματος εἰς ἕτερον σύστημα ἀναχωρήσῃ ἡ μελῳδία ἑτέραν μέσην κατασκευάζουσα, 'the transition which a melody makes from one scale into another by providing for itself a different Mese.' But a different Mese can mean nothing else than a tonic of different pitch, so this transition means simply modulation into a different key. The conditions of its possibility are given in the following passage of the *Isagoge* [ed. Meibom, p. 20, l. 33]:—

Γίνονται δὲ αἱ μεταβολαὶ ἀπὸ τῆς ἡμιτονιαίας ἀρξάμεναι μέχρι τοῦ διὰ πασῶν, ὧν αἱ μὲν κατὰ σύμφωνα γίνονται διαστήματα, αἱ δὲ κατὰ διάφωνα. τούτων δ' αἱ μὲν ἐμμελεῖς ἧττον ἢ ἐκμελεῖς, αἱ δὲ μᾶλλον. ἐν ὅσαις μὲν οὖν αὐτῶν πλείων ἡ κοινωνία, ἐμμελέστεραι· ἐν ὅσαις δὲ ἐλάττων, ἐκμελέστεραι· ἐπειδὴ ἀναγκαῖον πάσῃ μεταβολῇ κοινόν τι ὑπάρχειν, ἢ φθόγγον, ἢ διάστημα, ἢ σύστημα. λαμβάνεται δὲ ἡ κοινωνία καθ' ὁμοιότητα φθόγγων. ὅταν γὰρ ἐπ' ἀλλήλους ἐν ταῖς μεταβολαῖς πέσωσιν ὅμοιοι φθόγγοι κατὰ τὴν τοῦ πυκνοῦ μετοχήν, ἐμμελὴς γίνεται ἡ μεταβολή, ὅταν δὲ ἀνόμοιοι, ἐκμελής. 'Modulations begin with modulation by the semitone, and proceed to the octave. Some of these are by concords and others by discords. Some of them are more melodious than otherwise; others less so. The greater or less the community of elements, the more or less melodious the modulation. For every modulation demands some common element, whether note, interval, or scale. But this community is ascertained by the similarity of notes; for a modulation is melodious or unmelodious, according as the notes that coincide in pitch are similar or dissimilar as regards their participation in the Pycnum.'

262

NOTES

The last phrase of this passage requires some explanation. The Greeks considered that every note of every scale was actually or potentially the lowest, the middle, or the highest note of a Pycnum. Thus in the Enharmonic scale

E is actually the lowest, xE actually the middle and F actually the highest note of the Pycnum E-xE-F. Similarly b, xb and c are respectively the lowest, middle, and highest notes of the Pycnum b-xb-c. Similarly e is the lowest note of the Pycnum of the conjunct tetrachord by which we might extend the scale upwards. Finally A, though not actually participating in any Pycnum in the above scale, does so potentially as the lowest note of the Pycnum A-xa-♭b, in the possible conjunct tetra-

chord

Representing the lowest, middle, and highest notes of a Pycnum by the signs *LP*, *MP*, and *HP*, we find these notes thus distributed in the Enharmonic scale :

LP MP HP LP   LP MP HP LP

The same terms naturally apply to the Chromatic Genus; and may be applied *analogically* to the notes of the Diatonic Scale : thus—

LP MP HP LP   LP MP HP LP

This distinction in notes is a deep and essential one, in which the δύναμις of the note is conceived in relation to the tetrachord in general, abstraction being made of the difference between the individual tetrachords.

If then it be asked whether two scales admit of melodious intermodulation, the answer is 'Yes, if they have a common element; and the more common elements they possess, the more melodious will be the modulation.' But when we speak of a common element, we mean not only certain points of pitch common to both scales, but certain coincident points of pitch occupied in both scales alike by lowest, by middle, or by highest notes of a Pycnum. In other words there must be a coincidence in pitch of notes of the same δύναμις in relation to the tetrachord.

Let us consider then in particular the possibilities of intermodulation between the keys of the seven modes.

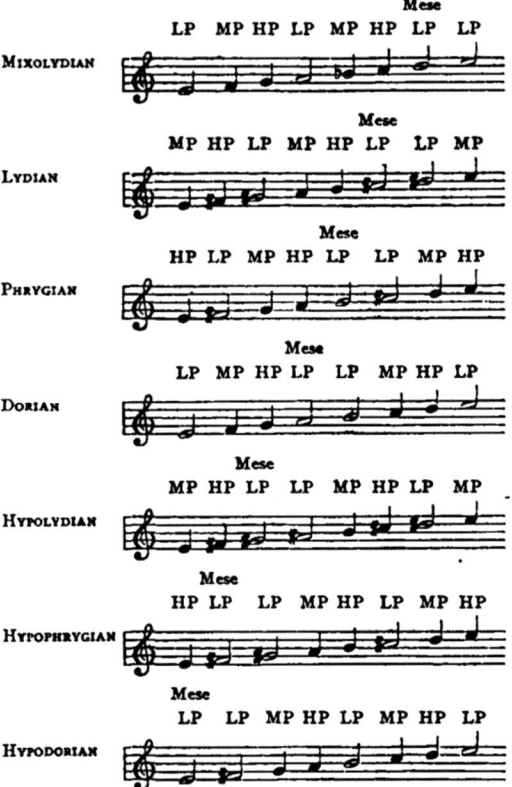

A semitone separates the tonics of the Mixolydian and Lydian

NOTES

keys. Similarly related are the Dorian and Hypolydian. Taking the first pair as typical we find that although there are several coincident points of pitch in the two scales such as E and A, there is no common element, because these points are occupied in the two scales by notes of different δύναμις in relation to the Pycnum, A for instance being LP in the Mixolydian key, but MP in the Lydian. Hence between scales separated by a semitone there is no direct modulation.

A tone separates the Lydian and Phrygian; the Phrygian and Dorian; the Hypolydian and Hypophrygian, the Hypophrygian and Hypodorian. Taking the first pair as typical we find that of the coincident points of pitch E, $\sharp F$, A, b, $\sharp c$, e, one alone, $\sharp c$, is occupied in the two scales by notes of the same δύναμις, namely the lowest notes of a Pycnum. Hence a melodious modulation is possible between scales separated by a tone, though the common element is the smallest possible.

A tone and a half separates the Mixolydian and Phrygian; the Phrygian and Hypolydian; the Dorian and Hypophrygian. In such pairs we find no common element; and hence they do not admit of direct intermodulation. Two tones separate the Lydian and Dorian; and the Hypolydian and Hypodorian. Here again we find no common element, and no direct modulation.

Two tones and a half, or the Concord of the Fourth, separate the Mixolydian and Dorian; the Lydian and Hypolydian; the Phrygian and Hypophrygian; the Dorian and Hypodorian. In the first pair we find several common elements E, F, G, A, e. In general, any two scales separated by a Fourth have many common elements, and modulation between them is highly melodious.

Three tones separate the Mixolydian and Hypophrygian keys. Here we find no common elements.

Three tones and a half, or the Concord of the Fifth, separate the Lydian and Hypophrygian; and the Phrygian and Hypodorian. In the first pair we find as common elements $\sharp G$, A, b, c. Hence in general one may modulate most melodiously between scales separated by a Fifth.

Four tones separate the Mixolydian and Hypophrygian. Here

there are no common elements. Four tones and a half separate
the Lydian and Hypodorian. Here again there are no common
elements.

Five tones separate the Mixolydian and Hypodorian. Here
we have E and e as common elements, and direct modulation
is p ssible.

The general result we arrive at is that when two scales are
separated by a Fourth or Fifth, modulation between them is
melodious in the highest degree; when they are separated by
a tone or five tones, modulation between them is again melodious though in an inferior degree; but when they are separated
by other intervals then.these, melodious modulation cannot be
effected between them directly, but only by the intervention of
other keys. It follows that the limits of indirect modulation are
strictly defined. Since direct modulation exists only between
keys whose tonics are spaced by a tone, by a Fourth, by a Fifth,
or by five tones, indirect modulation can only connect keys the
space between whose tonics can be arrived at by addition and
subtraction of these four intervals. But the only intervals that
can result from the addition and subtraction of a tone, two tones
and a half, three tones and a half, and five tones are the semitone and its multiples. Hence, if two keys have their tonics
separated by any other intervals than these, modulation between
them, direct or indirect, is impossible. See note on p. 101, l. 1.

Beside the μεταβολὴ συστηματική Bacchius (ed. Meibom, p. 13,
l. 26) mentions three other μεταβολαί affecting melody : γενική, 'of
genus'; κατὰ τρόπον, 'of mode'; κατὰ ἦθος, 'of emotional character.'

l. 6. I read τίνος for MSS τινός. λέγω δέ introduces an alternative statement, and the alternative statement of a question is
a question.

l. 7. κατὰ πόσα διαστήματα. The answer to this question as
appears from the last note is 'four,' κατὰ τὰ σύμφωνα διαστήματα,
καὶ κατὰ τὸν τόνον καὶ κατὰ τοὺς πέντε τόνους.

l. 10. μελοποιίας. The other parts of Harmonic science have
supplied the material of melody, notes, intervals, and scales;
it remains for the composer to make a judicious use of it. The
science of the use of musical material is the science of μελο-

ποιία. One of the functions of this science will be to determine which class of melody is adapted to any particular subject; whether the energetic style suits the chorus of a drama, or the Hypodorian tragedy, or the Enharmonic lamentation. But this function manifestly lies beyond the limits of ἁρμονική. To this latter science, however, belongs the classification of the several melodic figures by which a composition takes its shape.

In the *Isagoge* (ed. Meibom, p. 22, l. 3), we find the following account of this subject: Μελοποιία ἐστὶ χρῆσις τῶν προειρη-μένων μερῶν τῆς ἁρμονικῆς καὶ ὑποκειμένων δύναμιν ἐχόντων· δι' ὧν δὲ μελοποιία ἐπιτελεῖται τέσσαρά ἐστιν· ἀγωγὴ πλοκὴ πεττεία τονή. ἀγωγὴ [cp. above, p. 121, l. 7] μὲν οὖν ἐστὶν ἡ διὰ τῶν ἑξῆς φθόγγων ὁδὸς τοῦ μέλους, πλοκὴ δὲ ἡ ἐναλλὰξ τῶν τε διαστη-μάτων θέσις παράλληλος, πεττεία δὲ ἡ ἐφ' ἑνὸς τόνου πολλάκις γιγνο-μένη πλῆξις, τονὴ δὲ ἡ ἐπὶ πλείονα χρόνον μονὴ κατὰ μίαν γινομένη προφορὰν τῆς φωνῆς.

'Melopoeia is the employment of the above mentioned parts of Harmonic science which serve as a material to it. The figures through which Melopoeia takes final shape are four; the sequence, the zigzag, the repetition, and the prolongation.

The Sequence is the progression of the melody through consecutive notes; the Zigzag, the irregular progression with alternate location of the intervals [i. e. every second interval is ascending, every second descending]; the Repetition, the constant iteration of one note; the Prolongation, the dwelling for a length of time on one utterance of the voice.'

Ἀγωγή again is divided into three species (see Aristides Quint-ilianus, ed. Meibom, p. 29, l. 11), εὐθεῖα, or ἡ διὰ τῶν ἑξῆς φθόγγων τὴν ἐπίτασιν ποιουμένη (ascending by consecutive notes); ἀνακάμ-πτουσα or ἡ διὰ τῶν ἑπομένων ἀποτελοῦσα τὴν βαρύτητα (descending by consecutive notes); περιφερής or ἡ κατὰ συνημμένων μὲν ἐπι-τείνουσα, κατὰ διεζευγμένων δὲ ἀνιεῖσα· ἢ ἐναντίως (ascending by conjunction and descending by disjunction, or vice versa). A more general definition of πλοκή is supplied by Aristides Quint-ilianus (ed. Meibom, p. 19, l. 20), πλοκὴ δέ, ὅτε διὰ τῶν καθ' ὑπέρ-βασιν λαμβανομένων (ποιώμεθα τὴν μελῳδίαν), 'the zigzag occurs when our melody proceeds by notes that have been taken with a skip between them.'

267

If we accept this more general definition of πλοκή, and regard the more particular definition given in the *Isagoge* as descriptive of one special case of the class, it is easy to see that every melody is capable of being analysed into these four figures as final elements. I subjoin a few examples of such analysis.

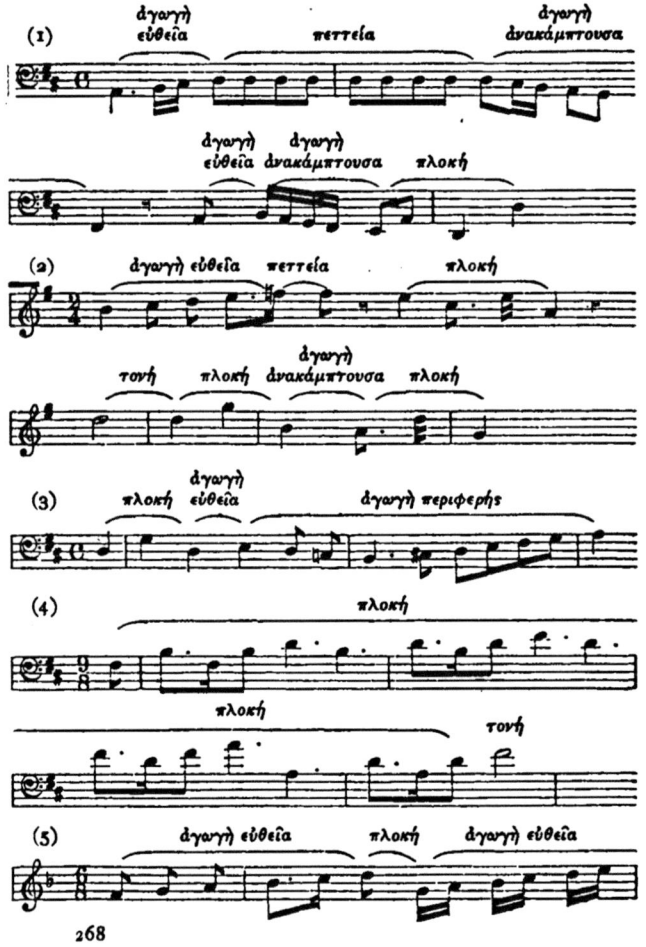

NOTES

l. 17. In this sentence I insert ἐστί after δέ, read παρακολουθεῖν for παρακολουθεῖ and insert δῆλον.

Either this paragraph is defective in the MSS, or its brevity amounts to obscurity. Yet it is not wholly unintelligible as it stands. In the first sentence Aristoxenus asserts that to understand a musical composition means to follow the *process* of its melody with ear and intellect. We have already learned from Aristoxenus what parts these two faculties play. The ear detects the magnitudes of the intervals as they follow one another, and the intellect contemplates the functions of the notes in the system to which they belong. But the phrase '*process* of the melody' turns the speculation of Aristoxenus into another channel. It reminds him of the difference that exists between music and such an art as architecture, the products of which present themselves to our senses complete at one moment. Melody, on the contrary, like everything in music, is a process of becoming, in which one passes, and another comes to be ; and we require here memory as well as sense, to retain the past as well as to apprehend the present.

But although this is undoubtedly the general sense of the passage, the logical connexion of the sentences is by no means obvious. Ἐν γενέσει γὰρ κ.τ.λ. justifies the previous use of τοῖς γιγνομένοις, but how is the sentence ἐκ δύο γὰρ τούτων κ.τ.λ. related to what goes before? The fact that the understanding of music requires memory as well as perception is a consequence rather than an explanation of the fact that melody is a process ; and τούτων implies that αἴσθησις and μνήμη, if not already mentioned, have at least been indicated.

Of course the contrast between ἀκοή and διάνοια [cp. p. 124, l. 17] must not be confused with the contrast between αἴσθησις and μνήμη.

P. 130, l. 1. ἃ δέ τινες ποιοῦνται τέλη κ.τ.λ. This paragraph contains a polemic against (*a*) the absurd theory that one who

can notate a melody has reached the pinnacle of musical knowledge; and (*b*) the equally absurd theory, which, basing the law
of harmony on the construction of clarinets, reduces musical
science to the knowledge of instruments and their construction.

l. 6. ὅλου τινός is governed by διημαρτηκότος, 'of one who has
missed some whole' = 'missed something completely.' But
perhaps we should read ὅλον, the accusative neuter used as
an adverb in the same sense as the cognate accusative ὅλον
ἁμάρτημα, and construe τινός in agreement with διημαρτηκότος.

l. 7. Marquard, followed by Westphal, inserts an οὐ between
ὅτι and πέρας, being ignorant apparently of the use of οὐχ ὅτι =
οὐ μόνον οὐ.

l. 13. Marquard is wrong in bracketing οὐ γὰρ ἀναγκαῖόν ἐστι
... ἐστι τὸ φρύγιον μέλος as a gloss. He does so on the supposition that its presence in the text involves a *petitio principii*;
because, he would say, Aristoxenus proves his statement 'that
the capacity to notate a melody does not necessarily imply the
understanding of it' by an appeal to a parallel case in metrical
science; and then proceeds to justify his analogy by assuming
the truth of the statement.

But Marquard has missed the course of the reasoning, which
is as follows: You admit that to mark a metre is not the
end-all of metrical science. On what grounds then? Because
it is a fact that a man may mark a metre, and yet not understand its nature. Very well then. The same fact holds good
with regard to melodic science (as I shall prove hereafter); it is
namely (γάρ) a fact that a man may notate a melody without
understanding its nature. Therefore you are logically bound
to admit that to notate a melody is not the end-all of melodic
science.

l. 17. This argument is based on two premises; (1) Notation
takes account of nothing beyond the bare magnitudes of intervals.
(2) Perception of the bare magnitude of intervals is no part of
musical knowledge.

In support of the first premiss he appeals to the following
facts :

(*a*) The notation makes no distinction of genus. Thus [see

table 22 in Introduction A] the notes $\begin{smallmatrix}T & O\\ \dashv & K\end{smallmatrix}$ stand for the

progression 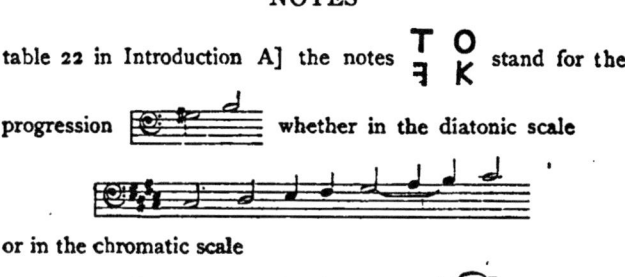 whether in the diatonic scale

or in the chromatic scale

though the interval in the first case is compound and diatonic, in the second case simple and chromatic.

(*b*) The notation makes no distinction of Figure. Thus the

notes $\begin{smallmatrix}\Phi & Z\\ \Gamma & L\end{smallmatrix}$ mark the interval of the sixth

both in the diatonic scale

where its schema is tone, semitone, tone, tone, tone; and in the diatonic scale

where its schema is tone, tone, tone, semitone, tone.

(*c*) The notation makes no distinction of the higher and lower

tetrachords of the scale. Thus the notes $\begin{smallmatrix}R & C\\ L & C\end{smallmatrix}$ apply to the

interval  whether in the scale

Hypatôn   Mesôn

or in the scale

Hypatôn   Mesôn

yet in the first case the interval belongs to the tetrachord Mesôn, in the second to the tetrachord Hypatôn.

The second premiss is evident from the undeniable fact that the perception of the distance between two sounds leaves all the vital distinctions of music untouched.

l. 25. To the reading adopted in the text Marquard would object (1) that Aristoxenus never refers to the tetrachords Hyperbolaeôn and Hypatôn; (2) that we know of no signs that were employed to denote tetrachords. But (1) in p. 99, l. 12 we have a reference to the Complete System of which the said tetrachords were parts; (2) when Aristoxenus speaks of the notation of a tetrachord, he means of course the notation of the notes of the tetrachord. The singular τῷ αὐτῷ σημείῳ is used because the sense is 'the same sign is used to represent *a* note of the tetrachord Hypatôn and *a* note of the tetrachord Mesôn,' &c.

Marquard's reading (given in the corrections at the beginning of his volume) τὸ γὰρ νήτης καὶ μέσης καὶ τὸ παραμέσης καὶ ὑπάτης has the fatal defect that these intervals are Fifths, not Fourths. Sense might be obtained by reading with Westphal τὸ γὰρ νήτης καὶ παραμέσης καὶ τὸ μέσης καὶ ὑπάτης, but this is rather far from the MSS.

P. 131, l. 6. οὔτε γὰρ . . . γνώριμον. An anacolouthon.

l. 10. τοὺς τῶν μελοποιιῶν τρόπους. See Aristides Quintilianus (ed. Meibom p. 29, l. 34), τρόποι δὲ μελοποιίας γένει μὲν τρεῖς· διθυραμβικός, νομικός, τραγικός. ὁ μὲν οὖν νομικὸς τρόπος ἐστὶ νητοειδής (i. e. its prevailing character is that of the tetrachord Netôn), ὁ δὲ διθυραμβικός, μεσοειδής (i. e. its prevailing character is that of the tetrachord Mesôn), ὁ δὲ τραγικὸς ὑπατοειδής (with the character of the tetrachord Hypatôn). εἴδει δὲ εὑρίσκονται πλείους, οὓς δυνατὸν δι᾽ ὁμοιότητα τοῖς γενικοῖς ὑποβάλλειν. ἐρωτικοί τε γὰρ καλοῦνταί τινες, ὧν ἴδιοι ἐπιθαλάμιοι, καὶ κωμικοί, καὶ ἐγκωμιαστικοί. τρόποι δὲ λέγονται διὰ τὸ συνεμφαίνειν πως τὸ ἦθος κατὰ τὰ μέλη τῆς διανοίας.

l. 21. Marquard, followed by Westphal, has made sad havoc of the following passage by changing the order of the sentences. In fact, the reading of the MSS calls for very little emendation. πέρας must be inserted in l. 22; and I have omitted ἢ before τάς in P. 132, l. 3, and inserted δέ after it; and omitted ἤ in l. 4, after πνεῦμα. No other changes are necessary, except in punctuation. The course of the argument is sufficiently clear from the translation.

P. 132, l. 12. μέγιστον μὲν οὖν. μὲν οὖν signifies a correction or strengthening of the preceding statement, 'No less absurd, nay rather most absurd of all.' I have followed Marquard in reading ἄτοπον though I am not at all sure that the addition is necessary. καθόλου μάλιστα τῶν ἁμαρτημάτων might mean 'the most *complete* mistake possible.' Cp. note on p. 130, l. 6.

l. 17. κοιλίας. The plural is very strange, if the word means, as it seems to mean, the main bore of the instrument.

Mr. Howard (*Harvard Studies in Class. Phil.* Vol. IV, p. 12) quotes in support of this rendering Porphyrius ad Ptol. p. 217, ed. Wallis: πάλιν δὲ ἐὰν λάβῃς δύο αὐλούς, τοῖς μὲν μήκεσιν ἴσους, ταῖς δὲ εὐρύτησι τῶν κοιλιῶν διαφέροντας· καθάπερ ἔχουσιν οἱ Φρύγιοι πρὸς τοὺς Ἑλληνικούς· εὑρήσεις παραπλησίως τὸ εὐρυκοίλιον ὀξύτερον προιέμενον φθόγγον τοῦ στενοκοιλίου· θεωροῦμεν γέ τοι τοὺς Φρυγίους στένους ταῖς κοιλίαις ὄντας ἐπὶ πολλῷ βαρυτέρους ἤχους προβάλλοντας τῶν Ἑλληνικῶν. Also Nicomachus (ed. Meibom, p. 8, l. 33), ἀνάπαλιν δὲ τῶν ἐμπνευστῶν αἱ μείζονες κοιλιώσεις καὶ τὰ μείζονα μήκη, νωθρὸν καὶ ἔκλυτον. He cites too the parallel use of the Latin *cavernae* by Servius ad Aen. ix, 615.

If it were not for the strength of these passages, one might suppose κοιλίας here to refer to the sidetubes with which some αὐλοί were furnished, and which served, when in use, to lower the pitch of the instrument (see Mr. Howard's article, p. 8).

l. 18. Marquard inserts ὁ αὐλητής unnecessarily. He assumes that οἷς in l. 19 must be an instrumental dative, and that πέφυκε must be used personally, in which case the construction will be ὁ αὐλὸς πέφυκεν ἐπιτείνειν καὶ ἀνιέναι, and ἐπιτείνειν and ἀνιέναι will be used intransitively. But there is no reason why οἷς may not be a dative after πέφυκεν ― [those other parts] to which it is natural [to raise and lower tone].

l. 24. ταῦτα. Cp. p. 122, l. 10.

l. 25. καὶ γὰρ ἀφαιροῦντες. For the violent ellipse by which γάρ is left without a finite verb, cp. p. 145, l. 6, ἢ γὰρ συμφωνεῖν.

Should we read παραιροῦντες for ἀφαιροῦντες? For this expedient of bringing the two pipes together, and drawing

ARISTOXENUS

them apart, and for its effect on the pitch, see the last clause of
the sentence from Plutarch (*non posse suaviter* 1096 a) quoted in
the note on p. 112, l. 15.

P. 133, l. 2. οὐδὲν διαφέρει λέγειν κ.τ.λ. Here Marquard's
translation is distinctly amusing, 'daher macht es offenbar
keinen Unterschied, ob man sagt "gut die Flöten" oder
"schlecht."' Westphal is equally ridiculous: 'sodass es meistens
eigentlich dasselbe besagen will, wenn das Publikum beim
Aulosspiel "gut" oder "schlecht" ruft.' The meaning simply
is that the goodness or badness of the music does not depend
upon the instrument.

l. 21. θαυμαστὸν δ' εἰ κ.τ.λ. One more argument. Clarinets
are changeable instruments, and their music must alter with the
alteration in themselves.

P. 134, l. 5. The MSS τὸ εἰρημένον ὄργανον cannot be right.
The argument plainly is (1) instruments in general will not
serve as bases for the laws of harmony; and (2) least of all will
that very defective instrument, the clarinet, do so. For ὄργανον
used alone cp. p. 133, l. 4.

l. 14. πρῶτον μὲν αὐτῶν κ.τ.λ. It is required of us firstly to
ascertain the phenomena correctly, secondly, to distinguish
truly in these phenomena what is primary and what is derived,
thirdly to grasp aright the result and conclusion. In other
words we must first observe accurately, then analyse our facts
and find the essentials, then sum the results of our observation
and analysis in a generalization. The generalizations, which
we shall thus obtain, will be the ἀρχαί, or fundamental principles
of our science, from which its other propositions will be deduced.
It is indispensable that such fundamental principles should be
(*a*) indisputably true; (*b*) recognizable by our sense perception
as primary truths of music.

The science of Harmonic then as conceived by Aristoxenus
starts from the observation of individual facts, and proceeds by
induction to general principles, which serve in turn as foundations
for a train of deductive reasoning.

l. 17. τοῦ συμβαίνοντος ... συνοφθέντος. This passage is mis-
translated by Marquard 'die methodische Beobachtung des
Zufälligen und Uebereinstimmenden,' that is 'the methodical

274

NOTES

observation of the contingent and constant'; by Westphal ' so muss der Sache gemäss erkannt werden was sich (erst) als Schlussfolge ergiebt, und was in die Kategorie des allgemein Angenommenen gehört,' that is, 'we must distinguish in accordance with the facts what is only arrived at as a conclusion, and what belongs to the category of the universally admitted.' But (1) τὸ συμβαῖνον and τὸ ὁμολογούμενον are technical terms for the result and conclusion; (2) συνορᾶν means 'to see the connexion of things' not to 'see the difference' between them ; (3) if τὸ συμβαῖνον and τὸ ὁμολογούμενον are distinct and contrasted classes, we should require τοῦ συμβαίνοντος καὶ τοῦ ὁμολογουμένου.

l. 25. καθόλου δ' ἐν τῷ κ.τ.λ. We must neither trace back our musical phenomena to physical and non-musical principles ; nor be content till we have resolved them into the ultimate laws of music.

l. 27. For ἡ of the MSS I read ᾗ in the sense of *qua* 'regarded as.'

P. 135, l. 1. κάμπτοντες ἐντός. A metaphor from the race-course.

l. 7. ἢ μικτὸν . . . ἢ κοινόν. See *Isagoge* [ed. Meibom, p. 9, l. 34], κοινὸν δὲ τὸ ἐκ τῶν ἑστώτων συγκείμενον. μικτὸν δὲ τὸ ἐν ᾧ δύο ἢ τρεῖς χαρακτῆρες γενικοὶ ἐμφαίνονται. A melody is common when it employs only the fixed notes, which, of course, are common to all three genera ; it is mixed, when it employs notes of different genus.

l. 12. περιέχεται δ' ἡ ὑστέρα . . . προτέρᾳ. That is the difference between concords and discords in one special case of the difference between larger and smaller intervals. The connotation of the διαφορά between concords and discords contains the connotation of the διαφορά of size, but the denotation of the διαφορά of size contains the denotation of the διαφορά between concords and discords.

l. 18. The MSS are corrupt here. It is absurd to say that the Fourth is determined as the smallest interval by its own nature. It is so determined by the nature of melody or' song, inasmuch as all the smaller intervals which the latter produces are discords. The correction is due to Westphal.

P. 136, l. 1. ταῦτα μὲν οὖν λέγομεν ἃ παρὰ τῶν ἔμπροσθεν παρειλήφαμεν. Marquard rejects this sentence on the ground that the sense required is not 'we say what we have learned,' but 'what we say, we have learned.' But, just as ταῦτα λέγομεν ἀληθῆ means 'in saying this we are speaking the truth' (the predicative force lying in the ἀληθῆ), so here the meaning is 'in the above statements we are repeating what we have learned from our predecessors.'

l. 6. πάθος. Cp. the use of πάσχω in p. 145, l. 17; p. 156, l. 5; p. 159, l. 8.

l. 10. οὔτε τὸ ἐξ ἑκατέρου κ.τ.λ. Meibom, Marquard and Westphal alike find this sentence unintelligible. Is it not a fact, they ask, that the sum of a Fourth or Fifth and an octave is a concord? Accordingly they correct the reading by inserting δὶς τεθέντος after ἑκατέρου αὐτῶν. But the MSS are perfectly right, and the commentators construed wrongly. Written in full with the ellipse supplied, the whole sentence runs, οὔτε γὰρ τὸ ἴσον ἑκατέρῳ αὐτῶν συντεθὲν τὸ ὅλον σύμφωνον ποιεῖ, οὔτε τὸ ἐξ ἑκατέρου αὐτῶν καὶ τοῦ διὰ πασῶν συγκείμενον ἑκατέρῳ αὐτῶν συντεθὲν τὸ ὅλον σύμφωνον ποιεῖ, and the meaning is 'Add to a Fourth or a Fifth an interval equal to itself; the result is a discord. Add to a Fourth or Fifth respectively the sum of an Octave and a Fourth or Fifth; again the result is a discord.'

According to the absurd misconstruction of Meibom, Marquard and Westphal, the second part of the sentence in its completeness is as follows: οὔτε τὸ ἐξ ἑκατέρου αὐτῶν δὶς τεθέντος καὶ τοῦ διὰ πασῶν συγκείμενον τὸ ὅλον σύμφωνον ποιεῖ. Now it is quite correct to say '4 added to 6 causes the whole to be 10' or 'the addition of 4 to 6 causes the whole to be 10,' but surely not to say 'the sum of 6 and 4 *causes* the whole to be 10.'

l. 18. Aristoxenus introduces two warnings. When he says that it is possible to sing the third or fourth part of a tone, he must not be misunderstood as saying that one can in singing divide a tone into three or four parts. For that would imply the possibility of singing three thirds of tones or four quarter-tones in succession which is against one of the fundamental laws of melody [see p. 119, l. 20].

Again, he has mentioned no smaller division of the tone than the quarter-tone, because the voice can sing and the ear dis-

criminate none smaller. But it must not be forgotten that in
the abstract there cannot be a minimum interval any more than
a minimum space or time.

P. 137, l. 4. ὁτὲ δὲ θατέρου κ.τ.λ. Between the Diatonic and
Chromatic scales there is only variation of the Lichanus, as
these genera have their Parhypatae in common.

P. 137, l. 18–P. 138, l. 6. Marquard is greatly disconcerted
by the abrupt transitions which he finds in this passage from the
indicative to the accusative and infinitive construction. Besides
correcting rightly δεῖ to δεῖν in p. 138, l. 3, he omits ἐστι in
p. 137, l. 20 to remove the incongruity. As a fact, with the
exception of the blunder δεῖ for δεῖν, the reading of the MSS is
quite unexceptionable, and the construction normal. The quoted
questions are in the indicative, the quoted *statements* in the
accusative and infinitive. The εἶναι that follows θετέον in p. 137,
l. 23 is grammatically dependent on it, and not the infinitive of
oratio obliqua, as Marquard supposes.

l. 18. The objection cited in this paragraph, and the answer
of Aristoxenus to it, raise again the conflict between the superficial view of notes as points of pitch, separated by certain spaces,
and the deeper view of Aristoxenus according to which notes
are essentially members of a system with special functions. The
objection is stated in l. 18–p. 138, l. 5 and here again Marquard
has quite wantonly perverted the order of the sentences. The
argument of the objection may be stated thus: 'We object to
applying one term, say the term Lichanus, to several points of
pitch at different distances from the Mese. The term Hypate
signifies one certain point at one certain distance from the
Mese; why not similarly restrict the term Lichanus to some
one point, say the point two tones below the Mese, your
Enharmonic Lichanus; and use other names for what you
call the Chromatic and Diatonic Lichani? For we hold that
notes which bound unequal magnitudes must be different notes;
or, to put it more plainly, that a difference in the size of the
contained interval necessarily implies a difference in the containing notes. We hold equally, by simple conversion of this
proposition, that different notes must bound different intervals,
or that a difference in the containing notes necessarily implies

a difference in the size of the contained intervals. Consequently a proper nomenclature will always employ the same terms to denote the points bounding the same magnitudes of intervals ; and will always employ different terms when the bounded intervals are unequal.'

l. 19. Marquard reads τεθέντος for κινηθέντος on the ground that it is when one posits, not when one changes, one of the possible intervals between the Lichanus and Mese that a Lichanus results. But the sense is rather this : The objectors urge that between any two notes there must be but one interval ; if this interval be *changed*, then there must, say they, be a change of notes also.

P. 138, l. 2. The addition of λιχανός is perhaps unnecessary ; κληθῇ might stand by itself for 'receives the name.'

l. 3. Probably S is right in omitting τό.

l. 5. The sentence τὰ γὰρ ἴσα τῶν μεγεθῶν τοῖς αὐτοῖς ὀνόμασι περιληπτέον εἶναι is the simple converse in sense, though not in form, of δεῖν γὰρ ἑτέρους εἶναι φθόγγους τοὺς τὸ ἕτερον μέγεθος ὁρίζοντας. For the former sentence = 'equal intervals should be bounded by identically-named notes' = 'no notes should have different names unless they bound unequal intervals' = 'no notes are really different unless they bound unequal intervals' = 'all different notes bound unequal intervals,' which is the simple converse of 'all notes that bound unequal intervals are different notes.'

l. 9. Before dealing with the original proposition of the objectors Aristoxenus disposes of its converse by insisting that the essential feature of a note is its δύναμις, and that nomenclature cannot overlook the distinction between the notes *a* and *e* in the scale

when they are Mese and Nete, and the notes *a* and *e* in the scale

when they are Lichanus and Paranete.

278

NOTES

l. 14. I read ἔν, τὸ for ἐν τῷ of the MSS.

l. 16. ὅτι δ᾽ οὐδὲ τοὐναντίον κ.τ.λ. Having disposed of the converse Aristoxenus turns to the original proposition, which requires a special refutation; for the two propositions are related to one another as a Universal Affirmative and its simple converse; and the falsity of one does not prove the falsity of the other. Aristoxenus has to prove not only that inequality in the contained intervals is not the sole ground for distinguishing notes by name, but also that it is no sufficient ground for doing so at all. His arguments are two:

'In the first place, if you insist on having different names wherever there is a difference of interval, you will require an infinite vocabulary. The voice, for example, may make its second resting place in the passage of the tetrachord at any point between a semitone above the Hypate and a tone below the Mese. The number of such points is infinite. We call them all Lichanus, but you who insist that a difference of interval demands a difference of name will require an infinity of names. Perhaps you will think that this is the quibble of a casuist; that as a matter of fact three terms would do, one for the Enharmonic Lichanus, one for the Chromatic, and one for the Diatonic. But it is no quibble. For consider seriously (ὡς ἀληθῶς): different schools or theorists assign different positions to the Lichani of the different genera; and there is no earthly reason for giving one's adherence to one of these schools rather than another. Take a special case. Some theorists locate the Enharmonic Lichanus at two tones below the Mese; some place it a little higher. Supposing, then, that we even went so far with you as to restrict the term Lichanus to the Enharmonic Lichanus, we should have just the same difficulty again. For here are two upper passing notes, one two tones below the Mese, and one a little higher; both of them to the ear give an Enharmonic scale, so that both have equal claims to the name of Lichanus: yet they bound unequal intervals from the Mese, therefore, on your theory, the one name will not apply to both.'

'In the second place, your demand ignores the fundamental character of sense perception which, abstracting from the petty distinctions of quantity, looks to the similarity of things through their possession of common qualities. Thus the juxtaposition of two small intervals produces on the ear an impression of a certain *sort*, which remains the same whatever the exact size of the intervals may be ; and one uses the general term Pycnum for this juxtaposition. But on your principle, one has no right to employ this term, since Pycna are of different sizes. Similarly, one has no right to speak of Enharmonic, or Chromatic, or Diatonic, for all these classes imply the ignoring of mathematical differences. If, on the other hand, we do admit a class Pycnum, a class Enharmonic, why not also a class Parhypate and a class Lichanus? For just as in the case of Pycna you have a general feature, namely, a certain compression, and as in each genus you have a certain character common to the particular cases of it, so here you have as common features the species or figure of the tetrachord, that is, a plan of four notes, the two outer fixed at an interval of a Fourth with the upper as tonic, and two passing notes between them.'

l. 17. For ἀκολουθητέον of the MSS I read ἀκολουθεῖν θετέον. The preceding sentence asserts that A is not a necessary result of B ; nor, continues Aristoxenus, must we allow that B is a necessary result of A. But ἀκολουθεῖν cannot mean 'to assert a necessary dependence.'

τοὐναντίον ἀκολουθεῖν ='the opposite order of dependence.'

l. 21. ὡς ἀληθῶς . . . ἐν ἑκατέρᾳ τῶν διαιρέσεων. I have transposed this passage from its unintelligible position after διαμένειν in p. 140, l. 1. In its proper place it is most serviceable in answering the certain objection that to talk of an infinity of Lichani is mere casuistry.

P. 189, l. 2. It is quite unnecessary to insert with Marquard and Westphal οὐ πάνυ ῥᾴδιον συνιδεῖν. ὥστε may very well introduce a conclusion pressed against an adversary in the form of a question.

l. 13. λέγω δέ is parenthetical, and τιθεῖσα agrees with ἐκείνη and stands in apposition to εἰς ὁμοιότητα . . . βλέπουσα.

l. 14. I read ἕως for ὡς in l. 14, and δὲ εἶδος ἕως ἄν for δὲ ἢ διέσεως ἄν in l. 17. For ἕως in the sense of 'to cover all cases in which' cp. p. 141, l. 1.

l. 16. πυκνοῦ τινὸς φωνή. If the reading is correct, πυκνοῦ

280

τινός must be construed as a genitive of the material: 'a voice-utterance consisting in a compression,' i.e. in a succession of close-lying notes.

l. 21. I insert μένειν after συμβαίνει.

P. 140, l. 9. Finally, Aristoxenus shows a palpable absurdity that would result from the acceptance of this principle—the absurdity of one note bearing more names than one in the same scale. In the first place let us take two equal intervals in succession; for instance, the interval between *e* and *f*, and

between *f* and ♯*f* in the Chromatic scale

If we insist on using the terms X and Y universally for the lower and higher notes of an interval of this size, the *f* of the above scale will be both X and Y.

In the second place, let us take two unequal intervals, the interval between *e* and *f* and that between *f* and *g* in the Diatonic

scale 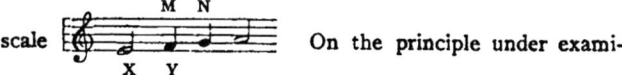 On the principle under exami-

nation, inasmuch as the names signify no function or intrinsic qualities of notes, but merely a space relation between two points whose only quality is that they are so far from one another, every such name of a point must connote its relation to another point at some certain distance; and cannot be employed outside this relation. Thus every change in the size of an interval will demand a new pair of note-names. Hence in the present case the intervals between *e* and *f* and between *f* and *g* will bear two distinct pairs of names, say XY and MN; and *f* will bear two names, *Y* and M.

P. 141, l. 1. In this paragraph we have another exposition of the genera and their 'shades.' See pp. 116-118.

P. 142, l. 23. The missing words have been well supplied by Westphal.

P. 143, l. 13. I have little doubt that we should read λεκτέον for δεικτέον. Cp. p. 147, l. 25, where all the MSS read λεκτέον instead of the plainly necessary δεικτέον.

l. 18. ἀγωγῆς: cp. p. 121, l. 7. The term is here used, not of a particular melodic figure, but of the general consecution of melody.

l. 19. I omit the words οὐ γὰρ διὰ τοσούτων δυνηθείη τις ἄν as a gloss which has crept into the text. They are meaningless by themselves, and require the addition of μελῳδεῖν, or the like; even when thus emended they present a singularly weak, and at the same time wholly unnecessary statement. The gloss was occasioned by the ambiguity of the following μέχρι.

l. 20. μέχρι here = 'up to, but excluding.' It more often means 'up to and including' (see p. 131, l. 3). The same ambiguity attaches to ἕως. Cp. p. 144, l. 1, and p. 140, l. 4. Perhaps, however, we should read ἀδυνατεῖ here.

l. 21. τὸ ἑξῆς οὔτ' ἐν κ.τ.λ. The nature of melody brings it to pass that (a) sometimes the next note to a given note is separated from it by the smallest possible interval, as in the Enharmonic scale 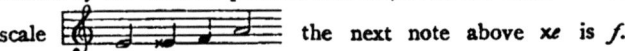 the next note above χε is ƒ. (b) Sometimes the next note to a given note is separated from it by an interval of considerable size, as for instance in the same scale the next note above ƒ is a. (c) Sometimes a consecutive progression moves by equal intervals as from ƒ to b in the

Diatonic scale  (d) Sometimes

a consecutive progression moves by unequal intervals as from ƒ to b in the Chromatic scale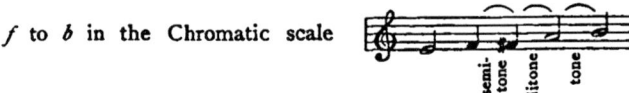

Consequently, the true conception of continuity is not derived from the notions of the minimum, the equality, or the inequality of intervals.

P. 144, ll. 8–9. After much hesitation I have accepted Marquard's reading, though I believe his interpretation of it to be quite erroneous. The difficulty lies in the genitive τοῦ προειρημένου ἀριθμοῦ: the general argument is clear. If we admit that the maximum number by which the distance AB can be divided is four

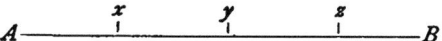

it is evident that the points A, x, y, z, B are consecutive, and admit of no intermediate points of section. Aristoxenus refers to these points A, x, y, z, B as 'the notes that bound fractions of the said number.' Marquard identifies the number with the distance AB, and regards τοῦ προειρημένου ἀριθμοῦ as a partitive genitive. But, to take the above illustration, ἀριθμοῦ evidently refers not to the distance AB but to the number four by which it has been divided. For it would not be true to say that the points which bound parts of the said interval are consecutive; A, y, B for example bound parts of it, and are not consecutive.

We must therefore understand the partitive genitive τοῦ διαστήματος with μέρη, and interpret τοῦ προειρημένου ἀριθμοῦ as 'having the said number as denominator.' To recur again to our illustration, the whole phrase τοῦ προειρημένου ἀριθμοῦ μέρη τοῦ διαστήματος would mean 'fractions-of-four' (or 'fourths') 'of the distance AB.'

l. 18. I read λαμβανέτω for λαμβάνεται of the MSS, as the middle voice is out of place. λαμβανέτω is parallel to ἐκμελὴς ἔστω that immediately follows.

Meibom wished to read μηδέτερον for μηδέτερα. But Marquard points out that each alternative here referred to comprehends two relations, those of any given note to a certain note above it and to a certain note below it.

l. 20. οὐ δεῖ δ᾽ ἀγνοεῖν κ.τ.λ. For instance, the scale

obeys the above law; yet it is illegitimate, because it violates the law of the tetrachord that the interval between the lower fixed note and the first passing note must never be greater than that between the two passing notes.

P. 145, l. 5. δεῖ γὰρ τοῖς κ.τ.λ. The law of the sequence of tetrachords is as follows: two tetrachords belong to the one scale either if the notes of one form some one concord with the corresponding notes of the other, or if the notes of both form a concord with the corresponding notes of a third tetrachord of which they are both alike continuations, but in opposite direc-tions, one upwards, one downwards.

Thus, in the Greater Complete System (see Introduction A, § 29)

the notes of any one tetrachord form some one concord (Fourth or Fifth or Octave) with the corresponding notes of any other.

Again, in the Lesser Complete System (see Introduction A, § 29)

the corresponding notes of the Hypatôn and Mesôn tetrachords form Fourths with one another; as do also the corresponding notes of the Mesôn and Synemmenôn tetrachords. But what about the Hypatôn and Synemmenôn tetrachords? They evidently belong to the one scale, and yet the notes of one do not form a concord with the corresponding notes of the other. Here the second clause of the law applies. The Hypatôn and Synemmenôn tetrachords are both continuous with the Mesôn, but in different directions (μὴ ἐπὶ τὸν αὐτὸν τόπον), one lying below it and one above, and the notes of the Hypatôn and Synemmenôn form concords with the correspond-ing notes of the Mesôn.

l. 9. Marquard, followed by Westphal, wrongly altered τὸν αὐτὸν τόπον to τῷ αὐτῷ τόπῳ, and supposing it to refer to the coincidence of the extremities of conjunct tetrachords proposed to omit the μή of l. 8.

l. 11. It is uncertain what are the other conditions of the legitimate synthesis of tetrachords, to which Aristoxenus here alludes. One may perhaps have been a certain order in the employment of conjunction and disjunction. Thus the scale

might be regarded as illegitimate, because the conjunction and disjunction do not occur alternately.

l. 15. The MSS here read ἀλλ' ἐν μεγέθει ὥρισται, which I have corrected to ἀλλ' ἐνὶ μεγέθει ὡρίσθαι. ὡρίσθαι is the infinitive after δοκεῖ, and with παντελῶς ἀκαριαῖόν τινα one repeats ἔχειν δοκεῖ τόπον. Marquard reads οὐκ ἔχειν δοκεῖ τόπον ἀλλ' ἢ εἰ μεγέθει ὥρισται, ἢ παντελῶς ἀκαριαῖόν τινα and translates absurdly ' seem only to take place when they are determined in magnitude, or at any rate only in a highly limited degree.' Of course ἔχειν τόπον means ' to have a locus of variation.' The same misconception under-lies Westphal's reading οὐκ ἔχειν δοκεῖ ἢ παντελῶς ἀκαριαῖόν τινα τόπον ἀλλ' ἢ εἰ τὰ μεγέθη ὥρισται.

l. 19. ἀκριβεστάτη κ.τ.λ. Note Aristoxenus' recognition of the truth that the determination of all intervals must in the last resort fall back upon the elementary relations of the concords.

δ', deleted by Marquard, may be an example of the δὲ ἀποδο-τικόν.

l. 22. τῶν δυνατῶν. Intervals smaller than semitones cannot be determined by concords. For the Fourth consists of two and a half tones, the Fifth of three and a half tones, and the Octave of six tones; and no repetition, addition, or subtraction of these numbers will lead to any fraction smaller than a half.

l. 23. ἐπὶ τὸ ὀξὺ κ.τ.λ. If it be required to ascertain by concords the note that lies two tones below G, the following will be the process :

The note that lies two tones above *G* is ascertained thus :

P. 146, l. 5. γίγνεται δὲ καὶ κ.τ.λ.   This is evident.   If in the

Fourth 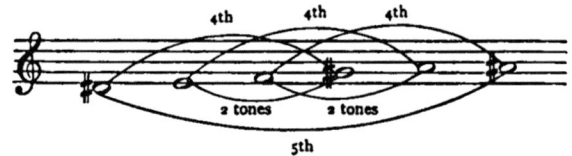 we determine the ditone between

a and *f* by concords we have in so doing also determined by concords the semitone between *e* and *f*. For *e* is given in concord with *a*, and *f* has now been determined by concord with *a*; and *e* and *f* are the bounding notes of the semitone.

l. 20. πότερον δ' ὀρθῶς κ.τ.λ.   The following is Aristoxenus' demonstration that a Fourth consists of two tones and a half (a tone being the excess of the Fifth over the Fourth).   Take

a Fourth *e-a*, and determine by concords the note *f* two tones below *a*, and the note ♯*g* two tones above *e*. It follows that the remainder *e-f*=the remainder ♯*g-a* because each of them=the whole Fourth, *e-a*, less by two tones. Now take the Fourth above *f* namely ♯*a*, and the Fourth below ♯*g* namely ♯*d*. There will now lie side by side at each extremity of the scale two remainders, which must be equal for the reason already given; that is, ♯*d-e*, *e-f*, ♯*g-a* and *a*-♯*a* are all equal, because each of them equals a Fourth less by two tones.

Now if ♯*d* and ♯*a*, the lowest and highest notes of the scale, be sounded, our ears will assure us that they form a concord. This concord, as greater than a Fourth by construction and obviously less than an octave, must be a Fifth. But since ♯*d*-♯*a* is thus found to be a Fifth, and ♯*d*-♯*g* by construction is a Fourth, ♯*g*-♯*a* must be the difference between a Fourth and a Fifth; in other words, a tone. But we have already seen that $\sharp g-a=a-\sharp a$ ∴ $\sharp g-a=$ a semitone. But by the construction $e-\sharp g=$ two tones; therefore $e-a$ being the sum of $e-\sharp g$ and $\sharp g-a$ must be equal to two tones and a semitone.

P. 147, l. 4. The MSS read δύο συνεχεῖς ἔσονται καὶ μὴ ἓν αἱ ὑπεροχαί which Marquard and Westphal following Meibom correct by changing ἕν to μία. But (1) how did the grammatically obvious μία come to be corrupted to ἕν? (2) what is the sense of insisting that the remainders are 'not one'? (3) the article before ὑπεροχαί is objectionable, as the meaning is 'there will be two remainders.' I read κείμεναι for καὶ μὴ ἓν αἱ. κείμεναι συνεχεῖς= 'lying side by side,' 'in juxtaposition.'

l. 9. The absurd τέτταρα in this line and in l. 15 arose of course from the scribe mistaking the δ of δῆλον and the δ' before ὀξύτατον for numerals.

P. 148, l. 1. The MSS read διτόνου· συγχωρεῖται παρὰ πάντων κ.τ.λ. Marquard followed by Westphal inserts ἀλλά before συγχωρεῖται; but I prefer συγχωρεῖται γάρ, because (1) the sentence supplies a reason, (2) γάρ might easily have been lost before παρά.

P. 149, l. 12. Before we consider Aristoxenus' exposition of the continuity of tetrachords, there are two points to be noticed. Firstly, whereas in his former sketch of the matter [p. 145, ll. 3–13] he considered the relation of *similar* tetrachords only, here his treatment takes into account the differences of Figure. Secondly there is an ambiguity in the terms συνεχής and ἑξῆς, which sometimes signify merely 'in the same line of succession,' at other times '*next* in the line of succession.'

In general, Aristoxenus asserts, tetrachords are in the same line of succession if their boundaries are in the same line of succession or coincide. In this general definition are explicitly given the two species of succession of which tetrachords are capable. We have a case of the one species when the lower boundary of the higher of two tetrachords coincides with the upper boundary of the lower; a case of the other species, when the lower boundary of the higher of two tetrachords is in the one line of succession with the upper boundary of the lower.

Now we must not confuse this distinction with the distinction between conjunct and disjunct tetrachords. The latter distinction divides successive tetrachords into (*a*) those whose extremities coincide; and (*b*) those whose extremities are divided by one tone. The former distinction divides successive tetrachords into (*x*) those whose extremities coincide; and (*y*) those whose extremities are in the same line of succession. Now the class (*a*) = the class (*x*), but (*b*) is only one subdivision of the class (*y*). Thus in the legitimate scale

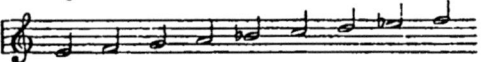

the tetrachords *E–F–G–A* and *c–d–♭e–f* fall into the class (*y*), since *A* and *c* are in the same line of succession, but not into the class (*b*), since they are separated not by one tone but by a tone and a half.

Now if two tetrachords belong to the class (*a*) (and consequently to (*x*) also) they must be similar in figure. Otherwise as in the pair

we shall find a violation of the fundamental law of continuity [p. 120, l. 16].

On the other hand, if tetrachords belong to the class (*y*) they will sometimes be similar, sometimes dissimilar in figure: similar, when they belong to the class (*b*), that is when their extremities are divided by a tone (and also, of course, if they are separated by a full concord); dissimilar, if they are separated by any other interval.

Thus in the scales

and

NOTES

E-F-G-A and ♭B-C-D-♭e, E-F-G-A and ♭e-f-g-♭a in the first, and E-F-G-A and C-D-e-f, E-F-G-A and f-g-a-b, E-F-G-A and B-C-D-e in the second are all examples of class (y); but only the last pair are examples of class (b) and only the last are similar in figure.

Since then we have seen that all successive tetrachords may be divided into (x) and (y), and since all (a) are (x) and are similar in figure and only those (y) are similar which are also (b), it follows that all similar tetrachords in the same line of succession are either (a) or (b). As Aristoxenus says, τὰ ἑξῆς τετράχορδα ὅμοια ὄντα ἢ συνημμένα ἀναγκαῖον εἶναι ἢ διεζευγμένα.

P. 140, l. 14. In general, tetrachords in the same line of succession cannot be separated by a tetrachord dissimilar to themselves; for

1. Similar tetrachords in the same line of succession cannot be separated by a tetrachord dissimilar to themselves.

For if it be possible, between the similar tetrachords E-F-G-A and d-♭e-f-g let the dissimilar tetrachord A-B-♯C-d be interposed.

The resulting scale is illegitimate, because f neither forms a Fourth with the fourth note below it, nor a Fifth with the fifth.

2. Dissimilar tetrachords in the same line of succession cannot be separated by a tetrachord of any figure.

For if it be possible, let the two dissimilar tetrachords E-xE-F-A and d-♯f-x ♯f-g be in the same line of succession and separated by a tetrachord of any of the three figures.

(a)

(b)

(c)

Any one of the resulting scales is illegitimate. In (*a*) for example x*A* neither forms a Fifth with the fifth note above it nor a Fourth with the fourth; and, the other scales suffer from the same defect.

P. 151, l. 4. For ὅν ἐστι I read ὅ γ' ἐστί for two reasons. Firstly, the sentence is thus made exactly parallel to the next; and Aristoxenus is fond of such parallelism. Secondly, if we read ὅν, the meaning is 'People take the ditone as simple and then wonder how it can be divided'; but we require rather 'People know that the ditone can be divided, and then wonder how it can be simple'; and this sense is secured by reading ὅ γ' ἐστί. The difficulty which Aristoxenus here resolves arose from the common misconception by which one decides an interval to be simple or compound by its dimension, without taking into account the scale to which it belongs, and the functions of its containing notes.

l. 17. I omit τὸ δ' ἴδιον τῆς διαζεύξεως ἀκίνητόν ἐστιν. The fact that the disjunctive interval (the tone) does not vary is used to prove the theorem, and therefore cannot be part of the statement of it.

l. 22. The disjunctive interval is constant because the notes that contain it are fixed notes.

P. 152, l. 14. For MSS ἀσύνθετα πλεῖστα I read ἀσύνθετα τὰ πλεῖστα. Cp. p. 153, l. 1.

l. 18. For the MSS ἔμπροσθεν τεθεῖσα Marquard and Westphal read προστιθεῖσα, supposing the ἔμπροσθεν to have crept in from l. 16. I read ἐν προστιθεῖσα; ἐν helps to account for the corruption, and strengthens the expression of the argument.

P. 153, l. 11. ὅτι δὲ καὶ ἐξ ἐλαττόνων κ.τ.λ. Defective or transilient scales [see Introduction A, § 26] contain fewer intervals than the simple parts of the Fourth. Also in the Enharmonic scale of Olympus [see note on p. 115, l. 2] the Fourth was only divided into two intervals.

l. 13. πυκνὸν δὲ πρὸς πυκνῷ κ.τ.λ. The next eleven pages are occupied by a series of special rules as to the succession of notes and intervals, all of which rules derive themselves immediately from two fundamental laws. One of these laws, that by which the order of intervals of the original tetrachord is

290

determined, is always presupposed by Aristoxenus; the other which demands a Fourth between fourth notes or a Fifth between fifth notes [see p. 120, l. 16] is explicitly quoted. To understand then all these special rules, it is only necessary to keep before one's mind (*a*) the form of the original tetrachord, and the functions of

its notes as regards the Pycnum , [see

note on p. 129, l. 4] and (*b*) the possibility of choosing between conjunction and disjunction both in the ascending scale

and in the descending scale

P. 156, l. 5. I read with M τοὐναντίον πέπονθεν ἁπλῶς οὐ δυνά-μενα. The other MSS have δυνάμεθα for δυνάμενα which Meibom retains, inserting ἃ before ἁπλῶς. Marquard, rightly urging that the explanation of the general phrase τοὐναντίον πέπονθεν would not be given in a relative sentence, reads τοὐναντίον πέπονθε καὶ ἁπλῶς, and is followed by Westphal. But the reading of M is quite unexceptionable. Marquard's objection to the two participles δυνάμενα and ἴσα ὄντα, which are not co-ordinated in sense, is groundless. In the active one might have οὐ δυνάμεθα ταῦτα τιθέναι ἴσα ὄντα ἐξῆς, which would become in the passive οὐ δύναται ταῦτα τίθεσθαι ἴσα ὄντα ἐξῆς, and if used participially οὐ δυνάμενα τίθεσθαι ἴσα ὄντα ἐξῆς. Another objection to the readings of Meibom and Marquard is that they would require τιθέναι, not τίθεσθαι.

P. 157, l. 6. Before ἀπὸ δὲ τοῦ διτόνου, the MSS have ἀπὸ ἡμι-τονίου μὲν ἐπὶ τὸ ὀξὺ δύο ὁδοὶ καὶ ἐπὶ τὸ βαρὺ δύο. This sentence cannot be retained; for in the first place it makes a false assertion, there being but one progression upwards from the semitone or first interval of the Diatonic tetrachord (that is, of course, in the scale of any one *shade*, see p. 159, l. 12); and in the second place, referring as it must, along with the preceding paragraph, to the Diatonic genus only, it could not stand in such close connexion with the following proposition, which as it concerns the ditone can only apply to the Enharmonic Genus.

l. 10. ἐπὶ δὲ τὸ βαρὺ πυκνὸν μόνον which in some of the MSS follows ἐπὶ τὸ ὀξύ is a most silly interpolation. The sentence in l. 11, λείπεται μὲν γὰρ κ.τ.λ., introduces the proof of the assertion πλείους δὲ τούτων οὐκ ἔσονται in l. 9. The consideration of the descent from the ditone does not begin till l. 13, ἐπὶ δὲ τὸ βαρὺ μία· δέδεικται γὰρ κ.τ.λ.

P. 158, l. 15. I read κατά with R. The other MSS have καί. But whichever we read, τὸ τοῦ πυκνοῦ μέγεθος is accusative (whether governed by καθ' or κατά) and not nominative, as Marquard and Westphal suppose. Evidently the chromatic interval that corresponds to the enharmonic ditone (which will differ in size as we pass from one *shade* to another) will vary inversely as the size of the Pycnum. τό γε μέσης. of the MSS, earlier in the sentence, is quite correct.

P. 159, l. 15. I have corrected εἰ to ᾖ. Cp. p. 101, l. 13, where Westphal has corrected εἴπερ to ᾖπερ. The MSS of Aristoxenus exhibit perpetual confusion of ι, ε, η, υ, ει, οι. Cp. note on p. 101, l. 7.

l. 18. δυνάμεις ... εἴδη ... θέσεις are used in a general not a technical sense here.

P. 161, l. 24. The absurd ἐπί which appears in the MSS is really the ἐπεί of p. 162, l. 1. This is proved by the Selden MS, the writer of which after the μία ὁδὸς ἐφ' ἑκάτερα ἔσται of ll. 23–24 missed a line, and proceeded to write the δεικτέον ἐπὶ (for ἐπεί) of p. 162, l. 1. Then discovering his mistake he drew his pen through these latter words.

P. 162, l. 4. Whether we retain κατ' οὐδέτερον τῶν τρόπων of the MSS or read as I prefer κατ' οὐδέτερον τῶν τόπων the sense is 'neither above nor below.'

l. 8. The MSS read ὁποτέρως ἂν τεθῇ τὸ δίτονον· τῷ τόπῳ τόνου

τεθειμένου. Marquard followed by Westphal reads ὁποτέρως ἂν
τεθῇ τὸ δίτονον· ἐπὶ δὲ τῷ αὐτῷ τόπῳ τόνου τεθειμένου κ.τ.λ., taking
ὁποτέρως in the sense of ' whether above or below' on the analogy
of κατ' οὐδέτερον τῶν τρόπων (l. 4) ; and ἐπὶ τῷ αὐτῷ τόπῳ in the
sense of πρὸς τῷ εἰρημένῳ φθόγγῳ. But this last is very hard
to accept; the phrase would much more naturally mean ' in
the same direction of pitch' i.e. either ascent or descent.
I prefer, having read κατ' οὐδέτερον τῶν τόπων in l. 4 = ' in
neither of the directions,' to read here ὁποτέρως ἂν τεθῇ τὸ
δίτονον τῶν τόπων = ' in whichever manner the ditone be placed
in regard of the directions.' The two τόποι are ὁ ἐπὶ τὸ ὀξύ and
ὁ ἐπὶ τὸ βαρύ.

l. 21. The MSS reading is obviously defective. The words
I have introduced restore the sense simply. Marquard's insertion of the article before φθόγγους is quite inadequate.
Westphal reads ἐπὶ τὴν αὐτὴν τάσιν τοὺς εἰρημένους ἐν πυκνῷ
φθόγγους.

P. 163, l. 4. ὅτι δὲ τὸ διάτονον σύγκειται ἤτοι κ.τ.λ. The proposition of this paragraph seems at first sight inconsistent
with Aristoxenus' exposition of the *shades* (see p. 142, ll. 9–14) ;
according to which exposition there are only two *shades* of the
Diatonic genus, (a) the soft Diatonic, the tetrachord of which
is thus divided

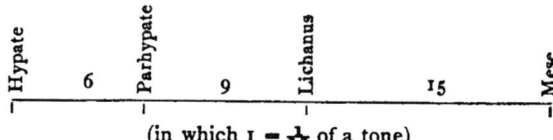

(in which 1 = $\frac{1}{12}$ of a tone)
(b) the sharp Diatonic with the tetrachord

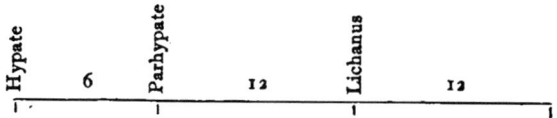

If we complete the Fifth by adding to each of these tetrachords the disjunctive tone = 12, we shall have in the sharp
Diatonic 12 and 6 as the only dimensions of intervals. In
the flat Diatonic, on the other hand, we shall have four

dimensions, 6, 9, 12, 15. But how can there be a Diatonic with three dimensions? In this way, that it is allowable for the Diatonic scale to borrow the Chromatic Parhypatae. Thus, by a combination of the Sharp Diatonic Lichanus and the soft Chromatic Parhypate we obtain a Fifth of the form

which may be called Diatonic from its prevailing character. In it there are three dimensions, 4, 12, 14.

P. 164, l. 13. εἶδος here = schema = the 'figure' or order of disposal of the given parts of a whole.

INDEX

ἀγαθός 122. 8, 10, 13.
'Αγήνωρ 127. 25.
ἀγνοέω 125. 3; 126. 26; 127. 2;
136. 19; 144. 21.
ἄγνοια 131. 12, 14; 151. 7.
ἄγω 104. 5, 6, 9, 24; 128. 11;
144. 16; 159. 22.
ἀγωγή = 'rate of movement' 105.
14; 125. 17.
= 'sequence' 121. 7; 143. 18.
= 'keeping,' 'observance'
128. 10.
ἀδιάφορος 129. 11.
ἀδυνατέω 106. 25.
ᾄδω 102. 25.
ἀήρ 134. 27.
ἀθεώρητος 126. 25; 127. 1.
'Αθηναῖος 128. 11.
αἰσθάνομαι 98. 20; 125. 1, 2, 7;
129. 22.
αἴσθησις 99. 21; 101. 22, 24; 102.
8; 103. 5; 104. 5; 111. 13;
124. 4, 23, 27; 129. 22; 139.
3, 10, 19; 140. 9; 145. 18.
αἰσθητός 99. 6.
αἰτία 98. 24; 114. 18; 123. 1;
124. 5, 9; 126. 18; 133. 1;
134. 2, 3; 138. 12; 145. 17;
151. 10; 153. 9; 159. 26; 160.
21; 161. 17, 20; 164. 7, 10.
αἴτιος 114. 9; 115. 6; 118. 22;
122. 16.
ἀκαριαῖος 145. 16.
ἀκίνητος 118. 23; 151. 17; 152.
6, 9, 11.
ἀκοή 102. 15; 106. 24; 107; 124.
16, 17; 129. 17.
ἀκολουθέω 126. 19; 138. 16, 17;
143. 23; 154. 14, 16.
ἀκούω 108. 8; 122. 8, 19; 123. 6,
12; 149. 12.

ἀκρίβεια 125. 1.
ἀκριβής 97. 8; 103. 6; 108. 9;
124. 5; 144. 1; 145. 19; 146.
23.
ἀκριβολογέομαι 126. 15.
ἀκριβῶς 119. 3; 124. 19.
ἀκροάομαι 123. 2.
ἀκρόασις 122. 8.
ἄκρος 121. 8; 137. 2; 141. 2;
147. 8, 20; 148. 7.
ἀλλοίωσις 130. 24; 164. 17.
ἀλλοτριολογέω 124. 4.
ἀλλότριος 124. 8.
ἄλογος 108. 23; 109. 12.
ἁμάρτημα 132. 13.
ἁμαρτία 123. 5.
ἀμελῳδητος 113. 12; 117. 8; 120. 1.
ἀμφισβητέω 138. 22.
ἀμφισβήτησις 118. 7.
ἀνάγω 124. 15; 132. 14; 133. 5,
11.
ἀναγωγή 133. 1; 134. 2.
ἀναιρέω 110. 24, 25; 145. 3.
ἀναμάρτητος 133. 6.
ἀναπόδεικτος 99. 2, 17, 19; 129. 9.
ἀνάρμοστος 110. 11, 17; 143. 6.
ἀναφορά 106. 23.
ἀνεπίληπτος 108. 14.
ἄνεσις (see note on 103. 16) 97.
10; 103; 104; 105. 19; 106.
11; 114. 9.
ἀνήρ 112. 18.
ἀνθρωπικός 106. 17.
ἀνίημι 103. 12; 104. 3, 5; 110. 7;
115. 17; 123. 24; 132. 19; 133.
1; 137. 15.
ἀνόμοιος 125. 18; 139. 7; 150. 16,
17; 162. 16, 23.
ἀντιστρέφω 138. 4.
ἀνώτερον 95. 11.
ἀνωτέρω 101. 12.

ἀνώτατος 111. 11.
ἀξιόλογος 98. 14.
ἀξιόω 95. 9; 138. 7; 140. 9; 143. 14.
ἀόριστος 99. 1.
ἀπαιτέω 134. 25.
ἀπαλλάττω 104. 10; 124. 22.
ἅπαξ 141. 12, 13.
ἀπειρία 160. 3.
ἄπειρος 97. 15; 104. 4; 106; 107; 112. 2; 188. 20, 21; 144. 3, 5; 158. 22, 24; 159. 5, 7, 15.
ἀπέχω 137. 7; 155. 6, 8.
ἁπλοῦς 109. 20, 22; 110. 25; 125. 24; 129. 3; 131. 9.
ἁπλῶς = (1) 'in plain speech, not in accordance with strict philosophical truth' 102. 14.
— (2) 'roughly speaking, overlooking particular exceptions' 125. 6; 126. 2, 25; 127. 5.
— (3) 'in general terms, summing up particulars' 131. 8; 143. 15.
= (4) 'absolutely, without exception' 127. 20; 150. 15; 153. 4; 156. 5.
— (5) 'in the abstract' 136. 24.
ἀποβάλλω 139. 6.
ἀποβλέπω 104. 1.
ἀπογιγνώσκω 122. 18.
ἀποδείκνυμι 99. 9, 11; 118. 4; 124. 13; 153. 9.
ἀποδεικτικός 99. 2; 129. 9.
ἀπόδειξις 124. 2, 10; 134. 25.
ἀποδίδωμι 98. 9, 10; 99. 13; 103. 15; 108. 8; 113. 3; 119. 16; 128. 9; 131. 17; 143. 17; 144. 1, 2.
ἀπόδοσις 128. 11.
ἀποθεσπίζω 124. 9.
ἀπολιμπάνω 135. 2.
ἀπορέω 149. 12; 164. 5.
ἀποτέμνω 96. 6.
ἀποφαίνω 105. 6; 119. 17.
ἅπτω 95. 17; 96. 10; 98. 16; 99. 24; 114. 6, 21.
ἄπυκνος 120. 13.
ἀρέσκω 122. 19.
'Αριστοτέλης 122. 7, 20.

ἁρμονία (see note on 95. 5) 95. 10; 115. 9; 116. 9; 118. 15; 126. 9, 11; 127. 23; 135. 5; 139. 1, 3, 9, 12; 142. 19; 154. 22; 155. 15; 160. 5, 16; 163. 19; 164. 8.
ἁρμονικός 123. 19; 130. 7; 134. 24.
ἁρμονικός, ὁ 95. 18; 96. 12; 98. 19; 101. 1; 119. 15; 128. 10, 13; 131. 13.
ἁρμονική, ἡ 95. 5; 101. 11; 126. 3; 130. 1; 134. 10.
ἁρμονικά, τά 123. 7.
ἁρμόττω 104. 2; 107. 23; 110. 8; 133. 17, 18, 19; 139. 1; 147. 13.
ἀρχαϊκός 115. 2.
ἀρχή 98. 13; 108. 14; 119. 4; 123. 4; 124. 11, 27; 131. 5; 134. 19, 20; 145. 2; 146. 21; 147. 21.
ἀρχοειδής 134. 22, 25.
ἄρχομαι 101. 13; 109. 16; 126. 11; 134. 26; 135. 1; 142. 7.
ἀστραβής 133. 6.
ἀστρολογία 122. 13.
ἀσύμμετρος 115. 23.
ἀσύμφωνος 120. 21; 144. 20.
ἀσύνθετος (see note on 108. 22) passim.
ἀταξία 99. 4.
ἀτοπία 131. 19.
ἄτοπος 131. 14, 21; 132. 12, 13; 140. 17.
αὐλέω 112. 16; 130. 5; 134. 2, 3.
αὐλοποιία 134. 8.
αὐλός (see note on 112. 13) 112. 13; 128. 17, 18; 130. 4; 132. 12, 16; 133. 3, 5, 7; 134. 1, 4, 7.
αὐξάνω 106. 20; 112. 2; 137. 14.
αὔξησις 97. 16; 107. 17; 119. 11; 138. 18.
αὐτάρκης 100. 13; 123. 16; 127. 3; 144. 21; 145. 10.
ἀφαιρέω 132. 25; 146. 7, 8, 19; 147. 1.
ἀφανής 103. 10.
ἀφίημι 100. 7; 108. 25.
ἀφικνέομαι 105. 24; 115. 9, 16; 137. 15.
ἀφίστημι 114. 13; 115. 14; 128. 22; 133. 22.

ἀφορίζω 98. 3; 108. 5; 109. 24;
111. 2, 20, 22; 113. 8, 15; 118.
13, 18; 143. 14; 144. 13; 146.
24; 151. 11; 164. 17.
ἀφορισμός 111. 3.
ἄχρηστος 129. 1; 145. 13.
ἄψυχος 132. 5.

βαδίζω 122. 4.
βαρύς ('low' in pitch) *passim*.
βαρύτης 97. 11; 103; 104; 105;
106.
βεβαιόω 133. 7; 134. 4.
βελτίων 122. 3; 123. 3, 7.
βραχύς 101. 4.

γένεσις 129. 19.
γένος (see Intr. A, § 6) *passim*.
γεωμέτρης 124. 22.
γεωμετρία 122. 13.
γλυκαίνω 115. 6.
γνωρίζω 127. 7.
γνώριμος 105. 4; 106. 13; 107. 20;
113. 7; 131. 12; 135. 10, 16.
γράμμα 119. 6, 8; 128. 2, 3.
γραμμή 124. 21.
γράφω 130. 9, 11, 13; 131. 1.

δεῖξις 123. 8.
δεικτικός 108. 2.
δέομαι 114. 19; 133. 20; 138. 20;
160. 9.
δέχομαι 118. 6.
δηλόω 96. 2.
διαβαίνω 102. 1, 16.
διάγνωσις 100. 14; 127. 4; 139. 7.
διάγραμμα 95. 21; 96. 2; 101. 6;
119. 16; 124. 20.
διαζεύγνυμι 109. 17; 149. 1, 15;
150. 14.
διάζευξις ('disjunction'; see Intr.
A, § 12) *passim*.
διαίρεσις and διαιρέω *passim*.
διαισθάνομαι 107. 5; 126. 10, 13;
130. 18; 131. 4.
διάκενος 118. 5.
διακριβόω 108. 14.
διαλέγομαι 96. 21; 102. 20, 25;
110. 7; 119. 7; 128. 3.
διαμαρτάνω 99. 21; 110. 18; 130.
7; 132. 9, 23; 136. 19.

διαμένω 122. 19; 133. 14; 139.
22; 140. 1, 6.
διανοέω 132. 5.
διάνοια 124. 16, 18; 126. 1; 129.
18.
διαπορία 140. 21.
διασαφέω 107. 4.
διασκοπέω 111. 16.
διάστασις 97. 15; 106. 14, 21;
107. 1, 9, 12, 15; 112. 12; 128.
24.
διάστημα ('interval') *passim*.
διαστηματικός *passim*.
διασώζω 133. 15.
διατείνω 112. 11; 125. 6.
διατελέω 102. 19.
διάτονος (see Intr. A, § 6) *passim*.
διατρίβω 115. 8; 126. 10.
διαφυλάττω 119. 13.
διαφωνέω 136. 12.
διαφωνία 111. 16.
διάφωνος (see note on 108. 21)
passim.
διέξειμι 96. 14; 101. 21; 103. 13.
διεξέρχομαι 103. 12; 106. 18; 134.
13.
διέρχομαι 97. 19; 101. 16; 106.
13; 126. 3; 142. 2.
δίεσις (any interval smaller than
a semitone) *passim*.
διέχω 119. 18.
διηγέομαι 122. 7.
διοράω 127. 10.
διορίζω *passim*.
διπλάσιος 117. 7; 120. 8; 137. 14.
διπλοῦς 109. 20, 22.
δίτονος *passim*.
δίχα 98. 22.
δόξα 96. 12; 104. 24.
δοξάζω 103. 25.
δύναμις 95. 6; 96. 14; 113. 4;
124. 18, 23; 125. 11; 127. 5,
9; 130. 24; 131. 2, 7; 138.
10; 140. 1; 159. 18, 20.
δωδεκατημόριον 117.
δώριος 128.

ἐάω 159. 15.
ἐγγίγνομαι 98. 8.
ἐγγύς 115. 9, 13; 120. 7.
ἐθίζω 124. 20, 23.

εἶδος 97. 1; 139; 150. 9, 16, 19; 159; 164.
ἐκατέρωθεν 121. 8.
ἔκκειμαι 95. 12; 135. 6, 16.
ἐκκλίνω 124. 4.
ἐκλαμβάνω 108. 7.
ἐκλιμπάνω 124. 4; 150. 24, 25.
ἐκμελής ('violating the laws of melody') passim.
ἐκτημόριον 117. 7.
ἐλάττωσις 97. 16; 138. 18.
ἐμβιβάζω 108. 12.
ἐμμελής ('musically legitimate') passim.
ἔμπειρος 123. 13; 124. 12; 126. 14.
ἐμπίπτω 134. 27; 150. 24; 160. 3.
ἐμφαίνομαι 139. 15, 17.
ἐνάλλαξ 102. 18; 154. 1; 156. 9.
ἐναργής 103. 14.
ἐναρμόνιος (see Intr. A, § 6) passim.
ἔνειμι 96. 23.
ἐνεργέω 133. 1.
ἐνίστημι 102. 10.
ἔννοια 95. 20; 98. 12.
ἐντείνω 133. 13.
ἐντός 135. 1.
ἐνυπάρχω 130. 20.
ἐξαδυνατέω 107. 3; 119. 23.
ἐξαίρετος 141. 4.
ἐξαριθμέω 99. 19, 24; 100. 8; 124. 10; 127. 19, 21, 24.
ἐξετάζω 99. 22; 115. 21; 146. 22.
ἕξις 98. 7; 123. 19.
ἐξορίζω 115. 5.
ἐπάγω 114. 16; 115. 1.
ἐπαγωγή 97. 23; 144. 4.
ἐπαλλάττω 115. 14; 150. 1, 12.
ἐπανάγω 147. 9.
ἐπαφάομαι 98. 2.
ἐπεθίζω 124. 19.
ἐπιβλέπω 126. 12; 159. 3.
Ἐπιγόνειοι 97. 6.
ἐπιμελής 96. 2.
ἐπιπλεῖον 105. 17.
ἐπιπολῆς 164. 7.
ἐπίσκεψις 111. 18; 127. 17, 23.
ἐπισκοπέω 96. 11; 98. 25; 103. 22; 107. 19; 114. 7; 130. 18; 160. 2.
ἐπιστατέω 132. 3; 133. 10.

ἐπιστήμη 95; 101. 11; 130. 8, 15; 131. 16, 20; 134. 18; 159. 15.
ἐπίτασις (see note on 103. 16) 97. 10; 103; 104; 106. 11; 114. 9.
ἐπιτείνω 103. 13; 104. 3, 4; 110. 6; 115. 16; 123. 23; 132. 19; 133. 1; 137. 16.
Ἐρατοκλῆς 98. 21; 99. 18.
ἔργον 131. 18; 132. 1, 2.
ἐριστικός 122. 17.
ἑρμηνεία 108. 14.
εὐδαιμονία 122. 11.
εὔδηλος 114. 21.
εὐθέως 125. 6; 159. 19.
εὐθύς 121. 9; 124. 21, 23.
εὐκαταφρόνητος 123. 14.
εὐσύνοπτος 96. 12.

Ζακύνθιος 127. 25.

ἦθος 115. 10; 123. 7, 10; 131. 13.
ἡλικία 112. 20.
ἡμέρα 128. 10; 133. 13.
ἡμιόλιος 116. 14; 117; 141; 143. 4, 5; 155. 7.
ἥμισυς 113. 10; 115. 14; 116. 1; 136. 14, 15; 146. 22; 147. 10, 12.
ἡμιτονιαῖος 142; 143. 4, 12.
ἡμιτόνιον passim.
ἠρεμέω 104. 13; 105. 1, 12, 23; 113. 21.
ἠρεμία 105. 13, 16, 20, 25.
ἡρμοσμένος (see note on 95. 3) 97. 23; 110. 8, 22, 23, 25; 111. 8; 125. 25; 129. 14; 132; 133; 134. 5; 145. 3; 151. 18.

θαυμάζω 151. 3; 158. 22.
θαυμαστός 99. 3; 122. 11; 133. 9, 21.
θέσις 99. 17; 145. 5; 156. 1, 24; 159. 18.
θεωρέω 95. 11, 14; 98. 4; 101. 18; 111. 4; 112. 21; 124. 18; 127. 12, 15.
θεωρητικός 95. 7.
θεωρία 95. 8; 101. 10; 123. 22; 124. 14; 130. 4.

ἰαμβικός 130. 11, 12.

INDEX

ἰδέα 95. 2; 101. 20.
ἴδιος 107. 13; 114. 4; 118. 14;
130. 20; 134. 8; 136. 6; 138.
8, 13, 19; 139. 18; 142. 19;
151. 17, 23; 152. 18.
ἰδιότης 110. 14.
ἰδιώτης 131. 17, 21.
ἱκανῶς 96. 15; 105. 17; 108. 11;
115. 2.
ἵστημι 101. 23; 102; 103; 104;
105; 106; 107. 24; 118. 4.
ἰσχυρός 131. 14.
ἰσχύς 122. 11.

καθαρῶς 127. 10.
καθήκω 101. 14.
καθίστημι 103. 11.
καθόλου 97. 17, 19; 98. 5; 99. 23;
100. 20; 101. 6, 8; 104. 24;
110. 21; 111. 5; 116. 10; 125.
22; 125. 21; 132. 13; 133. 8;
134. 25; 140. 3; 149. 13, 17.
καθοράω 96. 16.
καιρός 101. 14.
κάμπτω 135. 1.
καταγιγνώσκω 99. 5; 131. 19.
καταδύω 132. 6.
καταμανθάνω 96. 6; 100. 1, 12;
103. 25; 106. 1; 108. 11; 113.
16; 126. 16.
καταμέμφομαι 122. 15.
κατανοέω 104. 1, 21; 105. 22;
108. 10; 112. 19; 114. 15;
120. 4; 136. 22; 137. 14; 138.
17; 142. 26; 147. 23.
καταπυκνόω 101. 6.
καταπύκνωσις 101. 1; 119. 16;
128. 25; 143. 16.
κατασκευάζω 124. 5; 131. 20.
κατασπάω 112. 15.
κατέχω 113. 18; 114. 4; 115. 3;
120. 23; 139. 15; 141. 3.
κινέω and κίνησις passim.
κοιλία 132. 17.
κοινότης 151. 3.
κοινωνέω 118. 15; 150. 6; 163. 1.
Κορίνθιος 128. 11.
κρίνω 106. 24, 25; 107. 13; 124.
17, 19; 126. 1; 131. 22; 132.
3, 10, 11.
κριτής 131. 20.

κύριος 132. 10, 11; 133. 20.

λανθάνω 103. 13; 122. 6.
Λάσος 97. 6.
λείπω 116. 3; 120. 15, 24; 141.
19; 152. 2, 12; 157. 11, 15,
21; 158. 3, 10; 162. 23.
λέξις 110. 16; 119. 6.
λῆψις 143. 3; 145. 20; 146. 6.
λιχανοειδής 118. 6.
λιχανός (see Intr. A, § 11) passim.
λογικός 102. 20; 103. 7.
λόγος 98. 27; 99. 3; 107. 18;
108. 9, 12, 14; 122. 12; 123.
8, 16; 124. 6, 8; 125. 16; 127.
20; 129. 8; 133. 20; 138. 7;
144. 1; 149. 16; 151. 6; 160. 9.
λογώδης 110. 4, 5.
λύδιος 128.

μάθημα 122. 12; 123. 6, 15.
μαλακός 141; 142; 143; 155. 7.
μανθάνω 131. 21.
μελοποιΐα 114. 19; 115. 4; 123.
9; 126. 14; 129. 10, 14; 131.
10.
μέλος 95. 3; 96. 19; 97. 20, 22;
98. 3, 23; 99. 4; 100. 17;
101. 9; 103. 5; 107. 16, 23;
110; 111; 112. 3; 113. 2; 120.
6, 17; 121. 4; 123. 23; 124.
14; 129. 12, 19; 130. 2, 14;
134. 4; 135. 6; 143. 15, 18;
144. 16; 159. 17.
μελῳδέω passim.
μελῳδία 96. 3, 7; 101. 2; 119. 5;
120. 4; 129. 6; 144. 7.
μελῳδικός 103. 8.
μένω 106. 2; 116. 5; 125; 126. 2,
6; 137. 3; 139. 21; 140. 1, 4;
142. 2.
μερίζω 98. 5; 109. 15, 19.
μέση (see Intr. A, § 11) passim.
μεταβάλλω 134. 2.
μεταβολή 101. 8; 125. 14; 129. 4,
5, 7; 131. 9.
μετάβολος 129. 3.
μετακινέω 104. 6.
μεταλαμβάνω 133. 9; 158. 14.
μεταχειρίζομαι 99. 5; 100. 19.
μετέχω 160. 5-17; 163. 3.

μετοχή 162. 17.
μετρέω 115. 22; 141. 11, 12.
μετρική 123. 20; 130. 9.
μέτρον 112. 21; 130. 9, 11; 141. 11.
μηθείς 95. 9.
μίγνυμι 100. 9.
μικτός 109. 17; 135. 7.
μίξις 100. 12.
Μιξολύδιος 128. 14, 23.
Μιτυληναῖος 127. 25.
μνήμη 129. 22.
μνημονεύω 129. 23.
μόλις 111. 12.
μονή 104. 22.
μορφή 129. 12.
μουσικός 98. 3; 110. 4, 17; 111. 1; 124. 15.
μουσικός, ὁ 95. 15; 123. 6, 18, 19; 124. 27.
μουσική, ἡ 95. 15; 98. 3; 99. 4; 144. 6, 21; 123. 9, 11; 124. 12; 125. 4, 25; 129. 20, 21, 24; 133. 12; 159. 14.

νήτη (see Intr. A, § 11) 125. 10; 138. 9; 144. 11.
νητῶν (see Intr. A, § 29) 131. 1.
νοέω 97. 13; 107. 16; 108. 6; 113. 17, 20; 118. 3; 123. 22.
νοητός 124. 5.

ξυλλαβή 119. 8; 128. 4.
ξύνεσις 97. 10; 125. 4; 131. 4; 132. 2, 6.
ξυνίημι 107. 5; 108. 12; 129. 17; 130. 3; 131. 22.

ὁδός 122. 4; 157; 158; 159; 160; 161; 162.
οἰκεῖος 135. 1.
οἰκειότης 100. 23.
ὀκταπλάσιος 119. 23.
ὀκτάχορδος 96. 3; 127. 22.
ὀλιγωρέω 143. 18.
ὅλως 96. 14; 97. 13; 123. 12; 127. 21; 145. 15.
ὁμαλότης 105. 2.
ὅμοιος 139. 7; 145. 3; 149. 3, 4; 150. 7-19.

ὁμοίως 139. 21; 152. 9; 158. 13, 16.
ὁμολογέω 114. 15; 124. 3; 134. 17.
ὄνομα 105. 8; 110. 6; 114. 4; 122. 17; 138; 140; 164. 14.
ὀνομάζω 101. 25; 102. 22; 104. 20.
ὀξύς ('high' in pitch) passim.
ὀξύτης 97. 11; 103; 104; 105. 22, 24; 106.
ὀργανικός 106. 17.
ὀργανική, ἡ 123. 20.
ὄργανον 104. 4; 112. 9, 12; 124. 15; 126. 10; 132; 133; 134. 5, 6.
ὀρθός 133. 6.
ὀρθῶς 110. 13; 132. 5; 134. 16; 146. 21.
ὁρμάω 105. 6.
ὅρος 140. 3; 146. 12, 24; 149. 17; 150.
ὁσαχῶς 97. 18.
οὐθείς 133. 7.
ὄφελος 133. 4; 145. 2.
ὀφθαλμοειδής 131. 17.
ὀφθαλμοφανής 132. 2.
ὄψις 124. 23.

πάθος 102. 26; 104. 7; 129. 6; 136. 6; 159. 8.
παῖς 112. 18.
παλαιός 113. 19; 144. 11.
παντελῶς passim.
παντοδαπός 125. 22; 129. 12.
παραβάλλω 132. 25.
παράδοξος 103. 21; 122. 14.
παρακολουθέω 129. 18, 24.
παρακούω 123. 7, 11.
παραλαμβάνω 98. 14; 136. 2.
παραλιμπάνω 126. 24.
παραμέση (see Intr. A, § 11) 125. 9; 137. 20; 138. 12; 158. 20.
παρανήτη (see Intr. A, § 11) 138. 9, 10; 144. 12.
παραπλησίως 119. 11.
παρασημαίνω 130. 2, 17; 131. 15.
παρασημαντική 130. 8, 15.
παρατηρέω 108. 8; 134. 26; 139. 6.
παρθένιος 112. 13.
παρυπάτη (see Intr. A, § 11) passim.

INDEX

παρυπολαμβάνω 122. 6.
παύομαι 142. 6.
διὰ πέντε, τό ('the Fifth') passim.
περαίνω 106. 15; 159. 14, 19;
   161. 3, 16.
πέρας 101. 23; 107. 9; 112. 12;
   115. 15, 17; 122. 13; 130. 3,
   7; 131. 16, 22; 132. 2, 10.
περιγραφή 98. 5.
περιλαμβάνω 138. 6.
περιφερής 124. 24.
περιφορά 100. 1.
πιθανός 144. 4, 8.
πίπτω 146. 17; 156. 13, 16, 23;
   162. 6, 10, 21.
πιστεύω 145. 18.
πλανάομαι 134. 7.
πλάνη 151. 2; 158. 21.
πλάτος 97. 7.
Πλάτων 122. 8.
πλεοναχῶς 164. 21.
πλῆθος 143. 19.
πλοῦτος 122. 11.
πνεῦμα 132. 4. 25.
ποιητική 95. 12.
πολλαπλάσιος 120. 8.
πολλαπλούς 109. 21, 22.
πολυμερής 95. 3.
πορεύομαι 122. 5; 129. 15.
πορρωτέρω 96. 9; 131. 3.
πούς 125. 15-23.
πραγματεία and πραγματεύομαι
   passim.
πρεσβύτατος 111. 9.
προαποδείκνυμι 100. 2.
πρόβλημα 134. 18, 22; 151. 2;
   153. 3; 158. 21; 159. 3.
προγιγνώσκω 122. 4.
προδιαιρέω 109. 24.
προδιανοέω 134. 12.
προδιέρχομαι 122. 3; 134. 10.
πρόειμι 110. 25; 123. 16.
προεκτίθημι 122. 18.
προθυμέομαι 120. 5; 128. 25.
προκατασκευάζω 147. 7.
προσάγω 115. 9; 133. 17, 18.
προσδέομαι 110. 9; 145. 11.
πρόσειμι 122. 9, 17.
προσέρχομαι 115. 13.
προσέχω 120. 2; 134. 21.
προσηγορία 113. 19.

προσήκω 95. 9; 104. 9; 132. 21;
   134. 19.
πρόσκειμαι 147. 24; 148. 5.
προστάττω 145. 20; 141. 5.
προστυγχάνω 111. 10.
προσῳδία 110. 5.
προϋπάρχω 134. 14.
πρόχειρος 132. 6.
πτῶσις 107. 21.
Πυθαγόρας 127. 24.
πυκνόν (see note on 116. 1) passim.

ῥητός 108. 23; 109. 13.
ῥοπή 110. 13.
ῥυθμική 123. 20.
ῥυθμοποιία 125. 22.
ῥυθμός 125. 15, 23.

σαφής 105. 17.
σαφῶς 97. 9.
σημαίνω 100. 22; 125. 23.
σημεῖον 95. 20; 115. 7; 130. 19,
   20; 131. 1, 2; 135. 19.
σιωπή 101. 24.
σκέψις 102. 10.
στάσις ('stopping') 104. 22.
στοιχεῖον 120. 12; 134. 12.
στοιχειώδης 95. 6.
στοχάζομαι 115. 7.
σύγκειμαι 110. 5; 117. 17.
συγκεχυμένως 97. 14; 103. 25.
συγχορδία 114. 2.
συγχωρέω 114. 16, 17; 148. 3.
συζυγία 125. 19.
συμπίπτω 104. 25.
συμπληρόω 152. 20.
συμπροθυμέομαι 108. 10.
συμφωνέω, συμφωνία, and σύμφωνος (see note on 108. 21)
   passim.
συνάγω 106. 21.
συναμφότερος 109. 15; 159. 26.
συνάπτω 109. 16; 149. 1, 15; 150.
   13.
συναφή ('conjunction'; see Intr.
   A, § 10) passim.
συνεθίζω 111. 13; 115. 1; 125.
   25; 126. 14.
συνείρω 143. 21.
συνεπισπάω 115. 10.
συνέχεια 98. 7; 119. 3, 12.

συνεχής 101. 20, 21; 102. 15, 20;
103. 2, 7, 18; 109. 20; 119. 5,
15; 120. 3, 10; 143. 17; 144.
12; 145. 9; 147. 6; 149. 17.
συνεχῶς 101. 24; 102. 3, 19.
σύνθεσις, σύνθετος, and συντίθημι
passim.
συνίστημι 99. 11; 110. 8, 11; 144.
24; 151. 19; 163; 164.
συνοράω 106. 16; 113. 6; 114. 16;
131. 6, 15; 134. 17, 24; 141.
19; 147. 22; 151. 8; 160. 19;
164. 23.
συντείνω 95. 8; 101. 9; 144. 14.
συντόμως 107. 21.
σύντονος 115. 5; 116. 11, 24; 117;
118; 137. 6; 139. 3; 142. 9,
12; 143. 9, 10; 163. 10.
συνυπάρχω 106. 7.
σῦριγξ 112. 16.
συρίττω 112. 16.
σύστασις 99. 4; 107. 16; 110. 13.
σύστημα ('scale') passim.
σχῆμα 96. 4; 99. 15, 16, 25; 100.
2; 125. 12, 21; 130. 22; 149.
3, 5; 164. 13.
σχίζω 98. 22.

τάξις 95. 5; 96. 3; 99. 3, 7; 113.
20; 114. 3; 124. 27: 128. 1;
129. 6; 130. 23; 132. 16, 24;
133. 8, 15; 134. 5; 145. 2;
164. 16.
ταράττω 104. 23; 153. 3.
τάσις ('pitch') passim.
τάττω 107. 23; 117. 9; 159. 15,
19.
ταὐτότης 105. 3.
τάχος 105. 12, 13; 124. 6.
τείνω 108. 4.
τέκτων 124. 25.
τέλειος 99. 12; 101. 13.
τελευταῖος 111. 12; 129. 10; 146.
17.
τέλος 95. 10; 129. 16; 130. 1.
τέμνω 97. 20; 138. 21; 144. 5.
τεταρτημόριον 117. 16.
τετράχορδον passim.
διὰ τεττάρων, τό ('the Fourth')
passim.
τομή 138. 21.

τοιαῖος passim.
τόνος (= (1) 'interval of a tone,'
(2) 'key') passim.
τόπος ('compass,' 'locus of variation,' 'region or direction of
the voice-series') passim.
τορνευτής 124. 25.
τρίς 141. 12.
τρίτη (see Intr. A, § 11) 138. 11;
158. 20.
τρτημόριον 117. 5.
τρόπος (= (1) 'manner,'(2) 'style
of composition,' (3) 'character'
or 'motive') passim.
τρύπημα 132. 17; 133. 12, 18.
τρύπησις 128. 18.
τύπος 96. 16; 98. 5; 108. 1; 111.
3; 119. 4.
τυπόω 97. 21.
τυπώδης 108. 9.
τυχών, ὁ 100. 17; 110. 9.

ὑγίεια 122. 11.
ὑπάτη (see Intr. A, § 11) passim.
ὑπατῶν (see Intr. A, § 29) 131. 1.
ὑπερβαίνω 102. 3.
ὑπερβατός 109. 19.
ὑπερβολαίων (see Intr. A, § 29)
131. 1.
ὑπερέχω 117. 5; 120. 25; 146.
10; 148. 2.
ὑπερορία 134. 27.
ὑπεροχή 120. 24; 146; 147.
ὑπερτείνω 107. 7.
ὑπερτέλειος 112. 14.
ὑποδηλόω 97. 20.
ὑποδώριος 128. 13, 20.
ὑποκαταφρονέω 122. 15.
ὑπόληψις 122. 20; 131. 12, 18;
132. 12; 133. 22.
ὑποσημαίνω 119. 4.
ὑποτυπόω 110. 1; 143. 13.
ὑποφρύγιος 128. 17, 20.
ὑποχαίνω 122. 17.

φαντασία 101. 24; 102. 8; 139. 11.
φαῦλος 114. 20.
φαύλων 124. 24; 125. 1.
φθέγγομαι 102. 5; 103. 11; 106.
23; 107. 12.
φθόγγος ('note') passim.

φρύγιος 128; 130. 13, 14.
φυσικός 110. 6; 119. 10, 13; 123. 24.
φύσις 97. 21, 22; 98. 3; 100. 22; 110. 2; 111. 10, 22; 112. 1, 3; 113. 2; 119. 5, 7; 120. 4; 125. 24; 127. 17; 130. 25; 132. 14; 133. 8; 134. 9; 135. 19; 143. 15, 23.
φύω 97. 20; 102. 23; 108. 18; 114. 9; 120. 5; 123. 23; 132. 19.
φωνή (see note on 96. 18) passim.

χαλεπός 106. 16; 108. 13.
χειρουργία 132. 7, 18; 133. 17, 18; 134. 8.
χορδή 104; 133. 13, 16.
χράομαι 95. 11; 110. 16; 115. 5; 124. 22; 139. 19; 142. 17; 143. 12; 144. 11.

χρήσιμος 107. 1; 108. 19, 24.
χρῆσις 112. 7; 129. 13.
χρόα ('shade,' 'subdivision of genus'; see note on 116. 4); 115. 20; 126. 13; 138. 23; 152. 22; 158. 15, 19; 159. 12; 160. 1.
χρόνος 102. 3; 104. 6; 115. 8.
χρῶμα ('chromatic genus') passim.
χρωματικός (see Intr. A, § 6) passim.
χώρα 160. 19, 21.
χωρίζω 102. 12; 110. 4; 128. 20; 150. 8.
χωρισμός 98. 1.

ψευδής 99. 20.

ὠφελέω 123. 10, 12.

OXFORD
PRINTED AT THE CLARENDON PRESS
BY HORACE HART, M.A.
PRINTER TO THE UNIVERSITY

LaVergne, TN USA
24 November 2009

165194LV00004B/88/A